Computer Structure and Logic

Pearson Certification Team

Pearson
800 East 96th Street
Indianapolis, Indiana 46240 USA

Computer Structure and Logic

ISBN-13: 978-0-7897-4793-8
ISBN-10: 0-7897-4793-6

Library of Congress Cataloging-in-Publication data is on file.

Printed in the United States of America

Third Printing: October 2011

Trademarks

All terms mentioned in this book that are known to be trademarks or service marks have been appropriately capitalized. Pearson cannot attest to the accuracy of this information. Use of a term in this book should not be regarded as affecting the validity of any trademark or service mark.

Warning and Disclaimer

Every effort has been made to make this book as complete and as accurate as possible, but no warranty or fitness is implied. The information provided is on an "as is" basis. The authors and the publisher shall have neither liability nor responsibility to any person or entity with respect to any loss or damages arising from the information contained in this book or from the use of the CD or programs accompanying it.

Bulk Sales

Pearson offers excellent discounts on this book when ordered in quantity for bulk purchases or special sales. For more information, please contact

U.S. Corporate and Government Sales
1-800-382-3419
corpsales@pearsontechgroup.com

For sales outside the United States, please contact

International Sales
international@pearson.com

Associate Publisher
David Dusthimer

Acquisitions Editor
Betsy Brown

Development Editor
Dayna Isley

Managing Editor
Sandra Schroeder

Senior Project Editor
Tonya Simpson

Copy Editor
The Wordsmithery LLC

Indexer
Tim Wright

Proofreader
Water Crest Publishing, Inc.

Technical Editor
Aubrey Adams

Publishing Coordinator
Vanessa Evans

Book Designer
Gary Adair

Composition
Bronkella Publishing

Contents at a Glance

Table of Contents

About the Reviewer

Aubrey Adams is an electronic and computer system engineering lecturer and Cisco Networking Academy CCNA/IP Telephony instructor at Central Institute of Technology in Perth, Western Australia. Coming from a background in telecommunications design with qualifications in electronic engineering and management, and graduate diplomas in computing and education, he teaches across a broad range of related Vocational Education and Training areas. In 2007, Aubrey took leave from Central Institute to work as a member of the Networking Academy CCNA Exploration and Discovery course development teams. Since returning to teaching, he continues to contribute to Academy curriculum maintenance and development.

We Want to Hear from You!

As the reader of this book, *you* are our most important critic and commentator. We value your opinion and want to know what we're doing right, what we could do better, what areas you'd like to see us publish in, and any other words of wisdom you're willing to pass our way.

As an associate publisher for Pearson Certification, I welcome your comments. You can email or write me directly to let me know what you did or didn't like about this book—as well as what we can do to make our books better.

Please note that I cannot help you with technical problems related to the topic of this book. We do have a User Services group, however, where I will forward specific technical questions related to the book.

When you write, please be sure to include this book's title and author as well as your name, email address, and phone number. I will carefully review your comments and share them with the author and editors who worked on the book.

Email: feedback@pearsonitcertification.com

Mail: David Dusthimer
Associate Publisher
Pearson Certification
800 East 96th Street
Indianapolis, IN 46240 USA

Reader Services

Visit our website and register this book at www.pearsonitcertification.com/title/ 9780789747938 for convenient access to any updates, downloads, or errata that might be available for this book.

Introduction

Welcome to *Computer Structure and Logic*. This text is designed for those who want to learn about computers from the ground up. The book is planned so that each topic you learn builds on the last. From hardware to operating systems, basic security and networking, this book gives its readers a solid foundation from which to start their IT career.

This book also acts as a stepping stone to certifications from organizations such as CompTIA, Microsoft, and Cisco. Although further study is necessary to attain those certifications, this book creates a basis from which you can begin that process.

It's a pleasure for us to bring this text to you, and we wish you the best of success in your information technology (IT) endeavors.

Goals and Methods

The number one goal of this book is to establish the groundwork of computer knowledge and hands-on skills for the reader. To aid you in mastering an extensive list of computer concepts, each chapter first lists the topics to be discussed, thoroughly defines and describes each topic, and finally concludes with chapter review questions and case study problems that test your recall of the concepts.

In this book, we generally use a subsystem approach. Most of the chapters are devoted to a particular component of the computer. Each component discussed builds on the last one. Be sure to read the book in order, and don't skip any parts!

Who Should Read This Book?

This book is for entry-level IT students. The average reader should have a basic understanding of how to navigate through Windows and how to use the Internet. Readers will range from people who are very new to the IT field to people attempting to attain a position in the IT field.

This book is also aimed at the reader who ultimately wants to acquire certifications such as the CompTIA A+ and Network+, or certifications from organizations such as Microsoft or Cisco. The book is designed in such a way to offer easy transition to future certification studies.

How This Book Is Organized

This book is designed to be read in order, and in its entirety. As previously mentioned, the book's chapters and concepts build on each other as you progress throughout. There are 11 chapters in total, and they cover the following topics:

- **Chapter 1, "Introduction to Computers"**—This chapter gives a basic account of the history of computers through to today's modern computers. It also discusses the von Neumann model, and jumps right into the basics of personal computers (PCs).

- **Chapter 2, "Understanding Computer Math and Measurement"**—This chapter discusses the basics of computer math including the numbering systems used by computers, basic Boolean algebra, and how to measure data transfer.

- **Chapter 3, "I/O Ports and Devices"**—In this chapter, you learn about input and output devices, their connections and the ports they connect to, and how those ports communicate with the central processing unit.

- **Chapter 4, "Motherboards and Buses"**—Here you obtain important information about the motherboard and how it connects to everything else in the computer by way of buses. This chapter also demonstrates how to install adapter cards into a motherboard.

- **Chapter 5, "The CPU"**—This chapter talks about the "brain" of the computer: the central processing unit (CPU). Among the topics covered are CPU technologies, the differences between Intel and AMD processors, and how to install and troubleshoot processors.

- **Chapter 6, "Memory and Storage"**—This chapter delves into random access memory (RAM), magnetic hard drives, and optical drives. If you want to store information in a computer, RAM helps you do it over the short-term, and magnetic and optical drives help you do it over the long-term. The chapter also demonstrates how to install RAM and disk drives.

- **Chapter 7, "Computer Operation"**—In this chapter, you gain knowledge about how the computer boots with the help of the BIOS. The chapter also covers the boot process, and how to interpret and troubleshoot error messages and codes that might present themselves during bootup.

- **Chapter 8, "Operating Systems"**—This chapter examines the various Windows operating systems and their interfaces and tools. Linux and Mac are also briefly covered, but the emphasis of the chapter is on Windows.

- **Chapter 9, "Basic Security"**—Here you discover some basic security practices for your computer, from how to secure the computer physically, to protecting the data and wireless connections.

- **Chapter 10, "Troubleshooting"**—The ability to troubleshoot technology problems is what separates the good IT technicians from the not-so-good. This chapter discusses the tools you need, the concepts you should know, and how to troubleshoot in a logical and progressive way.

- **Chapter 11, "Networks"**—In this last chapter, you learn the basics of computer networking, how to connect to networks, Internet technologies, and of course, the all-powerful Transmission Control Protocol/Internet Protocol (TCP/IP).

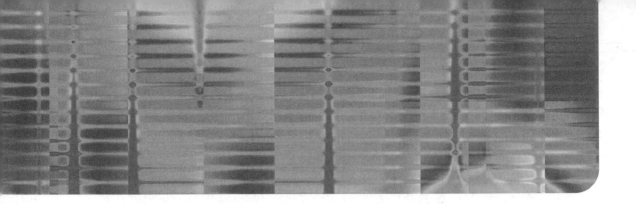

This chapter covers the following subjects:

- **History of Computers**—This section briefly describes the first computers such as the ENIAC, UNIVAC, and the Atanasoff-Berry computer.

- **The von Neumann Computer Model**—In this section, you learn about the computer architecture on which almost all computers today are based.

- **Modern Computers**—This section delves into today's computers, detailing the arrival of the transistor and the integrated circuit.

- **History of the PC**—The most common type of computer by far is the PC. This section discusses the birth of the PC, IBM's role in the growth of PCs in the 1980s, and today's PC industry leaders.

- **What Is a PC?**—This section details exactly what a PC is and who are the market leaders for PC hardware and software. It also defines white box systems and the main components of a PC.

Introduction to Computers

Welcome to Chapter 1, which discusses the progression of computers from the first systems in the 1940s to the modern computer of today. It also covers the von Neumann computer model—a computer architecture on which most computers are based. In addition, personal computers are defined and explained from a hardware and a software standpoint. This chapter is designed to give you a basic foundation of knowledge about computers. Many of the concepts in this chapter are covered in more depth in subsequent chapters. Let's begin!

History of Computers

A physicist named John V. Atanasoff (with associate Clifford Berry) is officially credited with creating the first true digital electronic computer during 1937 to 1942, while working at Iowa State University. The Atanasoff-Berry Computer (called the ABC) was the first to use modern digital switching techniques and vacuum tubes as switches, and it introduced the concepts of binary arithmetic and logic circuits. This was made legally official on October 19, 1973, when, following a lengthy court trial, U.S. Federal Judge Earl R. Larson voided the ENIAC patent of Eckert and Mauchly and named Atanasoff as the inventor of the first electronic digital computer.

Military needs during World War II caused a great thrust forward in the evolution of computers. In 1943, Tommy Flowers completed a secret British code-breaking computer called Colossus, which was used to decode German secret messages. Unfortunately, that work went largely uncredited because Colossus was kept secret until many years after the war.

Besides code-breaking, systems were needed to calculate weapons trajectory and other military functions. In 1946, John P. Eckert, John W. Mauchly, and their associates at the Moore School of Electrical Engineering at the University of Pennsylvania built the first large-scale electronic computer for the military. This machine became known as ENIAC, the Electrical Numerical Integrator and Calculator. It operated on 10-digit numbers and could multiply two such numbers at the rate of 300 products per second by finding the value of each product

from a multiplication table stored in its memory. ENIAC was about 1,000 times faster than the previous generation of electromechanical relay computers.

ENIAC used approximately 18,000 vacuum tubes, occupied 1,800 square feet (167 square meters) of floor space, and consumed around 180,000 watts of electrical power. Punched cards served as the input and output; registers served as adders and also as quick-access read/write storage.

The executable instructions composing a given program were created via specified wiring and switches that controlled the flow of computations through the machine. As such, ENIAC had to be rewired and switched for each program to be run. Although Eckert and Mauchly were originally given a patent for the electronic computer, it was later voided and the patent awarded to John Atanasoff for creating the Atanasoff-Berry Computer.

Earlier in 1945, the mathematician John von Neumann demonstrated that a computer could have a simple, fixed physical structure and yet be capable of executing any kind of computation effectively by means of proper programmed control without the need for any changes in hardware. In other words, you could change the program without rewiring the system. The stored-program technique, as von Neumann's ideas are known, became fundamental for future generations of high-speed digital computers and has become universally adopted. You can read more on the von Neumann architecture in the next section.

The first generation of modern programmed electronic computers to take advantage of these improvements appeared in 1947. This group of machines included EDVAC and UNIVAC, the first commercially available computers. These computers included, for the first time, the use of true random access memory (RAM) for storing parts of the program and the data that is needed quickly. Typically, they were programmed directly in machine language, although by the mid-1950s, progress had been made in several aspects of advanced programming. The standout of the era is the UNIVAC (Universal Automatic Computer), which was the first true general-purpose computer designed for both alphabetical and numerical uses. This made the UNIVAC a standard for business, not just science and the military.

The von Neumann Computer Model

When computer scientist John von Neumann designed his computer model in the 1940s, it was based on two main components: a central processing unit (CPU) and a storage structure (memory). This is the basis of most computers in use today. The purpose of this architecture was to show how a computer would access and run stored programs that contain programmed instructions and data. These are stored in random access memory (RAM), which can be read from and written to, similar to

today's computer RAM. Originally, the CPU was broken down into two components: the control unit and the arithmetic unit, as shown in Figure 1-1.

Figure 1-1   A basic diagram of the main components in the von Neumann computer model.

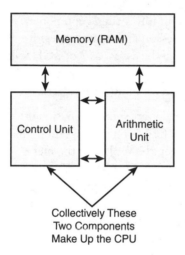

Each component had its own purpose. The control unit reads and interprets a program's instructions, which are converted into electrical signals that activate other components of the computer. The arithmetic unit (also known as a logic unit) takes care of arithmetic and logic operations. For example, the arithmetic unit deals with adding and subtracting, as well as Boolean logic operations such as AND, OR, and NOT which we speak about more in Chapter 2, "Understanding Computer Math and Measurement." The memory, which can be randomly accessed by the processor, stores data in cells. The data stored in each cell is a number between 0 and 255. Each one of these numbers is a byte of information. The numbers are actually stored in binary form instead of decimal form. For example, the decimal number 240 is stored in a memory cell as the binary equivalent: 11110000. We speak more about decimal and binary numbers and how to convert between them in Chapter 2.

RAM has many, many cells with which to store these bytes of information. Think about it—many of today's computers come with 1GB of RAM or more, allowing the computer to store more than a billion of these numbers, or bytes, of information. Data files, programs, graphics, and everything else you work with that is stored on the computer are based on bytes, which are simply any number between 0 and 255. Different values account for different data. A simple example of this is the capital letter "A." In the American Standard Code for Information Interchange (ASCII) character-encoding system, this letter is associated with the number 65. Capital "B" is associated with the number 66, and so on. Other characters, keys on the keyboard, colors, and everything else are associated with numbers in this fashion. Instruction sets consist of many bytes of information.

So, memory is used to store the numbers. The arithmetic unit calculates those numbers, and the control unit interprets what has been calculated and instructs the rest of the computer to take the necessary actions.

As time went on, the model went through some changes. The biggest change was the integration of the control unit and the arithmetic unit into a single component that we still refer to as the CPU. The terms CPU, processor, and microprocessor are often used interchangeably. Nowadays, processors can be as fast as 2 or 3GHz. If you were to build a computer, you wouldn't purchase a separate control unit and arithmetic unit; you would simply purchase a CPU, otherwise known as a *processor*.

On another note, one inherent problem with the original von Neumann design is the fact that the memory is physically separate from the CPU. This causes the "von Neumann bottleneck," a limit on the throughput between the CPU and the memory. The actual bottleneck is the pathways between the two. The CPU is powerful and can calculate lots of data; the memory can store lots of data, but those pathways between the two just can't handle the amount of data that needs to be sent back and forth. An analogy of a bottleneck is when you are driving on the highway, inevitably encounter construction, and the highway is constricted from three lanes to one, causing all of the vehicles to slow.

Several ways to alleviate the von Neumann bottleneck were developed. The most common of these was the concept of memory cache. Cache memory is located either on, or in, the processor core. It is usually far less in quantity compared to the main memory (RAM), but its proximity to the CPU enables the CPU to store and retrieve the most commonly used data more quickly as compared to storing and retrieving from RAM. Today's computers' CPUs might come with 1, 2, even 8 or 16MBs of cache memory. Finally, the architecture of the model was expanded to incorporate modern computer's devices. Von Neumann originally divided the computer system into five main groups, which are shown in Figure 1-2.

Figure 1-2 The five main groups within the von Neumann computer model.

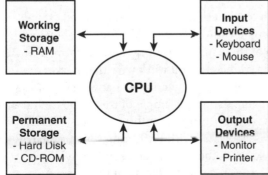

The following list describes the five groups:

- **CPU**—The "brain" of the computer, responsible for doing the math, and telling the rest of the computer what to do.

- **Working storage**—Generally this is RAM that stores information temporarily. This information is lost when the computer is shut down.

- **Permanent storage**—ROM, hard disks, and optical disks fall into this category. They store data permanently even if the computer is turned off.

- **Input devices**—Keyboards, mice, microphones, and other similar devices that are used to input information into the computer.

- **Output devices**—This includes display monitors, printers, speakers, and other devices used to output information from the computer.

This model can be associated with just about any type of computer from the historic ENIAC, EDVAC, and UNIVAC to modern computers such as today's PCs and Macs. The rest of this chapter discusses computers and computer technologies that are based on the von Neumann architecture.

Modern Computers

From UNIVAC to the latest desktop PCs, computer evolution has moved very rapidly. The first-generation computers were known for using vacuum tubes in their construction. The generation to follow would use the much smaller and more efficient transistor. Ultimately, individual transistors would be replaced by integrated circuits that contain multiple transistors—these would be the basis for the third generation of computers, which we still use today.

From Tubes to Transistors

Any modern digital computer is largely a collection of electronic switches. These switches are used to represent and control the routing of data elements called *binary digits* (or *bits*). Because of the on-or off nature of the binary information and signal routing the computer uses, an efficient electronic switch was required. The first electronic computers used vacuum tubes as switches, and although the tubes worked, they had many problems.

The type of tube used in early computers was called a *triode* and was invented by Lee De Forest in 1906 (see Figure 1-3). It consists of a cathode and a plate, separated by a control grid, suspended in a glass vacuum tube. The cathode is heated by a red-hot electric filament, which causes it to emit electrons that are attracted to the plate.

The control grid in the middle can control this flow of electrons. By making it negative, you cause the electrons to be repelled back to the cathode; by making it positive, you cause them to be attracted toward the plate. Thus, by controlling the grid current, you can control the on-off output of the plate.

Figure 1-3   The three main components of a basic triode vacuum tube.

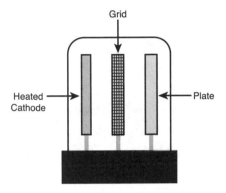

Unfortunately, the tube was inefficient as a switch. It consumed a great deal of electrical power and gave off enormous heat—a significant problem in the earlier systems. Primarily because of the heat they generated, tubes were notoriously unreliable—in larger systems, one failed every couple of hours or so.

The invention of the transistor was one of the most important developments leading to the personal computer revolution. The transistor was first invented in 1947 and announced in 1948 by Bell Laboratory engineers John Bardeen and Walter Brattain. Bell associate William Shockley invented the junction transistor a few months later, and all three jointly shared the Nobel Prize in Physics in 1956 for inventing the transistor. The transistor, which essentially functions as a solid-state electronic switch, replaced the less suitable vacuum tube. Because the transistor was so much smaller and consumed significantly less power, a computer system built with transistors was also much smaller, faster, and more efficient than a computer system built with vacuum tubes.

The conversion from tubes to transistors began the trend toward miniaturization that continues to this day. Today's small laptop (or palmtop) PC and even Tablet PC systems, which run on batteries, have more computing power than many earlier systems that filled rooms and consumed huge amounts of electrical power.

Although there have been many different designs for transistors over the years, the transistors used in modern computers are normally Metal Oxide Semiconductor Field Effect Transistors (MOSFETs).

MOSFETs are made from layers of materials deposited on a silicon substrate. Some of the layers contain silicon with certain impurities added by a process called doping or ion bombardment, whereas other layers include silicon dioxide (which acts as an insulator), polysilicon (which acts as an electrode), and metal to act as the wires to connect the transistor to other components. The composition and arrangement of the different types of doped silicon enables them to act both as a conductor or an insulator, which is why silicon is called a semiconductor.

MOSFETs can be constructed as either NMOS or PMOS types, based on the arrangement of doped silicon used. Silicon doped with boron is called P-type (positive) because it lacks electrons, whereas silicon doped with phosphorus is called N-type (negative) because it has an excess of free electrons.

MOSFETs have three connections, called the source, gate, and drain. An NMOS transistor is made by using N-type silicon for the source and drain, with P-type silicon placed in between (see Figure 1-4). The gate is positioned above the P-type silicon, separating the source and drain, and is separated from the P-type silicon by an insulating layer of silicon dioxide. Normally there is no current flow between N-type and P-type silicon, thus preventing electron flow between the source and drain. When a positive voltage is placed on the gate, the gate electrode creates a field that attracts electrons to the P-type silicon between the source and drain, thus changing that area to behave as if it were N-type silicon, creating a path for current to flow and turning the transistor "on."

Figure 1-4   Cutaway view of an NMOS transistor

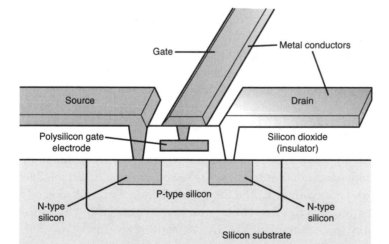

A PMOS transistor works in a similar but opposite fashion. P-type silicon is used for the source and drain, with N-type silicon positioned in between them. When a negative voltage is placed on the gate, the gate electrode creates a field that repels electrons from the N-type silicon between the source and drain, thus changing that area to behave as if it were P-type silicon and creating a path for current to flow and turning the transistor "on."

When both NMOS and PMOS field-effect transistors are combined in a complementary arrangement, power is used only when the transistors are switching, making dense, low-power circuit designs possible. Because of this, virtually all modern processors are designed using CMOS (Complementary Metal Oxide Semiconductor) technology.

Compared to a tube, a transistor is much more efficient as a switch and can be miniaturized to microscopic scale. Since the transistor was first invented, engineers have strived to make it smaller and smaller. In 2003, NEC researchers unveiled a silicon transistor only 5 nanometers (billionths of a meter) in size. Other technology, such as Graphene and carbon nanotubes, is being explored to produce even smaller transistors, down to the molecular or even atomic scale. In 2008, British researchers unveiled a Graphene-based transistor only 1 atom thick and 10 atoms (1nm) across, thus paving the way for future chips even more dense than possible with silicon-based designs.

Integrated Circuits

The third generation of modern computers is known for using integrated circuits instead of individual transistors. Jack Kilby at Texas Instruments and Robert Noyce at Fairchild are both credited with having invented the integrated circuit (IC) in 1958 and 1959. An IC is a semiconductor circuit that contains more than one component on the same base (or substrate material), which are usually interconnected without wires. The very first prototype IC constructed by Kilby at TI in 1958 contained only one transistor, several resistors, and a capacitor on a single slab of germanium, and featured fine gold "flying wires" to interconnect them. However, because the flying wires had to be individually attached, this type of design was not practical to manufacture. By comparison, Noyce patented the "planar" IC design in 1959, where all the components are diffused in or etched on a silicon base, including a layer of aluminum metal interconnects. The first planar IC was constructed in 1960 by Fairchild, consisting of a flip-flop circuit with four transistors and five resistors on a circular die only about 20mm2 in size. By comparison, the Intel Core i7 quad-core processor incorporates 731 million transistors (and numerous other components) on a single 263mm2 die! It's that reduction in the size of the IC, and the exponential increase in calculations per second that define the fourth generation of computers.

The fourth generation of the modern computer includes those that incorporate microprocessors in their designs. Of course, part of this fourth generation of computers is the personal computer (PC), which itself was made possible by the advent of low-cost microprocessors and memory. The next section discusses what many would argue as the most important step in the evolution of computers—the PC.

History of the PC

No other computer really defines the fourth generation of computers like the personal computer. From its birth in 1973, to the IBM PCs of the 80s and 90s, to modern PCs of today, it has been a mainstay in businesses worldwide, and in many homes as well. This section details the personal computer's evolution from 1973 to 2010.

Birth of the Personal Computer

In 1973, some of the first microcomputer kits based on the 8008 chip were developed. These kits were little more than demonstration tools and didn't do much except blink lights. In April 1974, Intel introduced the 8080 microprocessor, which was 10 times faster than the earlier 8008 chip and addressed 64KB of memory. This was the breakthrough the personal computer industry had been waiting for.

A company called MITS introduced the Altair kit in a cover story in the January 1975 issue of *Popular Electronics*. The Altair kit, considered the first personal computer, included an 8080 processor, a power supply, a front panel with a large number of lights, and 256 bytes (not kilobytes) of memory. The kit sold for $395 and had to be assembled. Assembly back then meant you got out your soldering iron to actually finish the circuit boards—not like today, where you can assemble a system of premade components with nothing more than a screwdriver.

NOTE Micro Instrumentation and Telemetry Systems was the original name of the company founded in 1969 by Ed Roberts and several associates to manufacture and sell instruments and transmitters for model rockets. Ed Roberts became the sole owner in the early 1970s, after which he designed the Altair. By January 1975, when the Altair was introduced, the company was called MITS, Inc., which then stood for nothing more than the name of the company. In 1977, Roberts sold MITS to Pertec, moved to Georgia, went to medical school, and became a practicing physician!

The Altair included an open architecture system bus called the *S-100 bus* because it had 100 pins per slot. The open architecture meant that anybody could develop

boards to fit in these slots and interface to the system. This prompted various add-ons and peripherals from numerous aftermarket companies. The new processor inspired software companies to write programs, including the CP/M (control program for microprocessors) operating system and the first version of the Microsoft BASIC (Beginners All-purpose Symbolic Instruction Code) programming language.

IBM introduced what can be called its first personal computer in 1975. The Model 5100 had 16KB of memory, a built-in 16-line-by-64-character display, a built-in BASIC language interpreter, and a built-in DC-300 cartridge tape drive for storage. The system's $8,975 price placed it out of the mainstream personal computer marketplace, which was dominated by experimenters (affectionately referred to as *hackers*) who built low-cost kits ($500 or so) as a hobby. Obviously, the IBM system was not in competition for this low-cost market and did not sell as well by comparison.

The Model 5100 was succeeded by the 5110 and 5120 before IBM introduced what we know as the IBM Personal Computer (Model 5150). Although the 5100 series preceded the IBM PC, the older systems and the 5150 IBM PC had nothing in common. The PC that IBM turned out was more closely related to the IBM System/23 DataMaster, an office computer system introduced in 1980. In fact, many of the engineers who developed the IBM PC had originally worked on the DataMaster.

In 1976, a new company called Apple Computer introduced the Apple I, which originally sold for $666.66. The selling price was an arbitrary number selected by one of Apple's cofounders, Steve Jobs. This system consisted of a main circuit board screwed to a piece of plywood; a case and power supply were not included. Only a few of these computers were made, and they reportedly have sold to collectors for more than $20,000. The Apple II, introduced in 1977, helped set the standard for nearly all the important microcomputers to follow, including the IBM PC.

The microcomputer world was dominated in 1980 by two types of computer systems. One type, the Apple II, claimed a large following of loyal users and a gigantic software base that was growing at a fantastic rate. The other type, CP/M systems, consisted not of a single system but of all the many systems that evolved from the original MITS Altair. These systems were compatible with one another and were distinguished by their use of the CP/M operating system and expansion slots, which followed the S-100 standard. All these systems were built by a variety of companies and sold under various names. For the most part, however, these systems used the same software and plug-in hardware. It is interesting to note that none of these systems was PC compatible or Macintosh compatible, the two primary standards in place today.

A new competitor looming on the horizon was able to see that to be successful, a personal computer needed to have an open architecture, slots for expansion, a modular design, and healthy support from both hardware and software companies other

than the original manufacturer of the system. This competitor turned out to be IBM, which was quite surprising at the time because IBM was not known for systems with these open-architecture attributes. IBM, in essence, became more like the early Apple, while Apple became like everybody expected IBM to be. The open architecture of the forthcoming IBM PC and the closed architecture of the forthcoming Macintosh caused a complete turnaround in the industry.

The IBM Personal Computer

At the end of 1980, IBM decided to truly compete in the rapidly growing low-cost personal computer market. The company established the Entry Systems Division, located in Boca Raton, Florida, to develop the new system. The division was intentionally located far away from IBM's main headquarters in New York, or any other IBM facilities, so that it would be able to operate independently as a separate unit. This small group consisted of 12 engineers and designers under the direction of Don Estridge and was charged with developing IBM's first real PC. (IBM considered the previous 5100 system, developed in 1975, to be an intelligent programmable terminal rather than a genuine computer, even though it truly was a computer.) Nearly all these engineers had come to the new division from the System/23 Data-Master project, which was a small office computer system introduced in 1980 and the direct predecessor of the IBM PC.

Much of the PC's design was influenced by the DataMaster design. In the DataMaster's single-piece design, the display and keyboard were integrated into the unit. Because these features were limiting, they became external units on the PC, although the PC keyboard layout and electrical designs were copied from the DataMaster.

Several other parts of the IBM PC system also were copied from the DataMaster, including the expansion bus (or input/output slots), which included not only the same physical 62-pin connector, but also almost identical pin specifications. This copying of the bus design was possible because the PC used the same interrupt controller as the DataMaster and a similar direct memory access (DMA) controller. Also, expansion cards already designed for the DataMaster could easily be redesigned to function in the PC.

The DataMaster used an Intel 8085 CPU, which had a 64KB address limit and an 8-bit internal and external data bus. This arrangement prompted the PC design team to use the Intel 8088 CPU, which offered a much larger (1MB) memory address limit and an internal 16-bit data bus, but only an 8-bit external data bus. The 8-bit external data bus and similar instruction set enabled the 8088 to be easily interfaced into the earlier DataMaster designs.

IBM brought its system from idea to delivery of functioning systems in one year by using existing designs and purchasing as many components as possible from outside vendors. The Entry Systems Division was granted autonomy from IBM's other divisions and could tap resources outside the company, rather than go through the bureaucratic procedures that required exclusive use of IBM resources. IBM contracted out the PC's languages and operating system to a small company named Microsoft. That decision was the major factor in establishing Microsoft as the dominant force in PC software today.

NOTE   It is interesting to note that IBM had originally contacted Digital Research (the company that created CP/M, then the most popular personal computer operating system) to have it develop an operating system for the new IBM PC. However, Digital was leery of working with IBM and especially balked at the nondisclosure agreement IBM wanted Digital to sign. Microsoft jumped on the opportunity left open by Digital Research and, consequently, became the largest software company in the world. IBM's use of outside vendors in developing the PC was an open invitation for the after-market to jump in and support the system—and it did. On August 12, 1981, a new standard was established in the microcomputer industry with the debut of the IBM PC. Since then, hundreds of millions of PC-compatible systems have been sold, as the original PC has grown into an enormous family of computers and peripherals. More software has been written for this computer family than for any other system on the market.

The PC Industry Nearly 30 Years Later

In the nearly 30 years since the original IBM PC was introduced, many changes have occurred. The IBM-compatible computer, for example, advanced from a 4.77MHz 8088-based system to 3GHz (3,000MHz) or faster Core i7–based systems—about 100,000 or more times faster than the original IBM PC (in actual processing speed, not just clock speed). The original PC had only one or two single-sided floppy drives that stored 160KB each using DOS 1.0, whereas modern systems can have several terabytes (trillion bytes) or more of hard disk storage.

A rule of thumb in the computer industry (called *Moore's Law*, originally set forth by Intel cofounder Gordon Moore) is that available processor performance and disk-storage capacity doubles every one and a half to two years, give or take. Since the beginning of the PC industry, this pattern has held steady and, if anything, seems to be accelerating.

Moore's Law

In 1965, Gordon Moore was preparing a speech about the growth trends in computer memory and made an interesting observation. When he began to graph the data, he realized a striking trend existed. Each new chip contained roughly twice as much capacity as its predecessor, and each chip was released within 18–24 months of the previous chip. If this trend continued, he reasoned, computing power would rise exponentially over relatively brief periods of time.

Moore's observation, now known as Moore's Law, described a trend that has continued to this day and is still remarkably accurate. It was found to not only describe memory chips, but also accurately describe the growth of processor power and disk drive storage capacity. It has become the basis for many industry performance forecasts. As an example, in 37 years, the number of transistors on a processor chip increased more than 356,000 times, from 2,300 transistors on the 4004 processor in 1971 to more than 820 million transistors on the Core 2 Quad processor in January 2008. During 2009, Intel released versions of the Core i7 processor with over one billion transistors.

In addition to performance and storage capacity, another major change since the original IBM PC was introduced is that IBM is not the only manufacturer of PC-compatible systems. IBM originated the PC-compatible standard, of course, but today it no longer sets the standards for the system it originated. More often than not, new standards in the PC industry are developed by companies and organizations other than IBM.

Today, it is Intel, Microsoft, and AMD who are primarily responsible for developing and extending the PC hardware and software standards. Some have even taken to calling PCs "Wintel" systems, owing to the dominance of the first two companies. Although AMD originally produced Intel processors under license and later produced low-cost, pin-compatible counterparts to Intel's 486 and Pentium processors (AMD 486, K5/K6), starting with the Athlon, AMD has created completely unique processors that have been worthy rivals to Intel's current models.

In more recent years, the introduction of hardware standards such as the Peripheral Component Interconnect (PCI) bus, Accelerated Graphics Port (AGP) bus, PCI Express bus, ATX and BTX motherboard form factors, as well as processor socket and slot interfaces show that Intel is really pushing PC hardware design these days. Intel's ability to design and produce motherboard chipsets as well as complete motherboards has enabled Intel processor–based systems to first adopt newer memory and bus architectures as well as system form factors. Although in the past, AMD has on occasion made chipsets for its own processors, the company's acquisition of ATI has allowed it to become more aggressive in the chipset marketplace.

PC-compatible systems have thrived not only because compatible hardware can be assembled easily, but also because the most popular operating system was available not from IBM but from a third party (Microsoft). The core of the system software is the basic input/output system (BIOS), and this was also available from third-party companies, such as AMI, Phoenix, and others. This situation enabled other manufacturers to license the operating system and BIOS software and sell their own compatible systems. The fact that DOS borrowed the functionality and user interface from both CP/M and Unix probably had a lot to do with the amount of software that became available. Later, with the success of Windows, even more reasons would exist for software developers to write programs for PC-compatible systems.

One reason Apple's Macintosh systems have never enjoyed the market success of PC systems is that Apple has often used proprietary hardware and software designs that it was unwilling to license to other companies. This proprietary nature has unfortunately relegated Apple to a meager 3%–5% market share in personal computers.

One fortunate development for Mac enthusiasts was Apple's shift to Intel x86 processors and PC architecture in 2006, resulting in greatly improved performance and standardization as compared to the previous non-PC-compatible Mac systems. Although Apple has failed to adopt some of the industry-standard component form factors used in PCs (rendering major components such as motherboards non-interchangeable), the PC-based Macs truly are PCs from a hardware standpoint, using all the same processors, chipsets, memory, buses, and other system architectures that PCs have been using for years. The move to a PC-based architecture could be considered the smartest move Apple has made in years—besides reducing Apple's component costs, it allows Macs to finally perform on par with PCs.

Apple could even become a real contender in the OS arena (taking market share from Microsoft) if the company would only sell its OS in an unlocked version that would run on non-Apple PCs. Unfortunately for now, even though Apple's OS X operating system is designed to run on PC hardware, it is coded to check for a security chip found only on Apple motherboards. There are ways to work around the check (see OSx86project.org), but they are not supported by Apple.

Apple's shift to a PC-based architecture is one more indication of just how popular the PC has become. After nearly 30 years, the PC continues to thrive and prosper. With far-reaching industry support and an architecture that is continuously evolving, it is a safe bet that PC-compatible systems will continue to dominate the personal computer marketplace for the foreseeable future.

What Is a PC?

"What exactly is a PC?" Most people immediately answer that PC stands for personal computer, which in fact it does. Many continue by defining a personal computer as any small computer system purchased and used by an individual. Although it is true that all PCs are personal computers, not all personal computers are PCs. For example, all of Apple's pre-2006 Motorola/IBM processor–based Macintosh systems, and older 8080/Z-80 processor–based CP/M machines are considered personal computers, but most people wouldn't call them PCs, least of all the Mac users! For the true definition of what a PC is, we must look deeper.

Calling something a PC implies that it is something much more specific than just any personal computer. One thing it implies is a family relation to the original IBM PC from 1981. It could be said that IBM literally invented the type of computer we call a PC today; that is, IBM designed and created the very first one, and IBM's definition set all the standards that made the PC distinctive from other personal computers. That's not to say that IBM invented the personal computer; many recognize the historical origins of the personal computer in the MITS Altair, introduced in 1975, even though other small computers were available prior. However, although IBM did not invent the personal computer, it did invent the type of personal computer that today we call the PC. Some people might take this definition a step further and define a PC as any personal computer that is "IBM compatible." In fact, many years back, PCs were called either IBM compatibles or IBM clones, in essence paying homage to the origins of the PC at IBM.

The reality today is that although IBM clearly designed and created the PC in 1981 and controlled the development and evolution of the PC standard for several years thereafter, IBM is no longer in control of the PC standard; that is, it does not dictate what makes up a PC today. IBM lost control of the PC standard in 1987 when it introduced its PS/2 line of systems. Up until then, other companies that were producing PCs literally copied IBM's systems right down to the chips, connectors, and even the shapes (form factors) of the boards, cases, and power supplies. After 1987, IBM abandoned many of the standards it created in the first place, and the designation "IBM compatible" started to be considered obsolete.

If a PC is no longer an IBM-compatible system, then what is it? The real question seems to be, "Who is in control of the PC standard today?" That question is best broken down into two parts. First, who is in control of PC software? Second, who is in control of PC hardware? The following sections provide the answers. We also define the standard components, system types, and design protocols that most PC manufacturers abide by. In addition, we discuss white-box systems and their effect on the PC market.

Who Controls PC Software?

Microsoft clearly controls the dominant operating systems used on PCs, which have evolved from the original MS-DOS to DOS/Windows 3.x, then to Windows 9x/Me, then to Windows NT/2000/XP, and now to Windows Vista.

Microsoft has effectively used its control of the PC operating systems as leverage to also control other types of PC software, such as drivers, utilities, and applications. For example, many utility programs originally offered by independent companies, such as disk caching, disk compression, file defragmentation, file structure repair, firewalls, and even simple applications such as calculator and notepad programs, are now bundled in Windows. Microsoft has even bundled more comprehensive applications such as web browsers, word processors, and media players, ensuring an automatic installed base for these applications—much to the dismay of companies who produce competing versions. Microsoft has also leveraged its control of the operating system to integrate its own networking software and applications suites more seamlessly into the operating system than others. That's why it now dominates most of the PC software universe—from operating systems to networking software to utilities, from word processors to database programs to spreadsheets.

In the early days of the PC, IBM hired Microsoft to provide most of the core software for the PC. IBM developed the hardware, wrote the basic input/output system (BIOS), and hired Microsoft to develop the disk operating system (DOS) as well as several other programs and utilities for the PC. In what was later viewed as perhaps the most costly business mistake in history, IBM failed to secure exclusive rights to the DOS it had contracted from Microsoft, either by purchasing it outright or by an exclusive license agreement. Instead, IBM licensed it nonexclusively, which subsequently allowed Microsoft to sell the same MS-DOS code it developed for IBM to any other company that was interested. Early PC cloners such as Compaq eagerly licensed this operating system code, and suddenly consumers could purchase the same basic MS-DOS operating system with several different company names on the box. In retrospect, that single contractual error made Microsoft into the dominant software company it is today and subsequently caused IBM to lose control of the very PC standard it had created.

It is interesting to note that in the PC business, software enjoys copyright protection, whereas hardware can be protected only by patents, which are much more difficult, time-consuming, and expensive to obtain. And in the case of U.S. patents, they also expire 20 years after filing. According to the U.S. patent office, "any new and useful process, machine, manufacture, or composition of matter, or any new and useful improvement thereof" can be patented. This definition made it difficult to patent most aspects of the IBM PC because it was designed using previously existing parts that anybody could purchase off the shelf. In fact, most of the important parts

for the original PC came from Intel, such as the 8088 processor, 8284 clock genera-
tor, 8253/54 timer, 8259 interrupt controller, 8237 DMA (direct memory access)
controller, 8255 peripheral interface, and 8288 bus controller. These chips made up
the heart and soul of the original PC motherboard.

Because the design of the original PC was not wholly patented and virtually all the
parts were readily available, almost anybody could duplicate the hardware of the
IBM PC. All one had to do was purchase the same chips from the same manufacturers and suppliers IBM used and design a new motherboard with a similar circuit.
IBM even made it easier by publishing complete schematic diagrams of its motherboards and adapter cards in very detailed and easily available technical reference
manuals. These manuals even included fully commented source code listings for the
ROM BIOS code as well. Although they are long out of print, they do turn up in the
used book market and online auction sites such as eBay.

The difficult part of copying the IBM PC was the software, which is protected by
copyright law. Both Compaq and Phoenix Software (today known as Phoenix Technologies) were among the first to develop a legal way around this problem, which
enabled them to functionally duplicate (but not exactly copy) software such as the
BIOS. The BIOS is defined as the core set of control software that drives the hardware devices in the system directly. These types of programs are normally called device drivers, so in essence, the BIOS is a collection of all the core device drivers used
to operate and control the system hardware. The operating system (such as DOS or
Windows) uses the drivers in the BIOS to control and communicate with the various hardware and peripherals in the system.

The method they used to legally duplicate the IBM PC BIOS was an ingenious form
of reverse engineering. They used two groups of software engineers, the second of
which were specially screened to consist only of people who had never before seen
or studied the IBM BIOS code. The first group studied the IBM BIOS and wrote a
detailed description of what it did. The second group read the description written
by the first group and set out to write from scratch a new BIOS that did everything
the first group had described. The end result was a new BIOS written from scratch,
and although the resulting code was not identical to IBM's, it had exactly the same
functionality.

This is called a "clean room" approach to reverse-engineering software, and if carefully conducted, it can escape any legal attack. Because IBM's original PC BIOS had
a limited and yet well-defined set of functions, and was only 8,096 bytes long, dupli-
cating it through the clean-room approach was not very difficult. As the IBM BIOS
evolved, keeping up with any changes IBM made was relatively easy. Discounting
the power-on self test (POST) and BIOS Setup (used for configuring the system)
portion of the BIOS, most motherboard BIOSs, even today, have only about

32KB–128KB of active code, and modern operating systems ignore most of it any-way by loading code and drivers from disk. In essence, the modern motherboard BIOS serves only to initialize the system and load the OS. Today, although some PC manufacturers still write some of their own BIOS code, most source their BIOS from one of the independent BIOS developers. Phoenix and American Megatrends (AMI) are the leading developers of BIOS software for PC system and motherboard manufacturers. A third major producer of BIOS software, Award Software, is owned by Phoenix Technologies, which continues to sell Award BIOS–based products.

After the motherboard hardware and BIOS of the IBM PC were duplicated, all that was necessary to produce a fully IBM-compatible system was MS-DOS. Reverse-en-gineering DOS, even with the cleanroom approach, seemed to be a daunting task at the time, because DOS is much larger than the BIOS and consists of many more programs and functions. Also, the operating system has evolved and changed more often than the BIOS, which by comparison has remained relatively constant. This means that the only way to get DOS on an IBM compatible back in the early 1980s was to license it. This is where Microsoft came in. Because IBM (who hired Mi-crosoft to write DOS in the first place) did not ensure that its license agreement with Microsoft was exclusive, Microsoft was free to sell the same DOS it designed for IBM to anybody else who wanted it. With a licensed copy of MS-DOS, the last piece was in place and the floodgates were open for IBM-compatible systems to be produced whether IBM liked it or not.

NOTE MS-DOS was eventually cloned, the first of which was DR-DOS, released by Digital Research (developers of CP/M) in 1988. By all rights, DR-DOS was more than just a clone; it had many features not found in MS-DOS at the time, inspiring Microsoft to add similar features in future MS-DOS versions as well. In 1991, Novell acquired DR-DOS, followed by Caldera in 1996 (who released a version of the source code under an open-source license), followed by Lineo in 1998, and final-ly by DRDOS (www.drdos.com) in 2002. Free and open source DOS versions have been independently produced, upgraded, and maintained by the DR-DOS/ OpenDOS Enhancement Project (www.drdosprojects.de) as well as the FreeDOS Project (www.freedos.org).

In retrospect, this is exactly why there were no clones or compatibles of the Apple Macintosh systems. It isn't that Mac systems couldn't be duplicated; in fact, the older Mac hardware was fairly simple and easy to produce using off-the-shelf parts, and current Macs now use the same hardware as PCs. The real problem is that Ap-ple owns the Mac OS, and so far has refused to license or allow its OS to run on non-Apple hardware. The earlier non-PC-compatible Macs also incorporated a rather large and complex BIOS that was very tightly integrated with the older Mac

OS. The greater complexity and integration combined with very low market share allowed the early non-PC-compatible Mac BIOS and OS to escape any clean-room duplication efforts.

NOTE   From 1996 to 1997, an effort was made by the more liberated thinkers at Apple to license its BIOS/OS combination, and several Mac-compatible machines were developed, produced, and sold. Companies such as Sony, Power Computing, Radius, and even Motorola invested millions of dollars in developing these systems, but shortly after these first Mac clones were sold, Apple canceled the licensing! By canceling these licenses, Apple virtually guaranteed that its systems would not be competitive with Windows-based PCs. Along with its smaller market share come much higher system costs, fewer available software applications, and fewer options for hardware repair, replacement, and upgrades as compared to PCs. The proprietary form factors also ensure that major components such as motherboards, power supplies, and cases are available only from Apple at very high prices, making out-of-warranty repair, replacement, and upgrades of these components not cost effective.

Now that Apple has converted its Mac systems over to PC architecture, the only difference between a Mac and a PC is the OS they run, so a PC running OS X essentially becomes a Mac, whereas a Mac running Windows becomes a PC. This means that the only thing keeping Mac systems unique is the ability to run OS X. To this end, Apple includes code in OS X that checks for an Apple-specific security chip, thus preventing OS X from running on non-Apple PCs. Although this does create an incentive to buy Apple-brand PCs, it also overlooks the huge market for selling OS X to non-Apple PC users. For example, if Apple had sold OS X to PC users while Microsoft was delaying the release of Vista, OS X would have taken a large amount of market share from Windows. However, despite Apple's attempts to prevent OS X from running, the OSx86 Project (www.osx86project.org) has information showing how to get OS X installed and running on standard PCs.

Who Controls PC Hardware?

Although it is clear that Microsoft has always had the majority control over PC software by virtue of its control over the dominant PC operating systems, what about the hardware? It is easy to see that IBM controlled the PC hardware standard up through 1987. After all, IBM invented the core PC motherboard design; the original expansion bus slot architecture (8/16-bit ISA bus); the ROM BIOS interface, serial and parallel port implementations; video card design through VGA and XGA standards; floppy and hard disk interface and controller implementations; power supply designs; keyboard interfaces and designs; the mouse interface; and even the physical shapes (form factors) of everything from the motherboard to the expansion cards, power supplies, and system chassis.

The real question is which company has been responsible for creating and inventing newer and more recent PC hardware designs, interfaces, and standards? Some people say Microsoft (but it controls the software, not the hardware), and some say HP/Compaq or Dell, or they name a few other big-name system manufacturers. Some, however, surmise the correct answer—Intel.

It is understandable that many people don't immediately realize this; for example, how many people actually own an Intel-brand PC? No, not just one that says "Intel inside" on it (which refers only to the system having an Intel processor), but a system that was designed and built by, or even purchased through, Intel. Believe it or not, many people today do have Intel PCs!

Certainly this does not mean that consumers have purchased their systems from Intel because Intel does not sell complete PCs to end users. You can't currently order a system from Intel, nor can you purchase an Intel-brand system from somebody else. What we are talking about are the major components inside, including especially the motherboard as well as the core of the motherboard—the chipset.

How did Intel come to dominate the interior of our PCs? Intel has been the dominant PC processor supplier since IBM chose the Intel 8088 CPU in the original IBM PC in 1981. By controlling the processor, Intel naturally controlled the chips necessary to integrate its processors into system designs. This naturally led Intel into the chipset business. It started its chipset business in 1989 with the 82350 Extended Industry Standard Architecture (EISA) chipset, and by 1993 it had become—along with the debut of the Pentium processor—the largest-volume major motherboard chipset supplier. Now imagine Intel sitting there, thinking that it makes the processor and all the other chips necessary to produce a motherboard, so why not just eliminate the middleman and make the entire motherboard too? The answer to this, and a real turning point in the industry, came about in 1994 when Intel became the largest-volume motherboard manufacturer in the world. By 1997, Intel made more motherboards than the next eight largest motherboard manufacturers combined, with sales of more than 30 million boards worth more than $3.6 billion!

After the industry downturn in 2001, Intel concentrated on its core competency of chip making, and began using Chinese contract manufacturers such as Foxconn to make Intel-branded motherboards. Since then, contract manufacturers such as Asus, Foxconn, ECS, MSI, and Gigabyte have essentially taken over the market for motherboard manufacturing. Regardless of which company actually manufactures the boards, the main part of any motherboard is the chipset, which contains the majority of the motherboard circuitry. These days, about 80% of PCs on the market use Intel processors, and the majority of those are plugged in to motherboards built using Intel chipsets.

Intel controls the PC hardware standard because it controls the PC motherboard and most of the components on it. It not only makes the majority of motherboards being used in systems today, but it also supplies the majority of processors and motherboard chipsets to other motherboard manufacturers.

Intel also has had a hand in setting several recent PC hardware standards, such as the following:

- Peripheral Component Interconnect (PCI) local bus interface.

- Accelerated Graphics Port (AGP) interface for high-performance video cards.

- PCI Express (originally known as 3GIO), the interface selected by the PCI Special Interest Group. (PCI SIG) to replace both PCI and AGP as the high-performance bus for newer PCs.

- Industry-standard motherboard form factors such as ATX (including variations such as microATX and FlexATX) and BTX (including variations such as microBTX, nanoBTX, and picoBTX). ATX is still the most popular, and beginning in 1996–1997 it replaced the somewhat long-in-the-tooth IBM-designed Baby-AT form factor, which had been used since the early 1980s.

- Desktop Management Interface (DMI) for monitoring system hardware functions.

- Dynamic Power Management Architecture (DPMA) and Advanced Power Management (APM) standards for managing power use in the PC.

Intel dominates not only the PC, but the entire worldwide semiconductor industry. According to the sales figures compiled by iSuppli, Intel has about one and a half times the sales of the next closest semiconductor company (Samsung) and more than four times the sales of competitor AMD (see Table 1-1).

Table 1-1 Top Semiconductor Companies Ranked by 2009 Semiconductor Sales

2009 Rank	Company Name	2009 Revenue[1]	Percent Total	2008 Rank	2008 Revenue	Percent Change
1	Intel Corporation	32,410	14.1%	1	33,767	–4.0%
2	Samsung Electronics	17,496	7.6%	2	16,902	+3.5%
3	Toshiba Semiconductors	10,319	4.5%	3	11,081	–6.9%
4	Texas Instruments	9,617	4.2%	4	11,068	–12.6%
5	STMicroelectronics	8,510	3.7%	5	10,325	–17.6%
8	AMD	5,207	2.3%	12	5,455	–4.6%

[1.] Ranking by revenue in millions of U.S. dollars.

As you can see by these figures, it is no wonder that a popular industry news website called *The Register* (www.theregister.com) uses the term *Chipzilla* when referring to the industry giant.

Whoever controls the operating system controls the software for the PC, and whoever controls the motherboard controls the hardware. Because Microsoft and Intel together seem to control software and hardware in the PC today, it is no surprise the modern PC is often called a "Wintel" system.

White-Box Systems

Many of the top-selling system manufacturers do design and make their own motherboards, especially for their higher-end systems. According to *Computer Reseller News* magazine, the top desktop systems manufacturers for the last several years have consistently been names such as HP, Dell, and Lenovo (formerly IBM). These companies both design and manufacture their own motherboards as well as purchase existing boards from motherboard manufacturers. In rare cases, they even design their own chips and chipset components for their own boards. Although sales are high for these individual companies, a large segment of the market is what those in the industry call the *white-box systems*.

White-box is the term used by the industry to refer to what would otherwise be called *generic* PCs—that is, PCs assembled from a collection of industry-standard, commercially available components. The white-box designation comes from the fact that historically most of the chassis used by this type of system have been white (or ivory or beige).

The great thing about white-box systems is that they use industry-standard components that are interchangeable. This interchangeability is the key to future upgrades and repairs because it ensures that a plethora of replacement parts will be available to choose from and will be interchangeable.

Companies selling white-box systems do not usually manufacture the systems; they assemble them. That is, they purchase commercially available motherboards, cases, power supplies, disk drives, peripherals, and so on, and assemble and market everything together as complete systems. Some companies such as HP and Dell manufacture some of their own systems as well as assemble some from industry-standard parts. In particular, the HP Pavilion and Dell Dimension lines are composed largely of mainstream systems made with mostly industry-standard parts. PC makers using mostly industry-standard parts also include high-end game system builders such as VoodooPC (owned by HP) and Alienware (owned by Dell). Other examples include Gateway and eMachines (owned by Gateway), whose PCs are also constructed using primarily industry-standard components. Note that there can be exceptions for all of these systems; for example, some of the Dell Dimension XPS systems use proprietary

parts such as power supplies. It is recommend that you avoid such systems, due to future upgrade and repair hassles.

Others using industry-standard components include Acer, CyberPower, Micro Express, and Systemax, but hundreds more could be listed. In overall total volume, this ends up being the largest segment of the PC marketplace today. What is interesting about white-box systems is that, with very few exceptions, anyone can purchase the same motherboards and other components any of the white-box manufacturers can (although we would probably pay more than they do because of the volume discounts they receive). We can assemble a virtually identical white-box system from scratch ourselves.

PC Design Guides

For several years, Intel and Microsoft released a series of documents called the "PC *XX* Design Guides" (where *XX* designates the year) as a set of standard specifications to guide both hardware and software developers creating products that work with Windows. The requirements in these guides were part of Microsoft's "Designed for Windows" logo requirement. In other words, if you produced either a hardware or software product and you want the official "Designed for Windows" logo to be on your box, your product had to meet the PC *XX* minimum requirements.

Following are the documents that have been produced in this series:

- "Hardware Design Guide for Microsoft Windows 95"

- "Hardware Design Guide Supplement for PC 95"

- "PC 97 Hardware Design Guide"

- "PC 98 System Design Guide"

- "PC 99 System Design Guide"

- "PC 2000 System Design Guide"

- "PC 2001 System Design Guide"

These documents are available for download from the Microsoft website (www.microsoft.com/whdc/system/platform/pcdesign/desguide/pcguides.mspx).

NOTE   These guides do not mean anything directly for the end user; instead, they were meant to be guides for PC manufacturers to design and build their systems. In some ways, they were a market-control tool for Intel and Microsoft to further wield their influence over PC hardware and software.

The "PC 2001 System Design Guide" is the most recent design guide produced by Microsoft and Intel together. Since then, these companies have produced individual whitepapers and other resources for this purpose. For updated system-design information, see the following websites:

■   The Microsoft Windows Hardware Developer Central site at http://microsoft.com/whdc

■   The Intel developer website at http://developer.intel.com

System Types

PCs can be broken down into many categories. We can break them down in two ways—by the design and/or width of the processor bus (often called the *front side bus*, or *FSB*) as well as by the width of the internal registers (the CPU's internal temporary storage), which dictates the type of software that can be run.

When a processor reads data, the data moves into the processor via the processor's external data connection. Traditionally this connection has been a parallel bus; however, in newer chips, it is a serialized point-to point link, transferring fewer bits at a time but at a much higher rate. Older designs often had several components sharing the bus, whereas the newer point-to-point links are exclusively between the processor and the chipset.

A common confusion arises in discussions of processor "widths." Some people take the width to refer to how many bits of data can be read or written at a time, whereas others refer to the size of the internal registers, which control how much data can be operated on at a time. Although many processors have had matching data bus widths and internal register sizes, they are not always the same, which can lead to more confusion. For example, most Pentium processors have 64-bit data bus widths and yet include internal registers that are only 32 bits wide. The newer AMD and Intel processors with x86-64 architecture have 64-bit internal registers and can run in both 32-bit and 64-bit modes. Thus, from a software point of view, there are PC processors capable of running 16-bit, 32-bit, and 64-bit instructions. For backward compatibility, those having 64-bit registers can also run 32-bit and 16-bit instructions, and those with 32-bit registers can run 16-bit instructions. Whereas the register size dictates what type of software instructions the processor can run, the data bus width is the major factor in motherboard and chipset design because it dictates how many bits move in and out of the chip in one cycle.

System Components

A modern PC is both simple and complicated. It is simple in the sense that over the years, many of the components used to construct a system have become integrated

with other components into fewer and fewer actual parts. It is complicated in the sense that each part in a modern system performs many more functions than did the same types of parts in older systems.

Table 1-2 briefly examines the components and peripherals necessary to assemble a modern PC system. Each item is discussed further in later chapters.

Table 1-2 Basic PC Components

Component	Description
Motherboard	The motherboard is the core of the system. It really is the PC; everything else is connected to it, and it controls everything in the system.
Processor	The processor is often thought of as the "engine" of the computer. It's also called the CPU (central processing unit).
Memory (RAM)	The system memory is often called RAM (for random access memory). This is the primary working memory, which holds all the programs and data the processor is using at a given time.
Case/chassis	The case is the frame or chassis that houses the motherboard, power supply, disk drives, adapter cards, and any other physical components in the system.
Power supply	The power supply feeds electrical power to the internal components in the PC.
Floppy drive	The floppy drive is a low-capacity, removable-media, magnetic-storage device. Many recent systems use other types of removable magnetic or USB-based flash memory devices instead of floppy drives for removable storage.
Hard drive	The hard disk is the primary high-capacity storage media for the system.
CD or DVD drive	CD (compact disc) and DVD (digital versatile disc) drives are relatively high-capacity, removable-media, optical drives; most newer systems include drives featuring write/rewrite capability.
Keyboard	The keyboard is the primary device on a PC that is used by a human to communicate with and control a system.
Mouse	Although many types of pointing devices are on the market today, the first and most popular device for this purpose is the mouse.
Video card*	The video card controls the information you see on the monitor.
Monitor	The monitor displays information and graphics that are sent to it by the video card.
Sound card*	A sound card enables the PC to generate complex sounds.
Network/modem*	Most prebuilt PCs ship with a network interface and possibly a modem.

Components marked with an asterisk (*) may be integrated into the motherboard on many recent systems, particularly entry-level systems.

Chapter Review Questions

The following questions test your recall of the concepts described in this chapter. The answers are listed at the end of the questions in the "Answers and Explanations" section.

1. Which of the following is an example of a PC?

    A. Colossus

    B. ENIAC

    C. 8088

    D. von Neumann

2. Who is credited with the patent for the first computer?

    A. Eckert and Mauchly

    B. Atanasoff

    C. Microsoft

    D. Intel

3. In the von Neumann architecture, what two components make up the CPU? (Select the two best answers.)

    A. Control unit

    B. Processor

    C. Arithmetic unit

    D. Memory

4. What technology alleviates the problem of the "von Neumann bottleneck"?

    A. Cache

    B. Main memory

    C. CPU

    D. Hard disk drive

5. Which of the following are groups within the von Neumann architecture? (Select the three best answers.)

   A. Working storage

   B. Monitor

   C. Output devices

   D. Permanent storage

   E. Keyboard

6. What are the three main connections in a transistor? (Select the three best answers.)

   A. Gate

   B. N-type silicon

   C. Source

   D. Drain

   E. Conductor

7. MOSFET is the most common type of what electronic component?

   A. Vacuum tube

   B. CPU

   C. Integrated circuit

   D. Transistor

8. Approximately how many transistors are incorporated into today's Intel processors?

   A. Hundreds

   B. Thousands

   C. Millions

   D. Billions

9. What made the 8088 Intel CPU special compared to its predecessors?

   A. 1MB address limit

   B. 33MHz processor

   C. 64KB address limit

   D. 1MHz processor

10. What does Moore's law state?

   A. Whatever can go wrong with computers will.

   B. Processor performance doubles every one and a half to two years.

   C. Total computer memory doubles with each new computer.

   D. Hard disks will fail.

11. Which two companies are most responsible today for the advancement of PC CPUs? (Select the two best answers.)

   A. Toshiba

   B. Intel

   C. Samsung

   D. AMD

12. Which company did IBM first hire to build their core operating system for their PCs?

   A. Intel

   B. Apple

   C. Microsoft

   D. Bell Labs

13. What company dominates the CPU and chipset market?

   A. Microsoft

   B. Asus

   C. Intel

   D. AMD

14. Which of the following components feeds power to the internal components in a PC?

   A. Hard disk drive

   B. Motherboard

   C. Power supply

   D. AC outlet

15. Which of the following are examples of input devices? (Select the two best answers.)

A. Hard disk drive

B. Keyboard

C. Mouse

D. Monitor

Case Study 1

There are many types of computers, computer hardware, and computer software. However, as we have discussed in the chapter, the most common type of computer is the PC, and the most common type of software is Windows.

Define what kind of computer you are using. This might be your home computer or the computer in your school's lab. Explain what type of computer it is. Identify the manufacturer of the CPU and the motherboard. Then classify each of the components of the computer within the von Neumann computer model. Put each component within its correct category. For example, a Samsung monitor goes in the output devices category.

Case Study 2

The CPU in a PC is just one example of a semiconductor. Use the Internet to research other types of semiconductors and their uses. For example, research other types of devices including cell phones, smartphones, gaming consoles, televisions, SOHO routers, adapter cards, and so on. Make a list of five other types of semiconductor usage. Identify at least one actual device for each category. Include the manufacturer of the device, model of the device, and type of semiconductor it uses.

Answers and Explanations

1. C. The 8088 was an early model PC powered by the integrated circuit. Colossus and ENIAC are much older computers powered by vacuum tubes.

2. B. John Atanasoff is credited with the patent for the first computer known as the Atansoff-Berry computer.

3. A and C. The control unit and the arithmetic unit make up the CPU in the von Neumann computer model. The CPU is the processor. The memory is separate and has a different function.

4. **A.** Cache memory, a special type of memory that resides on or in the processor, alleviates the problem of the von Neumann bottleneck by allowing the processor faster access to important data.

5. **A, C, and D.** The five groups in the von Neumann architecture are CPU, working storage, permanent storage, input devices, and output devices. Monitors are just one type of output device. Keyboards are just one type of input device.

6. **A, C, and D.** The three main connectors in a transistor are the gate, source, and drain. N-type silicon creates a path for the current to flow. The gate and drain are both metal conductors, but the conductor itself is not the connection.

7. **D.** The MOSFET is the most common type of transistor that takes the place of vacuum tubes. When transistors are grouped together in unison, it is known as an integrated circuit or IC. The most powerful ICs are CPUs.

8. **C.** Millions. For example, the Intel Core I7 processor incorporates 731 million transistors into on integrated circuit.

9. **A.** The 8088 Intel CPU could address 1MB of memory. The 8088 processor ran at 4.77MHz.

10. **B.** Moore's law stated that processing performance and disk storage capacity would double every one and a half to two years.

11. **B and D.** Intel and AMD are the two companies most responsible for the advancement of CPUs in PCs. Toshiba and Samsung are among the top five semiconductor companies.

12. **C.** Microsoft was the first big supplier of operating systems for IBM starting with MS-DOS.

13. **C.** Intel. The majority of computers have Intel CPUs and the majority of motherboards have Intel chipsets

14. **C.** The power supply feeds power to the internal components of the PC. Although the motherboard has some minor power connections, it is not the device in charge of feeding power to internal components such as hard disk drives, CD-ROMs, and so on. However, the motherboard does control the flow of data to those devices. The AC outlet powers the power supply, which in turn powers the internal components.

15. **B and C.** Keyboards and mice are examples of input devices. The hard disk drive is an example of permanent storage. The monitor is an example of an output device.

Case Study 1 Solution

A typical computer in a home or at a school would most likely be a PC that runs Windows (either Windows XP, Windows 7, or Windows Vista). The most common manufacturer of the CPU would be Intel. The motherboard could be of Intel make, or perhaps another manufacturer. This depends on what type of computer it is, either by a manufacturer such as Dell or HP, or a white-box.

A typical computer might have the following typical components, categorized using the five von Neumann groups:

- **CPU:** Intel 2.5GHz Core 2 Duo

- **Working storage:** 2GB of 800MHz DDR2 RAM

- **Permanent storage:** 500GB SATA version 2.0 hard drive, and a 24X DVD-RW drive

- **Input devices:** USB keyboard and mouse

- **Output devices:** 20" widescreen Samsung monitor, basic stereo computer speakers, and an HP Deskjet printer

Case Study 2 Solution

Semiconductors can be found in all kinds of gadgets. Each of the five categories mentioned has one example below:

- **Smartphones:** The Motorola Droid: Arm Cortex A8 processor at 550MHz.

- **Gaming console:** Xbox: Uses a 3.2GHz PowerPC Tri-Core Xenon processor.

- **Television:** Samsung LED TV: Uses an RMI Au1250 Ultra Low-Power processor.

- **SOHO router:** D-Link DIR-655: 275MHz 32-bit CPU.

- **Video card:** Nvidia GeForce GTX 580: Graphics Processing Unit (GPU) has a processor clock speed of 1544MHz, and a graphics clock speed of 772MHz.

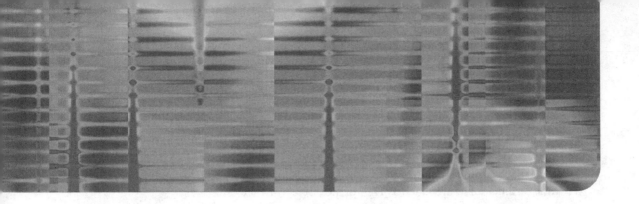

This chapter covers the following subjects:

- **Numbering Systems Used in Computers**—This section discusses the decimal, binary, and hexadecimal numbering systems, as well as conversions between those systems. The basics of bits and bytes are covered in this section as well.

- **Basic Boolean Operations**—In this section, you learn the basics about Boolean algebra that use three main operators: AND, OR, and NOT.

- **Measuring Data Transfer and Frequency**—Here the concepts of Hertz, bandwidth, frequency, and data transfer are discussed.

Understanding Computer Math and Measurement

In this chapter, we discuss computer math and measurement as they apply to today's operating systems and computer hardware. Concepts such as bits versus bytes, binary versus decimal, Boolean operators, Hertz, and data transfer are important to understand so that you have a solid foundation of computer knowledge.

Be sure to practice measuring data transfer and converting numbers from one system to another. The importance of these skills will be more apparent as we progress through the book, and as you continue with your training beyond this course.

Numbering Systems Used in Computers

Since the development of the first personal computers (PCs) more than 30 years ago, many terms such as bits, bytes, decimal, binary, and hexadecimal have become part of common language. However, these terms are not always used correctly. This section helps you understand the meaning of these terms and numbering systems and how they relate to the PC technologies you will be studying in future chapters.

Three numbering systems are used in computing: decimal, binary, and hexadecimal. You already are familiar with the decimal system: Look at your hands. Now, imagine your fingers are numbered from 0–9, for a total of 10 places. Decimal numbering is sometimes referred to as *base 10*.

The binary system doesn't use your fingers; instead, you count your hands: One hand represents 0, and the other 1, for a total of two places. Thus, binary numbering is sometimes referred to as *base 2*.

The hexadecimal system could be used by a pair of spiders who want to count: One spider's legs would be numbered 0–7, and the other spider's legs would be labeled 8, 9, A–F to reach a total of 16 places. Hexadecimal numbering is sometimes referred to as *base 16*.

> **TIP** Although all data in the computer is stored as a stream of binary values (0s and 1s), most of the time you will use decimal ("512MB of RAM") or hexadecimal ("memory conflict at C800 in upper memory") measurements. The typical rule of thumb is to use the system that produces the smallest *meaningful* number. If you need to convert between these systems, you can use any scientific calculator, including the Windows Calculator program (select **View, Scientific** from the Windows Calculator menu).

Decimal Numbering System

We use the decimal or base 10 system for everyday math. A variation on straight decimal numbering is to use "powers of 2" as a shortcut for large values. For example, drive storage sizes often are defined in terms of decimal bytes, but the number of colors that a video card can display can be referred to as *24-bit* (or 2^{24}), which is the same as 16,777,216 colors.

Binary Numbering System

All data used and stored by computers are processed as digital streams having only two values. Each value is considered as being on or off; high or low; or, as 1 (one) or 0 (zero). Because only two values (0 and 1) are used to represent data, this is called a *binary* numbering system. The ones and zeros in the binary numbering system are also known as bits. A bit is the smallest and most basic unit of measurement in computing; it is a contraction of the words binary and digit. Text is converted into its numerical equivalents before it is stored, so binary coding can be used to store all computer data and programs.

Table 2-1 shows how you would count from 1 to 10 (decimal) in binary.

Table 2-1 Decimal Numbers 1–10 and Binary Equivalents

Decimal	0	1	2	3	4	5	6	7	8	9	10
Binary	0	1	10	11	100	101	110	111	1000	1001	1010

Because binary numbers can occupy many places in comparison to decimal, the binary numbers are usually converted into hexadecimal or decimal numbers for calculations or measurements. In some cases, the leading zero can be removed from a binary number, leaving you with a truncated number. For example, an eight-bit number such as 01110011 can have the leading zero removed, resulting in the binary number 1110011. Although this is only seven bits, it is effectively the same as the number 01110011.

It is also important to understand the concepts of least significant bit (LSB) and most significant bit (MSB). In the binary number 1110011, the LSB is the last 1 shown. The MSB is the first 1 shown. LSB is often referred to as the *right-most bit*, and the MSB is often referred to as the *left-most bit*.

> **NOTE** After you understand how binary numbering works, you can appreciate the joke going around the Internet and showing up on T-shirts near you:
>
> "There are 10 kinds of people in the world—those who understand binary and those who don't."

There are several ways to convert a decimal number into binary:

- Use a scientific calculator with conversion
- Use the division method
- Use the subtraction method

To use the division method, follow these steps:

Step 1. Divide the number you want to convert by 2.

Step 2. Record the remainder: If there's no remainder, write down 0. If there's any remainder, write down 1.

Step 3. Divide the resulting answer by 2.

Step 4. Repeat the process, recording the remainder each time.

Step 5. Repeat the process until you divide 0 by 2. This is the last answer.

Step 6. When you divide the last answer, the binary appears from LSB to MSB. Reverse the order of bit numbers so that MSB is recorded first and the conversion is complete. For example, to convert the decimal number 115 to binary using the division method, follow the procedure shown in Figure 2-1.

If you use a scientific calculator (such as the scientific mode of the Windows Calculator) to perform the conversion, keep in mind that any leading zeros are suppressed. For example, the calculation in Figure 2-1 indicates the binary equivalent of 115 decimal is 01110011. However, a scientific calculator drops the leading zero and displays the value as 1110011.

Figure 2-1 Converting decimal 115 to binary with the division method.

115 (decimal) = 01110011 (binary)

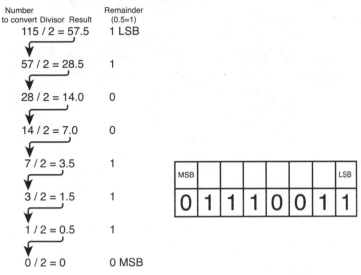

To use the subtraction method, follow these steps:

Step 1. Look at the number you want to convert and determine the smallest power of two that is greater than or equal to the number you want to subtract. Table 2-2 lists powers of two from 2^0 through 2^{17}. For example, 115 decimal is less than 2^7 (128) but greater than 2^6 (64).

Table 2-2 Powers of 2

Power of 2	Decimal Value	Power of 2	Decimal Value
2^0	1	2^9	512
2^1	2	2^{10}	1024
2^2	4	2^{11}	2048
2^3	8	2^{12}	4096
2^4	16	2^{13}	8192
2^5	32	2^{14}	16384
2^6	64	2^{15}	32768
2^7	128	2^{16}	65536
2^8	256	2^{17}	131072

Step 2. Subtract the highest power of two from the value you want to convert. Record the value and write down binary 1.

Step 3. Move to the next lower power of two. If you can subtract it, record the result and also write down binary 1. If you cannot subtract it, write down binary 0.

Step 4. Repeat Step 3 until you attempt to subtract 2^0 (1). Again, write down binary 1 if you can subtract it or binary 0 if you cannot. The binary values (0 and 1) you have recorded are the binary conversion for the decimal number. Unlike the division method, this method puts them in the correct order; there's no need to write them down in reverse order.

For example, to convert 115 decimal to binary using the subtraction method, see Figure 2-2.

Figure 2-2 Converting 115 decimal to binary with the subtraction method.

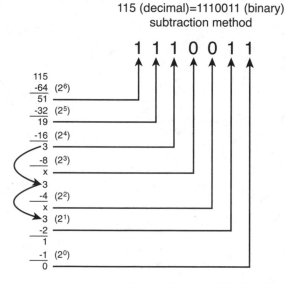

Table 2-2 provides a listing of powers of 2, but you can use the Windows Calculator in scientific view mode to calculate any power of two you want. To open the Windows Calculator, click **Start**, then **Run** and type **calc.exe**. (If you cannot see the Run option in Windows Vista, press the **Windows key** and **R** simultaneously.) Just enter **2**, click the **x^y** button, and enter the value for the power of 2 you want to calculate (such as 24). The results are displayed instantly (you add the commas). Use the Edit menu to copy the answer to the Windows Clipboard, and use your

program's Paste command to bring it into your document. Sure beats counting on your fingers!

You can also convert numbers easily with the Windows Calculator, which helps when checking your work. For example, Figure 2-3 shows the number 240 in decimal. Figure 2-4 shows that same number's equivalent in binary: 11110000, which you can discern by pressing the **F8** button or clicking the **Bin** radio button. (You can return to decimal by pressing **F6** or clicking the **Dec** radio button.)

Figure 2-3   Windows Calculator showing the number 240 in decimal.

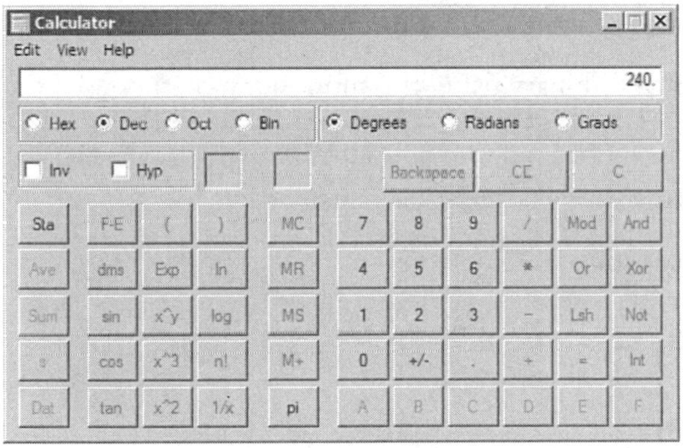

Figure 2-4   Windows Calculator showing the binary equivalent of 240.

Binary Versus Decimal MB/GB

Although a byte represents the basic "building block" of storage and RAM calculation, most measurements are better performed with multiples of a byte. All calculations of the capacity of RAM and storage are done in *bits* and *bytes*. A byte is the number of bits required to represent one character. In today's computers, one byte is equal to eight bits.

Table 2-3 provides the most typical values and their relationship to the byte.

Table 2-3   Decimal and Binary Measurements

Measurement	Type D=Decimal	Number of Bytes/Bits B=Binary
Bit	N/A	1/8 of a byte
Nibble	N/A	1/2 of a byte
Byte	N/A	8 bits
Kilobyte (kB)	D	1,000 bytes
	B	1,024 bytes
Megabit (Mb)	D	1,000,000 bits
	B	1,048,576 bits (131,072 bytes)
Megabyte (MB)	D	1,000,000 bytes
	B	1,048,576 bytes
Gigabit (Gb)	D	1,000,000,000 bits
	B	1,073,741,824 bits
Gigabyte (GB)	D	1,000,000,000 bytes
	B	1,073,741,824 bytes
Terabyte (TB)	D	1,000,000,000,000 bytes
	B	1,099,511,627,776 bytes

Decimal Versus Binary Numbering Confusion

The use of the terms kilobit, kilobyte, megabit, megabyte, gigabit, and gigabyte to refer both to decimal and binary values has caused widespread confusion about the capacities of magnetic, optical, and flash memory storage. Storage device manufacturers almost always rate drives and media in decimal megabytes (multiples of 1 million bytes) or decimal gigabytes (multiples of 1 billion bytes), which is also the standard used by disk utilities such as CHKDSK, ScanDisk, and FORMAT. However, most BIOS programs and Windows Disk Management utilities list drive sizes in binary megabytes or binary gigabytes.

continues

The differences in numbering between the decimal and binary versions of a numbering system often lead to a perception that device vendors are not properly describing the capacities of their drives or media. An attempt was made in late 1998 to use the prefixes kibi, mebi, and gibi to refer to binary numbers in place of kilo, mega, and giga. However, this numbering system has not been fully adopted by the industry.

Consider a hard disk rated by its maker as 160GB (decimal). This is 160,000,000,000 bytes (decimal). However, when the drive is detected and configured by the BIOS and partitioned with FDISK, its size is listed as only 149.01GB (binaryGB). At first glance, you might believe you've lost some capacity (see Figure 2-5).

Figure 2-5 The capacity of an 160GB hard disk size is 160 billion bytes (top bar), but most BIOS programs and Windows FDISK/Disk Management measure drives in binary gigabytes (bottom bar) and report a capacity of 149.01GB.

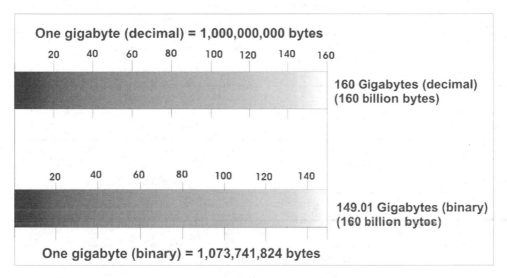

However, as you've already seen, there is a substantial difference between the number of bytes in a binary gigabyte and one billion bytes. This different numbering system, not any loss of bytes, accounts for the seeming discrepancy. Use this information to help explain to a customer that the "missing" capacity of the hard disk isn't really missing (see Figure 2-6).

Figure 2-6   A binary gigabyte has more than 73 million more bytes than a decimal gigabyte (1 billion bytes).

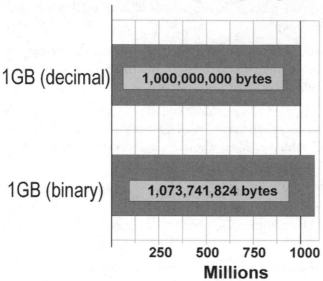

Decimal vs Binary Gigabytes

1GB (decimal) — 1,000,000,000 bytes

1GB (binary) — 1,073,741,824 bytes

250   500   750   1000

Millions

Data Storage and Overhead

As you learned earlier in this chapter, bits and bytes are the building blocks of measuring storage and memory capacities. However, why is it that when the same information is stored in different ways that the size of the file changes so much?

If you are storing text-only information in the computer, each character of that text (including spaces and punctuation marks) equals a byte. Thus, to calculate the number of bytes in the following sentence, count the letters, numbers, spaces, and punctuation marks:

```
"This book is published by Pearson."
12345678901234567890123456789012345678901234
         |         |         |         |
        10        20        30        40
```

From the scale, you can see that the sentence uses 36 bytes. You can prove this to yourself by starting Windows Notepad and entering the text just as you see it printed here. Save the text as EXAMPLE.TXT and view the File properties. You can see that the text is exactly 36 bytes.

Do most computer programs store just the text when you write something? To find out, start a word-processing program, such as Windows WordPad or Microsoft

Word. Enter the same sentence again, and save it as EXAMPLE. If you use Word-Pad, save the file as a Rich Text Format (.RTF) file. Depending upon whether you use WordPad or Microsoft Word, the file takes up a different amount of space. For example, WordPad for Windows XP saves text as an RTF file, using 193 bytes to store the file. The same sentence takes approximately 24 kilobytes (kB) when saved as a .DOC file by Microsoft Word!

When data you create is stored in a computer, it must be stored in a particular arrangement suitable for the program that created the information. This arrangement of information is called the *file format*.

In computer storage, however, pure text is seldom stored alone. WordPad and other word-processing programs such as Microsoft Word, OpenOffice Writer, and Corel WordPerfect enable you to **boldface**, <u>underline</u>, *italicize*, and make text larger or smaller. You can also use different fonts in the same document.

Most modern programs also enable you to insert tables, create columns of text, and insert pictures into the text. Some, such as Microsoft Word, have provisions for tracking changes made by different users. In other words, there's a whole lot more than text in a document.

To keep all this non-text information arranged correctly with the text, WordPad and other programs must store references to these additional features along with the text, making even a sentence or two into a relatively large file, even if none of the extra features is actually used in that particular file. Thus, for most programs, the bytes used by the data they create are the total of the bytes used by the text or other information created by the program and the additional bytes needed to store the file in a particular file format.

Because different programs store data in different ways, it's possible to have an apparent software failure take place because a user tries to use program B to open a file made with program A. Unless program B contains a converter that can understand and translate how program A stores data, program B can't read the file, and might even crash. To help avoid problems, Windows associates particular types of data files with matching programs, enabling you to open the file with the correct program by double-clicking the file in Windows Explorer.

Hexadecimal Numbering System

A third numbering system used in computers is hexadecimal. Hexadecimal numbering is also referred to as base 16. The hexadecimal numbering system is a convenient way to work with data because 16 is also the number of bits in 2 bytes or 4 nibbles (a nibble being 4 bits). Hexadecimal numbers use digits 0–9 and letters A–F to represent the 16 places (0–15 decimal). Hexadecimal numbers are used to represent locations in data

storage, data access, and RAM. Table 2-4 shows how decimal numbers are represented in hex.

Table 2-4   Decimal and Hexadecimal Equivalents

Decimal	0	1	2	3	4	5	6	7	8	9	10	11	12	13	14	15
Hexadecimal	0	1	2	3	4	5	6	7	8	9	A	B	C	D	E	F

The most typical uses for hexadecimal numbering are

- Upper memory addresses
- I/O port addresses
- MAC addresses and IPv6 addresses

One example of a hexadecimal number is 3F8. This is the I/O port address for Com Port 1 (COM1). Hexadecimal numbers are often used when it comes to storing data and programs within RAM. They are also important to programmers and developers. However, in this book, we deal with binary and decimal more often than hexadecimal.

Basic Boolean Operations

Boolean operations are processes used by computer programmers, mathematicians, and engineers. They are part of Boolean algebra (also known as Boolean logic) that was developed by the 19th-century mathematician George Boole. Boole's algebra was found to be of greatest value when it was applied to electronic logic circuits in the early 20th century.

There are three main Boolean operators: AND, OR, and NOT. These may be represented in different ways, as shown in Table 2-5. Let's discuss each one.

Table 2-5   Boolean Operators

Operator	Programmers' Representation	Mathematicians' Representation
AND	&	$\cdot$
OR	|	+
NOT	~	$\bar{x}$

AND

The AND operator is used to compare (or combine) two or more pieces of information. These are commonly known as *sets*. For example, Set A could consist of the elements (numbers) 1, 5, 9, 13, and 17. Set B could consist of the elements 2, 5, 10, 13, and 18. When sets A and B are compared, the AND operator will locate the numbers that are part of both sets: 5 and 13, as shown in Figure 2-7. This figure is an example of a Venn diagram, named after another 19th-century mathematician named John Venn.

Figure 2-7   The AND operator comparing Sets A and B.

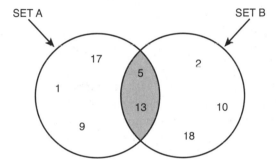

This operation can also be described in binary. When it comes down to it, Boolean operators are meant to be used with bits. For example, if we had two bit variables (known as A and B), there would be four possible combinations. However, the only result of 1 would occur when both A *and* B are equal to 1, as shown in Table 2-6.

Table 2-6   The AND Operation Shown with Bits

A	B	A & B
0	0	0
0	1	0
1	0	0
1	1	1

The preceding table is a basic example of a logic gate. A logic gate performs a logical operation from one or more inputs, and produces an output. In the table, on each row, two inputs are used to produce a single output. In computing, logic gates are implemented within digital circuits such as transistors and diodes. More advanced circuits such as integrated circuits (central processing units [CPUs]) can

have an output from one gate wired to several other gates' inputs. This is known as *cascading*.

Boolean operators are also used to define relationships between words. This applies to searching and retrieving records containing specific words. For example, the AND operator narrows the search by searching for records that contain all of the words it separates. When search terms such as "computer" and "hardware" are combined, the retrieved records must contain both of the terms. This can be shown as "computer AND hardware" and "computer & hardware". You can use the AND operator to search for more than two terms as well.

OR

The OR operator is used to broaden comparisons by including both sets of information. One or more sets of information *may* be included, but both are not necessary, as is the case with the AND operator.

This operation can be described in binary as well. Once again, if we had two bit variables (known as A and B), there would be four possible combinations. But this time, the result of 1 could occur if either A *or* B is equal to 1, as shown in Table 2-7. In this scenario, 3 of the 4 results are equal to 1.

Table 2-7   The OR Operation Shown with Bits

A	B	A | B
0	0	0
0	1	1
1	0	1
1	1	1

As it applies to searching records of information, the OR operator broadens the search by searching for records that contain any of the words that the OR separates. When search terms such as "music" and "lessons" are combined, the retrieved records can contain either or both of the terms. This can be shown as "music OR lessons" as well as "music | lessons". You can use the OR operator to search for more than two terms as well.

NOT

The NOT operator is used to narrow comparisons by excluding the second set of information. Generally, this operator is used only with two sets of information. In

binary, however, there are only two values possible, so applying the NOT operator to a 0 gives a 1, and applying it to a 1 gives a 0. Table 2-8 shows this single input and single output operation.

Table 2-8   The NOT Operation Shown with Bits

A	Not A
0	1
1	0

As it applies to searching records of information, the NOT operator narrows the search by searching for records that contain one term but *not* the other. When search terms such as "music" and "lessons" are combined, the retrieved records can contain information pertaining to music, but not information pertaining to music lessons. This can be shown as "music NOT lessons" as well as "music ~ lessons."

Mixed Boolean Operations

Quite often, the AND and OR operators will be mixed together to perform a more complex search. Here's an example:

music AND (lessons OR computer)

In this example, a search system will retrieve records containing the words "lessons and music" or the words "computer and music". The search could also be performed without parentheses. For example:

music AND lessons OR computer

In this example, the AND operation is completed first. Records will be retrieved containing the words "music and lessons" as well as the word "computer".

Keep in mind that different systems can (and will) process statements differently when it comes to mixing Boolean operators. The preceding examples are common, but not definitive. Consult your specific search system's help file for more information on mixing Boolean operators.

Measuring Data Transfer and Frequency

Data is constantly being transferred within a computer and between computers. But how much data, and how fast is it being computed? Data transfer is known as *bandwidth*, which specifies how much data is being sent per second. The speed at which data is computed is known as *Hertz*, which also dictates the frequency used to transfer data.

Bandwidth

Other than bits and bytes and their multiples, probably the second most significant concept to understand about computer measurements is bandwidth, also known as *data transfer rate*. Bandwidth refers to the amount of information that can be sent or received through a computer or network connection in one second. This can be measured in bits (with a lowercase b) or bytes (with an uppercase B). For example, the bandwidth of a USB 1.1 port running at full speed transfers a maximum of 11 megabits per second (11MBps; notice the lowercase b), while the bandwidth of a USB 2.0 port running at high speed is 480MBps, and an Internet user might download 300 kilobytes (300KBps; notice the upper case B) of data per second. Or an expansion card that goes into a PCI slot could transfer a maximum of 266MBps.

Bandwidth measurements like this are used for measuring the performance of serial, parallel, wired and wireless network connections, expansion slots, hard disk interfaces, and multipurpose device interfaces (such as the Universal Serial Bus [USB]). It defines the amount of information that can flow through the computer.

Information flows through the computer in many ways. The CPU is the central point for most information. When you start a program, the CPU instructs the storage device to load the program into RAM. When you create data and print it, the CPU instructs the printer to output the data.

Because of the different types of devices that send and receive information, two major types of data transfers take place within a computer: parallel and serial. These terms are used frequently, but if you're not familiar with the differences between them, check out Figure 2-8.

Figure 2-8   Parallel data transfers move data 8 bits at a time, whereas serial data transfers move 1 bit at a time.

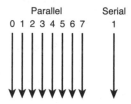

Parallel Information Transfers

Parallel transfers use multiple "lanes" for data and programs, and in keeping with the 8 bits = 1 byte nature of computer information, most parallel transfers use multiples of 8. Parallel transfers take place between the following devices:

- Processor (CPU) and RAM
- Processor (CPU) and interface cards

- LPT (printer) port and parallel printer

- SCSI port and SCSI devices

- PATA /IDE host adapter and PATA/IDE drives

- RAM and interface cards, either via the CPU or directly with direct memory access (DMA)

Before the development of high-speed interfaces such as serial ATA (SATA), universal serial bus (USB), and FireWire (IEEE 1394), parallel interfaces were the most common types of interfaces between peripherals and PC components. There were two reasons for this:

- Multiple bits of information are sent at the same time.

- At identical clock speeds, parallel transfers are faster than serial transfers because more data is being transferred.

However, parallel transfers also have problems:

- Many wires or traces (wire-like connections on the motherboard or expansion cards) are needed, leading to interference concerns and thick, expensive cables.

- Excessively long parallel cables or traces can cause data to arrive at different times. This is referred to as *signal skew* (see Figure 2-9).

- Differences in voltage between wires or traces can cause *jitter*, which can be described as shaky pulses of bits that can lead to loss of transmitted data.

Figure 2-9   Parallel cables that are too long can cause signal skew, allowing the parallel signals to become "out of step" with each other.

As a result of these problems, some compromises have had to be included in computer and system design:

- Short maximum lengths for parallel, PATA/IDE, and SCSI cables

- Dual-speed motherboards (running the CPU internally at much faster speeds than the motherboard or memory)

Fortunately, there is a second way to transmit information: serial transfers.

Serial Transfers

A *serial transfer* uses a single "lane" in the computer for information transfers. This sounds like a recipe for slowdowns, but it all depends on how fast the speed limit is on the "data highway."

The following ports and devices in the computer use serial transfers:

- Serial (also called RS-232 or COM) ports and devices

- Modems (which can be internal devices or can connect to serial or USB ports)

- USB (Universal Serial Bus) 1.1 and 2.0 ports and devices

- IEEE 1394 (FireWire, i.Link) ports and devices

- Serial ATA (SATA) host adapters and drives

Serial transfers have the following characteristics:

- One bit at a time is transferred to the device.

- Transmission speeds can vary greatly, depending on the sender and receiver.

- Very few connections are needed in the cable and ports (one transmit, one receive, and a few control and ground wires).

- Cable lengths can be longer with serial devices. For example, an UltraDMA/133 PATA/IDE cable can be only 18 inches long for reliable data transmission, whereas a Serial ATA cable can be almost twice as long.

Although RS-232 serial ports are much slower than any parallel interface, newer types of devices using serial transfers such as USB, SATA, and FireWire are much faster than parallel devices. The extra speed is possible because serial transfers don't have to worry about interference or other problems caused by running so many data lines together. As a result, parallel interfacing is used primarily for some types of internal connections between motherboard devices, while USB, SATA, and FireWire have almost completely replaced serial, parallel, PATA/IDE, and SCSI interfaces.

TIP Parallel data transfers are measured in bytes; serial data transfers are measured in bits.

Hertz (Hz)

Hertz (Hz) measures the transmission frequency of radio and electrical signals in cycles per second. For example, the common 115V alternating current (AC) electrical standard used in North America is transmitted at 60 cycles per second, or 60Hz; thus, 115V/60Hz AC.

Megahertz (MHz) is equal to 1,000,000Hz; Gigahertz (GHz) is equal to one billion Hertz, or 1000MHz. An example of a device that runs in the GHz speeds is the processor or CPU; a typical CPU might run at 2.4GHz. Table 2-9 shows the most common multiples for Hertz.

Table 2-9   Multiples for Hertz

Symbol	Name	Amount of Cycles per Second
Hz	Hertz	1
kHz	Kilohertz	1,000
MHz	Megahertz	1,000,000
GHz	Gigahertz	1,000,000,000

At this point, you should have a nice little foundation of knowledge concerning numbering systems and data transfer. Memorize and use these concepts as you read through the upcoming chapters to help you understand the more in-depth concepts that you will encounter.

Chapter Review Questions

The following questions test your recall of the concepts described in this chapter. The answers are listed at the end of the questions in the Answers and Explanations section.

1. How many combinations are there in a 4-bit binary number?

   A. 4

   B. 8

   C. 16 ✗

   D. 40

2. 24-bit color is the same as which of the following amounts of colors?

   A. 65,536

   B. 256

   C. 4,000,000,000

   D. 16,777,216 ✗

3. What is the binary equivalent of the decimal number 6?

   A. 11

   B. 110 ✗

   C. 1010

   D. 111

4. What is the binary equivalent of the decimal number 255?

   A. 00000000

   B. 01111111

   C. 11111111 ✗

   D. 11111110

5. What is the decimal value of 2^{12}?

   A. 512

   B. 1024

   C. 2048

   D. 4096 ✗

6. A gigabyte is equal to how many bytes in binary measurement?

   A. 2^{30}

   B. 2^{20}

   C. 2^{10}

   D. 2^{40}

7. In the hexadecimal numbering system, what is **D** equal to?

   A. 11

   B. 12 ˅

   C. 13

   D. 14

8. Which of the following operators is represented with the | (pipe) sign?

   A. AND

   B. OR ˟

   C. NOT

   D. EITHER

9. Using the binary numbering system, if A equals 1 and B equals 1, what is the solution to the following equation: **A AND B**.

   A. 0

   B. 1˟

   C. A

   D. B

10. You want to search for records containing "music lessons" and "computer music." Which of the following expressions would work best?

   A. music AND (lessons OR computer) ˟

   B. music AND lessons OR computer

   C. music AND lessons NOT computer

   D. (music AND lessons) OR computer

11. What does the following measurement mean?

266MBps

A. 266 megabits per second

B. 266 megabytes per minute

C. 266 megabytes per second ✓

D. 266 megabits per minute

12. Which of the following would be faster at an identical clock speed?

A. Parallel data transfer ✗

B. Serial data transfer

C. Dial-up modem data transfer over the Internet

D. Network adapter data transfer over the Internet

13. What is 1GHz equal to?

A. 1,000 Hertz

B. 1,000,000 Hertz

C. 1,000,000,000 Hertz ✗

D. 1,000,000,000,000 Hertz

14. Which numbering system has 16 values?

A. Binary 8

B. Decimal 10

C. Octal

D. Hexadecimal ✗ 16

15. What is the decimal equivalent of the binary number 11110000?

A. 224

B. 240 ✗

C. 248

D. 252

Case Study 1

Compare the ways that humans and computers count. The average human counts in decimal. This is derived from the fact that the human body has 10 fingers. The average computer counts in binary. This is derived from the fact that computers only have two fingers, so to speak. Computers only understand on and off, or 1 and 0—effectively positive or negative electricity. Which of the two is more efficient? Why?

Write a two-paragraph essay describing which you believe is more efficient and explain why you believe so. Use this chapter and the Internet as sources for the basis of your argument.

Case Study 2

Analyze the data transfer rate of your home Internet connection. Test the speed of the connection three times and average the three together to get a final result. Compare this result to others in your class. You can use tools from one of the following websites:

- Broadband Reports

  www.dslreports.com/speedtest

- Speedguide.net

  www.speedguide.net/speedtest/

Be sure to note which site you used, which type of test, and which server you connected to. Also note what kind of Internet connection you have, and if you know, what level of data transfer you are paying for.

Answers and Explanations

1. **C.** A 4-bit binary number has 16 combinations starting with 0000 and continuing on to 1111.

2. **D.** 24-bit color is a color scheme that deals with three bytes of colors (red, green, and blue). A binary number with 24 bits has 16,777,216 combinations. 65,536 colors is 16-bit. 256 colors is 8-bit, and 4 billion colors is approximate to 32-bit color.

3. **B.** 110 is the binary equivalent of the decimal number 6. 11 in binary equals 3 in decimal. 1010 in binary equals 10 in decimal. 111 equals 7 in decimal.

4. **C.** 11111111 is the binary equivalent of the decimal number 255. 00000000 in binary equals 0 in decimal (zero is always zero). 01111111 in binary equals 127 in decimal. 11111110 in binary equals 254 in binary.

5. D. 2^{12} is equal to 4096. 512 is equal to 2^{9}. 1024 is equal to 2^{10}. 2048 is equal to 2^{11}.

6. A. 2^{30} is a gigabyte. 2^{20} is a megabyte. 2^{10} is a kilobyte. 2^{40} is a terabyte.

7. C. In hexadecimal, **D** is equal to 13. 11 is equal to **B**; 12 is equal to **C**; and 14 is equal to **E**.

8. B. The OR operator can be represented with the | (pipe) sign or with a + (plus) sign.

9. B. 1. If both A and B equal 1, and the equation is A AND B, then the answer is 1.

10. A. music AND (lessons OR computer) is the best search expression to use in order to find records containing "music lessons" and "computer music".

11. C. 266MBps equals 266 megabytes per second. Bytes are shown with a capital B. Bits are represented with a lowercase b. Data transfers are normally measured by the second.

12. A. At identical clock speeds, parallel data transfers are faster than serial data transfers because more bits are sent per second. Dial-up modems and network adapters transfer information serially when sending that information over the Internet.

13. C. 1GHz (1 GigaHertz) is equal to 1,000,000,000 Hertz. 1,000 Hertz is 1KHz. 1,000,000 Hertz is 1MHz. 1,000,000,000,000 is 1THz.

14. D. The hexadecimal numbering system has 16 values (0–9 and A–F). You can remember this by thinking Hex (6) plus deci (10) equals 16. Binary has 2 values (0 and 1). Octal has 8 values. Decimal has 10 values (0–9).

15. B. 240 is the decimal equivalent of the binary number 11110000. 224 equals 11100000. 248 equals 11111000. 252 equals 11111100.

Case Study 1 Solution

From a pure calculating standpoint, a computer is more efficient at arithmetic and higher forms of math, not only because it is faster, but because it doesn't deal with as many values as a person does. However, in some cases, a human can put numbers into context much more efficiently than a computer can. So ensues a great debate. Your answer depends on what you are trying to accomplish and what kind of information you are working with.

Case Study 2 Solution

As an example, a typical cable modem Internet connection tested against Broadband Reports test servers might get the following results:

Test 1: Download speed = 5304KBps (5.3MBps), Upload speed = 1737KBps (1.7MBps).

Test 2: Download speed = 5865KBps (5.8MBps), Upload speed = 1912KBps (1.9MBps).

Test 3: Download speed = 4742KBps (4.7MBps), Upload speed = 1536KBps (1.5MBps).

Average results: Download speed = 5303KBps (5.3MBps), Upload speed = 1728KBps (1.7MBps)

This chapter covers the following subjects:

- **Understanding I/O Ports**—This section describes the types of I/O ports used to send information to and from the processor and memory.

- **Understanding Input Devices**—This section describes the important characteristics of keyboards, mice, biometric readers, and other input devices.

- **Understanding Display Types**—This section describes output devices such as CRTs, LCDs, and data projectors.

- **Understanding Video Connector Types**—This section talks about common video connectors such as VGA, DVI, and HDMI.

- **Printing Fundamentals**—This section describes the basics of laser, inkjet, impact, and thermal printers.

- **Understanding Multimedia Devices**—This section covers the basics of multimedia devices such as webcams, digital cameras, MIDI ports, microphones, sound cards, and video capture cards.

I/O Ports and Devices

Input/output (I/O) devices enable us to control the computer and display information in a variety of ways. There are a plethora of ports that connect these devices to the computer, for example, the well-known USB port. To fully understand how to install, configure, and troubleshoot input, output, and multimedia devices, you need to know the ports like the back of your hand. In this chapter you learn about serial, parallel, SCSI, USB, sound, and FireWire ports and their corresponding devices; the goal is to make you proficient with the various interfaces you see in the IT field.

Understanding I/O Ports

The word "port" is used often in the computer industry, and has many different meanings depending on what technology is being referred to. In this section, we detail input/output (I/O) ports. I/O ports allow for connections to hardware. This hardware could be internal or external. The ports are associated with copper circuits and memory ranges that allow the communication of data between the CPU, RAM, and the ports themselves. Common I/O ports include USB and FireWire. In this section, we also discuss SCSI, audio connections, MIDI, and RG-6 coaxial ports. Although the most important I/O port on recent systems is the USB port, you might also encounter other ports, including legacy ports such as serial and parallel, which we speak to in this section as well.

USB

Universal Serial Bus (USB) ports have largely replaced PS/2 (mini-DIN) mouse and keyboard, serial (COM), and parallel (LPT) ports on recent systems. Most recent desktop systems have at least four USB ports, and many systems support as many as eight or more front- and rear-mounted USB ports. Figure 3-1 shows the rear panel of a typical ATX system, including USB and other port types discussed in this chapter.

Figure 3-1   A typical ATX motherboard's I/O ports, complete with legacy (serial, parallel, PS/2 mouse, and keyboard), four USB, one IEEE 1394, two Ethernet, and audio ports.

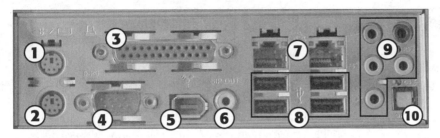

1. PS/2 mouse port
2. PS/2 keyboard port
3. Parallel port
4. Serial port
5. IEEE 1394a port
6. SPDIF coaxial digital audio port
7. Ethernet ports
8. USB ports
9. 1/8-inch mini-jack audio ports
10. SPDIF optical digital audio port

The following sections describe USB port types and how to add more USB ports.

USB Port Types, Speeds, and Technical Details

There are three standards types of USB ports you need to know:

- USB 1.1

- USB 2.0 (also called Hi-Speed USB)

- USB 3.0 (also called SuperSpeed USB)

The standards use the same cable and connector types, which are shown in Figure 3-2.

USB cables use two types of connectors: Series A (also called Type A) and Series B (also called Type B). Series A connectors are used on USB root hubs (the USB ports in the computer) and USB external hubs to support USB devices. Series B connectors are used for devices that employ a removable USB cable, such as a USB printer or a generic (external) hub. Generally, you need a Series A–to–Series B cable to attach most devices to a USB root or external hub. Cables that are Series A–to–Series A or Series B–to–Series B are used to extend standard cables, and can cause problems if the combined length of the cables exceeds recommended distances. Adapters are available to convert Series B cables into Mini-B cables, which support the Mini-B port design used on many recent USB devices.

Figure 3-2   USB plugs and sockets.

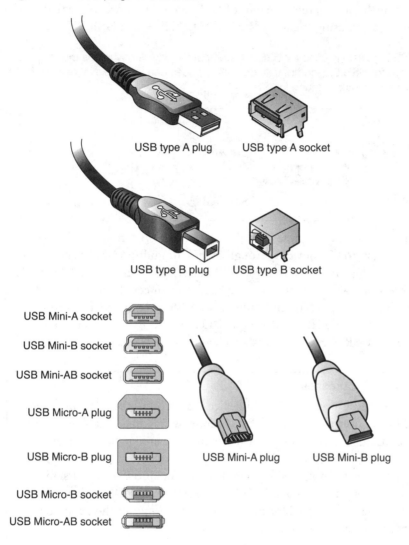

USB type A plug   USB type A socket

USB type B plug   USB type B socket

USB Mini-A socket

USB Mini-B socket

USB Mini-AB socket

USB Micro-A plug

USB Micro-B plug   USB Mini-A plug   USB Mini-B plug

USB Micro-B socket

USB Micro-AB socket

USB 1.1 ports run at a top speed (full-speed USB) of 12 megabits per second (Mbps), low-speed USB devices such as a mouse or a keyboard run at 1.5Mbps, and USB 2.0 (Hi-Speed USB) ports run at a top speed of 480Mbps. USB 2.0 ports are backward-compatible with USB 1.1 devices and speeds, and manage multiple USB 1.1 devices better than a USB 1.1 port does. USB 3.0 ports run at a top speed of 4,800Mbps.

USB packaging and device markings frequently use the official logos shown in Figure 3-3 to distinguish the different versions of USB in common use. Note that the industry is shifting from using the term "USB 2.0" to "Hi-Speed USB."

Figure 3-3 The USB logo (left) is used for USB 1.1–compatible devices, whereas the Hi-Speed USB logo (right) is used for USB 2.0–compatible devices. Devices bearing these logos have been certified by the USB Implementers Forum, Inc.

With either version of USB, a single USB port on an add-on card or motherboard is designed to handle up to 127 devices through the use of multiport hubs and daisy-chaining hubs. Starting with Windows 98, USB devices are Plug and Play (PnP) devices that are hot swappable (can be connected and disconnected without turning off the system). The USB ports (each group of two ports is connected to a root hub) in the computer use a single IRQ and a single I/O port address, regardless of the number of physical USB ports or devices attached to those ports.

IRQ Numbers and I/O Addresses

An IRQ is an Interrupt ReQuest, the act of a device interrupting the CPU in order to gain its attention in an effort to send data. This is done by way of an interrupt input line (an actual circuit). The devices, or ports and their associated controlling chips, are assigned IRQ numbers which help the CPU and interrupt controller to differentiate between devices. For example, the keyboard controller chip is always assigned IRQ 1. A PS/2 mouse is always assigned IRQ 12. The standard IRQ numbers range between 0 and 15. Some are reserved for future use by the owner of the computer; this helps with expansion and adding devices to the system.

I/O port addresses are ranges of circuits that a device uses to actually send the data after they have gained the CPU's attention. These are shown in hexadecimal because they are considered to be memory ranges. For example, the keyboard uses the I/O port address 60. This is known as the base address, or the first in the I/O range. The entire range for the keyboard is 60-6F, a total of 16 values (a 16-bit range). Another example would be the primary IDE controller; this uses the range 1F0-1F7, a total of 8 values (an 8-bit range). Because today's operating systems automatically configure these settings for devices, it is rare that you need to troubleshoot device conflicts associated with IRQs and I/O addresses.

The maximum length for a cable attached to 12Mbps or 480Mbps USB devices is five meters, whereas the maximum length for low-speed (1.5Mbps) devices such as mice and keyboards is three meters. When a USB root hub is enabled in a computer running Windows, two devices are visible in the Windows Device Manager: a USB root hub and a PCI-to-USB universal host controller (USB 1.1) or advanced host controller (USB 2.0), which uses the single IRQ and I/O port address required by USB hardware. If an external USB hub is attached to the computer, a generic hub also is listed in the Windows Device Manager (see Figure 3-4). A root hub supports two USB ports. In Figure 3-4, there are two root hubs listed, indicating that the system has four USB ports. You can access the Device Manager by clicking **Start**, right-clicking **Computer** (or **My Computer** in older Windows operating systems), and selecting **Manage**. The Computer Management window opens, and the Device Manager is located there. You can also access Device Manager from the Control Panel.

Figure 3-4   The USB section of the Windows XP Device Manager on a typical system. Note the fork-shaped USB logo next to the category and each device.

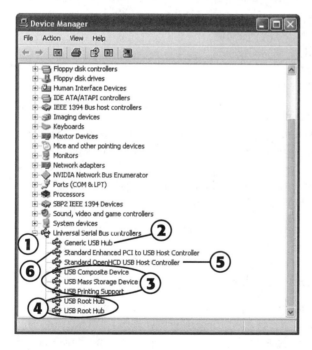

1. USB category
2. Generic (external) USB hub
3. Device-specific USB support
4. USB root hubs
5. USB universal host controller (USB 1.1 support)
6. USB enhanced host controller (USB 2.0 support)

Adding USB Ports

Need more USB ports? You can add USB ports with any of the following methods:

- Motherboard connectors for USB header cables
- Hubs
- Add-on cards

Some motherboards have USB header cable connectors, which enable you to make additional USB ports available on the rear or front of the computer. Some motherboard vendors include these header cables with the motherboard, whereas others require you to purchase them separately. Some recent case designs also include front-mounted USB ports, which can also be connected to the motherboard. Because of vendor-specific differences in how motherboards implement header cables, the header cable might use separate connectors for each signal instead of the more common single connector for all signals.

USB generic hubs enable you to connect multiple devices to the same USB port and to increase the distance between the device and the USB port. There are two types of generic hubs:

- Bus-powered
- Self-powered

Bus-powered hubs might be built into other devices, such as monitors and keyboards, or can be standalone devices. A bus-powered hub distributes both USB signals and power via the USB bus to other devices. Different USB devices use different amounts of power, and some devices require more power than others do. A bus-powered hub provides no more than 100 milliamps (mA) of power to each device connected to it. Thus, some devices fail when connected to a bus-powered hub.

A self-powered hub, on the other hand, has its own power source; it plugs into an AC wall outlet. It can provide up to 500mA of power to each device connected to it. A self-powered hub supports a wider range of USB devices, so it is recommended that you use it instead of a bus-powered hub whenever possible.

You can also add USB ports by way of an expansion card. If you have a free slot in the computer, and know what type of slot it is, you can easily snap in an adapter card that has an additional two, four, or eight USB ports. The key is to make sure that the adapter card is completely compatible with the expansion slot on the motherboard. For example, if you have a PCI Express x2 expansion slot, then you would need to purchase a PCI Express x2 adapter card. We talk more about expansion cards and slots in Chapter 4, "Motherboards and Buses."

Serial (COM)

The serial port, also known as RS-232 or COM (communication) ports, historically has rivaled the parallel port in versatility (see Figure 3-5).

Figure 3-5   A 9-pin serial port (DB-9M connector, top) and a 25-pin serial port (DB-25M connector, bottom) on a typical extension bracket from a multi-I/O card.

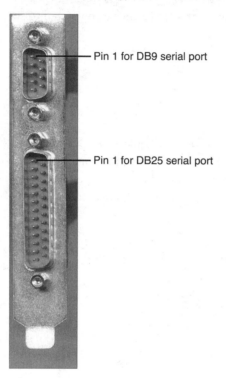

Pin 1 for DB9 serial port

Pin 1 for DB25 serial port

Serial ports have been used to connect the following:

- External modems
- Serial mouse or pointing devices such as trackballs or touchpads
- Plotters
- Label printers
- Serial printers
- PDA docking stations
- Digital cameras
- PC-to-PC connections used by file transfer programs such as Direct Cable Connection, LapLink, and Interlink

NOTE   The DB-9 is actually a DE-9 connector, but is colloquially known as "DB-9." The smaller the D-sub connector, the higher the letter.

Because USB ports provide greater speed than serial ports and support multiple devices connected to a single port via hubs, it's no wonder that USB is by far the most commonly used port on a PC, and many devices that were formerly connected to serial ports now utilize USB ports.

Serial ports come in two forms:

- DB-9M (male)

- DB-25M (male)

Either type can be adapted to the other connector type with a low-cost adapter (see Figure 3-6). The difference is possible because serial communications need only a few wires. Unlike parallel printers, which use a standard cable, each type of serial device uses a specially wired cable. DB-9M connectors are used on all but the oldest systems.

Figure 3-6   A typical DB-25F to DB-9M serial port converter. The DB-25F connector (lower left) connects to the 25-pin serial port and converts its signals for use by devices attaching to the DB-9M port at the other end (upper right).

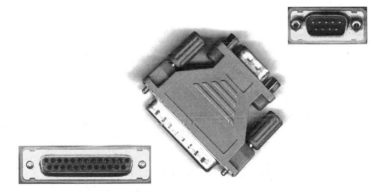

A serial connection needs to have a cable that connects the device to the port. The device then uses the IRQ and I/O port settings assigned to the serial port. Let's discuss the cables and settings now.

Types of Serial Cables

Serial cables can be constructed in many different ways. In fact, cables for serial devices are usually specified by device type rather than port type. This is because different devices use different pinouts.

Some of the most common examples of serial cables include

- Null-modem (data transfer) cable

- Modem cable

A null-modem cable enables two computers to communicate directly with each other by crossing the receive and transmit wires (meaning that two computers can send and receive data, much like a computer network, though much slower). The best known of these programs is LapLink, but the Windows Direct Cable Connection/Direct Serial Connection utilities can also use this type of cable. Although these programs support serial cable transfers, parallel port transfers are much faster and USB transfers are much faster than parallel; these methods for direct connection are recommended for most versions of Windows. However, Windows NT 4.0 and earlier do *not* support using the parallel port for file transfers, so you must use a null-modem cable, such as the one shown in Figure 3-7.

Figure 3-7   A LapLink serial cable with connectors for either 25-pin or 9-pin serial ports. Only three wires are needed, enabling the cable to be much thinner than the 9-pin serial extension cable also shown.

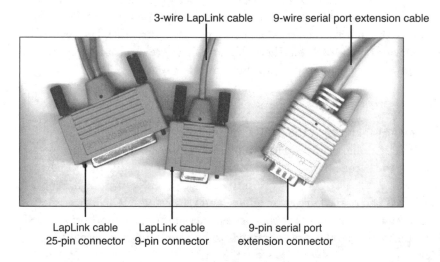

3-wire LapLink cable   9-wire serial port extension cable

LapLink cable   LapLink cable   9-pin serial port
25-pin connector   9-pin connector   extension connector

A modem cable is used to connect an external modem to a serial port. Some modems include a built-in cable, but others require you to use a DB-9F to DB-25M cable from the 9-pin connector on the serial port to the 25-pin port on the modem.

What about serial printers? These printers are used primarily with older terminals rather than with PCs, and because different printers use different pinouts, their cables must be custom-made. In fact, I've built a few myself. Fortunately, most recent terminals use parallel or USB printers.

Standard IRQ and I/O Port Addresses

Serial ports require two hardware resources: IRQ and I/O port address. Table 3-1 lists the standard IRQ and I/O port addresses used for COM ports 1–4. Some systems and add-on cards enable alternative IRQs to be used, either through jumper blocks (older cards) or via software/Device Manager configuration (newer cards).

Table 3-1   Standard Settings for COM (Serial) Ports 1–4

COM Port #	IRQ	I/O Port Address
1	4	3F8-3FFh
2	3	2F8-2FFh
3	4	3E8-3EFh
4	3	2E8-2EFh

IRQ conflicts have historically been the bane of PC technicians. For example, IRQ 4 is shared by default between COM 1 and COM 3; IRQ 3 is shared by default between COM 2 and COM 4. However, with serial ports that use the same IRQ, sharing does *not* mean that both serial ports can be used at the same time. If a device on COM 1 and a device on COM 3 that share the same IRQ are used at the same time, both devices stop working and they might shut down the system.

Parallel (LPT)

The parallel port, also known as the LPT (Line Printer) port, was originally designed for use with parallel printers. However, don't let the name "LPT port" fool you. Historically, the parallel port has been among the most versatile of I/O ports in the system because it was also used by a variety of devices, including tape backups, external CD-ROM and optical drives, scanners, and removable-media drives such as Zip drives. Although newer devices in these categories are now designed to use USB or IEEE 1394 ports, the parallel port continues to be an important external I/O device for older systems.

CAUTION   Devices other than printers that plug into the parallel (LPT) port have two connectors: one for the cable that runs from the device to the parallel port, and another for the cable that runs from the device to the printer. Although it's theoretically possible to create a long daisy-chain of devices ending with a printer, in practice you should have no more than one device plus a printer plugged into a parallel port. If you use more than one device, you could have problems getting the devices (not to mention the printer) to work reliably.

The parallel (LPT) port is unusual because it uses two completely different connector types:

- Since the first IBM PC of 1981, all IBM and compatible computers with parallel ports have used the DB-25F port shown in Figure 3-8, with pins 1–13 on the top and pins 14–25 on the bottom. This is also referred to as the type IEEE-1284-A connector. (IEEE 1284 is an international standard for parallel port connectors, cabling, and signaling.)

- The port used by parallel printers of all types, however, is the same Centronics 36-pin port used since the days of the Apple II and other early microcomputers of the late 1970s, as seen in Figure 3-8. This port is also referred to as the IEEE-1284-B port. It is an edge connector with 36 connectors, 18 per side.

Figure 3-8   Parallel devices such as printers use the Centronics port (top), whereas the computer's integrated parallel port is a DB-25F port (bottom). Some external devices also use a DB-25F port.

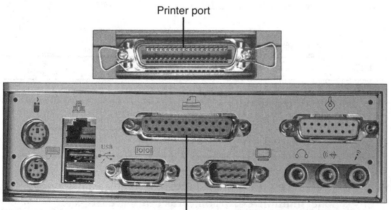

Printer port

Parallel port on computer

Some Hewlett-Packard LaserJet printers also use a miniature version of the Centronics connector known as the IEEE-1284-C, which is also a 36-pin edge connector. The 1284-C connector doesn't use wire clips.

Accordingly, a parallel printer cable also has different connectors at each end, as seen in Figure 3-9.

Figure 3-9   The ends of a typical IBM-style parallel cable. The Centronics 36-pin connector (upper left) connects to the printer; the DB-25M connector (lower right) connects to the computer's DB-25F parallel port.

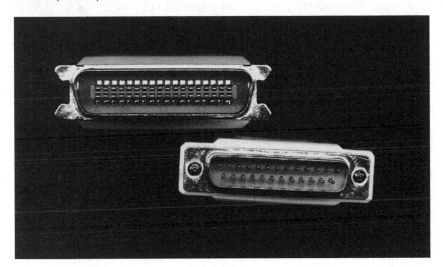

Parallel ports can be configured as LPT1, LPT2, and LPT3. When a single parallel port is found in the system, regardless of its configuration, it is always designated as LPT1. The configurations for LPT2 and LPT3, shown in Table 3-2, apply when you have a computer with more than one parallel port.

Table 3-2   Typical Parallel Port Hardware Configuration Settings

LPT Port #	IRQ	I/O Port Address Range
LPT1	7	378-37Fh or 3BC-38Fh
LPT2	5	278-27Fh or 378-37Fh
LPT3	5	278-27Fh

Some expansion multi-I/O cards can place the parallel port at any available IRQ. In some cases, when this is done, multiple expansion cards can share IRQs.

SCSI

SCSI (Small Computer Systems Interface) is a very flexible interface because it can accommodate many devices in addition to hard disk drives. Currently, SCSI interfaces, either on the motherboard or as add-on cards, are found primarily in servers

and are used for mass storage (hard disk, tape backup), although you might en-counter workstations and PCs that use SCSI interfaces for devices such as

- High-performance and high-capacity hard drives

- Image scanners

- Removable-media drives such as Zip, Jaz, and Castlewood Orb

- High-performance laser printers

- Optical drives

- Tape backups

So-called Narrow SCSI host adapters (which use an 8-bit data channel) can accom-modate up to seven devices of different varieties on a single connector. Wide SCSI host adapters use a 16-bit data channel and accommodate up to 15 devices on a sin-gle connector.

Multiple Device Support with SCSI Host Adapters

All true SCSI host adapters are designed to support multiple devices, although some low-cost SCSI host adapters made especially for scanners and Zip drives might not support multiple devices (also known as daisy-chaining). Several SCSI features per-mit daisy-chaining:

- External SCSI peripherals have two SCSI ports, enabling daisy-chaining of multiple devices.

- Internal SCSI ribbon cables resemble IDE data cables, only wider.

- Both internal and external SCSI peripherals enable the user to choose a unique device ID number for each device to distinguish one peripheral from another in the daisy-chain (see Figure 3-10).

Multiple device support enables the different types of devices listed previously to work on a single SCSI host adapter. To determine which device IDs are in use, you can

- Physically examine each SCSI device's device ID settings.

- Scan the SCSI bus with a software program such as Adaptec's SCSI Interrogator or with the BIOS routines built into some SCSI host adapters.

- View the properties for each SCSI device in the Windows Device Manager.

Figure 3-10   When a SCSI host adapter card with internal and external connectors is used, the SCSI daisy-chain can extend through the card. Note that the devices on each end of the chain are terminated, and each device (including the host adapter) has a unique device ID number.

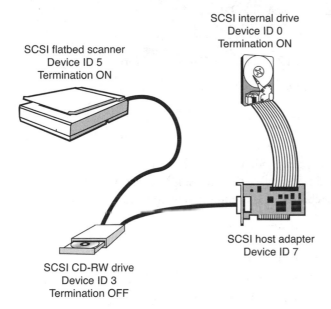

SCSI internal drive
Device ID 0
Termination ON

SCSI flatbed scanner
Device ID 5
Termination ON

SCSI host adapter
Device ID 7

SCSI CD-RW drive
Device ID 3
Termination OFF

Jumper Block and DIP Switch Settings for Device IDs

Each SCSI device must have a unique device ID to distinguish itself from other SCSI devices connected to the same SCSI channel. Narrow SCSI (50-pin data cable) devices use a set of three jumpers or DIP switches to set the device ID. Wide SCSI (68-pin data cable) devices use a set of four jumpers or DIP switches to set the device ID. Depending on the type of SCSI, you can have either 8 devices maximum (ID 0-7) or 16 devices maximum (ID 0-15).

SCSI Standards

SCSI actually is the family name for a wide range of standards, which differ from each other in the speed of devices, number of devices, and other technical details. The major SCSI standards are listed in Table 3-3.

Table 3-3   Popular SCSI Standards

Popular Name	Speed	Number of Devices	Data Bus	Signal Type
Fast	10MBps	7	8-bit	SE[1]
Fast-Wide	10MBps	15	16-bit	SE
Ultra	20MBps	7	8-bit	SE

Popular Name	Speed	Number of Devices	Data Bus	Signal Type
Ultra-Wide	20MBps	15	16-bit	SE
Ultra2	40MBps	7	8-bit	LVD[2]
Ultra2Wide	80MBps	15	16-bit	LVD
Ultra 160	160MBps	15	16-bit	LVD
Ultra 320	320MBps	15	16-bit	LVD

[1.] Single-ended
[2.] Low-voltage differential

8-bit versions of SCSI use a 50-pin cable or a 25-pin cable; wide (16-bit) versions use a 68-pin cable.

SCSI host adapters are generally backward compatible, enabling older and newer SCSI standards to be mixed on the same host adapter. However, mixing slower and faster devices can cause the faster devices to slow down unless you use a host adapter with dual buses that can run at different speeds.

IEEE 1394 (FireWire)

IEEE 1394 is a family of high-speed bidirectional serial transmission ports that can connect PCs to each other, digital devices to PCs, or digital devices to each other.

The most common version of IEEE 1394 is known as IEEE 1394a, and is also known as FireWire 400. Sony's version is known as i.LINK. At 400Mbps, IEEE 1394a is one of the fastest and most flexible ports used on personal computers. IEEE 1394a can be implemented either as a built-in port on the motherboard (refer to Figure 3-1) or as part of an add-on card (see Figure 3-11).

IEEE 1394 Ports and Cables

Standard IEEE 1394a ports and cables use a 6-pin interface (four pins for data, two for power), but some digital camcorders and all i.LINK ports use the alternative 4-pin interface, which supplies data and signals but no power to the device. Six-wire to four-wire cables enable these devices to communicate with each other.

A faster version of the IEEE 1394 standard, IEEE 1394b (also known as FireWire 800), runs at 800Mbps. IEEE 1394b ports use a 9-pin interface. There are two versions of the IEEE 1394b port: The Beta port and cable are used only for 1394b-to-1394b connections, whereas the Bilingual cable and port are used for 1394b-to-1394a or 1394b-to-1394b connections. Beta cables and ports have a wide notch at the top of the cable and port, whereas Bilingual cables and ports have a narrow notch at the 1394b end, and use either the 4-pin or 6-pin 1394a connection at the other end of the cable. All four cable types are shown in Figure 3-12.

Figure 3-11   A typical IEEE 1394a host adapter card with three external ports and one internal port.

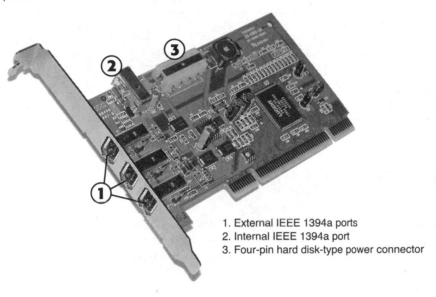

1. External IEEE 1394a ports
2. Internal IEEE 1394a port
3. Four-pin hard disk-type power connector

Figure 3-12   1394b and 1394a cable connectors compared.

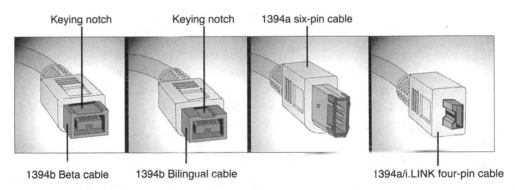

Keying notch   Keying notch   1394a six-pin cable

1394b Beta cable   1394b Bilingual cable   1394a/i.LINK four-pin cable

IEEE 1394–Compatible Devices and Technical Requirements

IEEE 1394–compatible devices include internal and external hard drives, digital camcorders (also referred to as DV camcorders), web cameras, MP3 players (such as older models of Apple's iPod), and high-performance scanners and printers, as well as hubs, repeaters, and SCSI to IEEE 1394 converters. IEEE 1394 ports support hot-swapping, enabling you to add or remove a device from an IEEE 1394 port without shutting down the system. 1394 ports can also be used for networking with Windows XP (but not Vista).

Up to 16 IEEE 1394 devices can be connected to a single IEEE 1394 port through daisy-chaining. Most external IEEE 1394 devices have two ports to enable daisy-chaining.

Windows 98 was the first version of Windows to include IEEE 1394 support. IEEE 1394 cards can use PCI or PCI Express buses (versions for laptops use ExpressCard or CardBus designs) and require the following hardware resources:

- One IRQ (it can be shared on systems that support IRQ sharing by PCI devices)

- One memory address range (must be unique)

You can determine the exact IRQ and memory address range used by a particular IEEE 1394 card by using the Windows Device Manager. When an IEEE 1394 card is installed, a device category called 1394 Bus Controller is added to the Device Manager, and the particular card installed is listed beneath that category.

PS/2 (Mini-DIN)

PS/2 ports (also referred to as Mini-DIN ports) are used by PS/2 keyboards, mice, and pointing devices. Most desktop systems, and many older laptop and portable systems, include PS/2 ports.

In a typical ATX/BTX port cluster, the bottom PS/2 port is used for keyboards, and the top PS/2 port is used for mice and pointing devices. On systems and devices that use the standard PC99 color coding for ports, PS/2 keyboard ports (and cables) are purple, and PS/2 mouse ports (and cables) are green. Refer to Figure 3-1 for the location of these ports.

Centronics

Centronics ports are used by parallel (LPT) printers and by some older narrow SCSI devices. Centronics parallel ports use a 36-pin edge connector (refer to Figure 3-9), and Centronics SCSI ports use a 50-pin edge connector.

For more information about parallel (LPT) ports, see the section "Parallel (LPT)," earlier in this chapter. For more information about SCSI ports, see the section "SCSI," earlier in this chapter.

1/8-Inch Audio Mini-Jack

The 1/8-inch audio mini-jack is used by sound cards and motherboard-integrated sound for speakers, microphone, and line-in jacks, as shown in Figure 3-1.

To avoid confusion, most recent systems and sound cards use the PC99 color coding listed as follows:

- **Pink**—Microphone in

- **Light Blue**—Line in

- **Lime Green**—Stereo/headphone out

- **Brown**—Left to right speaker

- **Orange**—Subwoofer

SPDIF Digital Audio

Many systems include both analog audio (delivered through 1/8-inch audio mini-jacks) and digital audio. Sony/Philips Digital Interconnect Format (SPDIF) ports output digital audio signals to amplifiers, such as those used in home theater systems, and come in two forms: optical and coaxial.

Optical SPDIF uses a fiber optic cable, while coaxial SPDIF uses a shielded cable with an RCA connector. The cables are shown in Figure 3-13. To see SPDIF ports, refer to Figure 3-1.

Figure 3-13   SPDIF optical (top) and coaxial (bottom) cables.

Sound cards might incorporate SPDIF ports into the card itself or into drive bay or external extension modules.

TIP By default, systems with both analog and digital output use analog output. To enable digital output, use the Sounds and Audio Devices dialog in Windows Control Panel or the proprietary mixer provided with some sound cards or onboard audio devices.

MIDI Port

Some sound cards feature MIDI ports. MIDI ports are used to communicate with MIDI keyboards. Older devices with MIDI support use MIDI ports that use a five-pin DIN design similar to the original IBM PC keyboard jack, and newer devices use the smaller Mini-DIN design, but with five pins instead of the six pins used by PS/2 keyboards and mice.

Figure 3-14 illustrates a drive bay-mounted module that contains MIDI ports. Note that some older sound cards use adapters that connect to the joystick port.

Figure 3-14   MIDI ports in a Creative Labs add-on module for sound cards.

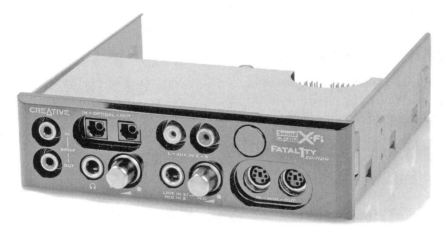

RG-6 Coaxial

RG-6 coaxial connections are used by TV and FM radio tuners to receive signals from broadcast and cable TV and radio. Figure 3-15 illustrates a typical TV tuner card with an F-connector and an RG-6 cable.

To enjoy TV broadcasts on your PC, you must also use software that can tune in the appropriate station, display the video, and play back the audio. To enjoy FM radio broadcasts on your PC, you must also use software that can tune in the appropriate station and play back the audio. Most recent TV and radio tuner cards and devices are bundled with suitable software and drivers for Windows Media Center.

Figure 3-15   TV tuner cards use RG-6 cables for video sources such as broadcast and cable TV.

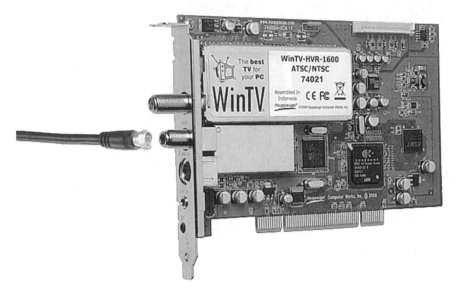

Understanding Input Devices

Modern PCs use many different types of input devices, including keyboards and mice, bar code readers, biometric devices, and touch screens. The following sections cover the important characteristics of each of these devices.

Keyboard

The keyboard remains the primary method used to send commands to the computer and enter data. You can even use it to maneuver around the Windows Desktop if your mouse or other pointing device stops working.

Keyboards can be connected through dedicated keyboard connectors or through the USB port. Extremely old systems use the 5-pin DIN connector, whereas newer systems use the smaller 6-pin mini-DIN connector (also called the PS/2 keyboard connector) shown in Figure 3-1.

Most recent systems use the USB port for the keyboard, and any system with USB ports can be equipped with a USB keyboard if the system BIOS supports USB Legacy mode and if the system runs an operating system that supports USB ports (Windows 98 or newer).

Most recent systems use the 104-key keyboard layout, which includes Windows keys on each side of the space bar and a right-click key next to the right Ctrl key. Otherwise, the standard 104-key keyboard's layout is the same as the older standard 101-key keyboard.

Mouse and Pointing Devices

Next to the keyboard, the mouse is the most important device used to send commands to the computer. For Windows users who don't perform data entry, the mouse is even more important than the keyboard. Mouse alternatives, such as trackballs or touchpads, are considered mouse devices because they install and are configured the same way.

Current mice and pointing devices use the USB 1.1 or USB 2.0 port, but older models used the 6-pin PS/2 (mini-DIN), serial (COM) ports, or 8-pin bus mouse port.

Some mice sold at retail work with either the USB port or the PS/2 port and include a PS/2 adapter. This adapter and others are shown in Figure 3-16.

Figure 3-16   A USB keyboard–to–PS/2 keyboard port adapter (top) compared to a USB mouse–to–PS/2 mouse port adapter (middle) and serial mouse–to–PS/2 mouse port adapter (bottom).

Connects to USB keyboard

Plugs into PS/2 keyboard port

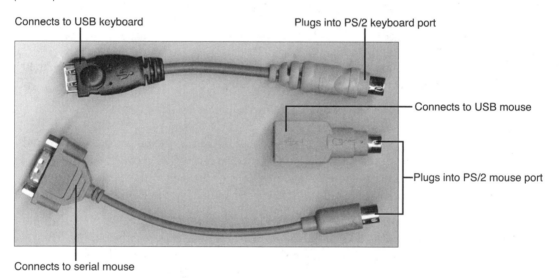

Connects to USB mouse

Plugs into PS/2 mouse port

Connects to serial mouse

NOTE   Adapters cannot be used successfully unless the mouse (or keyboard) is designed to use an adapter. A mouse designed to use an adapter is sometimes called a hybrid mouse.

A USB mouse uses the IRQ and I/O port address of the USB port to which it is connected. Because a single USB port can support up to 127 devices through the use of hubs, a USB mouse doesn't tie up hardware resources the way other mouse types do.

A PS/2 mouse uses IRQ 12; if IRQ 12 is not available, the device using that IRQ must be moved to another IRQ to enable IRQ 12 to be used by the mouse. A serial mouse uses the IRQ and I/O port address of the serial port to which it is connected.

Game Controllers

Game controllers are handheld devices that provide input to computer games and other applications. They are most common in gaming consoles but can also be connected to PCs by way of a USB or 15-pin parallel connector, often found on sound-cards.

The most common type of game controller is the game pad, which is held with both hands and is manipulated by a person's fingers and thumbs. Many computer games are developed to work with gamepads, but some games require the use of a keyboard and mouse. On the other side of the spectrum, applications such as browsers can often be manipulated by gamepads. This all depends on application support, and the programming strength of the gamepad driver software.

Bar Code Reader

Bar code readers are used in a variety of point-of-sale retail, library, industrial, medical, and other environments to track inventory.

Bar code readers use one of the following technologies:

- **Pen-based readers**—Use a pen-shaped device that includes a light source and photo diode in the tip. The point of the pen is dragged across the bar code to read the varying thicknesses and positions of the bars in the bar code and translate them into a digitized code that is transmitted to the POS or inventory system.

- **Laser scanners**—Commonly used in grocery and mass-market stores. They use a horizontal-mounted or vertical-mounted prism or mirror and laser beam protected by a transparent glass cover to read bar codes.

- **Charge-coupled device (CCD) readers**—Use a hand-held gun-shaped device to hold an array of light sensors mounted in a row. The reader emits light that is reflected off the bar code and is detected by the light sensors.

- **Camera-based readers**—Contain many rows of CCD sensors that generate an image of the sensor that is processed to decode the barcode information.

Biometric Devices

A biometric device is used to prevent access to a computer or other electronic device by anyone other than the authorized user. It does so by comparing the fingerprint or

other biometric marker of the prospective user to the information stored by the authorized user during initial setup. Some keyboards and laptop computers include built-in fingerprint readers, and some vendors also produce USB-based fingerprint readers.

To learn more about fingerprint readers and other biometric devices, see Chapter 9, "Basic Security."

Voice-Activated Typing

For those who want to dictate documents instead of typing them and issue commands to the computer by voice instead of with the keyboard and mouse, voice-activated typing is a viable alternative. Also known as voice-to-text recognition software, voice recognition, and dictation software, these programs take a person's speech and interpret it to the computer. This can manifest itself as the automatic display of words in a Microsoft Word document, or as the control of a browser and other applications, even the operating system.

For the voice-activated typist, a few items are necessary, including software (a commonly used program is Dragon Naturally Speaking), a headset with microphone, and a fairly powerful computer (due to the fact that most of these programs are quite resource intensive).

The user first needs to train the software with their speaking style. Afterward, the user's inflection, and other nuances, are stored in a user profile. The more a person uses software such as this, the better the software will be able to recognize the user's words and commands. User profiles can be moved from one computer to another as long as the other computer has the same voice-activated software installed.

Organizations that want to implement voice-activated typing software should look for a solution that meets the Americans with Disability Act (ADA) requirements. This ensures that everyone in the organization who wants to use the software can do so easily and efficiently.

Understanding Display Types

There are three major types of displays you should be knowledgeable of:

- CRT monitors
- LCD monitors
- Data projectors

The following sections help you understand the common and unique features of each.

CRT Monitor

Cathode ray tube (CRT) displays are now fading in popularity but are still in widespread use on older systems. CRTs use a picture tube that is similar to the picture tube in a tube-based TV set. The narrow end of the tube contains an electron gun that projects three electron beams (red, blue, green) toward the wide end, which is coated with phosphors that glow when they are hit by the electron beams. Just before the phosphor coating, a metal plate called a shadow mask is used to divide the image created by the electron guns into red, green, and blue pixels or stripes that form the image. Shadow masks use one of three technologies:

■   A phosphor triad (a group of three phosphors—red, green, and blue). The distance between each triad is called the dot pitch.

■   An aperture grill, which uses vertical red, green, and blue phosphor strips. The distance between each group is called the stripe pitch.

■   A slotted mask, which uses small blocks of red, green, and blue phosphor strips. The distance between each horizontal group is also called stripe pitch.

If you look closely at a CRT display, you can see the individual triads or strips. However, from normal viewing distances, they blend into a clear picture.

Figure 3-17 shows the design of a typical CRT monitor.

Figure 3-17   A cutaway of a typical CRT display.

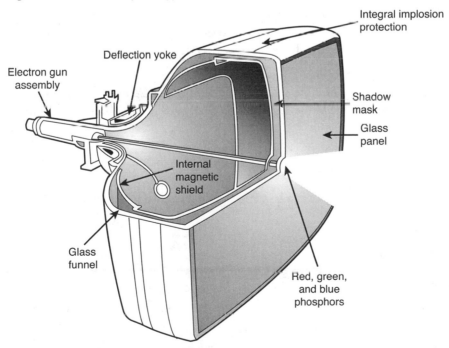

Generally, the smaller the dot or stripe pitch, the clearer and sharper the onscreen image will be. Typical standards for CRT monitors call for a dot pitch of .28 millimeters (mm) or smaller. Generally, low-cost monitors have poorer picture quality than higher-cost monitors of the same size because of wider dot pitch, low refresh rates at their highest resolutions, and poor focus at their highest resolutions.

Typical CRT displays range in size from 15 inches (diagonal measure) to 19 inches, and feature support for a wide range of resolutions. CRTs are analog display devices that can display an unlimited range of colors, and use the 15-pin VGA connector. To learn more about VGA connectors, see the section "VGA," later in this chapter.

LCD Monitor

Liquid crystal displays (LCD) use liquid crystal cells to polarize light passing through the display to create the image shown on the monitor. In color LCD displays, liquid crystal cells are grouped into three cells for each pixel: one each for red, green, and blue light.

All LCD displays use active matrix technology, which uses a transistor to control each cell, as the basic technology. Variations in how quickly a display can refresh, how wide the viewing angle, and how bright the display help distinguish different brands and models from each other.

An LCD monitor is a digital design, but many models, particularly low-end models and older designs, use the same VGA analog interface as CRTs. In such cases, the monitor must include an analog-digital converter to change the analog signal received by the VGA cable into a digital signal. High-end LCD displays and most recent midrange models also support digital signals and use DVI-D ports. To learn more about DVI-D connectors, see the section "DVI," later in this chapter.

Compared to CRT monitors, LCDs are much lighter, require much less power, emit less heat, and use much less desk space.

An LCD display has only one native resolution; it must scale lower resolutions to fit the panel, or, depending upon the options configured in the video card driver, might use only a portion of the display when a lower resolution is selected. When a lower resolution is scaled, the display is less sharp than when the native resolution is used.

LCD displays are found in both standard (4:3 or 1.33:1) and widescreen (16:9 or 16:10) aspect ratios, and range in size from 14 inches (diagonal measure) to 24 inches or larger.

Data Projector

Data projectors can be used in place of a primary display or can be used as a clone of the primary display to permit computer information and graphics to be displayed on a projection screen or a wall.

Data projectors use one of the following technologies:

- Liquid crystal display (LCD)

- Digital light processing (DLP)

LCD projectors use separate LCD panels for red, green, and blue light, and combine the separate images into a single RGB image for projection, using dichroic mirrors. A dichroic mirror reflects light in some wavelengths, while permitting light in other wavelengths to pass through. In Figure 3-18, red and blue dichroic mirrors are used to split the image into red, blue, and green wavelengths. After passing through the appropriate LCD, a dichroic combiner cube recombines the separate red, green, and blue images into a single RGB image for projection.

Figure 3-18   How a typical three-LCD data projector works.

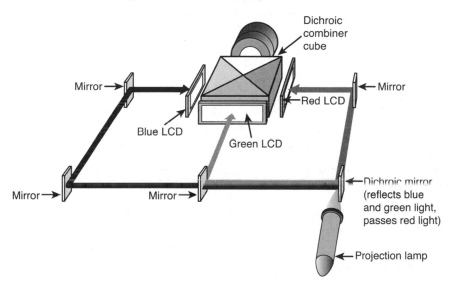

LCD projectors use a relatively hot projection lamp, so LCD projectors include cooling fans that run both during projector operation and after the projector is turned off to cool down the lamp.

DLP projectors use a spinning wheel with red, green, and blue sections to add color data to light being reflected from an array of tiny mirrors known as a digital micromirror device (DMD). Each mirror corresponds to a pixel, and the mirrors

reflect light toward or away from the projector optics. The spinning wheel might use only three segments (RGB), four segments (RGB+clear), or six segments (RGB+RGB). More segments help improve picture quality. Figure 3-19 illustrates how a DLP projector works.

Figure 3-19   How a typical DLP projector works.

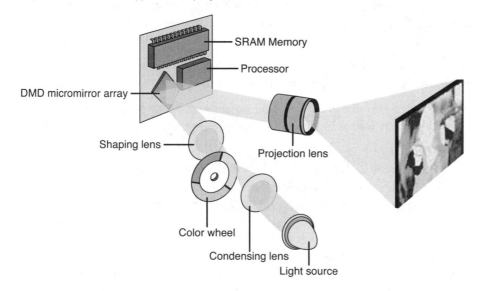

Touch Screens

Touch screen (or touchscreen) monitors enable the user to transfer data into the computer by pressing onscreen icons. Touch screen monitors are popular in public-access and point-of-sale installations.

Touch screen monitors use liquid crystal display (LCD) or cathode ray tube (CRT) technology and also incorporate one of the following surface treatments to make the monitor touch sensitive:

■ **Four-wire resistive technology**—Uses a glass panel coated with multiple layers that conduct and resist electricity. A flexible polyester cover sheet fits over the glass panel and is separated from the panel with insulating separator dots. The outer side of the cover has a durable coating; the inner side has a conductive coating. When the cover is pressed, an electrical signal is generated and is sent through the interface to the computer. The lowest-cost touch screen technology, this type of screen is designed for public use.

■ **Five-wire resistive technology**—A more sensitive and more accurate version of four-wire resistive technology suitable for use by trained personnel (offices, point-of-sale, and so on).

- **Surface wave**—Uses horizontal and vertical piezoelectric transducers to create ultrasonic waves. Touching the screen overlay disrupts the waves and the coordinates of the touch determine what signal is sent to the computer. It's a durable surface able to compensate for surface damage and dirt and is suitable for self-service applications such as banking or information kiosks.

- **Touch-on-tube**—Combines surface wave technology with direct touch contact to the CRT; no overlay is necessary. LCDs use an overlay with a simple air gap between the overlay and the panel surface. Suitable for self-service applications.

- **Scanning infrared**—A light grid created by infrared (IR) signals is used to sense touches. Works with plasma as well as other types of displays.

Touch screens are available in freestanding versions similar to normal desktop CRT and LCD displays as well as in kiosk and built-in designs.

Touch screens, like ordinary LCD and CRT monitors, use standard VGA analog or DVI digital interfaces to the video card. However, the touch signals are transmitted to the computer through a separate interface known as the touch screen controller. Touch screen controllers can use either of the following interfaces:

- **Serial (RS-232)**—Some touch screen monitors have an internal serial controller; others use an external serial controller. The internal serial controller might use a standard 9-pin serial cable or a special PS/2–to–9-pin serial cable to connect the controller to a serial (COM) port on the computer, depending upon the monitor model. The external serial controller uses a controller with a built-in serial cable.

- **USB**—A touch screen monitor with an internal USB interface uses a standard USB cable to connect to a USB port on the computer.

Understanding Video Connector Types

When selecting a monitor or projector for use with a particular video card or integrated video port, it's helpful to understand the physical and feature differences between different video connector types, such as VGA, DVI, HDMI, Component/RGB, S-video, and composite.

VGA

VGA is an analog display standard. By varying the levels of red, green, or blue per dot (pixel) onscreen, a VGA port and monitor can display an unlimited number of colors. Practical color limits (if you call more than 16 million colors limiting) are based on the video card's memory and the desired screen resolution.

All VGA cards made for use with standard analog monitors use a DB-15F 15-pin female connector, which plugs into the DB-15M connector used by the VGA cable from the monitor. Figure 3-20 compares these connectors.

Figure 3-20   DB15M (cable) and DB15F (port) connectors used for VGA video signals.

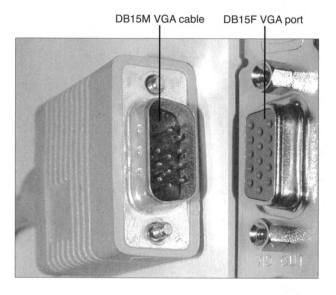

DB15M VGA cable   DB15F VGA port

DVI

The DVI port is the current standard for digital LCD monitors. The DVI port comes in two forms: DVI-D supports only digital signals, and is found on digital LCD displays. Most of these displays also support analog video signals through separate VGA ports. However, video cards with DVI ports use the DVI-I version, which provides both digital and analog output and supports the use of a VGA/DVI-I adapter for use with analog displays. Figure 3-21 illustrates a DVI-D cable and DVI-I port.

HDMI

Video cards and systems with integrated video that are designed for home theater use support a unique type of digital video standard known as High-Definition Multimedia Interface (HDMI). HDMI is unique in its ability to support digital audio as well as video through a single cable. HDMI ports are found on most late-model HDTVs as well as home theater hardware such as amplifiers and DVD players.

The most recent HDMI standard, version 1.3b, supports up to 1080p HDTV, 24-bit or greater color depths, and various types of uncompressed and compressed digital audio. However, all versions of HDMI use the cable shown in Figure 3-22 and the port shown in Figure 3-23.

Figure 3-21 DVI-I video port and DVI-D video cable.

DVI-D video cable supports digital signals only

DVI-I video port supports
analog and digital signals

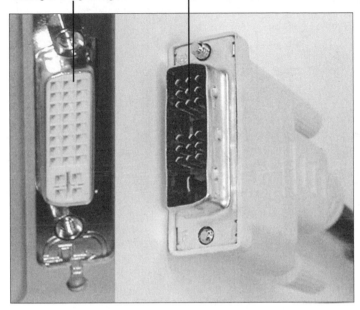

Figure 3-22 HDMI cable (right) compared to DVI-D cable (left).

DVI-D cable (for comparison)

HDMI cable

Figure 3-23   HDMI, DVI-D, and VGA ports on the rear of a typical PC built for use with Windows Media Center and home theater integration.

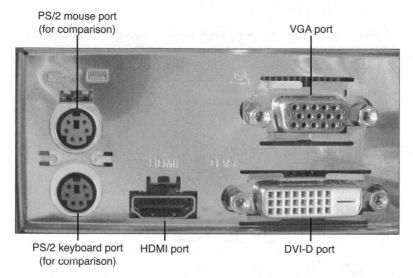

PS/2 mouse port
(for comparison)

VGA port

PS/2 keyboard port
(for comparison)

HDMI port

DVI-D port

Systems and video cards with integrated HDMI ports might also feature DVI-I or VGA ports, as in Figure 3-23.

A converter cable with a DVI connector on one end and an HDMI connector on the other end can be used to interface a PC with an HDTV if the PC doesn't have an HDMI port.

Component/RGB

Some data projectors and virtually all HDTVs support a high-resolution type of analog video known as component video. Component video uses separate RCA cables and ports to carry red, green, and blue signals, and can support up to 720p HDTV resolutions.

S-Video

S-video divides a video signal into separate luma and chroma signals, providing a better signal for use with standard TVs, projectors, DVD players, and VCRs than a composite signal. The so-called "TV-out" port on the back of many video cards is actually an S-video port.

Composite

The lowest-quality video signal supported by PCs is composite video, which uses a single RCA cable and port to transmit a video signal. Video cards sold in Europe usually use a composite signal for their TV-out signal.

Composite video can be used by standard definition TVs (SDTVs) and VCRs. If you need to connect a PC with an S-video port to a TV or VCR that has a composite port, you can use an S-video to composite video adapter.

Figure 3-24 compares component, S-video, and composite video cables and ports to each other. Note that composite video cables are often bundled with stereo audio cables, but can also be purchased separately.

Figure 3-24   Composite video and stereo audio, S-video, and component video cables and ports compared.

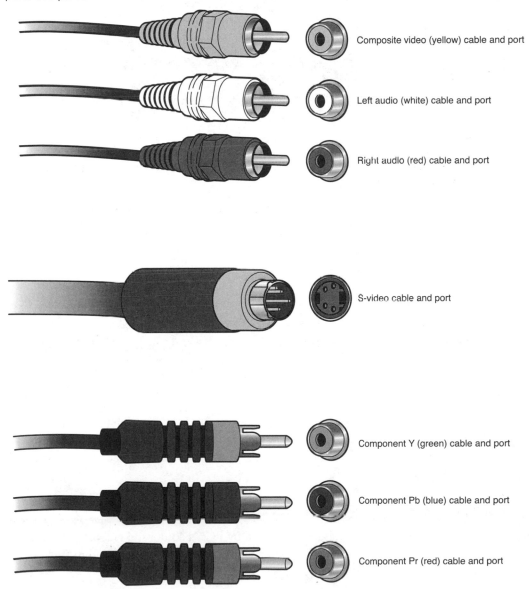

Composite video (yellow) cable and port

Left audio (white) cable and port

Right audio (red) cable and port

S-video cable and port

Component Y (green) cable and port

Component Pb (blue) cable and port

Component Pr (red) cable and port

Printing Fundamentals

There are four types of printers you should be aware of:

- Laser
- Inkjet
- Thermal
- Impact

The following sections introduce you to the basic features of each printer type:

- How printers create a page (note in particular the steps used by a laser printer to create a page)
- Major components of each printer type covered (thermal printers as well as impact, inkjet, and laser/LED)
- Typical printer operation and output problems and their solutions
- How printers are interfaced to the computer

Laser Printers

Laser printers are similar in many ways to photocopiers:

- Both use an electrostatically charged drum to receive the image to be transferred to paper.
- Both use a fine-grained powdered toner that is heated to adhere to the paper.
- Both must feed the paper through elaborate paper paths for printing.

However, significant differences exist between the photocopier and its computer-savvy sibling:

- Laser printers produce images digitally, turning individual dots on and off; most copiers, however, are still analog devices.
- Laser printers work under the control of a computer; copiers have a dedicated scanner as an image source.
- Laser printers use much higher temperatures than copiers to bond printing to the paper; using copier labels or transparency media in a laser printer can result in damage to the printer due to melted label adhesive, labels coming off in the printer, or melted transparency media.

One type of laser printer is the LED printer. LED stands for light-emitting diode, which the LED printer uses as its light source. The essential difference between a laser and an LED printer is in the imaging device. The laser printer uses a laser to transfer the image to the drum, whereas an LED printer uses an LED array to perform the same task. Otherwise, these technologies are practically identical.

Although the technology of laser printers is interesting, we cannot forget what they use to print and what they print on. Laser printers use toner cartridges that can be replaced when they are empty. These printers print their information best on paper that is optimized for laser printers. Let's discuss toner cartridges and laser printing paper now.

Toner Cartridges

Most monochrome laser printers use toner cartridges that combine the imaging drum and the developer with black toner. This provides you with an efficient and easy way to replace the laser printer items with the greatest potential to wear out.

Depending on the model, a new toner cartridge might also require that you change a wiper used to remove excess toner during the fusing cycle. This is normally packaged with the toner cartridge.

NOTE   Recycled toner cartridges are controversial in some circles, but I've used a mixture of new and rebuilt toner cartridges for several years without a problem. Major manufacturers, such as Apple, HP, and Canon, place a postage-paid return label in cartridge boxes to encourage you to recycle your toner cartridges.

Reputable toner cartridge rebuilders can save you as much as 30% off the price of a new toner cartridge.

When you install the toner cartridge, be sure to follow the directions for cleaning areas near the toner cartridge. Depending on the make and model of the laser printer, this can involve cleaning the mirror that reflects the laser beam, cleaning up stray toner, or cleaning the charging corona wire or conditioning rollers inside the printer. If you need to clean the charging corona wire (also called the *primary corona wire* on some models), the laser printer contains a special tool for this purpose. The printer instruction manual shows you how to clean the item.

Keep the cartridge closed; it is sensitive to light, and leaving it out of the printer in room light can damage the enclosed imaging drum's surface. Figure 3-25 shows a typical laser printer toner cartridge and mirror cleaning tool. The tool above the toner cartridge is used to clean the printer's mirror.

Figure 3-25 A typical laser printer toner cartridge. The inset shows the mirror cleaning tool in use after the old toner cartridge has been removed and before the new cartridge is put into position.

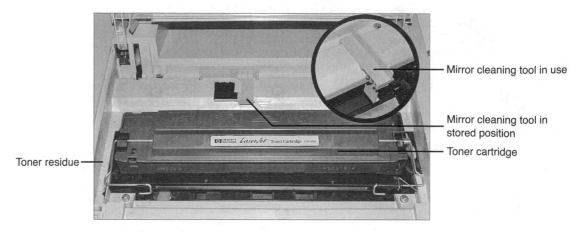

Mirror cleaning tool in use

Mirror cleaning tool in stored position

Toner cartridge

Toner residue

CAUTION When you change a toner cartridge, take care to avoid getting toner on your face, hands, or clothing. It can leave a messy residue that's hard to clean.

Color laser printers differ from monochrome laser printers in two important ways: They include four different colors of toner (cyan, magenta, yellow, and black), and the imaging drum is separate from the toner. Thus, instead of waste toner being reused as in a monochrome laser printer that has a toner cartridge with an integrated imaging drum, waste toner in a color printer is sent to a separate waste toner container.

Depending upon the toner transfer technology used, a color laser printer might require four passes to print a color page (one pass per color), or only one pass to print all four colors.

Laser Printer Paper and Media

For best results with laser printing, use these guidelines when selecting paper and media:

- Use paper made for laser or photocopier use. Extremely rough-surfaced specialty papers might not enable the toner to fuse correctly to the paper.

- Use envelopes made for laser printing, especially if the printer doesn't offer a straight-through paper path option. Standard envelopes can lose some of their flap adhesive or have the flap stick to the back of the envelope when used in a laser printer.

■ Use only labels made for laser printers; these labels have no exposed backing, requiring you to separate the labels from the backing after printing.

CAUTION   Labels made for copiers have exposed backing, and the labels can come off inside the printer, leading to expensive repairs.

■ Use only laser-compatible transparency stock; it can resist the high heat of the fuser rollers better than other types, which can melt and damage the printer.

■ Avoid using paper with damaged edges or damp paper; this can cause paper jams and lead to poor-quality printing.

■ Load paper carefully into the paper tray; fan the paper and make sure the edges are aligned before inserting it.

Inkjet Printers

Inkjet printers (also known as ink dispersion printers) represent the most popular type of printer in small-office/home-office (SOHO) use today and are also popular in large offices. Their print quality can rival laser printers, and virtually all inkjet printers in use today are able to print both color and black text and photographs.

From a tightly spaced group of nozzles, inkjet printers spray controlled dots of ink onto the paper to form characters and graphics. On a typical 5,760×1,440 dots per inch (dpi) printer, the number of nozzles can be as high as 180 for black ink and more than 50 per color (cyan, magenta, yellow). The tiny ink droplet size and high nozzle density enables inkjet printers to perform the seemingly impossible at resolutions as high as 1,200dpi or higher: fully formed characters from what is actually a high-resolution, non-impact, dot-matrix technology.

Inkjet printers are character/line printers. They print one line at a time of single characters or graphics up to the limit of the printhead matrix. Inkjet printers are functionally fully formed character printers because their inkjet matrix of small droplets forming the image is so carefully controlled that individual dots are not visible.

Larger characters are created by printing a portion of the characters across the page, advancing the page to enable the printhead to print another portion of the characters, and so on until the entire line of characters is printed. Thus, an inkjet printer is both a character and a line printer because it must connect lines of printing to build large characters. Some inkjet printers require realignment after each ink cartridge/printhead change to make sure that vertical lines formed by multiple printhead passes stay straight; with other models, alignment can be performed

through a utility provided as part of the printer driver when print quality declines due to misalignment.

Ink Cartridges

Many inkjet printers, especially low-cost models, use a large tank of liquid ink for black and a separate tank with separate compartments for each color (typically cyan, magenta, and yellow; some models feature light versions of some of these colors for better photo-printing quality). However, the trend in most recent models has been to use a separate cartridge for each color. This improves print economy for the user because only one color at a time needs to be replaced. With a multicolor cartridge, the entire cartridge needs to be replaced, even when only one of the colors runs out.

NOTE Inkjet printers are sometimes referred to as CMYK devices because of the four ink colors used on most models: cyan, magenta, yellow, and black.

Figure 3-26 shows some of the typical components of an inkjet printer.

Figure 3-26 A typical inkjet printer with its cover open.

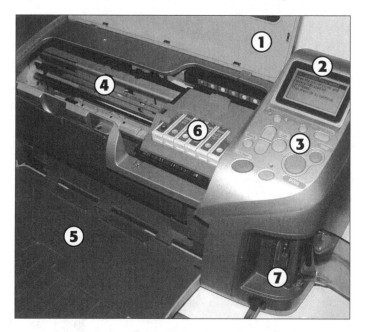

1. Dust cover
2. LCD instruction panel
3. Control panel
4. Printhead drive belt
5. Output tray
6. Ink cartridges
7. Flash memory card reader

Depending on the printer, the printhead might be incorporated into the ink tank; be a separate, user-replaceable item; or be built into the printer.

Some inkjet printers feature an extra-wide (more nozzles) printhead or a dual printhead for very speedy black printing. Some models enable the user to replace either the ink cartridge only or an assembly comprising the printhead and a replaceable ink cartridge.

An inkjet printer is only as good as its printhead and ink cartridges. Clogged or damaged printheads or ink cartridges render the printer useless. If an inkjet printer fails after its warranty expires, you should check service costs carefully before repairing the unit. Failed inkjet printers are often "throwaway" models and can be replaced, rather than repaired, even during the warranty period.

CAUTION   Inkjet printers should never be turned off with a surge protector; doing so prevents the printer from self-capping its ink cartridges, which is a major cause of service calls and printer failures. Cleaning the printhead, either with the printer's own cleaning feature, a cleaning utility built into the printer driver, or with a moistened cleaning sheet, restores most printers to service.

Always use the printer's own power switch, which enables the printer to protect the ink cartridges and perform other periodic tasks (such as self-cleaning) properly.

Inkjet Printer Paper and Media

Although papers made for copiers and laser printers provide adequate results, you must use inkjet-specific media of the following types to achieve best print quality:

- Glossy photos
- Transparencies
- Business cards
- Labels (especially clear labels)

It is also critical to use the correct print setting for the media type to avoid smudging, lines, and other print defects.

Thermal Printers

Thermal printers use heat transfer to create text and graphics on the paper. Thermal printers are used in point-of-sale and retail environments, as well as for some types of portable printing.

Thermal printers are available using three different technologies:

- Thermal transfer
- Direct thermal
- Dye sublimation

Thermal printers can use a dot-matrix print mechanism or a dye-sublimation technology to transfer images. Some thermal printers use heat-sensitive paper, and others use an ink ribbon to create the image. Let's start by discussing the thermal printer ribbon.

Thermal Printer Ribbons

Thermal transfer printers use wax or resin-based ribbons, which are often bundled with paper made especially for the printer. The most common type of thermal transfer printer uses dye-sublimation (dye-sub) technology to print 4×6 continuous-tone photographs. Examples of dye-sublimation printers include Kodak printer docks and Canon's Selphy CP series.

Figure 3-27 illustrates a typical dye-sublimation ribbon for a Canon Selphy CP printer.

Figure 3-27   A dye-sublimation ribbon for a 4×6-inch photo printer (Canon Selphy CP).

Thermal transfer printers used in point-of-sale or retail environments typically use non-impact dot-matrix printheads.

Thermal Printer Paper

Direct thermal printers use heat-sensitized paper, and thermal transfer printers might use either standard copy paper or glossy photo paper, depending upon their intended use.

If the printer uses direct thermal printing, heat-sensitive paper with characteristics matching the printer's design specifications must be used. For portable printers using direct thermal printing such as the Pentax PocketJet series, the usual source for such paper is the printer vendor or its authorized resellers. If the direct thermal printer is used for bar codes or point-of-sale transactions, you can get suitable paper or label stock from bar code or POS equipment suppliers and resellers.

If the printer uses thermal transfer and is not designed for photo printing, most smooth paper and label stocks are satisfactory, including both natural and synthetic materials. However, dye-sublimation photo printers must use special media kits that include both a ribbon and suitable photo paper stocks.

Impact Printers

Impact printers are so named because they use a mechanical printhead that presses against an inked ribbon to print characters and graphics. Impact printers are the oldest printer technology, and are primarily used today in industrial and point-of-sale applications.

NOTE Years ago, many impact printers used a daisy-wheel printhead similar to those used in electronic typewriters. This type of printhead created typewriter-style fully formed characters. However, virtually all recent impact printers use a dot-matrix printhead.

Dot-matrix printers, the most common form of impact printers, are so named because they create the appearance of fully formed characters from dots placed on the page.

Dot-matrix printers use a thermal or impact print head containing multiple pins that are used to form characters and graphics. Dot-matrix and other printers that print a line at a time are sometimes referred to as line printers. Typically, the term "page printers" refers to laser or LED array to change the electrostatic charge on a drum to attract toner, which is then transferred to paper to form the page.

The print mechanism of the dot-matrix printer is almost always an impact mechanism: A printhead containing various numbers of fine wires (called *pins*) arranged in one or more columns is used along with a fabric ribbon, similar to typewriter technology. The wires are moved by an electromagnet at high speed against the ribbon

to form dot patterns that form words, special characters, or graphics. Figure 3-28 shows actual print samples from a typical 9-pin printer's draft mode, a typical 24-pin printer's draft mode, and the Near Letter Quality (NLQ) mode of the same 24-pin printer. The narrower pins of the 24-pin printhead produce a reasonably good NLQ printout but hard-to-read results in draft mode.

NOTE   The print samples shown in Figure 3-28 are taken from printers that use 8.50×110-inch or wider paper sizes. The printhead design and print quality vary greatly on printers that use smaller paper sizes in point-of-sale applications.

Figure 3-28   Actual print samples illustrating the differences in 24-pin and 9-pin impact dot-matrix printers.

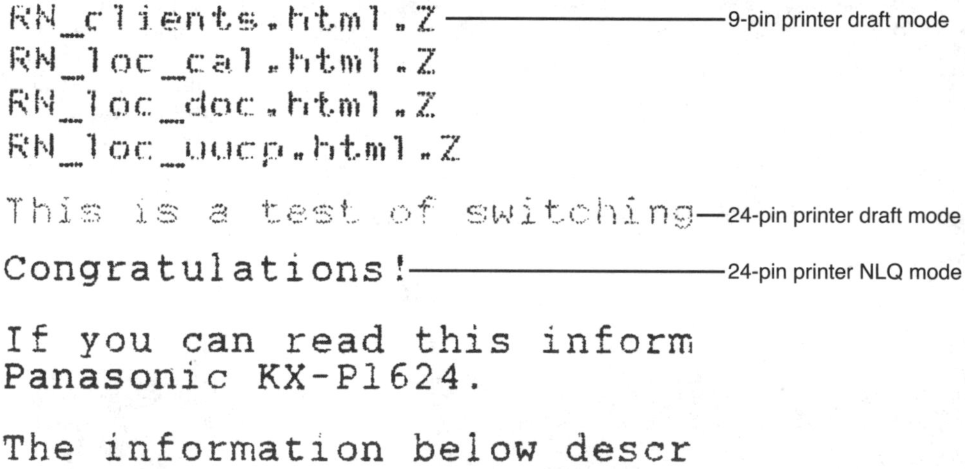

RN_clients.html.Z ——————————————9-pin printer draft mode
RN_loc_cal.html.Z
RN_loc_doc.html.Z
RN_loc_uucp.html.Z

This is a test of switching—24-pin printer draft mode

Congratulations!——————————24-pin printer NLQ mode

If you can read this inform
Panasonic KX-P1624.

The information below descr

Figure 3-29 illustrates a typical impact dot-matrix printer.

Impact Printer Ribbons

Printer ribbons for impact printers use various types of cartridge designs. Some span the entire width of the paper, and others snap over the printhead. Figure 3-30 compares various types of ribbons for impact printers.

Figure 3-29 Components of a typical impact dot-matrix printer. The model pictured is a wide-carriage version, but its features are typical of models using either standard or wide-carriage paper.

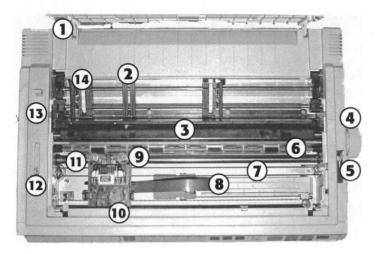

1. Rear cover (top cover removed, not shown)
2. Paper supports for tractor-feed paper path
3. Platen for using single sheets of paper
4. Manual paper advance knob
5. Paper bail lifter
6. Paper bail
7. Timing/drive belt
8. Printhead signal control cable
9. Printhead with heat sink
10. Ribbon holder
11. Printhead support rod
12. Head gap adjustment
13. Tractor/friction-feed selector lever
14. Tractor feed

Figure 3-30 Some typical ribbons for impact dot-matrix printers.

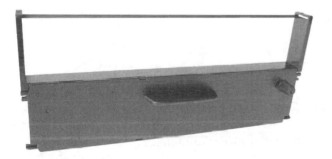

Impact Printer Paper and Media

Impact printers use plain uncoated paper or labels in various widths and sizes. Impact printers designed for point-of-sale receipt printing might use roll paper or larger sizes of paper. When larger sizes of paper are used, these printers typically use a tractor-feed mechanism to pull or push the paper past the printhead. Paper used with tractor-fed printers has fixed or removable sprocket holes on both sides of the paper.

Understanding Multimedia Devices

Multimedia devices such as webcams, digital cameras, MIDI ports, microphones, sound cards, and video capture cards are used by both home and business-oriented PCs. The following sections discuss the characteristics of each of these devices.

Webcam

A webcam is a simple digital camera capable of taking video or still images for transmission over the Internet. Unlike digital cameras (next section), webcams don't include storage capabilities.

Most webcams plug into a USB port, but a few have used IEEE 1394 or parallel ports.

Webcams are generally used in live chat situations, such as with AOL Instant Messenger or other IM clients. They offer resolutions ranging from sub-VGA to as high as 2 million pixels (2 megapixels). Some offer autofocus and zoom features for better image clarity, and some have built-in microphones.

Digital Camera

Digital cameras have largely replaced film cameras for both amateur and professional photography. They use CMOS or CCD image sensors to record images onto internal or card-based flash memory form factors such as Compact Flash, SD, Memory Stick, xD-Picture Card, and Smart Media.

Digital cameras transfer images to computers for emailing, printing, or storage via either flash memory card readers or direct USB port connections.

MIDI Music and MIDI Ports

Musical instrument digital interface (MIDI) music is created from digitized samples of musical instruments that are stored in the ROM or RAM of a MIDI device (such as a sound card) and played under the command of a MIDI sequencer. MIDI sequences can be stored as files for future playback, and can be transferred between sound cards and MIDI-enabled devices such as keyboards via the MIDI port. To learn more about MIDI ports, see the section "MIDI Port," earlier in this chapter.

Sound Card

Sound cards are used to record and play back analog audio, and most can also play back digital audio sources as well. When recording analog audio sources such as CDs, line in or microphone in, sound cards digitize the audio at varying sample

rates and store files in either uncompressed forms such as WAV or compressed forms such as WMA or MP3.

Most recent sound cards support 5.1 or 7.1 surround audio, and many sound cards also support digital stereo or surround audio playback standards via SPDIF ports. In recent years, sound cards have become less popular due to the popularity of onboard audio, but sound cards are preferred by users who create audio recordings.

Figure 3-31 illustrates a typical sound card.

Figure 3-31   Typical input and output jacks on a typical sound card (the Creative Labs X-Fi Xtreme Gamer).

1. Proprietary "Flexjack" for use with various input devices
2. Line out 1 (front left/right, stereo, and headphone jack)
3. Line out 2 (rear and side speakers in home theater systems)
4. Line out 3 (center, subwoofer, and side speakers in home theater systems)
5. Proprietary connector to external I/O breakout box
6. Proprietary connector
7. Aux-In from internal analog audio (CD/DVD drives, TV tuners)
8. Power connector for internal I/O breakout box
9. Data connector for internal I/O breakout box
10. 32-bit PCI slot connector

Microphone

Microphones plug into the 1/8-inch mini-jack microphone jack on a sound card or integrated motherboard audio. The most common microphones used on PCs include those built into headsets (see Figure 3-32) or those that use a stand.

Figure 3-32   A typical PC stereo headset with microphone.

Microphone volume is controlled by the Windows Sounds and Audio Devices applet's mixer control. Open the Recording tab to adjust volume, to mute or unmute the microphone, or to adjust microphone boost.

NOTE   The microphone jack is monaural, whereas the line-in jack supports stereo. Be sure to use the line-in jack to record from a stereo audio source.

Video Capture Card

As the name suggests, video capture cards are used to capture live video from various sources, including analog camcorders, VCRs, analog output from DV camcorders, broadcast TV, and cable TV. Most recent cards with video capture capabilities are actually multi-purpose cards that include other functions. These include ATI's All-in-Wonder series of video (graphics) cards with onboard TV tuner and video capture functions, video (graphics) cards with VIVO (video-in/video-out) S-video or composite video ports, and TV tuner cards and USB devices. Video can be stored in a variety of formats, including MPEG, AVI, and others for use in video productions.

Chapter Review Questions

The following questions test your recall of the concepts described in this chapter. The answers are listed at the end of the questions in the Answers and Explanations section.

1. Which of the following can be used with the SCSI-based technology? (Choose two.)

   A. High-performance and high-capacity hard drives

   B. Image scanners

   C. Hubs

   D. Switches

2. What are two ways that USB version 2.0 ports can be added to a computer? (Choose two.)

   A. Implement a USB hub

   B. Add a USB 1.1 expansion card

   C. Add a USB 2.0 expansion card

   D. Use an Ethernet hub

3. A serial port can hook up devices such as external modems and label printers. What is this port usually called?

   A. SCSI port

   B. COM port

   C. PS/2 ports

   D. Parallel port

4. Which of the following devices can be used for a printer port, scanner, or removable media?

   A. PS/2 port

   B. Parallel port

   C. NIC card

   D. I/O port

5. Which device is known as IEEE 1394?

    A. USB

    B. Parallel port

    C. FireWire

    D. PS/2

6. Some desktop systems and many of the older laptop and portable systems include a port to connect a mouse or keyboard. What is this port called?

    A. USB

    B. FireWire

    C. BIOS

    D. PS/2

7. What is the standard size of the audio mini-jack used by sound cards?

    A. 1 1/2 inch

    B. 1/8 inch

    C. 2 1/2 inch

    D. 1 inch

8. There are currently three standards for USB ports. What are they? (Choose three.)

    A. USB 1.1

    B. USB 3.0

    C. USB 1.0

    D. USB 2.0

9. If you run out of USB ports and need more, which of the following devices are available? (Choose all that apply.)

    A. Motherboard connectors

    B. USB hubs

    C. Add-on cards

    D. Extra PCI slots

10. Which device still remains the primary method used to enter data and send commands to the computer?

   A. Mouse

   B. Gamepad

   C. Stylus

  ✗ **D.** Keyboard

11. Which of the following is used to transfer data into a computer by pressing on screen icons?

  ✗ **A.** Touch screen monitors

   B. CRT monitors

   C. LCD monitors

   D. Serial ports

12. Which of the following are considered multimedia devices? (Choose all that apply.)

   A. Webcam

   B. Sound card

   C. Microphone

  ✗ **D.** All of these options are correct.

13. You are in the process of installing a new keyboard to a new PC. Which of the following is the most common type of connector to use?

   A. Serial connector

   B. PS/2 connector

  ✗ **C.** USB connector

   D. IEEE1394 connector

14. What is the major difference between a laser printer and an LED printer? (Choose all that apply.)

  ✗ **A.** LED printers use an LED array to perform the transfer of images.

   B. LED printers use an LED drum.

   C. Laser printers are of better print quality.

  ✗ **D.** Laser printers use a laser to transfer the image to the drum.

15. Most inkjet, laser, and thermal printers use this interface to connect a printer to a computer. (Choose two.)

    A. RJ-45

    B. USB

    C. Parallel

    D. LED

16. What are three major types of display devices that are in use in today's industry? (Choose all that apply.)

    A. CRT monitors

    B. LCD monitors

    C. Data projectors

    D. USB monitors

17. Identify three types of video connectors.

    A. VGA type

    B. DMI type

    C. HDMI type

    D. USB type

Case Study 1

As discussed in this chapter, today's typical PC can have many different input and output devices. From keyboards, mice, writing tablets, and game pads, to monitors, printers, and speakers, the computer would be unusable without these I/O devices.

Examine your home (or lab) computer, and identify the different input and output devices. List each one, and identify the type of device and its characteristics.

For example, your PC will most likely have a monitor. List the manufacturer name, model, size, maximum resolution, and so forth. Create a detailed list of the input/output devices that you possess.

Case Study 2

Today's PCs have many different connections. In order to input information and have corresponding information outputted by the computer, all of the devices need to be connected to the correct ports.

Examine your home (or lab) computer and identify the various ports associated with it. Make a quick sketch of the back of the computer. Document each port, what they look like, their orientation, and any identifiable characteristics.

For example, a standard serial port is often blue or black with nine pins (one row of five and a row below with four). That particular port is known as a DB-9 port (or DE-9) port and transmits at five volts.

Answers and Explanations

1. **A, B.** High-performance hard drives, image scanners, removable-media drives—such as Zip, Jaz, and Castlewood Orb—and other devices use SCSI interfaces.

2. **A, C.** You can add USB ports to a computer by implementing a USB hub and by installing an add-on USB expansion card. However, if you require USB 2.0 ports, a USB 1.1 expansion card does not work. Any devices connected to the USB 1.1 card are limited to USB 1.1 speeds. Ethernet hubs enable a person to connect more computers to a network, usually by way of RJ-45 ports.

3. **B.** A PC's serial ports are usually called COM ports. Serial ports can also be used to connect docking stations and digital cameras.

4. **B.** You can use a parallel port to hook up all the items listed in the question. Most motherboards still come with this port, even though USB is much faster and more popular.

5. **C.** FireWire is Apple Inc.'s brand name for the IEEE 1394 standard. IEEE 1394 is a family of high-speed, bidirectional, serial transmission ports that can connect PCs to each other, digital devices to PCs, or digital devices to each other.

6. **D.** In some ATX/BTX port clusters, the bottom PS/2 port is used for keyboards, and the top PS/2 port is used for mice and pointing devices. On systems and devices that use the standard PC99 color coding for ports, PS/2 keyboard ports (and cable ends) are purple, and PS/2 mouse ports (and cable ends) are green.

7. **B.** The 1/8-inch audio mini-jack is used by sound cards and motherboard-integrated sound for speakers, microphone, and line-in jacks. Also, to avoid confusion, most recent systems have color-coded jacks.

8. **A, B, and D.** USB 1.1, USB 2.0, and USB 3.0 are the three current standards for USB ports. USB 3.0 is the newer and faster of the three.

9. **A, B, and C.** If you need more ports for USB devices, your options are motherboard connectors, USB hubs, and add-on cards.

10. **D.** The keyboard remains the primary method used to send commands to the computer and enter data. There are many shortcuts that can take the place of actions that would be otherwise accomplished with the mouse—for example, Ctrl+X is cut, Ctrl+C is copy, and so on. You can even use it to maneuver around the Windows Desktop if your mouse or other pointing device stops working.

11. **A.** Touch screen monitors enable the user to transfer data into the computer by pressing on-screen icons. Touch screen monitors are very popular in public-access and point-of-sale installations.

12. **D.** All listed devices are considered multimedia devices. The webcam, sound card, and microphone give you the ability to make Internet phone calls, for example.

13. **C.** The Universal Serial Bus (USB) connector is by far the most common keyboard and mouse connector in today's computers. Unlike older DIN or Mini-Din jacks, you do not have to turn off the PC's power to connect the keyboard. To install a USB keyboard, you just plug it in to an empty USB port. Most of the newer computers only have USB ports. PS/2 ports have become very rare on new computers. Keyboards historically have not connected to serial or IEEE1394 ports.

14. **A, D.** The essential difference between a laser and an LED printer is in the imaging device. The laser printer uses a laser to transfer the image to the drum, whereas an LED printer uses an LED array to perform the same task. Otherwise, these technologies are practically identical.

15. **B, C.** Interface types used by printers and scanners include USB and parallel. USB 2.0 is used by most inkjet, dye-sublimation, thermal, and laser printers, either when connected directly to a PC or connected to a network via a print server. The parallel interface works for older inkjet and laser printers.

16. **A, B, and C.** The three main types of display devices in use today are LCD monitors (the most common), CRT monitors, and data projectors.

17. **A, B, and C.** VGA, DMI, and HDMI are the three main types of connectors you will be dealing with. You can also use S-Video for a connection.

Case Study 1 Solution

An example of a typical PC would be one with a keyboard, mouse, monitor, printer, and speakers. Details follow:

- **Keyboard**: Logitech Wave Keyboard

- **Mouse**: Microsoft Intellimouse Optical Mouse

- **Monitor**: Samsung P2450H 24" Widescreen LCD monitor. HDMI port, maximum resolution = 1920 × 1080.

- **Printer**: HP Officejet Pro 8000. 32MB RAM, 384MHz CPU speed, 15 pages per minute (PPM), USB 2.0 connectivity.

- **Speakers**: Logitech Z-2300 THX-Certified 2.1 speaker system and subwoofer. 200 watts.

Case Study 2 Solution

Refer to Figure 3-1 in the beginning of the chapter. This displays a typical computer with an ATX form factor. It details most of the common ports you would find on a computer. Most ports are color-coded. For example, the 5.1 sound ports use the following color scheme:

- **Light blue**—Line input. Sometimes this seconds as a microphone input.

- **Pink**—Microphone input.

- **Lime green**—Main output for stereo speakers or headphones. Can also act as a line out.

- **Black**—Output for surround sound speakers (rear speakers).

- **Gray/Brown**   Output for additional two speakers in a 7.1 system (middle surround speakers).

- **Orange**—Output for center speaker and subwoofer.

These colors are derived from the PC 99 System Design Guide. See the following link to download the entire guide:
www.microsoft.com/whdc/archive/pcguides.mspx

This chapter covers the following subjects:

- **Motherboards and Their Components**—This section talks about the foundation of the computer, form factors, integrated ports and interfaces, memory slots, and expansion slots, and demonstrates how to install and troubleshoot motherboards.

- **Installing Adapter Cards**—This section demonstrates how to install video and sound cards, and how to troubleshoot common adapter card issues.

Motherboards and Buses

In this chapter, we talk about some of the core components of the computer—the guts of the computer—including the motherboard, the various bus technologies, and interfaces that you might encounter. Deciding on a motherboard should be your first task when you build a PC. Adapter cards are vital because they allow video, audio, and network capabilities. It is important to know how many and what type of adapter card slots are available on your motherboard before selecting specific adapter cards.

Within these pages, you learn some of the considerations to take into account when building the core of a PC.

Motherboards and Their Components

The motherboard represents the logical foundation of the computer. In other words, everything that makes a computer a computer must be attached to the motherboard. From the CPU to storage devices, from RAM to printer ports, the motherboard provides the connections that help them work together. Figure 4-1 shows an example of a typical motherboard. The various components of the motherboard are called out in the figure. We will be referring to this figure throughout the chapter.

The motherboard is essential to computer operation in large part because of the two major buses it contains: the system bus and the I/O bus. Together, these buses carry all the information between the different parts of the computer. The location and orientation of these buses varies depending on the type of form factor used. The form factor is the design of the motherboard, which the case and power supply must comply with. Motherboards can come with integrated I/O ports; these are usually found as a rear port cluster. The motherboard also has memory slots, which enable a user to add sticks of RAM, thus increasing the computer's total resources. Of course, the motherboard also has expansion slots most commonly used by audio and video cards, although the slots can be utilized by many other types of cards as well. You also find mass storage ports for hard drives, CD-ROMs, and DVD-ROMs on the motherboard. After we cover

all of these concepts, we show how to select, install, and troubleshoot the motherboard. As you can see, the motherboard is the central meeting point of all technologies in the computer. There is a lot to cover concerning motherboards. Let's begin by discussing the system and I/O buses.

Figure 4-1 A typical motherboard.

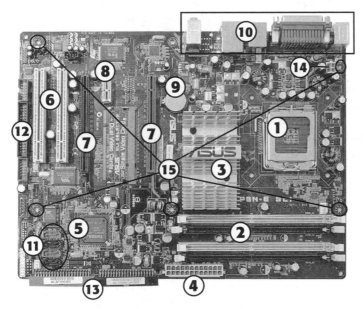

1. Socket 775 processor socket
2. Dual-channel DDR2 memory slots
3. Heat sink over North Bridge
4. 24-pin ATX v2.0 power connector
5. South Bridge chip
6. PCI slot (2)
7. PCI Express x16 slot (2)
8. PCI Express x1 slot
9. CMOS battery
10. Port cluster
11. SATA host adapter (4)
12. Floppy drive controller
13. PATA host adapter (2)
14. 4-pix ATX12 power connector
15. Mounting holes

The System Bus and I/O Bus

The system bus carries four different types of signals throughout the computer:

- Data
- Power
- Control
- Address

To help you understand this concept, let's take an imaginary trip to Chicago and compare the city to a typical motherboard. If you were on the Willis Tower observation deck overlooking downtown Chicago one evening, you would first notice the endless stream of cars, trucks, and trains carrying people and goods from everywhere to everywhere else along well-defined surface routes (the expressways and tollways, commuter railroads, Amtrak, and airports). You can compare these routes to the data bus portion of the system bus, which carries information between RAM and the CPU. If you've ever listened to the traffic reports on a radio station such as

Chicago's WBBM (760 AM), you've heard how traffic slows down when expressway lanes are blocked by construction or stalled traffic. In your computer, wider data buses that enable more "lanes" of data to flow at the same time promote faster system performance.

Now, imagine that you've descended to street level, and you've met with a local utility worker for a tour of underground Chicago. On your tour, you find an elaborate network of electric and gas lines beneath the street carrying the energy needed to power the city. You can compare these to the power lines in the system bus, which transfer power from the motherboard's connection to the power supply to the integrated circuits (ICs or chips) and expansion boards connected to the motherboard.

Go back to street level, and notice the traffic lights used both on city streets and on the entrance ramps to busy expressways, such as the Eisenhower and the Dan Ryan. Traffic stops and starts in response to the signals. Look at the elevated trains or at the Metra commuter trains and Amtrak intercity trains; they also move as directed by signal lights. These signals, which control the movement of road and rail traffic, can be compared to the control lines in the system bus, which control the transmission and movement of information between devices connected to the motherboard.

Finally, as you look around downtown, take a close look at the men and women toting blue bags on their shoulders or driving electric vans and Jeeps around the city. As these mail carriers deliver parcels and letters, they must verify the correct street and suite addresses for the mail they deliver. They correspond to the address bus, which is used to "pick up" information from the correct memory location among the gigabytes of RAM in computer systems and "deliver" new programs and changes back to the correct memory locations.

The I/O bus connects storage devices to the system bus and can be compared to the daily flow of commuters and travelers into the city in the morning, and out again in the evening. Between them, the system and I/O buses carry every signal throughout the motherboard and to every component connected to the motherboard.

The Chipset

In a general sense, the chipset *is* the motherboard, incorporating all the controllers on the motherboard; many technicians refer to it in this way. But in the more specific sense, the chipset is composed of two main components:

- **Memory Controller Hub (MCH)**—On Intel motherboards, this provides the connection between the processor (also known as the CPU), the RAM, and some PCI Express devices, and it handles the communications between them. Historically it has been known as the MCC or memory controller chip and is

informally referred to as the northbridge. The MCH is used by devices that require a high speed of data transfer. It is important to note that on many AMD-based motherboards, this chip doesn't connect to the RAM; instead, the RAM is accessed directly by the processor; therefore, on those AMD-based motherboards, this chip is simply referred to as the northbridge.

NOTE   Newer Intel Core i7 setups have a redesigned chipset that uses the Input/Output Hub (IOH) in place of the MCH. We speak more to this in Chapter 5, "The CPU."

- **I/O Controller Hub (ICH)**—This provides the central connection point between all the secondary systems such as USB, FireWire, hard drives, and so on. It connects to the MCH through the Direct Media Interface (DMI), which is a high-speed point-to-point interconnection for the two hubs. The ICH is also known as the southbridge.

Because there are several different types of processors and manufacturers of processors, the two main chips in the chipset might be referred to as different things. In general, you can get away with using the terms northbridge, which basically connects to the CPU, and southbridge, which connects all the secondary systems.

Form Factors

Although all motherboards have some features in common, their layout and size varies a great deal. The most common motherboard designs in current use include ATX, Micro ATX, BTX, and NLX. Some of these designs feature riser cards and daughterboards. The following sections cover the details of these designs.

ATX and Micro ATX

The ATX family of motherboards has dominated desktop computer designs since the late 1990s. ATX stands for "Advanced Technology Extended," and it replaced the AT and Baby-AT form factors developed in the mid 1980s for the IBM PC AT and its rivals. ATX motherboards have the following characteristics:

- A rear port cluster for I/O ports

- Expansion slots that run parallel to the short side of the motherboard

- Left side case opening (as viewed from the front of a tower PC)

There are four members of the ATX family, listed in Table 4-1. In practice, though, the Mini-ATX design is not widely used.

Table 4-1   ATX Motherboard Family Comparison

Motherboard Type	Maximum Width	Maximum Depth	Maximum Number of Expansion Slots	Typical Uses
ATX	12"	9.6"	Seven	Full tower
Mini-ATX	11.2"	8.2"	Seven	Full tower
microATX	9.6"	9.6"	Four	Mini tower
FlexATX	9.0"	7.5"	Four	Mini tower, small form factor

BTX

One problem with the ATX design has been the issue of system cooling. Because ATX was designed more than a decade ago, well before the development of today's faster components, it's been difficult to properly cool the hottest-running components in a typical system: the processor, memory modules, and the processor's voltage regulator circuits.

To enable better cooling for these devices, and to promote better system stability, the BTX family of motherboard designs was introduced in 2004. Compared to ATX motherboards, BTX motherboards have the following:

■ Heat-producing components, such as the process, or memory, chipset, and voltage regulator, are relocated to provide straight-through airflow from front to back for better cooling.

■ The processor socket is mounted at a 45-degree angle to the front of the motherboard to improve cooling.

■ A thermal module with a horizontal fan fits over the processor for cooling.

■ The port cluster is moved to the rear left corner of the motherboard.

■ BTX cases include multiple rear and side air vents for better cooling.

■ Because of the standardization of processor and memory locations, it's easy to use the same basic design for various sizes of BTX motherboards; the designer can just add slots.

■ BTX tower cases use a right-opening design as viewed from the front.

Although BTX designs are easier to cool than ATX designs, the development of cooler-running processors has enabled system designers to continue to favor ATX. There are relatively few BTX-based motherboards and systems currently on the market.

Figure 4-2 compares typical ATX and BTX motherboard layouts to each other.

Figure 4-2 The ATX motherboard family includes ATX (largest), microATX, and flexATX (smallest). The BTX motherboard family includes BTX, microBTX, nanoBTX, and picoBTX (smallest).

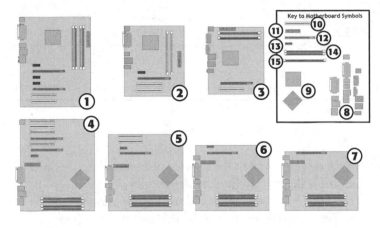

1. ATX motherboard
2. microATX motherboard
3. FlexATX motherboard
4. BTX motherboard
5. microBTX motherboard
6. nanoBTX motherboard
7. picoBTX motherboard
8. Port cluster (at rear of system)
9. Processor (CPU) socket
10. PCI 32-bit slot
11. Motherboard power connector
12. PCI Express x16 slot
13. PCI Express x1 slot
14. Pair of memory sockets
15. Single memory sockets

NOTE The motherboard examples shown in Figure 4-2 are simplified examples of actual motherboards. Onboard ports, port headers, and additional motherboard power connectors are not shown. Also, motherboards using a particular design might have components in slightly different positions than shown here.

NLX

NLX motherboards are designed for quick replacement in corporate environments. They use a riser card that provides power and expansion slots that connect to the right edge of the motherboard (as viewed from the front). NLX motherboards have a two-row cluster of ports along the rear edge of the motherboard.

Most systems that use NLX motherboards are considered obsolete. Figure 4-3 illustrates a typical NLX motherboard and riser card.

Riser Cards and Daughterboards

Riser cards and daughterboards provide two different methods for providing access to motherboard–based resources. In current slimline or rackmounted systems based on ATX or BTX technologies, riser cards are used to make expansion slots usable that would otherwise not be available because of clearances inside the case. Riser card designs can include one or more expansion slots, and are available in PCI, PCI-X (used primarily in workstation and server designs), and PCI-Express designs. Figure 4-4 shows two typical implementations of riser card designs.

Figure 4-3   A typical NLX motherboard and riser card.

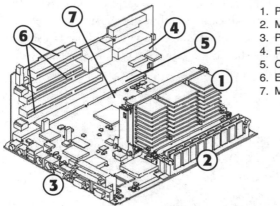

1. Processor and passive heat sink
2. Memory modules
3. Port cluster
4. Riser card
5. Connection to motherboard
6. Expansion slots
7. Motherboard

Figure 4-4   Examples of single-slot and multi-slot riser cards.

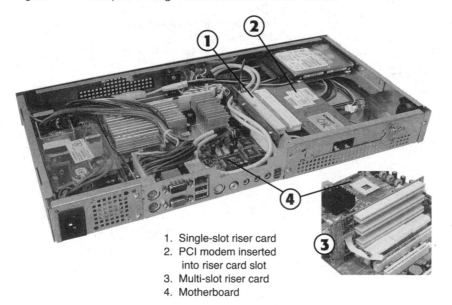

1. Single-slot riser card
2. PCI modem inserted
   into riser card slot
3. Multi-slot riser card
4. Motherboard

The term daughterboard is sometimes used to refer to riser cards, but daughter-board can also refer to a circuit board that plugs into another board to provide extra functionality. For example, some small form factor motherboards support daughter-boards that add additional serial or Ethernet ports, and some standard-size mother-boards use daughterboards for their voltage regulators.

Integrated I/O Ports

Motherboards in both the ATX and BTX families feature a variety of integrated I/O ports. These are found in as many as three locations: All motherboards feature a rear port cluster (see Figure 4-5 for a typical example), and many motherboards also have additional ports on the top of the motherboard that are routed to header cables accessible from the front and rear of the system.

Figure 4-5   A port cluster on a late-model ATX system.

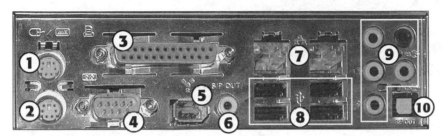

1. PS/2 mouse port
2. PS/2 keyboard port
3. Parallel (LPT) port
4. Serial (COM) port
5. FireWire 400 (IEEE-1394a) port
6. Coaxial SPDIF (digital audio) port
7. RJ-45 Ethernet port
8. Hi-Speed USB port
9. 5.1 surround audio ports
10. Fiber Optic SPDIF port

Most recent motherboards include the following ports in their port cluster:

- Serial (COM)
- Parallel (LPT)
- PS/2 mouse
- PS/2 keyboard
- USB 2.0 (Hi-Speed USB)
- 10/100 or 10/100/1000 Ethernet (RJ-45)
- Audio

So-called "legacy-free" motherboards might omit some or all of the legacy ports (serial, parallel, PS/2 mouse, and keyboard), a trend that will continue as devices using these ports have been replaced by devices that plug into USB ports.

Some high-end systems might also include one or more FireWire (IEEE-1394a) ports, and systems with integrated video include a VGA or DVI-I video port and an S-Video or HDMI port for TV and home theater use.

Figure 4-5 illustrates a port cluster from a typical ATX system, but note that BTX systems use similar designs.

Some integrated ports use header cables to provide output. Figure 4-6 shows an example of 5.1 surround audio ports on a header cable. The header cable plugs into the motherboard and occupies an empty expansion slot.

Figure 4-6 This header cable provides support for 5.1 surround analog audio and digital audio.

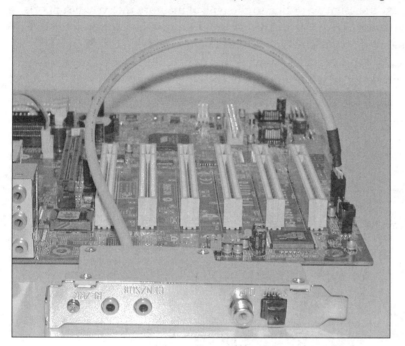

Integrated Port Considerations

Why integrated ports? They provide clear benefits to both users and technicians who set up a system. For users, integrated ports provide lower system purchase prices, faster component performance, centralized control of components through the ROM BIOS and CMOS, and an interior that is less crowded with add-on cards. In other words, you might have a slot or two available in a brand-new system for future upgrades.

For technicians, the greatest benefits of integrated components come during initial setup. Fewer components need to be installed to make a system meet standard requirements and components can be enabled or disabled through the BIOS setup program. Very handy!

However, when systems must be repaired or upgraded, integrated components can be troublesome. If an integrated component that is essential to system operation fails, you must either replace the motherboard or disable the component in question (if possible) and replace it with an add-on card.

Memory Slots

Modern motherboards include two or more memory slots, as seen in Figures 4-1 and 4-2. At least one memory slot must contain a memory module, or the system cannot start or function.

Memory slots vary in design according to the type of memory the system supports. Older systems that use SDRAM use three-section memory slots designed for 168-pin memory modules. Systems that use DDR SDRAM use two-section memory slots designed for 184-pin modules. Systems that use DDR2 SDRAM use two-section memory slots designed for 240-pin modules.

Each memory slot includes locking levers that secure memory in place. When memory is properly installed, the levers automatically swivel into place (see Figure 4-7).

Figure 4-7   Installing memory modules.

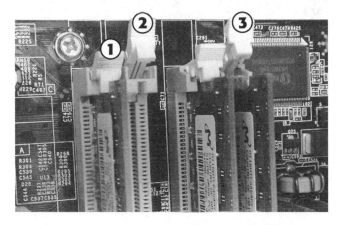

1. Installed module
   (locking lever closed)
2. Empty slot
   (locking lever open)
3. Module being installed
   (locking lever open)

To learn more about memory types and slots, see Chapter 6, "Memory and Storage."

Expansion Slots

Motherboards use expansion slots to provide support for additional I/O devices and high-speed video/graphics cards. The most common expansion slots on recent systems include peripheral component interconnect (PCI), advanced graphics port (AGP), and PCI-Express (also known as PCIe). Some systems also feature audio modem riser (AMR) or communications network riser (CNR) slots for specific purposes.

PCI Slots

The PCI slot can be used for many types of add-on cards, including network, video, audio, I/O, and storage host adapters for SCSI, PATA, and SATA drives. There are several types of PCI slots, but the one found in desktop computers is the 32-bit slot running at 33MHz (see Figure 4-8 in the next section).

AGP

The AGP slot was introduced as a dedicated slot for high-speed video (3D graphics display) in 1996. Since 2005, the PCI Express x16 slot (described in the next section) has replaced it in most new systems. There have been several versions of the AGP slot, reflecting changes in the AGP standard, as shown in Figure 4-8. Note that all types of AGP slots can temporarily "borrow" system memory when creating 3D textures.

Figure 4-8   PCI slots compared to an AGP 1x/2x slot (top), an AGP 4x/8x slot (middle), and an AGP Pro/Universal slot (bottom).

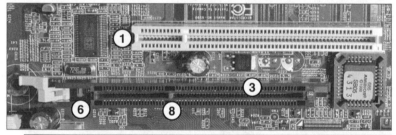

1. PCI slots	5. AGP Pro slot cover
2. AGP 1x/2x (3.3v) slot	6. AGP 4x/8x retaining latch
3. AGP 4x/8x (1.5v) slot	7. AGP 1x/2x key
4. AGP Pro/Universal slot	8. AGP 4x/8x key

Note that the AGP 1x/2x and AGP 4x/8x slots have their keys in different positions. This prevents installing the wrong type of AGP card into the slot. AGP 1x/2x cards use 3.3V, whereas most AGP 4x cards use 1.5V. AGP 8x cards use 0.8 or 1.5V. The AGP Pro/Universal slot is longer than a normal AGP slot to support the greater electrical requirements of AGP Pro cards (which are used in technical workstations). The protective cover over a part of the slot is intended to prevent normal AGP cards from being inserted into the wrong part of the slot. The slot is referred to as a universal slot because it supports both 3.3V and 1.5V AGP cards.

CAUTION An AGP Pro slot cover might be removed after a system has been in service for awhile, even if an AGP Pro card wasn't inserted in a computer. If you see an AGP Pro slot without a cover and you're preparing to install an AGP card, cover the extension with a sticker to prevent damaging a standard AGP card by inserting it improperly.

PCIe (PCI Express) Slots

PCI Express (often abbreviated as PCIe) began to replace both PCI and AGP slots in new system designs starting in 2005. PCI Express slots are available in four types:

- x1
- x4
- x8
- x16

The most common versions include the x1, x4, and x16 designs, as shown in Figure 4-9.

It is important to understand the concept of lanes. PCI Express sends information serially over one or more lanes. A lane is a group of signal paths that can collectively transmit and receive data simultaneously. When sending and receiving data at the same time, it is known as *full-duplex*. x1 (pronounced "by one") PCIe slots and cards are considered to be a single lane. x4 is 4 lanes, and so on. At the time of publication of this book, there are three versions of PCI Express. V1.0 is rated at 250MBps per lane, V2.0 at 500MBps per lane, and V3.0 at 1GBps per lane. Currently, the standard allows for a maximum of 32 lanes, but 16 lanes is the highest scenario that is commonly found. So, the data transfer rate of a PCI Express x1 V2.0 card is 500MBps. A PCI Express x4 V2.0 card would be 2,000MBps.

Figure 4-9 PCIe versions: x1, x4, and x16

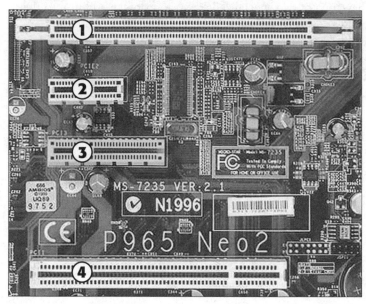

1. PCI Express x16 slot
2. PCI Express x1 slot
3. PCI Express x4 slot
4. PCI slot (32-bit, 33MHz)

PCI Express x1 and x4 slots are designed to replace the PCI slot, and x8 and x16 are designed to replace the AGP slot. Table 4-2 compares the performance of PCI, AGP, and PCI Express slots.

Table 4-2 Technical Information About Expansion Slot Types

Slot Type	Typical Performance
PCI	133MBps
AGP 1x	266MBps
AGP 2x	533MBps
AGP 4x	1,066MBps
AGP 8x	2,133MBps
PCIe x1	500MBps
PCIe x4	2,000MBps
PCIe x8	4,000MBps
PCIe x16	8,000MBps

AMR and CNR Slots

Some motherboards have one of two specialized expansion slots in addition to the standard PCI, PCI Express, or AGP slots. The audio modem riser (AMR) slot enables motherboard designers to place analog modem and audio connectors and the codec chip used to translate between analog and digital signals on a small riser card. AMR slots are frequently found on older systems with chipsets that integrate software modems and audio functions.

The AMR was replaced by the communications network riser (CNR) slot, a longer design that can support up to six-channel audio, S/PDIF digital audio, and home networking functions. Some vendors have used the CNR slot to implement high-quality integrated audio.

Figure 4-10 compares the AMR, PCI, and CNR slots. Figure 4-11 illustrates the AMR and CNR riser cards.

Figure 4-10   An AMR slot and PCI slot (left) compared to a CNR slot and PCI slot (right).

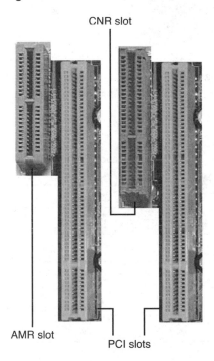

Very few AMR riser cards were ever sold, but some motherboard vendors have bundled CNR riser cards with their motherboards to provide six-channel audio output and other features.

Figure 4-11   An AMR riser card used for soft modem support (left) and a CNR riser card used for six-channel (5.1) analog and digital audio support (right).

AMR Riser Card   CNR Riser Card

The AMR or CNR slot, when present, is usually located on the edge of the motherboard. The AMR slot was often found on Pentium III or AMD Athlon processor-based systems, while the CNR slot was used by some Pentium 4-based systems. Current systems integrate network and audio features directly into the motherboard and its port cluster, making both types of slots obsolete.

NOTE   AMR and CNR riser cards were generally provided by motherboard makers because they are customized to the design of particular motherboards. Although some parts suppliers have sold AMR and CNR cards separately, it's best to get the riser card from the same vendor as the motherboard to ensure proper hardware compatibility and driver support.

Mass Storage Interfaces

Motherboards also include mass storage interfaces such as EIDE/PATA, SATA, and SCSI. The following sections compare and contrast the appearance and functionality of these interfaces. Table 4-3 provides a quick overview of technical information about these interfaces.

Table 4-3 Technical Information About Mass Storage Interfaces

Interface	Performance	Suggested Uses
SATA 1st generation	1.5Gbps	Hard disk, rewritable DVD
SATA 2nd generation	3.0Gbps	Hard disk, rewritable DVD
EIDE/PATA	1.0–1.3Gbps	Rewritable DVD, rewritable CD, Zip, JAZ, REV, tape
SCSI	1.6–3.2Gbps*	Hard disk, tape backup

*Current Ultra 160 and Ultra 320 SCSI standards; older standards are much slower.

The following sections describe each of these interfaces in greater detail.

EIDE/PATA

Until recently, most motherboards included two or more EIDE/PATA (also known as ATA/IDE) host adapters for PATA devices such as hard disks, CD or DVD drives, tape backups, and removable-media drives. Each host adapter uses a 40-pin interface similar to the one shown in Figure 4-12, and can control up to two drives.

Figure 4-12 PATA host adapter on a typical motherboard.

EIDE/PATA host adapter

Most recent systems use a plastic skirt around the PATA connector with a notch on one side. This prevents improper insertion of a keyed PATA (ATA/IDE) cable. However, keep in mind that some older systems have unskirted connectors and some older ATA/IDE cables are not keyed. To avoid incorrect cable connections, be sure to match pin 1 on the PATA host adapter to the red-striped edge of the PATA ribbon cable.

On systems with a third EIDE/PATA host adapter, the additional host adapter is typically used for a RAID 0 or RAID 1 drive array. See your system or motherboard documentation for details. Most current systems now have only one EIDE/PATA host adapter, as the industry is transitioning away from EIDE/PATA to SATA interfaces for both hard disk and DVD drives.

SATA

Most recent systems have anywhere from two to as many as eight Serial ATA (SATA) host adapters. Each host adapter controls a single SATA drive, such as a hard disk or rewritable DVD drive.

The original SATA host adapter design did not have a skirt around the connector, making it easy for the cable to become loose. Many late-model systems now use a skirted design for the host adapter (see Figure 4-13).

Figure 4-13   Most late model systems include multiple SATA host adapters with skirted connectors.

Sata host adapters

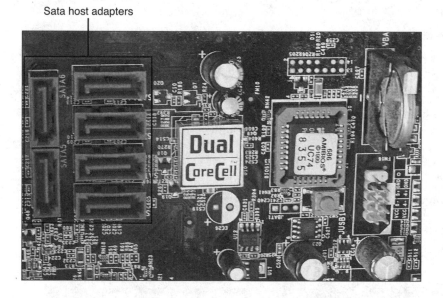

SCSI

SCSI (Small Computer Systems Interface) is a more flexible drive interface than PATA (ATA/IDE) because it can accommodate many devices that are not hard disk drives. The fastest versions of SCSI are comparable in speed to today's SATA. However, SCSI

systems are usually used in servers and power workstations, as opposed to regular PCs. The following have been common uses for SCSI:

- High-performance and high-capacity hard drives

- Image scanners

- Removable-media drives such as Zip, Jaz, and Castlewood Orb

- High-performance laser printers

- High-performance optical drives, including CD-ROM, CD-R, CD-RW, DVD-ROM, and others

So-called Narrow SCSI host adapters (which use an 8-bit data channel) can accommodate up to seven devices of different varieties on a single connector on the host adapter through daisy-chaining. Wide SCSI host adapters use a 16-bit data channel and accommodate up to 15 devices on a single connector on the host adapter through daisy-chaining. Narrow SCSI devices and host adapters use a 50-pin or (rarely) a 25-pin cable and connector, and Wide SCSI devices use a 68-pin cable and connector.

Several years ago, SCSI host adapters were found on some high-end desktop and workstation motherboards. However, most recent systems use SATA in place of SCSI, and SCSI host adapters and devices are now primarily used by servers. Currently, SCSI is used primarily for high-performance hard disks and tape backups.

Systems with onboard SCSI host adapters might have one or more 50-pin or 68-pin female connectors similar to those shown in Figure 4-14.

Figure 4-14 SCSI HD50 and HD68 cables and connectors are typically used on systems with onboard SCSI host adapters.

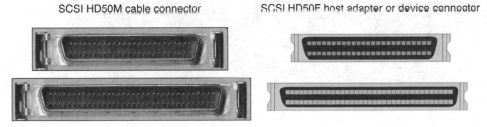

SCSI HD50M cable connector

SCSI HD50F host adapter or device connector

SCSI HD68M cable connector

SCSI HD68F host adapter or device connector

Choosing the Best Motherboard for the Job

So, how do you go about choosing the best motherboard for the job? Follow this process:

Step 1. Decide what you want the motherboard (system) to do. Because most of a computer's capabilities and features are based on the motherboard, you need to decide this first.

Some examples:

If you need high CPU performance, you must choose a motherboard that supports the fastest dual-core or multi-core processors available.

If you want to run a 64-bit (x64) operating system, you need a motherboard that supports 64-bit processors and more than 4GB of RAM.

If you want to run fast 3D gaming graphics, you need a motherboard that supports NVIDIA's SLI or ATI's CrossFire multi-GPU technologies.

If you want to support multimedia uses such as video editing, you'll prefer a motherboard with onboard IEEE-1394a (FireWire 400).

If you are building a system for use as a home theater, a system with HDMI graphics might be your preferred choice.

Step 2. Decide what form factor you need to use. If you are replacing an existing motherboard, the new motherboard must fit into the case (chassis) being vacated by the old motherboard and (ideally) be powered by the existing power supply. If you are building a new system, though, you can choose the form factor needed.

Some examples:

Full-size ATX or BTX motherboards provide the most room for expansion but require mid-size or full-size tower cases.

If no more than three expansion slots are needed, micro ATX or micro BTX systems fit into mini-tower cases that require less space and can use smaller, less-expensive power supplies.

If only one slot (or no slots) is needed, picoATX or picoBTX systems that fit into small form factor cases require little space.

Installing Motherboards

What keeps a motherboard from sliding around inside the case? If you look at an unmounted motherboard from the top, you can see that motherboards have several holes around the edges and one or two holes toward the middle of the motherboard.

Most ATX-family and BTX-family motherboards are held in place by screws that are fastened to brass spacers that are threaded into holes in the case or a removable motherboard tray. Before you start working with motherboards or other static-sensitive parts, see the section "Preventing Electrostatic Discharge (ESD)," in Chapter 10, "Troubleshooting," for ESD and other precautions you should follow.

Step-by-Step Motherboard Removal (ATX and BTX)

Removing the motherboard is an important task for the computer technician. For safety's sake, you should remove the motherboard before you install a processor upgrade as well as if you need to perform a motherboard upgrade.

To remove ATX- or BTX-family motherboards from standard cases, follow these steps:

Step 1.   Turn off the power switch and disconnect the AC power cable from the power supply.

Step 2.   Disconnect all external and internal cables attached to add-on cards after labeling them for easy reconnection.

Step 3.   Disconnect all ribbon cables attached to built-in ports on the motherboard (I/O, storage, and so on) after labeling them for easy reconnection.

Step 4.   Disconnect all cables leading to internal speakers, key locks, speed switches, and other front-panel cables. Most recent systems use clearly marked cables as shown in Figure 4-15, but if the cables are not marked, mark them before you disconnect them so you can easily reconnect them later.

Figure 4-15   Front-panel cables attached to a typical motherboard, which control system power to the motherboard, case speaker, drive and power lights, and so on.

TIP You can purchase premade labels for common types of cables, but if these are not available, you can use a label maker or blank address labels to custom-make your own labels.

Step 5.   Remove all add-on cards and place them on an antistatic mat or in (not on top of) antistatic bags.

Step 6.   Disconnect header cables from front- or rear-mounted ports and remove them from the system (see Figure 4-16).

Figure 4-16   A typical dual-USB header cable that uses an expansion slot bracket.

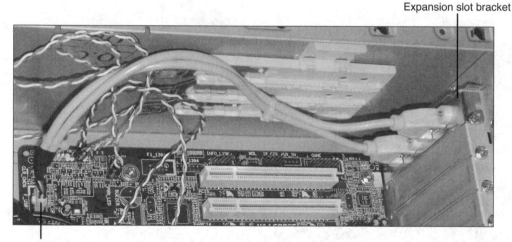

Expansion slot bracket

USB header cable connected to motherboard

Step 7.   Disconnect the power-supply leads from the motherboard. The new motherboard must use the same power-supply connections as the current motherboard.

Step 8.   Remove the heat sink and the processor before you remove the motherboard and place them on an anti-static mat. Removing these items before you remove the motherboard helps prevent excessive flexing of the motherboard and makes it easier to slip the motherboard out of the case. However, skip this step if the heat sink requires a lot of downward pressure to remove and if the motherboard is not well supported around the heat sink/processor area.

Step 9.   Unscrew the motherboard mounting screws (refer to Figure 4-1) and store for reuse; verify that all screws have been removed.

CAUTION   Easy does it with the screwdriver! Whether you're removing screws or putting them back in, skip the electric model and do it the old-fashioned way to avoid damaging the motherboard. If your motherboard is held in place with hex screws, use a hex driver instead of a screwdriver to be even more careful.

Step 10.   Lift the motherboard and plastic stand-off spacers out of the case and place them on an antistatic mat. Remove the I/O shield (the metal plate on the rear of the system that has cutouts for the built-in ports; refer to Figure 4-17) and store it with the old motherboard.

Figure 4-17   An ATX I/O shield and motherboard during installation.

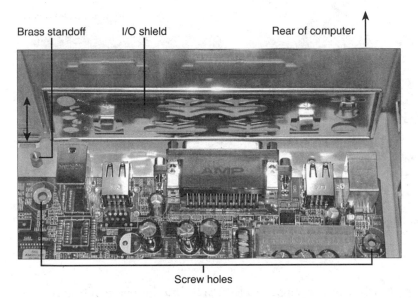

Step-by-Step Motherboard Removal (NLX)

NLX motherboards are designed for fast, easy removal. Follow this procedure:

Step 1.   As described earlier, disconnect cables from any installed add-on cards.

Step 2.   Remove any add-on cards, remembering to handle the cards by their edges.

Step 3.   Pull the motherboard release lever to disconnect the motherboard from the NLX riser.

Step 4.   Slide the motherboard out of the case.

Preparing the Motherboard for Installation (ATX/BTX)

Before you install the new motherboard into the computer, perform the following steps:

Step 1.   Review the manual supplied with the new motherboard to determine correct sizes of memory supported, processor types supported, and configuration information.

Step 2.   Install the desired amount of memory. See Chapter 6 for details.

Step 3.   Install the processor (CPU) and heat sink as described in Chapter 5.

Step 4.   Configure CPU speed, multiplier, type, and voltage settings on the motherboard if the motherboard uses jumpers or DIP (Dual Inline Pin) switches. Note that many recent motherboards use BIOS configuration options instead.

Making these changes after the motherboard is installed in the computer is normally very difficult.

Step-by-Step Motherboard Installation (ATX/Baby-AT)

After you have prepared the motherboard for installation, follow these steps to install the motherboard:

Step 1.   Place the new motherboard over the old motherboard to determine which mounting holes should be used for standoffs (if needed) and which should be used for brass spacers. Matching the motherboards helps you determine that the new motherboard fits correctly in the system.

Step 2.   Move brass spacers as needed to accommodate the mounting holes in the motherboard.

Step 3.   Place the I/O shield and connector at the back of the case. The I/O shield is marked to help you determine the port types on the rear of the motherboard. If the port cutouts on some I/O shields are not completely removed, remove them before you install the shield.

Step 4.   Determine which holes in the motherboard have brass stand-off spacers beneath them and secure the motherboard using the screws removed from the old motherboard (refer to Figure 4-17).

Step 5.   Reattach the wires to the speaker, reset switch, IDE host adapter, and power lights.

Step 6.   Reattach the ribbon cables from the drives to the motherboard's IDE and floppy disk drive interfaces. Match the ribbon cable's colored side to pin 1 on the interfaces.

Step 7.   Reattach cables from the SATA drives to the SATA ports on the motherboard. Use SATA port 1 for the first SATA drive, and so on.

Step 8.   Reattach the power supply connectors to the motherboard.

Step 9.   Insert the add-on cards you removed from the old motherboard; make sure your existing cards don't duplicate any features found on the new motherboard (such as sound, ATA/IDE host adapters, and so on). If they do, and you want to continue to use the card, you must disable the corresponding feature on the motherboard.

Step 10.   Mount header cables that use expansion card slot brackets into empty slots and connect the header cables to the appropriate ports on the motherboard.

Step 11.   Attach any cables used by front-mounted ports such as USB, serial, or IEEE-1394 ports to the motherboard and case.

Step-by-Step Motherboard Installation (NLX)

After you have prepared the motherboard for installation, follow these steps to install the motherboard:

Step 1.   Line up the replacement motherboard with the motherboard rails located at the bottom of the case.

Step 2.   Slowly push the motherboard into place. After the motherboard is connected to the riser card, it stops moving.

Step 3.   Lift and push the motherboard release lever to lock the motherboard into place.

Step 4.   Replace the side panel. If the side panel cannot be replaced properly, the motherboard is not installed properly.

Troubleshooting Motherboards

When you're troubleshooting a computer, there is no shortage of places to look for problems. However, because the motherboard is the "home" for the most essential system resources, it's often the source of many problems. If you see the following problems, consider the motherboard as a likely place to look for the cause:

- **System does not start**—When you push the power button on an ATX or BTX system, the computer should start immediately. If it doesn't, the problem could be motherboard–related.

- **Devices connected to the port cluster don't work**—If ports in the port cluster are damaged or disabled in the system BIOS configuration (CMOS setup), any devices connected to the port cluster do not work.

- **Devices connected to header cables don't work**—If ports connected to the header are not plugged into the motherboard, are damaged, or are disabled in the system BIOS configuration (CMOS setup), any devices connected to these ports do not work.

- **Mass storage drives are not recognized or do not work**—If mass storage ports on the motherboard are not properly connected to devices, are disabled, or are not configured properly, drives connected to these ports do not work.

- **Memory failures**—Memory failures could be caused by the modules themselves, or they could be caused by the motherboard.

- **Problems installing aftermarket processor heat sinks or replacement cards**—You cannot assume that every device fits every system.

The following sections help you deal with these common problems.

System Does Not Start

If the computer does not start, check the following:

- Incorrect front panel wiring connections to the motherboard

- Loose or missing power leads from power supply

- Loose or missing memory modules

- Loose BIOS chips

- Incorrect connection of PATA/IDE cables to onboard host adapter

- Dead short in system

- Incorrect positioning of a standoff

- Loose screws or slot covers

The following sections describe each of these possible problems.

Incorrect Front Panel Wiring Connections to the Motherboard

The power switch is wired to the motherboard, which in turn signals the power supply to start. If the power lead is plugged into the wrong pins on the motherboard, or has been disconnected from the motherboard, the system does not start and you will not see an error message.

Check the markings on the front panel connectors, the motherboard, or the motherboard/system manual to determine the correct pinouts and installation. Figure 4-18 shows typical motherboard markings for front panel connectors (refer to Figure 4-15 for typical markings on front-panel wires).

Figure 4-18   A typical two-row front panel connector on a motherboard.

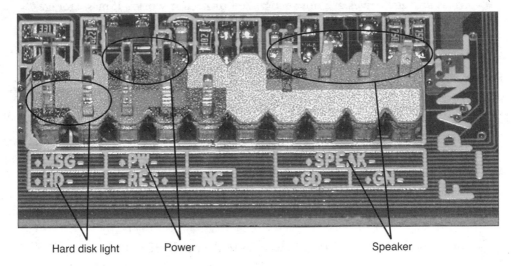

Hard disk light   Power   Speaker

Loose or Missing Power Leads from Power Supply

Modern power supplies often have both a 20- or 24-pin connection and a 4- or 8-pin connection to the motherboard. If either or both connections are loose or not present, the system cannot start and you will not see an error message.

Loose or Missing Memory Modules

If the motherboard is unable to recognize any system memory, it does not start properly. Unlike the other problems, you see a memory error message.

Make sure memory modules are properly locked into place, and that there is no corrosion on the memory contacts on the motherboard or on the memory modules themselves. To remove corrosion from memory module contacts, remove the memory modules from the motherboard and gently wipe the contacts off to remove any

built-up film or corrosion. An Artgum eraser (but not the conventional rubber or highly abrasive ink eraser) can be used for stubborn cases. Be sure to rub in a direction away from the memory chips to avoid damage. Reinsert the modules and lock them into place.

CAUTION Never mix tin memory sockets and gold memory module connectors, or vice versa. Using different metals for memory socket and module connectors has been a leading cause of corrosion with SIMM-based systems.

Loose BIOS Chips

Socketed motherboard chips that don't have retaining mechanisms, such as BIOS chips, can cause system failures if the chips work loose from their sockets. The motherboard BIOS chip (see Figure 4-19) is responsible for displaying boot errors, and if it is not properly mounted in its socket, the system cannot start and no error messages are produced (note that many recent systems have surface-mounted BIOS chips).

Figure 4-19 If a socketed BIOS chip like this one becomes loose, the system does not boot.

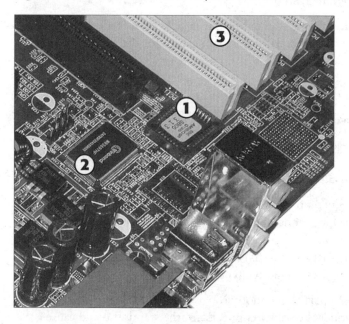

1. System BIOS chip
2. LPC I/O chip (for comparison)
3. PCI slots (for comparison)

The cycle of heating (during operation) and cooling (after the power is shut down) can lead to chip creep, in which socketed chips gradually loosen in the sockets. To cure chip creep, push the chips back into their sockets. Use even force to press a

square BIOS chip into place. On older systems that use rectangular BIOS chips, alternately push on each end of the chip until the chip is securely mounted.

> **NOTE**   Check your system or motherboard documentation to determine the location of the BIOS chip.

Incorrect Connection of EIDE/PATA Cables to Onboard Host Adapter

Many systems are designed to wait for a response from a device connected to an EIDE/PATA host adapter on the motherboard before continuing to boot. If the EIDE/PATA cable is plugged in incorrectly, the system never gets the needed response, and some systems do not display an error message.

Make sure pin 1 on the cable is connected to pin 1 on the EIDE/PATA device and the corresponding host adapter on the system. Check the motherboard manual for the position of pin 1 on the motherboard's host adapter if the host adapter is not marked properly.

Dead Short (Short Circuit) in System

A dead short (short circuit) in your system prevents a computer from showing any signs of life when you turn it on. Some of the main causes for dead shorts that involve motherboards include

- Incorrect positioning of a standoff
- Loose screws or slot covers

The following sections describe both possible causes.

Incorrect Positioning of a Standoff

Brass standoffs should be lined up with the mounting holes in the motherboard (refer to Figure 4-1 for typical locations). Some motherboards have two types of holes: plain holes that are not intended for use with brass standoffs (they might be used for heat sink mounting or for plastic standoffs) and reinforced holes used for brass standoffs. Figure 4-20 compares these hole types.

If a brass standoff is under a part of the motherboard not meant for mounting, such as under a plain hole or under the solder connections, the standoff could cause a dead short that prevents the system from starting.

Figure 4-20   Mounting holes compared to other holes on a typical motherboard.

Plain hole (not used
for motherboard
installation)

Metal-reinforced hole designed to ground the
motherboard when mounted with brass standoffs

Loose Screws or Slot Covers

Leaving a loose screw inside the system and failing to fasten a slot cover or card in place are two common causes for dead shorts, because if these metal parts touch live components on the motherboard, your system shorts out and stops working.

The solution is to open the case and remove or secure any loose metal parts inside the system. Dead shorts also can be caused by power supply–related problems.

Devices Connected to the Port Cluster Don't Work

The port cluster (refer to Figure 4-5) provides a "one-stop shop" for most I/O devices, but if devices plugged into these ports fail, check the disabled ports and possible damage to a port in the port cluster, as described in the following sections.

Disabled Port

If a port hasn't been used before, and a device connected to it doesn't work, be sure to check the system's BIOS configuration to determine if the port is disabled. This is a particularly good idea if the port is a legacy port (serial/COM, parallel/LPT) or is the second network port. Ports can also be disabled using Windows Device Manager.

Damage to a Port in the Port Cluster

If a port in the port cluster has missing or bent pins, it's obvious that the port is damaged, but don't expect all types of damage to be obvious. The easiest way to see if a port in the port cluster is damaged is to follow these steps:

Step 1.   Verify that the port is enabled in the system BIOS and Windows Device Manager.

Step 2.   Make sure the device cable is connected tightly to the appropriate port. Use the thumbscrews provided with serial/COM, parallel/LPT, and VGA or DVI video cables to assure a proper connection.

Step 3.   If the device fails, try the device on another port or another system. If the device works, the port is defective. If the device doesn't work, the device or the device's cable is defective.

To solve the problem of a defective port, use one of these solutions:

- **Replace the motherboard with an identical model**—This is the best solution for long-term use. Note that if you replace the motherboard with a different model, you might need to reinstall Windows, or, at a minimum, reinstall drivers and reactivate Windows and some applications.

- **Install an add-on card to replace the damaged port**—This is quicker than replacing the motherboard, but if you are replacing a legacy port such as serial/COM or parallel/LPT, it can be expensive. If the device that plugged into a legacy port can also use a USB port, use a USB port instead.

- **Use a USB/legacy port adapter**—Port adapters can be used to convert serial/COM or parallel/LPT devices to work on USB ports. However, note that some limitations might be present. Generally, this is the least desirable solution.

Devices Connected to Header Cables Don't Work

Before assuming that a port that uses a header cable is defective or disabled, make sure the header cable is properly connected to the motherboard. If the system has just been assembled, or if the system has recently undergone internal upgrades or servicing, it's possible the header cable is loose or disconnected.

If the header cable is properly connected to the motherboard, follow the steps in the previous section to determine the problem and solution.

NOTE   Check system or motherboard documentation to determine how to properly connect header cables to the motherboard.

Mass Storage Devices Do Not Work Properly

Mass storage devices that connect to SATA, PATA/IDE, or SCSI host adapters on the motherboard do not work if either of the following are true, as described in the next sections:

- Mass storage ports are disabled in system BIOS or Windows.

- Data cables are not properly connected to the motherboard or drives.

Mass Storage Ports Disabled in System BIOS or Windows

Before assuming a mass storage device is defective, be sure to verify whether the port has been disabled in the system BIOS configuration (CMOS setup or in Windows Device Manager). If you cannot connect the device to another port, enable the port and retry the device.

Data or Power Cables Are Not Properly Connected to the Motherboard or Drives

If internal upgrades or servicing has taken place recently, it's possible that data or power cables have become loose or disconnected from the mass storage host adapters on the motherboard or the drives themselves. Before reconnecting the cables, shut down the computer and disconnect it from AC power.

Memory Failures

Memory failures could be caused by the modules themselves, or they could be caused by the motherboard. For more information on memory problems and motherboards, see the section "Loose or Missing Memory Modules," earlier in this chapter.

Card, Memory, or Heat Sink Blocked by Motherboard Layout

Internal clearances in late-model systems are tight, and if you attempt to install some types of hardware in some systems, such as an oversized processor heat sink or a large video card, it might not be possible because of the motherboard's layout.

Before purchasing an aftermarket heat sink, check the clearances around the processor. Be especially aware of the location of capacitors and the voltage regulator; if the heat sink is too large, it could damage these components during installation. To help verify that an aftermarket heat sink fits properly, remove the original heat sink from the processor and take it with you to compare its size to the aftermarket models you are considering.

Before purchasing an expansion card, check the slot clearance to be sure the card fits into the desired expansion slot. In some cases, you might need to move a card from a

neighboring slot to make room for the cooling fan shroud on some high-performance graphics cards.

Installing Adapter Cards

Although most desktop systems are equipped with a variety of I/O ports and integrated adapters, it is still often necessary to install adapter cards to enable the system
to perform specialized tasks or to achieve higher performance. The following sections show you how to perform typical installations.

General Installation

Before installing an adapter card, you should determine the following:

- **Does the adapter card perform the same task as an integrated adapter?**—
  For example, if you are installing a display adapter (also called a graphics card or
  video card), does the system already have an integrated adapter? If you are installing a sound card, does the system already have a sound card? Depending
  upon the type of card you are installing, it might be necessary to disable the
  comparable onboard feature first to avoid hardware resource conflicts.

- **What type(s) of expansion slots are available for expansion cards?**—A typical system today might have two or three different types of expansion slots, such
  as PCI Express x16, PCI Express x1 and PCI, or PCI and AGP, as shown in Figure 4-21. You can use PCI Express x1 and PCI slots for a variety of adapter
  cards, but PCI Express and AGP slots are designed for display adapters. The
  adapter card you select must fit into an available slot.

- **When PCI and PCI Express x1 slots are available, which slot should be
  used?**—PCI Express x1 slots provide higher performance than PCI slots, and
  you should use them whenever possible.

The general process of installing an adapter card works like this:

Step 1. Shut down the system.

Step 2. Disconnect it from AC power, either by unplugging the system or by
turning off the power supply with its own on/off switch.

Step 3. Remove the system cover. Depending upon the motherboard design and
case design, the exact method varies:

- If the case has a one-piece design, remove the entire case.

- If the case is a tower design with removable side panels, remove the
  left side panel (as seen from the front) to install cards into an ATX system. Remove the right side panel to install cards into a BTX system.

Figure 4-21   AGP, PCI, PCI Express x1, and x16 slots on typical motherboards. Arrow indicates rear of motherboard.

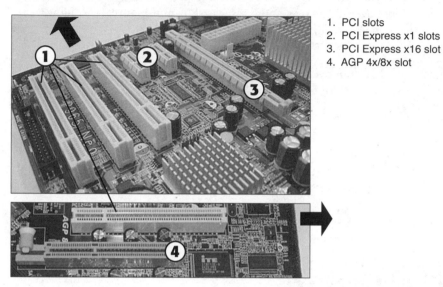

1. PCI slots
2. PCI Express x1 slots
3. PCI Express x16 slot
4. AGP 4x/8x slot

Step 4.   Locate the expansion slot you want to use. If the slot has a header cable installed in the slot cover, you need to move the header cable to a different slot. Figure 4-22 illustrates a typical system that has some available slots.

Figure 4-22   A typical system has some available slots and some that are not available for various reasons.

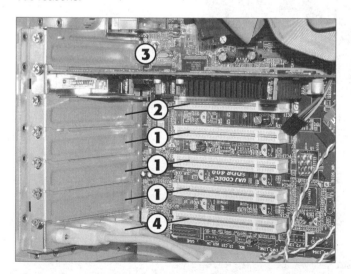

1. Available slots and slot covers
2. Not available; too close to neighboring card
3. Available for header cable only; no matching slot
4. Not available; header cable blocks slot

Step 5.   Remove the slot cover corresponding to the slot you want to use for the adapter card. Most slot covers are held in place by set screws that fasten the slot cover to the rear of the case, as shown in Figure 4-22. However, some systems use different methods.

TIP   If you are unable to remove the slot cover after removing the set screw, loosen the set screw on the adjacent slot cover. Sometimes the screw head overlaps the adjacent slot cover.

Step 6.   Remove the card from its antistatic packaging. Hold the card by the bracket, not by the circuit board, chips, or card connector. Figure 4-23 illustrates a typical card and where to hold it safely.

Figure 4-23   A typical adapter card. Callouts indicate where it is safe and not safe to hold the card.

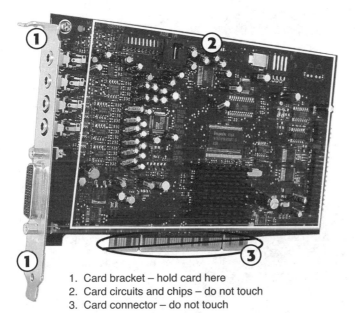

1. Card bracket – hold card here
2. Card circuits and chips – do not touch
3. Card connector – do not touch

Step 7.   Insert the card into the expansion slot, lining up the connector on the bottom.

Step 8.   Push the card connector firmly into the slot.

Step 9.   Secure the card bracket; on most systems, you secure the card bracket by replacing the set screw. See Figure 4-24.

Figure 4-24 An improperly installed card compared with a properly installed card.

A Incorrect installation   B Correct installation

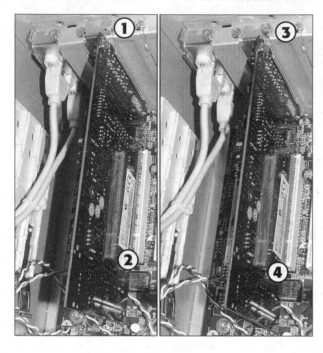

1. Bracket not secured to rear of system
2. Card connector not completely inserted
3. Bracket secured
4. Card connector completely inserted

Step 10.   Connect any cables required for the card.

Step 11.   Reconnect AC power and restart the system.

Step 12.   When the system restarts, provide drivers as prompted.

The following sections discuss some special installation considerations that apply to some types of adapter cards.

Display Adapters

Display adapters are available for PCI Express x16, AGP, and PCI expansion slots. Display adapters in PCI form factor are intended for use in systems that don't have PCI Express or AGP slots, or to provide support for additional displays on systems that already have PCI Express or AGP cards installed.

When you install a card into an AGP slot, make sure the card-locking mechanism on the front of the slot is open before you install the card. Locking mechanisms sometimes use a lever that is moved to one side, flips up and down, or has a locking tab that is pulled to one side.

After installing the display adapter, install the drivers provided by the graphics card vendor. If possible, use updated drivers downloaded from the vendor's website rather than the ones provided on CD.

When connecting the monitor(s) to the display adapter, keep in mind that CRT and some LCD monitors use the 15-pin VGA connector, but many LCD monitors use the larger DVI connector. You can use an adapter to enable a DVI-I connector on a display adapter to connect to a monitor that uses the VGA connector.

Sound Cards

After installing a sound card, you must connect 1/8-inch mini-jack cables from the speakers and the microphone to the sound card. Most sound cards use the same PC99 color-coding standards for audio hardware that are used by onboard audio solutions, as described in Table 4-4.

Table 4-4   PC99 Color Coding for Audio Jacks

Usage	Color	Jack Type
Microphone input (mono)	Pink	Mini-jack
Line in (stereo)	Light blue	Mini-jack
Speaker or headphone (front/stereo)	Lime green	Mini-jack
Speaker out/subwoofer	Orange	Mini-jack
Game port/MIDI out	Gold	15-pin DIN

After installing the sound card, you are prompted to install drivers when you restart the system. The driver set might also include a customized mixer program that is used to select speaker types and speaker arrangement (stereo, 5.1, and so on), and provides speaker testing and diagnostics. Be sure to test the speakers to assure they are plugged into the correct jack(s) and are working properly.

Video Capture Cards

Video capture cards are used to capture video from analog or digital video sources. Video capture card types include

- **IEEE 1394 (FireWire) cards**—These capture video from DV camcorders. You can also use these cards for other types of 1394 devices, such as hard disks and scanners. You can use an onboard IEEE 1394 port for video capture.

- **Analog video capture cards**—These capture video from analog sources, such as cable or broadcast TV, composite video, or S-video. Many of these cards also include TV tuners. Examples include the Hauppauge WinTV PVR series and the ATI Theater Pro series.

- **Digital video capture card**—These capture digital video from HDMI sources, such as HDTV.

- **The ATI All-in-Wonder series**—These cards incorporate accelerated 3D video display output to monitors, video capture, and TV tuner support.

After installing any type of video capture card, you need to install the drivers provided with the card, connect the card to video sources, and, in the case of cards with onboard TV tuners, set up the TV tuner feature.

Troubleshooting Adapter Cards

Adapter card problems can be detected in the following ways:

- A device connected to the adapter card doesn't work.

- The adapter card listing in Device Manager indicates a problem.

To solve these problems, see the following sections.

Device Connected to Adapter Card Doesn't Work

If a device connected to an adapter card doesn't work, it could indicate a variety of issues. After verifying that the device works on another system, check the following:

Step 1. Check Device Manager and make sure the adapter card is listed as working. Windows XP uses the yellow ! symbol to indicate devices that are not working, and the red X mark to indicate devices that have been disabled. In some cases, an adapter card works after you install a driver upgrade. To learn more about driver and firmware upgrades, see "Performing Driver and Firmware Upgrades," later in this chapter. To learn more about using Device Manager, see Chapter 10.

Step 2. Check the system BIOS setup to ensure that any onboard devices that might interfere with the adapter card's operation have been disabled.

Step 3. Make sure the adapter card is properly secured in the expansion slot. Refer to Figure 4-24.

Step 4.   If the adapter card requires additional power, make sure an appropriate power cable is connected from the power supply to the card. Some IEEE-1394 and display adapter cards require additional power to operate properly.

Performing Driver and Firmware Upgrades

A device is only as good as the software that makes it work. Device drivers are found in two forms:

- Driver files

- Firmware

You can update the drivers for most devices installed in Windows through the Update Driver Wizard found in the properties sheet for the device in Device Manager. The wizard can locate updated drivers on the Internet or can be directed to install drivers from a location you provide, such as drivers on a floppy disk, CD, or a particular folder on a hard disk.

Firmware, which is software stored on a flash memory chip, can also be upgraded, although most adapter cards don't use upgradeable firmware. If a firmware upgrade is available from the adapter card vendor, follow the vendor's instructions for installing the upgrade.

Some upgrades are installed by creating a special boot disk from the downloaded file provided by the vendor, but others are installed from within Windows. Regardless of how firmware is upgraded, it's important to keep in mind that the upgrade process can take two or three minutes and must not be interrupted. If the firmware process is interrupted, the card no longer functions, and it must be repaired or replaced.

Chapter Review Questions

The following questions test your recall of the concepts described in this chapter. The answers are listed at the end of the questions in the "Answers and Explanations" section.

1. The system bus and I/O bus carry four different types of signals throughout the computer. Which of the following are the signals? (Choose all that apply.)

   A. Data

   B. Power

   C. Control

   D. Adapters

   E. Address

2. Which of the following are considered expansion slots? (Choose all that apply.)

   A. PCI

   B. FireWire

   C. AGP

   D. USB

3. Which of the following can you use with SCSI (Small Computer Systems Interface)? (Choose all that apply.)

   A. Hard drives

   B. Scanners

   C. Laser printers

   D. DVD-ROMs

   E. A dot-matrix printer

4. Which of the following are in the ATX family of motherboards? (Choose all that apply.)

   A. ATX

   B. Mini-ATX

   C. FlexATX

   D. ATX and Mini-ATX only

   E. None of the options provided is correct

5. Which of the following are considered integrated I/O ports?

    A. Serial port

    B. Parallel port

    C. USB port

    D. PS/2 mouse and keyboard

    E. Audio port

    F. Ethernet port

    G. All of these options are correct

6. To connect speakers to the sound card, which of the following must you use?

    A. 1/2-inch jack

    B. 1 1/4-inch jack cable

    C. 2/3-inch jack cable

    D. 1/8-inch mini-jack cable

    E. None of these options is correct

7. How many pins are DDR SDRAM two-section memory slots designed for?

    A. 168

    B. 184

    C. 240

    D. 255

8. Which of the following is a common speed for PCI?

    A. 33MHz

    B. 133MHz

    C. 266MHz

    D. 1066MHz

9. Which of the following expansion bus technologies would be described as x16 (spoken as "by sixteen")?

    A. PCI

    B. AGP

    C. PCIe

    D. PCI-X

10. Which of the following expansion buses has the fastest data transfer rate?

   A. PCIe x1

   B. AGP 4x

   C. PCI

   D. PS/2

11. Which of the following is the fastest mass storage interface?

   A. SATA 2nd generation

   B. SCSI Ultra 160

   C. IDE

   D. PATA

12. Which of the following should you do first before disconnecting all ribbon cables that are attached to built-in ports on the motherboard? (Select the two best answers.)

   A. Turn off the power switch and disconnect the AC power cable from the power supply

   B. Disconnect all cables leading to internal speakers, key locks, speed switches, and other front-panel cables

   C. Disconnect all external and internal cables attached to add-on cards after labeling them for easy reconnection

   D. Remove all add-on cards and place them on an antistatic mat or in (not on top of) antistatic bags

13. If your computer does not start, which of the following should you check for? (Select the two best answers.)

   A. Loose or missing memory modules

   B. Whether the OS is installed

   C. CD/DVD drive is connected

   D. Power to the motherboard

14. If the sound ports are color-coded, what color should the headphone connection be?

  A. Pink

  B. Lime green

  C. Light blue

  D. Gold

15. When installing an adapter card, what should you do just prior to reconnecting power?

  A. Restart the system

  B. Push the card firmly into the slot

  C. Connect any cables required for the card

  D. Secure the card bracket

Case Study 1

As discussed earlier in this chapter, a motherboard can have many different connections. They can include connections for power, hard drives, optical drives, and much more.

Examine your home computer, and identify the various ports and connections of your motherboard. Diagram what you see on the motherboard and list each of the connections and their distinguishing characteristics.

For example, your motherboard probably has a main power connection with either 20 or 24 wires (pins) bundled together.

Case Study 2

Different adapter cards use different expansion buses. Define which expansion buses today's adapter cards would normally utilize, including video cards, sound cards, and network adapters.

Use the Internet to help define which expansion buses would most often be used. Manufacturer's websites and online computer pricing guides can be helpful in finding out what is commonly used in the field.

Answers and Explanations

1. **A, B, C, and E.** The motherboard is essential to computer operation in large part because of the two major buses it contains: the system bus and the I/O bus. Together, these buses carry all the information between the different parts of the computer.

2. **A, C.** Motherboards use expansion slots to provide support for additional I/O devices and high-speed video/graphics cards. The most common expansion slots on recent systems include PCI, AGP, and PCI-Express (also known as PCIe). Some systems also feature AMR or CNR slots for specific purposes.

3. **A, B, C, and D.** SCSI (Small Computer Systems Interface) is a more flexible drive interface than PATA (ATA/IDE) because it can accommodate many devices that are not hard disk drives. Devices are high-performance hard drives, image scanners, and removable media, as well as laser printers and CD-ROM/DVD-ROM drives.

4. **A, B, and C.** The ATX family of motherboards has dominated desktop computer designs since the late 1990s. ATX stands for Advanced Technology Extended, and it replaced the AT and Baby-AT form factors developed in the mid 1980s for the IBM PC AT and its rivals. The ATX family includes Mini-ATX and FlexATX.

5. **G.** Motherboards in both the ATX and BTX families feature a variety of integrated I/O ports, including serial, parallel, USB, PS/2, audio, and Ethernet. These are found in as many as three locations. All motherboards feature a rear port cluster, and many motherboards also have additional ports on the top of the motherboard that are routed to header cables that are accessible from the front and rear of the system.

6. **D.** After installing a sound card, you must connect 1/8-inch mini-jack cables from speakers and the microphone to the sound card. Most sound cards use the same PC99 color-coding standards for audio hardware that are used by onboard audio solutions.

7. **B.** DDR SDRAM memory modules and their corresponding slots have 184 pins. Older SDRAM modules are 168 pin. DDR2 SDRAM modules are 240 pin. There are no 255-pin memory modules.

8. **A.** A common speed for PCI is 33MHz. PCI might also operate at 66MHz depending on several factors. Other faster expansion buses can operate at speeds of 133MHz, and beyond.

9. C. PCIe (PCI Express) has four main types: x1, x4, x8, and x16. PCI (and its derivative PCI-X), and AGP are not described in this manner. AGP shows the x after the number.

10. B. AGP 4x can transmit 1,066MBps whereas PCIe x1 only transmits 500MBps. PCI is far slower at 133MBps, and PS/2 sends a very small amount of information, only what is needed to input information from a keyboard or mouse.

11. A. SATA 2nd generation is the fastest at 3.0GBps. SCSI Ultra 160 comes in second at 1.6GBps. IDE/PATA is limited to a maximum of 1.3GBps.

12. A, C. Before disconnecting the ribbon cables, you should turn off the power switch and disconnect the AC power cable from the power supply, and disconnect all external and internal cables attached to add-on cards after labeling them for easy reconnection.

13. A, D. If the computer does not start, make a quick check of the main power connections and important devices such as CPU, RAM, and video card. Whether or not the CD/DVD drive is connected or OS is installed should not affect the computer *starting*. However, these things could affect the computer trying to *boot*.

14. B. The headphone connection should be lime green according to the PC99 color-coding standard. Pink is the microphone input, light blue is the line in, and gold is the game port.

15. C. Just prior to reconnecting the AC power, you should connect any cables required for the card. Previous to this, the card should be inserted, pushed firmly into the slot, and any card brackets should be secured. Restarting (or starting) the system should be the first thing you do.

Case Study 1 Solution

Refer to Figure 4-1, repeated here. This shows a typical ATX form factor motherboard. All of the components are labeled. If you haven't already, memorize the components you see in the figure. Then compare them to your motherboard components.

Figure 4-1   A typical motherboard.

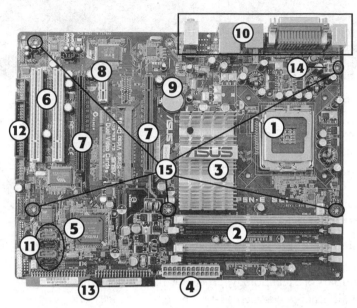

1. Socket 775 processor socket
2. Dual-channel DDR2 memory slots
3. Heat sink over North Bridge
4. 24-pin ATX v2.0 power connector
5. South Bridge chip
6. PCI slot (2)
7. PCI Express x16 slot (2)
8. PCI Express x1 slot
9. CMOS battery
10. Port cluster
11. SATA host adapter (4)
12. Floppy drive controller
13. PATA host adapter (2)
14. 4-pix ATX12 power connector
15. Mounting holes

Case Study 2 Solution

Although there are lots of different scenarios when it comes to adapter cards, the following shows some common expansion buses used by adapter cards. Keep in mind that these technologies arc constantly being updated!

■   Video cards: PCIe x16

■   Sound cards: PCIe x1 or PCI (could also be integrated into the motherboard)

■   Network cards: PCIe x1 or PCI (could also be integrated into the motherboard)

Some websites that can offer some more information include manufacturers' websites, such as

■   www.intel.com

■   www.creative.com

■   www.nvidia.com

Online computer pricing guides that can be of assistance include

■   www.pricewatch.com

■   www.cyberguys.com

■   www.amazon.com

This chapter covers the following subjects:

- **Intel and AMD Processors**—The two most common processor manufacturers are Intel and AMD. This section discusses the various types of CPUs that each company makes. It also covers the different connections that processors make to the motherboard.

- **CPU Technologies**—This section delves into the technologies that govern a CPU. It is important to understand topics such as clock rate, hyperthreading, multiple core technology, processor throttling, overclocking, cache, and the differences between 32-bit and 64-bit processors.

- **Choosing the Best Processor for the Job**—After you know about the different processors available, and the technologies that processors utilize, it's time to select the processor for your application. Here you want to think about what you will be using the computer for. You don't always need the most powerful computer!

- **Installing and Upgrading Processors**—This section gets into the hands-on of installing processors. They are expensive and delicate, and so you should follow some basic rules and step-by-step procedures when installing them.

- **Troubleshooting Processors**—Finally, if a processor (or its supporting hardware) fails, the entire computer is not able to boot. This is the most catastrophic of failures that can occur, and although it's less common than other failures, you should troubleshoot it in a methodical way. The most common failure is due to overheating; this section shows how to overcome these failures, and protect against them happening again.

The CPU

In Chapter 4, we talked about the foundation of the computer: the motherboard. Just as important to the computer is the processor. The processor (or CPU) is the "brain" of the computer and takes care of the bulk of the PC's calculations. Deciding on a CPU and motherboard should be the first tasks at hand when building a PC, and these choices depend on how the computer is to be used. Some users only need basic access to the Internet. Others run resource-intensive applications such as voice recognition software or powerful games. The applications that the user works with help dictate what CPU to select. Just be sure that the CPU is compatible with the motherboard!

This chapter covers processor terminology, the major types of processors available for recent systems, their technologies, how to install them, and how to troubleshoot them.

Intel and AMD Processors

The two most common types of CPUs on the market today are manufactured by Intel and Advanced Micro Devices (AMD). Intel is the largest global supplier of microprocessors for the x86 architecture (PCs), and AMD is the second largest. AMD concentrates primarily on CPUs, chipsets, and other microprocessors, but Intel delves into many other markets including networking technologies, motherboards, and much more. The two companies are constantly waging a battle for superior CPU technology; this competition has helped the CPU market to quickly grow and become more sophisticated over the past two decades.

It is important to know some of the processors that each manufacturer develops so that you can differentiate between the various types of PCs you see in the field. Let's begin with Intel.

Intel Processors

Intel processors developed from 2000 to 2010 include the following product families:

- Pentium III

- Pentium 4

- Pentium D

- Celeron

- Core 2 Duo

- Core 2 Quad

- Core 2 Extreme

- Core 2 i3

- Core 2 i5

- Core 2 i7

- Core 2 i7 Extreme

NOTE You might also see the term "Centrino." Intel's Centrino technology refers to a combination of the Core 2 Duo and certain Intel chipsets made for mobile computers.

All processors must connect to the motherboard in some way. This is generally done by way of a socket. The processor is gently placed in the socket, and then locked in place by some kind of retention mechanism. Older processors used a cartridge system; the processor was integrated into a cartridge and would be pressed straight down into a slot, kind of like some older gaming consoles, and quite similar to the usage of an expansion slot.

The Pentium III processor was the last Intel processor produced in both a slot-based and socket-based design. Slot-based versions use Slot 1, the same slot design used by the Pentium II and slot-based Celeron processors. Socketed versions use Socket 370, which is mechanically the same as the socket used by the first socketed Celeron processors. However, some early Socket 370 motherboards are not electrically compatible with the Pentium III. We speak more to slots and sockets later in this chapter.

The Pentium 4 replaced the Pentium III and ran at much higher clock speeds. Early versions used Socket 423, a socket used by no other Intel processor. Most Pentium 4 designs used Socket 478, and late-model Pentium 4 designs used Socket 775, which is also used by current Intel processors. The different sockets used by the Pentium 4 were necessary because of substantial design changes throughout the processor's lifespan, including the introduction of 64-bit extensions (x64).

The Pentium 4's successor was the Pentium D, which is essentially two Pentium 4 processor cores built into a single physical processor. Although it used the same Socket 775 as late-model Pentium 4 processors, it required support from different chipsets because data was transferred between processor cores via the Memory Controller Hub (northbridge) component. The Pentium D was Intel's first dual-core processor. The Pentium Extreme Edition is a faster version of the Pentium D designed for gaming or other high-performance tasks. The Pentium D and Pentium Extreme Edition both support x64 extensions, as does the Core 2 Duo.

The Pentium D was replaced by the Core 2 family of processors. The Core 2 family switched to a new processor architecture that emphasizes real-world performance over clock speed. The first Core 2 processors were the Core 2 Duo (featuring two processor cores), followed by the Core 2 Quad models with four processor cores. Although Core 2 processors run at much slower clock speeds than the fastest Pentium 4 or Pentium D processors, they perform much better in real-world operations. As of the writing of this book, the latest processors by Intel are the Core "i" series; for example, i7. These processors communicate in a new and faster way to the RAM and the rest of the computer. They also include additional cores—as many as eight!

Celeron is actually a brand name rather than a specific processor design. Celeron processors have been based on the Pentium II, Pentium III, Pentium 4, and Core 2 processors. However, they feature lower clock speeds, slower front side bus speeds (the clock speed of the memory bus), and smaller L2 caches, making them less powerful (and less expensive) processors than the designs they're based on. Few Celeron models support x64 extensions.

Because most Intel processor families have gone through many changes during their lifespans, specific models are sometimes referred to by their code names. In an attempt to make it easier to understand the performance and feature differences of models in a particular processor family, Intel has assigned processor numbers to recent versions of the Pentium 4, as well as all models of the Celeron D, Pentium D, Pentium 4 Extreme Edition, Pentium Extreme Edition, Core 2 Duo, Core 2 Quad, and Core i3, i5, and i7 series.

Table 5-1 provides a summary of Intel desktop processors produced from 1998 to 2010. For additional details, see *Upgrading and Repairing PCs*, 19th Edition, by Scott Mueller (Que Publishing).

Table 5-1   Intel Desktop Processors from Pentium III Through Core 2 Extreme

Processor	Clock Speed Range	FSB Speed	Processor Socket or Slot	L2 Cache Sizes
Pentium III	450MHz–1.3GHz	100MHz, 133MHz	Slot 1, Socket 370	256KB or 512KB
Celeron	533MHz–1.4GHz	66MHz, 100MHz	Slot 1, Socket 370	128KB, 256KB
Pentium 4	1.4GHz–3.8GHz	400MHz, 533MHz, 800MHz	Socket 423, Socket 478, Socket 775	256KB, 512KB, 1MB, 2MB
Pentium 4 Extreme Edition	3.2GHz–3.733GHz	800MHz	Socket 775	512KB+2MB L3 or 2MB
Celeron	1.7GHz–2.8GHz	400MHz	Socket 478	128KB
Celeron D	2.13GHz–3.6GHz	533MHz	Socket 478, Socket 775	256KB, 512KB
Pentium D	2.66GHz–3.66GHz	533MHz, 800MHz	Socket 775	1MB×2 or 2MB ×2
Pentium Extreme Edition	3.73GHz	800MHz	Socket 775	2MB×2
Core 2 Duo	1.80GHz–3.33GHz	800MHz, 1066MHz, 1333MHz	Socket 775	2MB, 4MB, 6MB
Core 2 Extreme	2.93GHz	1066MHz	Socket 775	4MB
Celeron	1.2–2.2GHz	800MHz	Socket 775	512KB
Celeron	1.6–2.4GHz	800MHz	Socket 775	512KB
Core 2 Quad	2.4–2.6GHz	1066MHz	Socket 775	4MB×2
Core 2 Quad	2.26–3.0GHz	1333MHz	Socket 775	3MB×2, 6MB×2
Core 2 Extreme	2.66–3.0GHz	1066MHz, 1333MHz	Socket 775	4MB×2

Processor	Clock Speed Range	FSB Speed	Processor Socket or Slot	L2 Cache Sizes
Core 2 Extreme	3.0–3.2GHz	1333MHz, 1600MHz	LGA-771	6MB×2
Core i3	2.93–3.06GHz	n/a	LGA-1156	4MB
Core i5	2.66–3.6GHz	n/a	LGA-1156	4 and 8MB
Core i7	2.66–3.06	n/a	LGA-1156/ LGA-1366	4, 8 and 12MB
Core i7 Extreme	3.33GHz	n/a	LGA-1156/ LGA-1366	8 and 12MB

Socket 775 is also referred to as LGA-775 because the socket contains leads that connect with solder balls on the bottom of the processor.

The processor code names and performance in this table are effective as of mid 2010.

NOTE   The Core i7 does away with the FSB. This is because Intel added an on-die memory controller (memory controller added directly to the CPU). Core i7 setups use a different chipset; within this chipset the QuickPath Interconnect (QPI) makes the connection between the CPU and the northbridge. The northbridge is referred to as the IOH (Input/Output Hub).

AMD Processors

AMD processors contemporary with the Intel Pentium III and its successors include the following processor families as of mid 2010:

- Athlon
- Duron
- Athlon XP
- Sempron
- Athlon 64
- Athlon 64 FX
- Athlon 64 X2
- Phenom X3
- Phenom X4
- Phenom II X2

- Phenom II X3

- Phenom II X4

- Phenom II x6

The Athlon processor was the first (and last) AMD processor produced in a slot-based design. It uses Slot A, which physically resembled Slot 1 used by Intel Pentium II and Pentium III models, but was completely different in its pinout. Later versions of the Athlon switched to Socket A, a 462-pin socket, which was also used by the Duron, Athlon XP, and Socket A versions of the Sempron.

The Athlon XP replaced the Athlon, and featured higher clock speeds and larger L2 cache. The lower-performance counterpart of the Athlon and Athlon XP was the Duron, which featured a smaller L2 cache and slower FSB speed.

The Athlon XP design was used for the Socket A versions of the Sempron when AMD moved to 64-bit processing with the introduction of the Athlon 64, AMD's first x64 64-bit desktop processor.

The Athlon 64 family initially used Socket 754, but because the memory controller is built into the processor, rather than into the northbridge as on conventional processors, it was necessary to develop a new Socket 939 to support dual-channel memory.

The Athlon 64 FX is a faster performance–oriented version of the Athlon 64. Initial versions were based on the Opteron workstation and server processor, and thus used Socket 940. Later versions used Socket 939 and its successor, Socket AM2.

AMD's first dual-core processor was the Athlon 64 X2, which uses a design that permits both processor cores to communicate directly with each other, rather than using the northbridge (Memory Controller Hub) as in the Intel Pentium D. This enabled upgrades from Socket 939 Athlon 64 to the X2 version after performing a BIOS upgrade.

AMD's economy version of the Athlon 64 is also called the Sempron, various versions of which have used Socket 754 and Socket 939.

AMD's Phenom series is based on the AMD K10 processor architecture, and all Phenoms include multiple processor cores that are built as a single unit. The first two Phenom processors are the quad-core Phenom X4 and the three-core Phenom X3. The Phenom II series utilizes a more efficient socket, and increases the total possible amount of processor cores to six. Processor speeds are also increased in this series. These processors use a more powerful chipset. The chipset is the main controller of the motherboard. When selecting an AMD processor, the motherboard's chipset should be taken into account to ensure compatibility.

Because most AMD processor families have gone through many changes during their lifespans, specific models are sometimes referred to by their code names.

Table 5-2 provides a brief summary of AMD desktop processors produced over the last decade. For additional details, see *Upgrading and Repairing PCs*, 19th Edition.

Table 5-2 AMD Desktop Processors from Athlon Through Phenom

Processor	Clock Speed Range	HyperTransport (Also Known as FSB Speed)	Processor Socket or Slot	L2 Cache Sizes
Athlon	500MHz–1.4GHz	200–266MHz	Slot A, Socket A (also known as Socket 462)	256–512KB
Athlon XP	1.333–2.2GHz	266–400MHz	Socket A	256–512KB
Duron	550MHz–1.8GHz	200–266MHz	Socket A	64KB
Sempron	1.5–2.2GHz	166–200MHz	Socket A	256KB (Thorton), 512KB (Barton)
Sempron	11.4–2.0GHz	800MHz–1GHz	Socket 754	128–256KB
Athlon 64	1–2.6GHz	800MHz–1GHz	Socket 754, Socket 939, Socket 940, Socket AM2	512KB–1MB
Sempron	1.8–2.0GHz	800MHz	Socket 939	128KB–256KB
Athlon 64 FX	2.2–2.8GHz	800MHz–1GHz	Socket 939, Socket 940	1MB
Sempron	1.6–2.3GHz	800MHz	Socket AM2	128-256-512KB
Athlon 64 X2	1.9–3.2GHz	1GHz	Socket 939 (Manchester, Toledo), Socket AM2 (Windsor, Brisbane)	256KB×2; 512KB×2; 1MB×2
Athlon 64 FX	2.0–3.2GHz	1GHz	Socket 939 (Toledo), Socket AM2 (Brisbane)	1MB×2
Phenom X4	1.8–2.6 GHz	1.6–2GHz	Socket AM2	512KB×4 + 2MB L3
Phenom X3	2.1–2.5GHz	1.6–1.8GHz	Socket AM2	512KB×3 + 2MB L3

Table 5-2 AMD Desktop Processors from Athlon Through Phenom

Processor	Clock Speed Range	HyperTransport (Also Known as FSB Speed)	Processor Socket or Slot	L2 Cache Sizes
Phenom II X2	2.8–3.3GHz	2.0–2.2GHz	Socket AM3	512KB×2
Phenom II X3	2.4–3.2GHz	2GHz	Socket AM3	512KB×3
Phenom II x4	2.4–3.5GHz	1.8–2.0GHz	Socket AM2+ and AM3	512KB×4
Phenom II x6	2.7–3.2GHz	2GHz	Socket AM3	512KB×6

The processor code names and performance in this table are effective as of mid 2010.

NOTE All the AMD models listed have an on-die memory controller and use HyperTransport technology instead of a front side bus. AMD CPUs utilize L3 cache whereas Intel CPUs do not; however, AMD CPUs in general use less L2 cache than Intel.

Processor Sockets and Packaging

Most processors listed in the previous sections use some form of the pin grid array (PGA) package, in which pins on the bottom of the processor plug into holes in the processor socket. The exceptions include slot-mounted processors (Slot 1 and Slot A) and the current LGA771 and LGA775 sockets, which use a different type of processor package called the land grid array (LGA). LGA packaging uses gold pads on the bottom of the processor package to connect with raised leads in the processor socket.

Figure 5-1 compares processor packages and sockets to each other.

Overview of Processor Differences

Although Intel and AMD processors share two common architectures, x86 (used for 32-bit processors and for 64-bit processors running in 32-bit mode) and x64 (an extension of x86 that enables larger files, larger memory sizes, and more complex programs), these processor families differ in many ways from each other, including

- Different processor sockets
- Different types of instruction sets
- Differences in dual-core and multi-core designs
- Cache sizes
- Performance versus clock speed

Figure 5-1   Intel and AMD processors and sockets.

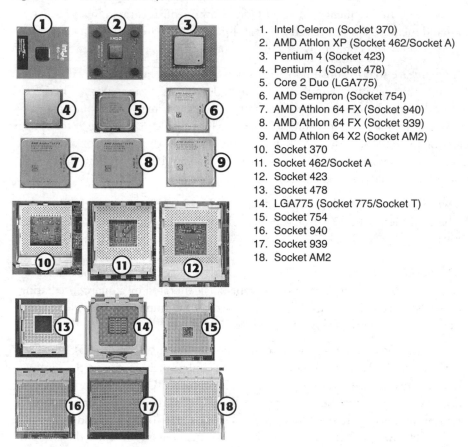

1. Intel Celeron (Socket 370)
2. AMD Athlon XP (Socket 462/Socket A)
3. Pentium 4 (Socket 423)
4. Pentium 4 (Socket 478)
5. Core 2 Duo (LGA775)
6. AMD Sempron (Socket 754)
7. AMD Athlon 64 FX (Socket 940)
8. AMD Athlon 64 FX (Socket 939)
9. AMD Athlon 64 X2 (Socket AM2)
10. Socket 370
11. Socket 462/Socket A
12. Socket 423
13. Socket 478
14. LGA775 (Socket 775/Socket T)
15. Socket 754
16. Socket 940
17. Socket 939
18. Socket AM2

Keep these differences in mind when deciding on the best processor for your applications. Also, remember that different processors require different motherboards. When designing a computer, the CPU and motherboard must be compatible.

CPU Technologies

The processor technologies described in the following sections might be used by AMD only, by Intel only, or by both vendors. These technologies are used to help distinguish different processors from each other in terms of performance or features.

CPU Clock Rate

The *clock rate* is the frequency (or speed) of a component. It is rated in cycles per second and measured in Hertz (Hz). For all practical purposes, the term clock rate is the same as the more commonly used term *clock speed*.

Components are sold to consumers with a *maximum* clock rate, but they don't always run at that maximum number. To explain, let me use a car analogy. The CPU is often called the "engine" of the computer, like a car engine. Well, your car's speedometer might go up to 120MPH, but you'll probably never drive at that maximum—for a variety of reasons! When it comes to CPUs, the stated clock rate is the *maximum* clock rate, and the CPU usually runs at a speed less than that; in fact, it can run at any speed below the maximum.

Now, we're all familiar with speeds such as 2.4GHz, 3.0GHz, or 3.2GHz. But what is the basis of these speeds? Speed can be broken down into three categories that are interrelated:

- **Motherboard clock speed**—The base clock speed of the motherboard. Also referred to as the *system bus speed*, this speed is generated by a quartz oscillating crystal soldered directly to the motherboard. For example, the base clock speed of a typical motherboard might be 333MHz.

- **External clock speed**—This is the speed of the front side bus (FSB), which connects the CPU to the memory controller hub (northbridge) on the motherboard. This is usually variable and depends on the CPU you install. In addition, it is determined from the base clock speed of the motherboard. For example, a typical motherboard's maximum external clock speed (or FSB) could be 1333MHz. Simply put, this means that it is transferring four times the amount of data per cycle as compared to the original base clock speed. $333\text{MHz} \times 4 = 1{,}333\text{MHz}$.

- **Internal clock speed**—This is the internal speed of the CPU. As an example, the Intel Q8400 CPU is rated at 2.66GHz. The CPU uses an internal multiplier that is also based off the motherboard base clock. The multiplier for this CPU is eight. The math is as follows:

    base clock speed × multiplier = internal clock speed.

    In our example, that would be

    $333\text{MHz} \times 8 = 2.66\text{GHz}$

A motherboard can possibly support faster CPUs also; for example, the Intel Q9650 that has an internal clock speed of 3.00GHz. This means that it has a multiplier of nine (3.00GHz /333MHz = 9). Some motherboards allow for overclocking, which enables the user to increase the multiplier within the BIOS,

thereby increasing the internal clock speed of the CPU. This could possibly cause damage to the system, analogous to blowing the engine of a car when attempting to run a 10-second one-fourth mile. So approach overclocking with caution.

> **NOTE**   Quite often, motherboard manufacturers state only the internal and external clock speeds (CPU and FSB); you might need to dig for more information concerning the base clock speed. To make matters more confusing, some manufacturers refer to the FSB as the system bus, but you can tell the difference. Just remember that the FSB is calculated from the base clock of the motherboard. It's often multiplied by four. Currently, FSBs are between 800MHz and 1600MHz. However, the external clock speed (FSB) isn't actually a factor for AMD CPUs or newer Intel Core i7 CPUs because they have essentially done away with the FSB. Intel just recently started using the QPI technology in newer motherboards.

Hyperthreading (HT Technology)

Hyperthreading (HT Technology) is a technology developed by Intel for processing two execution threads within a single processor. Essentially, when HT Technology is enabled in the system BIOS and the processor is running a multithreaded application, the processor is emulating two physical processors. The Pentium 4 was the first desktop processor to support HT Technology, which Intel first developed for its Xeon workstation and server processor family.

Pentium 4 processors with processor numbers (meaning newer Pentium 4 versions) all support HT Technology, as do older models with 800MHz FSB and a clock speed of 3.06GHz or higher. HT Technology is not needed (and is therefore not present) in dual-core, three-core, and quad-core processors because each processor core is capable of handling separate execution threads in a multithreaded application.

Dual-Core and Multi-Core

Two or more physical processors in a system enable it to perform much faster when multitasking or running multithreaded applications. However, systems with multiple processors are very expensive to produce and some operating systems cannot work with multiple processors. Dual core processors, which combine two processor cores into a single physical processor, provide virtually all of the benefits of two physical processors, and are lower in cost and work with any operating system that supports traditional single-core processors.

The first dual-core desktop processors were introduced by Intel (Pentium D) and AMD (Athlon 64 X2) in 2005. Athlon 64 X2's processor cores communicate directly

with each other, enabling systems running single-core Athlon 64 processors to swap processors after a simple BIOS upgrade. The Pentium D, on the other hand, required new chipsets to support it. The Core 2 Duo is Intel's current dual-core processor, and, like the AMD Athlon 64 X2, the Core 2 Duo's processor cores communicate directly with each other.

Both Intel and AMD have released processors that include more than two cores. Intel's Core 2 Quad and some versions of the Core 2 Extreme contain four processor cores, and AMD's Phenom x4 contains four processor cores and the Phenom x3 contains three.

Processor Throttling

Processors do not need to run at full speed when they have little, or no, work to perform. By slowing down—or throttling—the processor's clock speed when the workload is light, the processor runs cooler, the system uses less energy, and—in the case of mobile systems—the computer enjoys a longer battery life. Throttling, sometimes referred to as thermal throttling, can also take place when a processor gets too hot for the computer's cooling system to work properly.

Intel uses the terms SpeedStep or Enhanced SpeedStep for its throttling technologies. AMD uses the term Cool'n'Quiet for its throttling technology.

MMX and 3DNow! Instruction Sets

An *instruction set* is a list of instructions that a processor can execute. These basic instructions are wired into the CPU and can be performed directly by it, without the need for communication with any other device. Today's more advanced processors incorporate powerful types of instruction sets that enable such functionality as computation of multiple data units concurrently within a single instruction, increased security, and boosted multimedia performance.

All Intel and AMD processors in current use include various ways of boosting multimedia performance. The first processor to include this was the Pentium MMX, which included 57 new instructions (known as MMX) for working with multimedia. According to Intel, MMX doesn't stand for anything, but it has commonly become known as *MultiMedia eXtensions*. MMX was the first example of what is known as single instruction, multiple data (SIMD) capability.

Later Intel processors included enhanced versions of MMX known as SSE (MMX+70 additional instructions, introduced with the Pentium III), SSE2 (MMX+SSE+144 new instructions, introduced with the Pentium 4), SSE3

(MMX+SSE+SSE2+13 new instructions, introduced with the Pentium 4 Prescott), and, most recently, SSSE3 (MMX+SSE+SSE2+SSE3+32 new instructions, introduced with the Core 2 Duo).

AMD also provides multimedia-optimized instruction sets in its processors, starting with 3DNow! (introduced by the K6, which was roughly equivalent to the Pentium MMX). However, AMD's version differs in details from Intel's, offering 21 new instructions. The AMD Athlon introduced 3DNow! Enhanced (3DNow!+24 new instructions), and the Athlon XP introduced 3DNow! Professional (3DNow!+Enhanced+51). 3DNow! Professional is equivalent to Intel's SSE. Starting with the Athlon 64 family, AMD now supports SSE2, and added SSE3 support to the Athlon 64 X2 and newer versions of the Athlon 64 family.

Overclocking

Overclocking refers to the practice of running a processor or other components, such as memory or the video card's graphics processing unit (GPU) at speeds higher than normal. Overclocking methods used for processors include increasing the clock multiplier or running the front side bus (FSB) at faster speeds than normal. These changes are performed by altering the normal settings in the computer's Basic Input Output System (BIOS) setup for the processor's configuration. Figure 5-2 is a typical BIOS processor configuration screen. The BIOS is firmware that is loaded on a chip on the motherboard; it keeps track of the time and date, and verifies what hardware is on the system. You can access it by pressing a special key when the computer is first turned on. This key needs to be pressed before the operating system boots. We talk more about the BIOS in Chapter 7, "Computer Operation."

Most processors feature locked clock multipliers. That is, the clock multiplier frequency cannot be changed. In such cases, the only way to overclock the processor is to increase the front side bus speed, which is the speed at which the processor communicates with system memory. Increasing the FSB speed can lead to greater system instability than changing the clock multipliers.

Some processors from Intel and AMD feature unlocked clock multipliers so that the user can choose the best method for overclocking the system. Overclocked processors and other components run hotter than normal, so techniques such as using additional cooling fans, replacing standard active heat sinks with models that feature greater cooling, and adjusting processor voltages are often used to help maintain system stability at faster speeds.

Figure 5-2 Preparing to overclock a system running an AMD Athlon 64x2 processor.

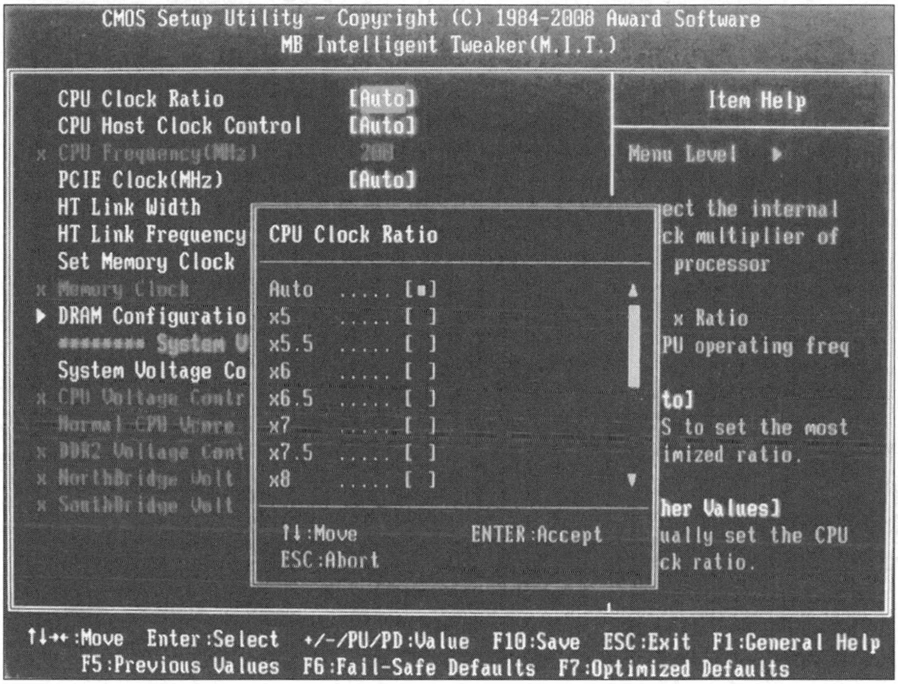

Cache

Cache memory improves system performance by enabling the processor to reuse recently retrieved memory locations without needing to fetch them from main memory. Processors from AMD and Intel feature at least two levels of cache:

- Level 1 (L1) cache is built into the processor core. L1 cache is relatively small (8KB–64KB). When the processor needs to access memory it checks the contents of L1 cache first.

- Level 2 (L2) cache is built onto the processor. On older slot-mounted processors, L2 cache was external to the processor die, and ran at slower speeds than the processor. On socketed processors, L2 cache is built onto the processor. If the processor does not find the desired memory locations in L1 cache, it checks L2 cache next.

- Level 3 (L3) cache is found on a few high-performance processors and is also built onto the processor. On systems with L3 cache, the processor checks L3 cache after checking L1 and L2 caches.

If cache memory does not contain the desired information, the processor retrieves the desired information from main memory, and stores copies of that information in

its cache memory (L1 and L2, or L1, L2, and L3). Processors with larger L2 caches (or L2 and L3 caches) perform most tasks much more quickly than processors that have smaller L2 caches for two reasons. Cache memory is faster than main memory, and the processor checks cache memory for needed information before checking main memory.

VRM

Starting with Socket 7 versions of the Intel Pentium, processors have not received their power directly from the power supply. Instead, a device called a voltage regulator module (VRM) has been used to reduce 5V or 12V DC power from the power supply to the appropriate power requested by the processor through its voltage identification (VID) logic.

Although some motherboards feature a removable VRM, most motherboards use a built-in VRM that is located next to the processor socket, as shown in Figure 5-3.

Figure 5-3   A portion of the VRM on an Athlon 64 motherboard.

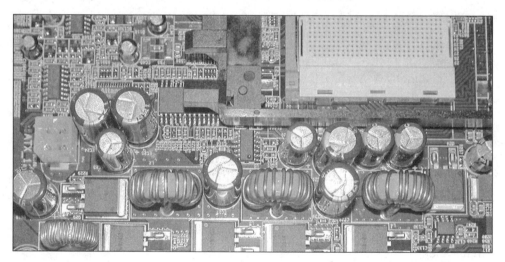

TIP   Be sure to determine the free space around a processor before ordering or installing a third-party active heat sink. Some motherboards have VRM components located so close to the processor that some heat sinks do not fit.

32-Bit Versus 64-Bit

Processors developed before the AMD Athlon 64 were designed for 32-bit operating systems and applications. 32-bit software cannot access more than 4GB of RAM (in fact, 32-bit Windows programs can use only 3.25GB of RAM), which makes

working with large data files difficult as only a portion of a file larger than the maximum memory size can be loaded into memory at one time.

The Athlon 64 was the first desktop processor to support 64-bit extensions to the 32-bit x86 architecture. These 64-bit extensions, commonly known as x64, enable processors to use more than 4GB of RAM and run 64-bit operating systems, but maintain full compatibility with 32-bit operating systems and applications.

Late-model Pentium 4 processors from Intel also support x64, as do subsequent processors such as the Pentium 4 Extreme Edition, Pentium D, Pentium Extreme Edition, Core 2 Duo, Core 2 Quad, Core 2 Extreme, Phenom x4, and Phenom x2. Most processors made today support x64 operation.

NOTE   To learn more about a particular processor's support for x64 operation, hardware virtualization, and other features, look up the processor specifications at the manufacturer's website.

Choosing the Best Processor for the Job

If you are buying or building a new system, you have free rein in the choice of a processor to build the system around. This section describes important considerations, including performance, thermal issues, compatibility, and other features.

Performance

If you need a system that can handle high-resolution graphics and video, and can perform heavy-duty number crunching, get the fastest dual-core or multi-core processor you can afford. However, if your requirements are less extreme, you can save money for your clients by opting for a processor from the same family with slower clock speed or less cache memory.

Thermal Issues

Many processor models are available in two or more versions that differ in their thermal requirements; that is, the type of active heat sink necessary to cool them and the amount of power (in watts) needed to operate them. In a mid-tower or full tower system, these considerations might be less important than in a micro-tower or small form factor system, or a system that might need to run as quietly as possible.

32-Bit Versus 64-Bit (x64) Compatibility

Unless you are trying to build the least-expensive system possible, you will find it difficult to find 32-bit only processors today. However, if you are repurposing

existing systems, you might need to determine which systems include processors with support for 64-bit operation, and which support only 32-bit operation.

Other Processor Features

Processor features such as NX (no execute, which provides hardware-based protection against some types of viruses and malware) and hardware-based virtualization (which enables a single processor to be split into multiple virtual machines with little or no slowdown) are also important to consider in business environments. Check the specification sheets provided by processor vendors to determine the exact features supported by a particular processor.

TIP   To help determine detailed information for current and late-model installed Intel processors (Pentium 4, Celerons based on the Pentium 4 and newer), use the Intel Processor Identification Utility available from the Intel website (www.intel.com).

For older Intel processors, use the Intel Processor Frequency ID Utility, also available from the Intel website.

To help determine detailed information for installed AMD processors, download and install CPUInfo from the AMD website (www.amd.com).

Installing and Upgrading Processors

Processors are one of the most expensive components found in any computer. Because a processor can fail, or more likely, might need to be replaced with a faster model, knowing how to install and remove processors is important. If you are building a new computer, you don't have to worry about the removal of the processor (and its additional parts), but chances are you will be upgrading a computer with a new processor. In this case, you should know how to properly remove the processor, heat sink, and fan. The methods used for CPU removal vary according to two factors: the processor type and the socket/slot type.

As you saw in Tables 5-1 and 5-2, most recent processors are socketed. Before the development of the ZIF socket, the processor was held in place by tension on the chip's legs, pins, or leads. Thus, to remove these chips, you must pull the chip out of the socket. Because the chip's legs, pins, or leads are fragile, special tools are strongly recommended for removing chips that are not mounted in ZIF sockets.

Before removing and installing any CPU or other internal component, be sure to review and follow the electrostatic discharge (ESD) precautions discussed in Chapter 10, "Troubleshooting."

Removing the Heat Sink

ZIF sockets are used on almost all desktop systems using Pentium III-class or newer socketed processors (except for processors using LGA 771 or 775). They enable easy installation and removal of the processor.

What makes ZIF sockets easy to work with? They have a lever that, when released, loosens a clamp that holds the processor in place.

If the processor has a removable heat sink, fan, or thermal duct that is attached to the motherboard, you must remove these components before you can remove the processor.

Heat sinks used on Socket 370 and Socket A processors have a spring-loaded clip on one side and a fixed lug on the other side. To release this clip, press down on it using a screwdriver, as shown in Figure 5-4.

Figure 5-4   Releasing the spring clip on a Socket A processor's heat sink.

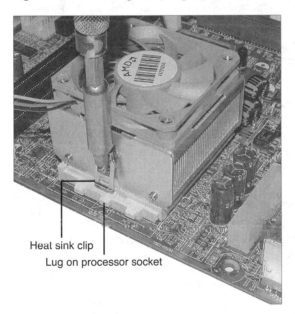

Heat sink clip
Lug on processor socket

Most newer processors use heat sinks that are attached to a frame around the processor or are mounted through the motherboard. To release these heat sinks, you might need to flip up a lever on one side of the heat sink or release the locking pins. Figure 5-5 illustrates a typical installation on an Athlon 64 processor, and Figure 5-6 illustrates the components of a typical heat sink for LGA 775 processors.

Figure 5-5   Typical heat sink assembly on Athlon 64 processor.

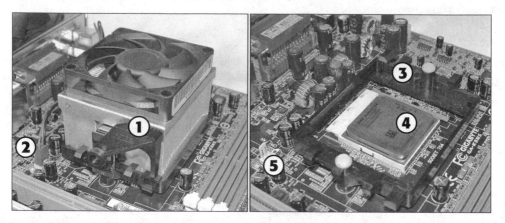

1. Locking lever
2. Power lead for heat sink fan
3. Heat sink frame
4. Processor
5. Motherboard power connector for heat sink fan

Figure 5-6   Stock heat sink assembly for Intel Core 2 Duo LGA 775 processor.

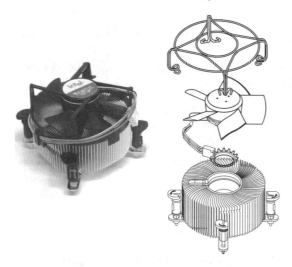

BTX systems use a horizontally mounted thermal module that is equipped with a fan. The thermal module also helps cool other components such as the motherboard chipset and memory. Figure 5-7 illustrates a typical thermal module installed on a motherboard. Note that the front of the thermal module extends below the edge of the motherboard to provide cooling for both top and bottom.

Figure 5-7   Thermal module placement on a typical BTX motherboard. Figure courtesy of Formfactors.org.

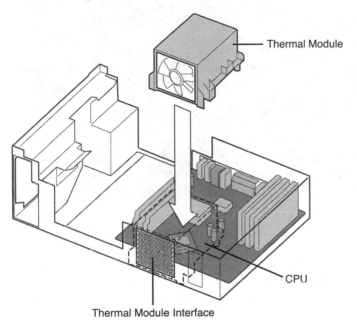

To remove a thermal module from a BTX motherboard, follow these steps:

Step 1.   Remove the screws that attach the module to the retention bracket on the underside of the motherboard.

Step 2.   Disconnect the thermal module's fan power lead.

Step 3.   Lift the thermal module off the processor.

Be careful when removing this component. Be careful not to drop the heat sink on the CPU or on the motherboard. The thermal module is bulky and heavy and can easily damage the expensive parts of your computer.

Removing the Processor

After removing the heat sink, follow these instructions to complete the processor removal process:

Step 1.   Disconnect the active heat sink (if included) from its power source and lift the assembly away.

Step 2.   Push the lever on the ZIF socket slightly to the outside of the socket to release it.

Step 3.   Lift the end of the lever until it is vertical (see Figure 5-8). This releases the clamping mechanism on the processor's pins.

Step 4.   Grasp the processor on opposite sides, making sure not to touch the pins, and remove it from the socket. Put it into antistatic packaging.

Figure 5-8   After the heat sink fan is disconnected from power (left) to reveal the processor (center), the lever on the ZIF socket (right) can be lifted to release the processor.

The process of removing an LGA 775 processor is a bit different:

Step 1.   Disconnect the active heat sink (if included) from its power source and lift the assembly away.

Step 2.   Lift the locking lever to release the load plate, which holds the processor in place.

Step 3.   Carefully lift the processor away and place into antistatic packaging.

Be quite careful when removing the processor and when unlocking any sockets. These components are delicate. Think of yourself as a watchmaker when dealing with these parts!

Installing a New Processor

Before installing a new processor, verify that the processor you plan to install is supported by the motherboard. Even though a particular combination of processor and motherboard might use the same socket, issues such as BIOS, voltage, or chipset considerations can prevent some processors from working on particular motherboards. You can destroy a processor or motherboard if you install a processor not suitable for a particular motherboard.

After verifying compatibility by checking the system or processor manual (and installing any BIOS updates required for processor compatibility), check a PGA-type processor for bent pins, and the socket of an LGA775 processor for bent leads. Correct these problems before continuing.

To insert a PGA-type CPU into a ZIF socket, find the corner of the chip that is marked as pin 1 (usually with a dot or triangle). The underside of some chips might be marked with a line pointing toward pin 1. Then follow these steps:

Step 1.   Line up the pin 1 corner with the corner of the socket also indicated as pin 1 (look for an arrow or other marking on the motherboard). If you put the chip in with pin 1 aligned with the wrong corner and apply the power, you destroy the chip.

Step 2.   Make sure the lever on the ZIF socket is vertical; insert the CPU into the socket and verify that the pins are fitting into the correct socket holes.

Step 3.   Lower the lever to the horizontal position and snap it into place to secure the CPU.

Step 4.   Before attaching the heat sink or fan, determine if the heat sink has a thermal pad (also called a phase-change pad) or if you need to apply thermal compound to the processor core (refer to Figure 5-8). Remove the protective tape from the thermal pad or apply thermal compound as needed. Attach the heat sink or fan. You must use some type of thermal compound between the processor and the bottom of the heat sink.

Step 5.   Attach the heat sink to the processor as directed by the processor vendor (for heat sinks supplied with the processor) or heat sink vendor (for aftermarket heat sinks). In some cases, you might need to attach mounting hardware to the motherboard before you can attach the heat sink.

Step 6.   If you are installing an active heat sink (a heat sink with a fan), plug the fan into the appropriate connector on the motherboard.

To insert an LGA775 processor, locate the notches on each side of the processor. These correspond with key tabs in the processor socket. Then follow these steps:

Step 1.   Make sure the load plate assembly is completely open. It has a plastic cover that you can remove at the end of Step 5.

Step 2.   Line up the notches in the processor with the key tabs in the processor socket. This ensures that the processor's Pin 1 is properly aligned with the socket.

Step 3.   Lower the processor into place, making sure the metal heat spreader plate faces up and the gold pads face down. Do not drop the processor, as the lands in the processor socket could be damaged.

Step 4.   Push down the load plate and close the load plate assembly cam lever.

Step 5.   Lock the lever in place on the side of the socket. Remove the plastic cover and save it for future use.

Step 6.   Before attaching the heat sink or fan, determine if the heat sink has a thermal pad (also called a phase-change pad) or if you need to apply thermal compound to the processor core (refer to Figure 5-8). Remove the protective tape from the thermal pad or apply thermal compound as needed. Attach the heat sink or fan. You must use some type of thermal compound between the processor and the bottom of the heat sink.

Step 7.   Attach the heat sink to the processor as directed by the processor vendor (for heat sinks supplied with the processor) or heat sink vendor (for aftermarket heat sinks). In some cases, you might need to attach mounting hardware to the motherboard before you can attach the heat sink.

Step 8.   If you are installing an active heat sink (a heat sink with a fan), plug the fan into the appropriate connector on the motherboard.

Check the processor installation by booting the computer, and by checking the speed of the processor in the BIOS and in Windows.

Slot-Type CPU (Early Pentium III, Early AMD Athlon, and Others)

You won't see many slot-type CPUs anymore, but if you need to install one on a motherboard, make sure the motherboard has a retention mechanism attached. If the motherboard doesn't have one, you need to remove the motherboard from the case to attach a retention mechanism if it is not already attached.

To remove a slot-type CPU, follow these steps:

Step 1.   Push down on the retainers at each end of the CPU to release the CPU from the retention mechanism.

Step 2.   Disconnect the power lead to the CPU fan (if present).

Step 3.   Remove the CPU and fan/heat sink from the retention mechanism. The CPU slides straight up from the slot.

To attach a slot-type CPU, follow these steps:

Step 1.   Attach the CPU retention mechanism to the motherboard. Leave the foam backing on the bottom of the motherboard while pushing the supports into place. Lift up the motherboard and secure the retention mechanism with the screws supplied.

Some motherboards are shipped with the retention mechanism already installed, so this step might not apply to you. If the retention mechanism is folded against the motherboard, unfold it so the supports stand straight up.

Step 2.   Attach the fan and heat sink to the CPU if it is not already attached; some CPUs have a factory-attached heat sink/fan, whereas others require you to add it in the field.

Step 3.   Match the pinouts on the bottom of the CPU to the motherboard's slot; note that the slot has two sides of unequal length, making it easy to match the slot with the CPU.

Step 4.   Insert the CPU into the retention mechanism; push down until the retaining clips lock the CPU into place. Figure 5-9 shows the CPU in place.

Step 5.   Connect the power lead from the fan (if present) to the motherboard or drive power connector as directed.

Figure 5-9   A Slot 1-based Celeron CPU after installation. The heat sink and fan are attached to the rear of the CPU.

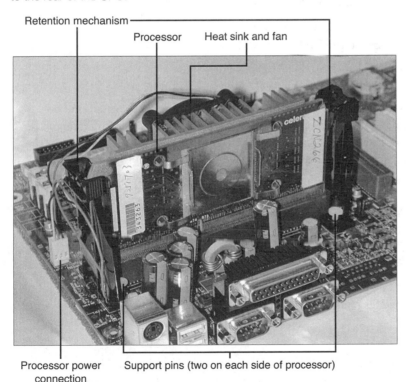

Troubleshooting Processors

Keeping the processor running reliably is vital to correct system operation. This section focuses on some common problems and solutions.

System Runs Slower Than Rated Speed

A system running slower than its rated speed might do so because of processor throttling due to overheating, or incorrect BIOS timing.

Causes for Overheating

Overheating issues directly related to the processor can include fan failure and incorrect heat sink for the processor type.

Fan Failure

Heat sink fans don't have to stop turning to fail; if they turn more slowly than they are specified to run, they can cause processor overheating.

Incorrect Heat Sink for Processor Type/Speed

If the processor overheats and the heat sink is properly attached and the fan is running, make sure the heat sink is designed for the processor type and speed in use. Heat sinks made for lower-speed processors might not provide adequate cooling for faster processors, which often run at higher temperatures.

Use the heat sink provided by the processor vendor, or, if you are using a separately purchased heat sink, make sure the heat sink is designed for the processor type and speed in use.

Overheating of the Processor or System

A system that overheats stops operating, and with some older processors, serious damage can result. Most processors today are fitted with active heat sinks that contain a fan. If the fan stops working, the processor overheats.

Fan failures can be caused by dirt in the fan, worn-out bearings, or a bad connection to the motherboard or drive-cable power. In most cases, it's better to replace the heat sink fan than to try to clean it. If you must clean it, follow these steps:

Step 1.   Remove the heat sink from the CPU.

Step 2.   Place it on a surface covered with old newspapers or waste paper.

Step 3.   Blow it out with compressed air.

Before reattaching the heat sink, clean the old thermal material from the processor and the heat sink and reapply a small amount of thermal material to the top center of the processor cap. For specific thermal material installation recommendations for a particular processor, check the processor manufacturer's website.

If you opt for a replacement fan, improve reliability and life by specifying a ball-bearing fan rather than the typical (and cheap) sleeve-bearing units. Overheating can also be caused by a dirty power supply or case fan, or by missing slot covers. Clean or replace the fans, and replace the slot covers. Don't overlook cleaning out the inside of the case, because a dirty case interior eventually clogs other components due to the system's airflow.

The hardware monitor feature in the system BIOS can warn of overheating or fan failure. This is most effective if the motherboard or system vendor's monitoring software is also installed so you can be warned of problems while Windows is running.

Underclocked System

Some systems revert to a "fail-safe" setting in which the CPU frequency and/or clock multiplier default to low-speed settings if the system fails to boot properly or is shut off before starting. Check the system speed reported on the System properties sheet in Windows XP or the CPU frequency/multiplier values in the BIOS. If these values are incorrect, set the CPU frequency and multiplier values according to the processor manufacturer's guidelines.

If the system is configured to automatically detect the correct values for CPU frequency and clock multiplier but does not report the correct speed, the system might need a BIOS upgrade to properly support the processor, or you might be using a re-marked processor (one that has had its original model number and technical information altered to make it appear as if it's a faster processor).

Processor Failure

If the processor is not locked into place, you cannot attach the heat sink. Never run the system if the processor is not properly installed, including heat sink installation.

Chapter Review Questions

The following questions test your recall of the concepts described in this chapter. The answers are listed at the end of the questions in the "Answers and Explanations" section.

1. Which one of the listed processors was the last slot-based processor designed by Intel?

    A. Celeron

    B. Core 2 Duo

    C. Pentium D

    D. Pentium III

2. Which of the following processors was the first dual-core design by AMD?

    A. Athlon 64 X2

    B. Athlon

    C. Duron

    D. Sempron

3. Which of the following best describes hyperthreading?

    A. Overclocking your CPU

    B. Processing two execution threads simultaneously

    C. Having more than one processor

    D. None of these options is correct

4. Before you remove the processor from the motherboard, what device should you remove first?

    A. Power supply

    B. RAM chip

    C. Heat sink

    D. Thermal compound

5. You have been dispatched to a client's computer. You have decided that the processor is overheating. Which of the following steps can you take to help with the air flow around the processor?

   A. Blow it out with compressed air.

   B. Remove the heat sink from the CPU.

   C. Place it on a surface covered with old newspapers or waste paper.

   D. Clean off the old thermal paste and reapply a small amount to the processor.

   E. All of these options are correct.

6. Which of the following are causes of overheating? (Choose all that apply.)

   A. Fan failure

   B. The power supply fan is too large

   C. Incorrect heat sink

   D. Incorrect processor

7. Which of the following is also known as the FSB?

   A. Base clock speed

   B. External clock speed

   C. Internal clock speed

   D. Motherboard clock speed

8. Which of the following is the executing of two or more threads within a single processor core?

   A. Dual core technology

   B. Hyperthreading

   C. Processor throttling

   D. MMX

9. Which of the following is best described as the practice of running a processor at higher speeds than normal?

   A. Hyperthreading

   B. Processor throttling

   C. Overclocking

   D. SpeedStep

10. Which of the following types of cache memory is built into the processor core?

   A. L1

   B. L2

   C. L3

   D. L4

11. Which of the following (known as extensions) allows a processor to access more than 4GB of RAM?

   A. 32-bit

   B. 64-bit

   C. x64

   D. Athlon 64

12. Which type of socket allows a processor to simply be dropped in without the need for any pressure?

   A. ZIF

   B. Slot 1

   C. Slot A

   D. LGA 771

13. What should you do if a processor's fan fails because it is clogged with dirt? (Select the two best answers.)

   A. Blow it out with compressed air

   B. Re-seat the processor

   C. Purchase a new processor

   D. Reapply thermal compound

14. Your computer system overheats. You find that the fan is clogged. What should you do?

   A. Replace the fan

   B. Use compressed air

   C. Replace the CPU

   D. Use a vacuum cleaner

15. If the base speed of the motherboard is 333MHz and your processor is using an internal multiplier of eight, what would be the internal speed of the processor?

A. 2.33GHz

B. 2.66GHz

C. 3.0GHz

D. 3.33GHz

Case Study 1

Processor technology is constantly changing. Research the following websites:

- www.intel.com

- www.amd.com

List the latest types of processors that both manufacturers offer and describe the characteristics of each. For example, what are the speeds of the new class of processors, do they have multiple cores, do they use hyperthreading, what kind of cache memory do they utilize, and so on.

Case Study 2

Analyze your processor. Using your home or lab computer, analyze the speed and other characteristics of the processor with the CPU-z program, which can be downloaded from www.cpuid.com/softwares/cpu-z.html.

Download and install the program. Then define the speed of the processor, number of cores, cache memory, and voltage.

Answers and Explanations

1. **D.** The Pentium III processor was the last Intel processor produced in both a slot-based and socket-based design. Slot-based versions use Slot 1, the same slot design used by the Pentium II and slot-based Celeron processors. Socketed versions use Socket 370, which is mechanically the same as the socket used by the first socketed Celeron processors. However, some early Socket 370 motherboards are not electrically compatible with the Pentium III.

2. **A.** AMD's first dual-core processor was the Athlon 64 X2, which uses a design that permits both processor cores to communicate directly with each other, rather than using the northbridge (Memory Controller Hub) as in the Intel Pentium D.

3. B. Hyperthreading is a technology developed by Intel for processing two execution threads simultaneously within a single processor. Essentially, when HT Technology is enabled in the system BIOS and the processor is running a multithreaded application, the processor is emulating two physical processors.

4. C. If the processor has a removable heat sink, fan, or thermal duct that is attached to the motherboard, you must remove these components before you can remove the processor.

5. E. A system that overheats stops operating, and with some older processors, serious damage can result. Most processors today are fitted with active heat sinks that contain a fan. If the fan stops working, an overheated processor follows.

6. A, C. Heat sink fans don't have to stop turning to fail; if they turn more slowly than they are specified to run, they can cause processor overheating. So keep them clean. If the heat sink is incorrect for the processor model or if the heat sink is not attached correctly, it can also cause overheating.

7. B. The external clock speed is also known as the front side bus (FSB) speed. The base clock speed and motherboard clock speed are one and the same and are also referred to as the system bus speed. The base clock speed is generated by a quartz crystal on the motherboard. The Internal clock speed is the internal speed of the CPU, the speed at which processors are normally rated.

8. B. Hyperthreading is when two or more threads are executed within a single core simultaneously.

9. C. Overclocking is the practice of running a processor at higher speeds than normal. SpeedStep is a type of processor throttling by Intel.

10. A. L1 cache is built into the processor core. L2 cache is built onto the processor but not directly within the core.

11. C. The x64 extensions are 64-bit extensions that allow a processor to access more than 4GB of RAM (the standard limitation of 32-bit processors).

12. A. ZIF (Zero insertion force) is a type of socket used to allow for the easy installation of processors. No force is necessary when installing the processor; it can be gently slid across the socket until it drops in.

13. A, D. If the fan is clogged with dirt, it should be removed and cleaned; compressed air is a great tool for this. After it is cleaned, the old thermal compound on the CPU should be removed, and new thermal compound should be applied.

14. B. Use compressed air to clean out a clogged fan. However, remember to remove the fan (and heat sink) from the CPU first. Then work over newspapers or outside. Vacuum cleaners are not recommended near computers due to the fact that they generate ESD. The fan should only be replaced if you find it has failed completely. The CPU is not the cause of the problem in this scenario and should not be replaced unless the computer overheating caused it to become defective.

15. B. The internal speed of the processor would be 2.66GHz. This is derived by multiplying the base speed by the multiplier, in this case, 333MHz × 8 = 2.66GHz.

Case Study 1 Solution

As of 2010, the current link to learn more about Intel's processors is

www.intel.com/products/processor/index.htm

The current link to learn more about AMD's processors is

www.amd.com/us/products/Pages/processors.aspx

As of October 2010, the latest Intel processor is the Core i7, which has a maximum of six cores, 12MB L2 cache, and a top speed of 3.33GHz. The latest AMD processor is the Phenom II X6, which has six cores, 3MB L2 cache, 6MB L3 cache, and can run at a maximum speed of 3.2GHz.

Case Study 2 Solution

The CPU-Z program can be downloaded from

www.cpuid.com/softwares/cpu-z.html

After it is downloaded and installed, it can be run in Windows by accessing the program from **Start > All Programs > CPUID > CPU-Z > CPU-Z.**

After the program has run, it should automatically analyze the processor(s). An example of this is shown in Figure 5-10. Note that the processor is a Intel Mobile Core 2 Duo T9300 CPU that runs at 2.5GHz (the mobile tells us that the computer analyzed is a laptop). Also note that there is 64KB of L1 cache, and 6MB of L2 cache. It also shows the various clock speeds as they correspond to the CPU.

Figure 5-10 Example of CPU-Z analyzing a processor.

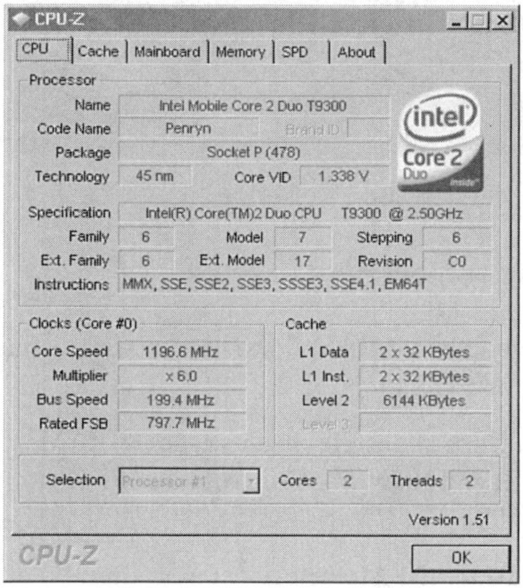

This chapter covers the following subjects:

- **RAM Basics**—This section talks about what RAM does, how it works, and how it relates to the rest of the computer system.

- **RAM Types**—In this section, you learn about the various types of RAM available, including SDRAM, DDR, and Rambus. Their architecture, capacity, and speed is also described.

- **Installing DIMMs and Rambus RDRAM Modules**—This section demonstrates how to install DIMMs properly.

- **Hard Disk Drives**—Hard drives are the most common and most important storage device. You learn about SATA, PATA (IDE), jumpering, installation, creating arrays of redundant disks, and optimizing performance.

- **CD and DVD Optical Drives**—This section describes the various types of CDs and DVDs, how to install optical drives, optical drive interfaces, how to record to CD and DVD, and any possible installation issues you might encounter.

Memory and Storage

When it's time for the CPU to process something, RAM (random access memory) is the workspace it uses. RAM is one of two types of memory found in your computer; the other type of memory is ROM (read-only memory). What's the difference? RAM's contents can be changed at any time, but ROM's contents require special procedures to change. Think of RAM as a blank sheet of paper and a pencil: You can write on it, erase what you've done, and keep making changes. On the other hand, ROM is like a newspaper. If you want to change what's printed on the newspaper, you must recycle it so it can be reprocessed into newsprint and sent through the newspaper's printing presses again. This chapter focuses on the types, installation, and troubleshooting of RAM. We cover more about ROM in Chapter 7, "Computer Operation."

After information has been processed and stored in RAM, you might decide that it needs to be stored for a longer period of time. That is where the hard disk drive comes in. These magnetic drives offer high capacities at low prices for long-term storage. This type of solution is known as fixed media. However, hard drives fail over time, so you might decide to store information to a longer-term storage media such as CD or DVD. These optical solutions are known as removable media.

As you can see, data can be stored in many ways, not all of which were mentioned thus far. Let's start with the memory that works in direct concert with the processor—the RAM.

RAM Basics

RAM is used for programs and data, and by the operating system for disk caching (using RAM to hold recently accessed disk sectors). Thus, installing more RAM improves transfers between the CPU and both RAM and disk drives. If your computer runs short of RAM, Windows can also use the hard disk as a slow substitute for RAM. The swapfile (Windows 9x/Me) or paging file (Windows NT/2000/XP/Vista) is a file on the hard disk used to hold part of the contents of memory if the installed RAM on the system isn't large enough for the tasks currently being performed.

Although the hard disk can substitute for RAM in a pinch, don't confuse RAM with magnetic storage devices such as hard disks. Although the contents of RAM and magnetic storage can be changed freely, RAM loses its contents as soon as you shut down the computer, but magnetic storage can hold data for years. Although RAM's contents are temporary, RAM is much faster than magnetic storage: RAM speed is measured in nanoseconds (billionths of a second), and magnetic storage is measured in milliseconds (thousandths of a second).

Even though every computer ever made is shipped with RAM, you will probably need to add more RAM to a computer as time passes. Ever-increasing amounts of RAM are needed as operating systems and applications get more powerful and add more features. Because RAM is one of the most popular upgrades to add to any system during its lifespan, you need to understand how RAM works, what types of RAM exist, and how to add it to provide the biggest performance boost to the systems you maintain.

When you must specify memory for a given system, there are several variables you need to know:

- **Memory module type (240-pin DIMM, 184-pin DIMM, 168-pin DIMM, and so on)**—The module type your system can use has a great deal to do with the memory upgrade options you have with any given system. Although a few systems can use more than one memory module type, in most cases if you want to change to a faster type of memory module, such as from 184-pin DIMM (used by DDR SDRAM) to 240-pin DIMM (DDR2 SDRAM), you need to upgrade the motherboard first.

- **Memory chip type used on the module (SDRAM, DDR SDRAM, RDRAM, and so on)**—Today, a particular memory module type uses only one type of memory. However, older memory module types such as 72-pin SIMM and early 168-pin DIMMs were available with different types of memory chips. You need to specify the right memory chip type in such cases to avoid conflicts with onboard memory and provide stable performance.

- **Memory module speed (60ns, PC-133, PC800, PC2700, and so on)**—There are three ways to specify the speed of a memory module: the actual speed in ns (nanoseconds) of the chips on the module (60ns), the clock speed of the data bus (PC-133 is 133MHz; PC800 is 800MHz), or the throughput (in MBps) of the memory (PC2700 is 2,700MBps or 2.7GBps). The throughput method is used by current memory types.

- **Error checking (parity, non-parity, ECC)**—Most systems don't perform parity checking (to verify the contents of memory) or correct errors, but some

motherboards and systems support these functions. Although parity-checked memory mainly slows down the system, ECC memory can detect memory errors as well as correct them. If a system is performing critical work (high-level mathematics or financial functions, departmental or enterprise-level server tasks), ECC support in the motherboard and ECC memory are worthwhile options to specify. Some systems also support registered or non-registered modules. Registered modules are more reliable, but are slower because they include a chip that boosts the memory signal.

- **Allowable module sizes and combinations**—Some motherboards insist you use the same speeds and sometimes the same sizes of memory in each memory socket, but others are more flexible. To find out which is true about a particular system, check the motherboard or system documentation before you install memory or add more memory.

- **The number of modules needed per bank of memory**—Systems address memory in banks, and the number of modules per bank varies with the processor and the memory module type installed. If you need more than one module per bank, as with SIMM memory on a Pentium-class system, and only one module is installed, the system ignores it. Systems that require multiple modules per bank require that modules be the same size and speed.

- **Whether the system requires or supports dual-channel memory (two identical memory modules instead of one at a time)**—Dual-channel memory treats two matched modules as a single unit, similar in some ways to the way that older systems use two or more modules per bank. However, dual-channel memory is faster than single-channel memory, and is becoming common on more and more systems.

- **The total number of modules that can be installed**—The number of sockets on the motherboard determines the number of modules that can be installed. Very small-footprint systems (such as those that use microATX, flexATX, or Mini-ITX motherboards) often support only one or two modules, but systems that use full-size ATX motherboards often support three or four modules.

When it comes to memory, compatibility is important. The memory module type must fit the motherboard; speed must be compatible, and the module storage size/combination must match your computer system as well. To find out exactly what type of memory modules are compatible with your motherboard, visit a memory manufacturer's website and check within their database. Be sure to have the model number of the motherboard, or the model of the computer handy.

RAM Types

Although today's systems use memory modules built from a combination of chips, rather than individual chips plugged into the motherboard as with early PC systems, it's still necessary to understand the different types of memory chips that have been and are used to build memory modules.

DRAM

Virtually all memory modules use some type of *dynamic* RAM, or DRAM chips. DRAM requires frequent recharges of memory to retain its contents. Early types of DRAM, including variations such as fast-page mode (FPM) and extended data-out (EDO), were speed rated by access time, measured in nanoseconds (ns; smaller is faster). Typical speeds for regular DRAM chips were 100ns or slower; FPM memory, used primarily in 30-pin and 72-pin SIMM modules, ran at speeds of 70ns, 80ns, and 100ns. EDO DRAM, which was used primarily in 72-pin SIMM modules and a few 168-pin DIMM modules, typically ran at 60ns.

Although these types of DRAM are long obsolete, other types of DRAM, including SDRAM, DDR SDRAM, DDR2 SDRAM, and Rambus, are used in more recent systems.

SRAM

Static random-access memory (SRAM) is RAM that does not need to be periodically refreshed. Memory refreshing is common to other types of RAM and is basically the act of reading information from a specific area of memory and immediately rewriting that information back to the same area without modifying it. Due to SRAM's architecture, it does not require this refresh. You will find SRAM being used as cache memory for CPUs, as buffers on the motherboard or within hard drives, and as temporary storage for LCD screens. Normally, SRAM is soldered directly to a printed circuit board (PCB) or integrated directly to a chip. This means that you probably won't be replacing SRAM. SRAM is faster than, and is usually found in smaller quantities than, its distant cousin DRAM.

SDRAM

Synchronous DRAM (SDRAM) was the first type of memory to run in sync with the processor bus (the connection between the processor, or CPU, and other components on the motherboard). Most 168-pin DIMM modules use SDRAM memory. To determine if a DIMM module contains SDRAM memory, check its speed markings. SDRAM memory is rated by bus speed (PC66 equals 66MHz bus speed; PC100 equals 100MHz bus speed; PC133 equals 133MHz bus speed).

Depending upon the specific module and motherboard chipset combination, PC133 modules can sometimes be used on systems that are designed for PC100 modules.

DDR SDRAM

Many recent systems use double-data-rate SDRAM (DDR SDRAM). DDR SDRAM performs two transfers per clock cycle, instead of one as with regular SDRAM. 184-pin DIMM memory modules use DDR SDRAM chips.

Although DDR SDRAM is sometimes rated in MHz, it is more often rated by throughput (MBps). Common speeds for DDR SDRAM include PC1600 (200MHz/1600MBps), PC2100 (266MHz/2100MBps), PC2700 (333MHz/2700MBps), and PC3200 (400MHz/3200MBps), but other speeds are available from some vendors.

DDR2 SDRAM

Double-double data rate SDRAM (DDR2 SDRAM) is the successor to DDR SDRAM. DDR2 SDRAM runs its external data bus at twice the speed of DDR SDRAM, enabling faster performance. However, DDR2 SDRAM memory has greater latency than DDR SDRAM memory. Latency is a measure of how long it takes to receive information from memory. 240-pin memory modules use DDR2 SDRAM.

DDR2 SDRAM memory might be referred to by the effective memory speed of the memory chips on the module (the memory clock speed ×4 or the I/O bus clock speed ×2); for example, DDR2-533 (133MHz memory clock×4 or 266MHz I/O bus clock ×2)=533MHz) or by module throughput (DDR2-533 is used in PC2-4200 modules, which have a throughput of more than 4200MBps). PC2- indicates the module uses DDR2 memory, and PC- indicates the module uses DDR memory.

Other common speeds for DDR2 SDRAM modules include PC2-3200 (DDR2-400; 3200MBps throughput), PC2-5200 (DDR2-667), PC2-6400 (DDR2-800), and PC2-8500 (DDR2-1066).

Rambus

Rambus Direct RAM (RDRAM) memory was used by early Pentium 4-based chipsets from Intel, including the i820, i840, and E7205 Granite Bay workstation chipset, but has not been used by more recent systems. RDRAM modules are known as RIMMs and were produced in 16-bit and 32-bit versions.

16-bit RIMMs use a 184-pin connector, and 32-bit RIMMs use a 232-pin connector. 32-bit motherboards that use RIMMs must use pairs of 16-bit modules. Empty

RIMM sockets must be occupied by a continuity module (resembles a RIMM but without memory; also known as a CRIMM).

Common Rambus 16-bit module speeds include PC600 (1200MBps bandwidth); PC700 (1420MBps bandwidth); PC800 (1600MBps bandwidth); PC1066 (also known as RIMM 2100; 2133MBps bandwidth); and PC1200 (also called RIMM 2400; 2400MBps bandwidth).

32-bit (dual-channel) RIMM modules use the RIMM xxxx identifier, listing the throughput inMBps as part of the name; for example, RIMM 3200 (3200MBps bandwidth); RIMM 4200 (4200MBps bandwidth); RIMM 4800 (4800MBps bandwidth); and RIMM 6400 (6400MBps bandwidth).

Table 6-1 shows a comparison of the types of RAM you should know.

Table 6-1 RAM Comparisons

RAM Type	Pins	Common Type and Speed	Defining Characteristic
DRAM	30 and 72	33 or 66MHz	Obsolete.
SDRAM	168	PC133 = 133MHz	This original version of SDRAM is rarely used on new computers, and has given way to DDR.
DDR SDRAM	184	PC3200 = 400MHz/ 3200MBps	Double the transfers per clock cycle compared to regular SDRAM.
DDR2 SDRAM	240	DDR2-800 (PC2-6400) = 800MHz/6400MBps	External data bus speed (I/O bus clock) is 2x DDR SDRAM.
Rambus (RDRAM)	184 and 232	PC800 = 1600MBps	Not used in new computers, but you still might see existing systems using Rambus memory modules.

Comparison of Memory Modules

All systems built since the early 1990s have used some form of memory module, and most of these systems have used standard versions of these modules. These modules come in these major types:

■ **Single Inline Memory Module (SIMM)**—Has a single row of 30 or 72 edge connectors on the bottom of the module. Single refers to both sides of the module having the same pinout.

- **Single Inline Pin Package (SIPP)**—A short-lived variation on the 30-pin SIMM, which substituted pins for the edge connector used by SIMM modules.

- **Dual Inline Memory Module (DIMM)**—These are available in 168-pin, 184-pin, and 240-pin versions. Dual refers to each side of the module having a different pinout.

- **Small Outline DIMM (SODIMM)**—A compact version of the standard DIMM module, available in various pinouts for use in notebook computers and laser/LED printers.

- **Rambus RDRAM Module**—A memory module using Direct Rambus memory (RDRAM) chips. Kingston Technology has copyrighted the name RIMM for its Rambus RDRAM modules, but Rambus RDRAM modules are often referred to as RIMMs, regardless of their actual manufacturer.

- **Small Outline Rambus Module**—A compact version of the standard Rambus module for use in notebook computers.

Figure 6-1 illustrates SIMM, SIPP, and DIMM modules used in desktop computers.

Figure 6-1 Desktop memory modules (SIMM, SIPP, and DIMM) compared.

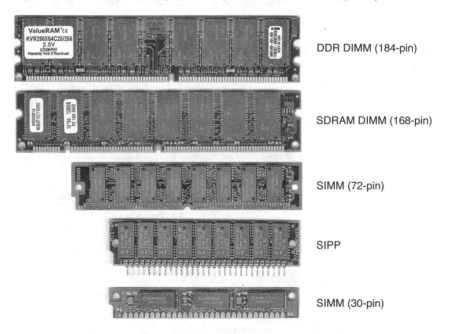

Installing DIMMs and Rambus RDRAM Modules

Memory modules are the memory "sticks" that are installed into the slots of a motherboard. Installing memory modules is fairly easy, and can be a fun initial task for people who have never worked on a computer before. However, precautions must be taken not to damage the memory module or the motherboard. Before working with any memory modules, turn the computer off, and unplug it from the AC outlet. Be sure to employ electrostatic discharge (ESD) protection in the form of an antistatic strap and antistatic mat. Use an antistatic bag to hold the memory modules while you are not working with them. Before actually handling any components, touch an unpainted portion of the case chassis in a further effort to ground yourself. Try not to touch any of the chips, connectors, or circuitry of the memory module; instead, hold them from the sides.

DIMM and Rambus RDRAM module sockets have an improved keying mechanism and a better locking mechanism compared to SIMMs.

To install the DIMM or Rambus RDRAM module, follow these steps:

Step 1. Line up the modules' connectors with the socket. Both DIMMs and Rambus modules have connections with different widths, preventing the module from being inserted backward.

Step 2. Verify that the locking tabs on the socket are swiveled to the outside (open) position.

Step 3. After verifying that the module is lined up correctly with the socket, push the module straight down into the socket until the swivel locks on each end of the socket snap into place at the top corners of the module (see Figure 6-2). A fair amount of force is required to engage the locks. Do not touch the gold-plated connectors on the bottom of the module; this can cause corrosion or ESD.

For clarity, the memory module installation pictured in Figure 6-2 was photographed with the motherboard out of the case. However, the tangle of cables around and over the DIMM sockets in Figure 6-3 provides a much more realistic view of the challenges you face when you install memory in a working system.

When you install memory on a motherboard inside a working system, use the following tips to help your upgrade go smoothly and the module to work properly:

■ If the system is a tower system, consider placing the system on its side to make the upgrade easier. Doing this also helps to prevent tipping the system over by accident when you push on the memory to lock it into the socket.

Figure 6-2   A DIMM partly inserted (top) and fully inserted (bottom). The memory module must be pressed firmly into place before the locking tabs will engage.

Locking clips not engaged

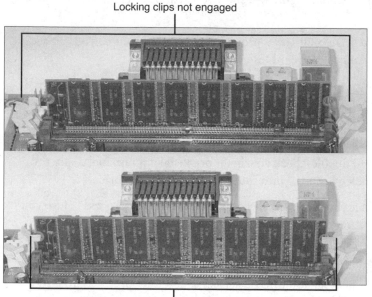

Locking clips engaged; module locked in place

Figure 6-3   DDR DIMM sockets in a typical system are often surrounded and covered up by drive and power cables, making it difficult to properly install additional memory.

Installed DIMM modules

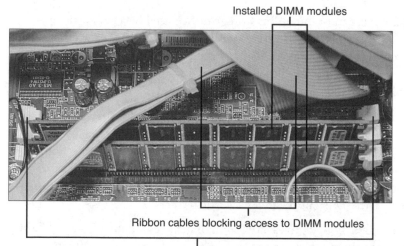

Ribbon cables blocking access to DIMM modules

Locking mechanism on empty DIMM socket in closed position; must be opened before another module can be installed

- Move the locking mechanisms on the DIMM sockets to the open position before you try to insert the module. In Figure 6-3, the locks on the empty socket are in the closed position. Figure 6-2 shows open and closed locks for comparison.

- Move power and drive cables away from the memory sockets so you can access the sockets. Disconnect drive cables if necessary.

- Use a flashlight to shine light into the interior of the system so you can see the memory sockets and locking mechanisms clearly; this enables you to determine the proper orientation of the module and to make sure the sockets' locking mechanisms are open.

- Use a flashlight to double-check your memory installation to make sure the module is completely inserted into the slot and locked into place.

- Replace any cables you moved or disconnected during the process before you close the case and restart the system.

TIP   Note the positions of any cables you need to remove before you remove them to perform an internal upgrade. You can use self-stick colored dots on a drive and its matching data and power cables. You can purchase sheets of colored dots at most office-supply and discount stores.

Hard Disk Drives

Hard disk drives are the most important storage device used by a personal computer. Hard disk drives store the operating system (Windows, Linux, or others) and load it into the computer's memory (RAM) at startup. Hard disk drives also store applications, system configuration files used by applications and the operating system, and data files created by the user.

Hard disk drives use one or more double-sided platters formed from rigid materials such as aluminum or glass. These platters are coated with a durable magnetic surface that is divided into sectors. Each sector contains 512 bytes of storage along with information about where the sector is located on the disk medium. Sectors are organized in concentric circles from the edge of the media inward toward the middle of the platter. These concentric circles are called *tracks*.

Hard disk drives, unlike floppy drives, are found in many computers. Internal hard disk drives for desktop computers use the same 3.5-inch form factor as floppy drives, but are installed into internal drive bays. Their capacities range up to 1TB, but most desktop drives in recent systems have capacities ranging from 160GB to 500GB.

The most common types of hard disk interfaces in current PCs are Serial ATA (SATA) and Parallel ATA (PATA). PATA is also known as ATA/IDE. Both SATA and PATA interfaces can also be used by optical drives (CD and DVD), removable-media drives such as Zip and REV, and tape backup drives.

Figure 6-4 compares typical SATA and PATA hard disks to each other.

Figure 6-4   The power and data cable connectors on SATA and PATA (ATA/IDE) hard disks.

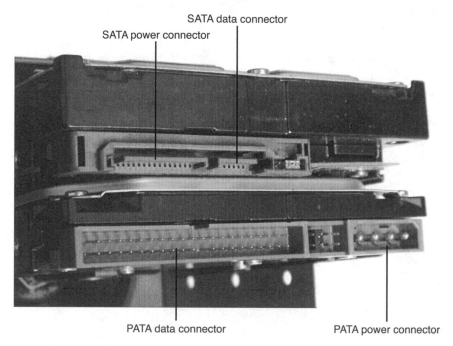

In the following sections, you learn about the data and power cables used by SATA and PATA drives, how PATA drives are configured by jumper blocks, the various ATA specifications, how PATA and SATA drives are installed, how to configure PATA and SATA drives in the system BIOS, and how to improve PATA drive performance.

PATA and SATA Data and Power Cables

PATA drives use a 40-pin data cable, and SATA drives use an L-shaped seven-wire data cable. PATA drives use a five-pin Molex power cable, and SATA drives use an L-shaped power cable. Figure 6-5 compares PATA and SATA power and data cables.

Figure 6-5   The power and data cables used by SATA and PATA (ATA/IDE) hard disks.

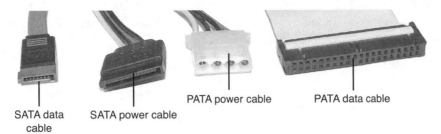

PATA power cable

PATA data cable

SATA data
cable

SATA power cable

One or two PATA hard disks or other types of ATA/IDE drives can be connected to a single data cable. Current hard disk designs use an 80-wire cable, and CD/DVD and removable-media drives can use either the 80-wire cable or the older 40-wire design. Figure 6-6 compares these cables to each other.

Figure 6-6   40-wire and 80-wire PATA data cables. 80-wire cables are required by modern PATA hard disks and recommended for other types of PATA devices.

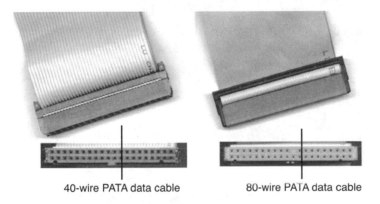

40-wire PATA data cable

80-wire PATA data cable

PATA Drive Jumpering and Cable Select

PATA drives are identified as primary/secondary or master/slave. To make this determination, jumper blocks on the drive (usually on the rear, but occasionally on the bottom) are used. Figure 6-7 shows PATA drives configured for cable select. Some drives, such as the one on the left, require the user to consult a chart on the drive's top plate or in the system documentation for correct settings, whereas others silk-screen the jumper settings on the drive's circuit board.

With an 80-wire cable, jumper blocks on both drives are set to Cable Select (CS), and the drive's position on the cable determines primary/secondary:

■   The blue connector on the cable plugs into the PATA host adapter on the motherboard or add-on card.

Figure 6-7   Two typical PATA (ATA/IDE) drives configured for cable select.

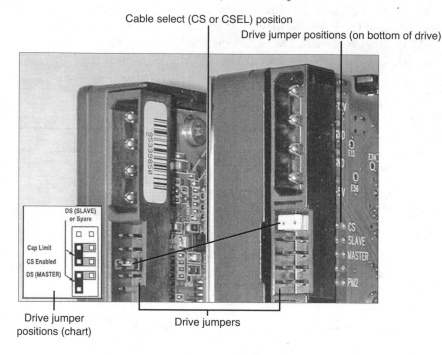

The gray connector in the middle of the cable is used for the secondary (slave) drive.

- The gray connector in the middle of the cable is used for the secondary (slave) drive.

- The black connector on the far end of the cable is used for the primary (master) drive.

The older 40-wire cable uses only jumper blocks to determine drive configuration. When a single drive is installed on a cable, the drive is configured as master or single. When two drives are installed on a cable, one is configured as master (primary) and the other as slave (secondary).

Only one SATA drive can be connected to an SATA host adapter port, so jumper blocks are unnecessary.

ATA Specifications

A series of standards for ATA/IDE and SATA drives are referred to as the *ATA specifications* (AT Attachment). Table 6-2 provides an overview of the differences in the various ATA specifications. Note a couple new terms in this table including PIO and UDMA. PIO stands for programmed input/output. The higher the PIO mode number, the higher the data transfer rate from the hard drive and the CPU. UDMA stands for Ultra DMA (Direct Memory Access). This is a protocol for transmitting

data between the hard drive and RAM directly, bypassing the CPU; it is sometimes referred to simply as "DMA." UDMA modes correspond to ATA levels; for example, the specification ATA-4 uses the mode UDMA 33, which means that it can transfer 33MB of data per second. The higher the UDMA mode, the higher the data transfer rate. The oldest version of UDMA (UDMA 33) is faster than the fastest PIO mode.

Table 6-2   ATA Specifications and Features

ATA Specification	Major Features
ATA-1 (original)	Standardized master/slave jumpers
	IDE Identify command for automatic configuration and detection of parameters
	PIO modes 0-2
	CHS (standard cylinder head sector) and LBA (logical block addressing, sector-translated) parameters
ATA-2	PIO modes 3–4
	Power management
	CHS/LBA translation for drives up to 8.4GB
	Primary and secondary IDE channels
	IDE block mode
ATA-3	S.M.A.R.T. self-diagnostics feature for use with monitoring software
	Password protection
	Improved reliability of PIO mode 4
ATA-4	UDMA 33 (33MBps)
	ATAPI support
	80-wire/40-pin cable
	BIOS support for LBA increased to 136.9GB
ATA-5	UDMA 66 (66MBps)
	Required use of 80-wire/40-pin cable with UDMA 66
ATA-6	UDMA 100 (100MBps)
	Increased capacity of LBA to 144 petabytes (PB; 1PB = 1 quadrillion bytes)

ATA Specification	Major Features
ATA-7	UDMA 133 (133MBps)
	Serial ATA (SATA)
ATA-8	SATA-II (300MBps)

ATA/IDE Drive Physical Installation

The following steps apply to typical ATA/IDE drive installations of hard disks, optical (CD/DVD) drives, removable-media drives, or tape drives:

Step 1.   Open the system and check for an unused 3.5" drive bay or an unused 5.25" drive bay. The 3.5" drive bay is used for hard disks and some tape and removable-media drives. The 5.25" drive bay is used for optical drives and can be used for other types of drives as well.

Step 2.   For 3.5" drives: If a 3.5"drive bay is not available but a 5.25" drive bay is, attach the appropriate adapter kit and rails as needed, as shown in Figure 6-8.

Figure 6-8   A typical adapter kit for a 3.5" drive. Screw a attaches the frame at hole #1; screw b attaches the frame at hole #2, with corresponding attachments on the opposite side of the drive and frame. Drive rails used by some cases can be attached to the adapter kit.

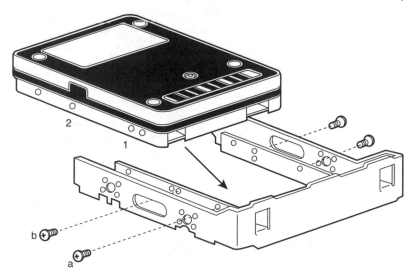

For 5.25"drives: If the 5.25" drive bays on the system use rails to hold drives in position, attach the appropriate rails.

Step 3.   Jumper the drive according to the cable type used: 40-wire cables use master and slave; 80-wire cables use cable select or master and slave. Use only 80-wire cables for hard disks. Other types of drives can use 40-wire or 80-wire cables, but 80-wire cables are preferred.

Step 4.   Attach the appropriate connector to the drive, making sure to match the colored marking on the edge of the cable to the end of the drive connector with pin 1. Pin 1 might be marked with a square solder hole on the bottom of the drive or silk-screening. If no markings are visible, pin 1 is usually nearest the drive's power connector. Disconnect the cable from the host adapter or other ATA/IDE drive if necessary to create sufficient slack.

Step 5.   Slide the drive into the appropriate bay and attach as needed with screws or by snapping the ends of the rails into place.

Step 6.   Attach the power connector; most PATA hard drives use the larger four-wire (Molex) power connector originally used on 5.25" floppy disk drives. Use a Y-splitter to create two power connectors from one if necessary.

Step 7.   Reattach the data cable to the other ATA or ATAPI drive and host adapter if necessary.

Step 8.   Change the jumper on the other ATA or ATAPI drive on the same cable if necessary. With 80-wire cables, both drives can be jumpered as Cable Select, with the drive at the far end of the cable being treated as master, and the middle drive as slave. With 40-wire cables, only Master and Slave jumper positions are used with most brands. See the drive markings or documentation for details.

NOTE Move the jumper simply by grasping it with a pair of tweezers or small needle-nose pliers and gently pulling straight backward. It's always best to change jumper settings before inserting the drive into the PC because they can be especially difficult to reach after the drive is installed.

Step 9.   Verify correct data and power connections to all installed drives and host adapters.

Step 10.   Turn on the system and start the BIOS configuration program.

Figure 6-9 shows a typical ATA/IDE drive before and after power and data cables are attached.

Figure 6-9   Attaching power and data cables to a typical ATA/IDE drive.

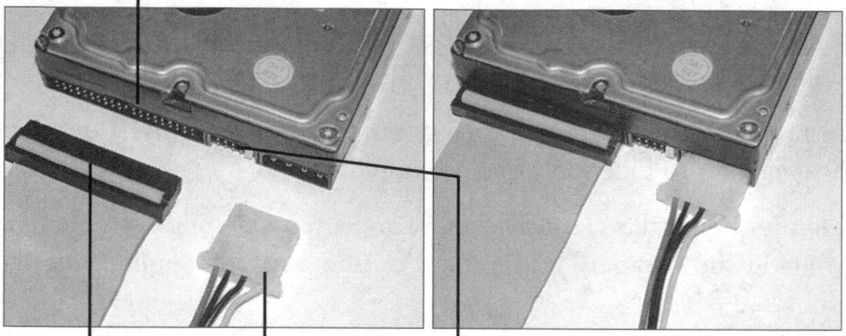

ATA/IDE data connector on drive

ATA/IDE data cable (80-wire)   Drive jumper (set to Cable Select)

Molex power cable

SATA Hard Drive Physical Installation

The process of installing an SATA drive differs from that used for installing an ATA/IDE drive because there are no master or slave jumpers and the SATA data cable goes directly from host adapter to drive. The following instructions assume the system has an onboard or add-on card SATA host adapter already installed. If you need to install an SATA host adapter, see the next section for details.

Step 1.   Open the system and check for an existing 3.5" drive bay; use an internal bay if possible.

Step 2.   If a 3.5" drive bay is not available but a 5.25" drive bay is, attach the appropriate adapter kit and rails as needed, as shown previously in Figure 6-8.

Step 3.   Attach the SATA cable to the drive; it is keyed so it can only be connected in one direction.

Step 4.   Slide the drive into the appropriate bay and attach as needed with screws or by snapping the ends of the rails into place.

Step 5.   Attach the power connector; use the adapter provided with the drive to convert a standard Molex connector to the edge connector type used by SATA. If the drive didn't include a power connector, purchase one.

Step 6.   Attach the data cable to the host adapter.

Step 7.   Verify correct data and power connections to IDE drives and host adapters.

Step 8.   Turn on the system and start the BIOS configuration program if the SATA host adapter is built into the motherboard. Enable the SATA host adapter, save changes, and restart your system.

Step 9.   If the SATA drive is connected to an add-on card, watch for messages at startup indicating the host adapter BIOS has located the drive.

Step 10.   Install drivers for your operating system to enable the SATA drive and host adapter to function when prompted.

Figure 6-10 shows a typical SATA drive before and after attaching power and data cables. Figure 6-11 shows typical PATA and SATA host adapter connections on a recent motherboard.

Figure 6-10   Attaching power and data cables to a typical SATA drive.

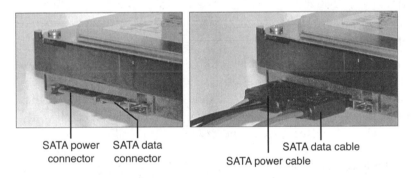

SATA power   SATA data   SATA data cable
connector   connector   SATA power cable

Figure 6-11   PATA and SATA host adapters on a recent motherboard.

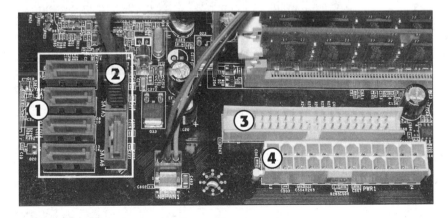

1. SATA host adapters
2. SATA data cable
3. PATA host adapter
4. ATX 24-pin power connector (for size comparison)

Installing an SATA Host Adapter

Some older systems don't include an SATA host adapter on the motherboard. Thus, to add an SATA drive to these systems, you also need to install an SATA host adapter card such as the one pictured in Figure 6-12.

Figure 6-12 A typical SATA host adapter card that supports two SATA drives. The inset shows how this host adapter appears in the Windows XP Device Manager after installation.

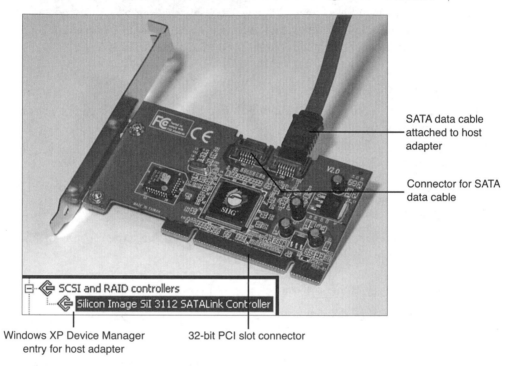

SATA data cable attached to host adapter

Connector for SATA data cable

Windows XP Device Manager entry for host adapter

32-bit PCI slot connector

Follow this procedure:

Step 1. Shut down the system and disconnect the power cable from the outlet to cut all power to the system.

Step 2. Use ESD protection equipment, such as a wrist strap and work mat, if available.

Step 3. Open the computer and locate an unused PCI slot.

Step 4. After removing the slot cover, insert the SATA card into the slot.

Step 5. Secure the card into place with the screw removed from the slot cover.

Step 6. Connect the card to the SATA drive with an SATA data cable. The cable might be provided with the card or with the drive.

Step 7. Connect an SATA power cable to the hard drive. This power cable usually comes from the power supply.

Step 8. Reconnect the power cord and restart the computer.

Step 9. Install drivers when prompted.

Step 10. Restart your computer if prompted.

Step 11. Open Windows Device Manager to verify that the SATA host adapter is working. It should be listed under the category SCSI Controllers, SCSI Adapters, or SCSI and RAID Controllers (refer to Figure 6-12).

Configuring PATA BIOS

For PATA drives controlled by the motherboard BIOS, the following information must be provided to the BIOS:

- Hard drive geometry
- Data transfer rate
- Logical Block Addressing (LBA) translation

Hard drive geometry refers to several factors used to calculate the capacity of a hard drive. These factors include the following:

- The number of sectors per track
- The number of read/write heads
- The number of cylinders

The surface of any disk-based magnetic media is divided into concentric circles called tracks. Each track contains multiple sectors. A sector contains 512 bytes of data and is the smallest data storage area used by disk drives.

NOTE Although floppy disks also have tracks and sectors, modern operating systems do not require you to specify the track layout of the disk when formatting the media.

Each side of a hard disk platter used for data storage has a read-write head that moves across the media. There are many tracks on each hard disk platter, and all the tracks on all the platters are added together to obtain the cylinder count.

Figure 6-13 helps you visualize sectors, tracks, and cylinders.

Before the drive can be prepared by the operating system, it must be properly identified by the system BIOS.

Figure 6-13 Tracks, sectors, and cylinders compared.

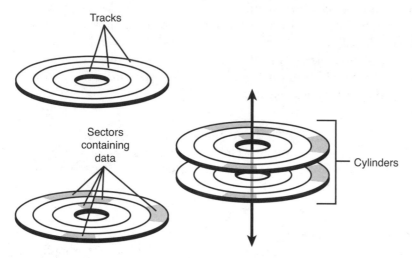

Most system BIOS programs are designed to perform auto-detection, reading the appropriate configuration from the drive itself. When installing a drive, make sure the system detects the hard disk (see Figure 6-14). After the drive is detected, the changes to the CMOS setup should be saved, the system rebooted, and the drive prepared for use.

Figure 6-14 Configuring a 160GB Maxtor PATA drive with the auto-detection feature in a typical system BIOS.

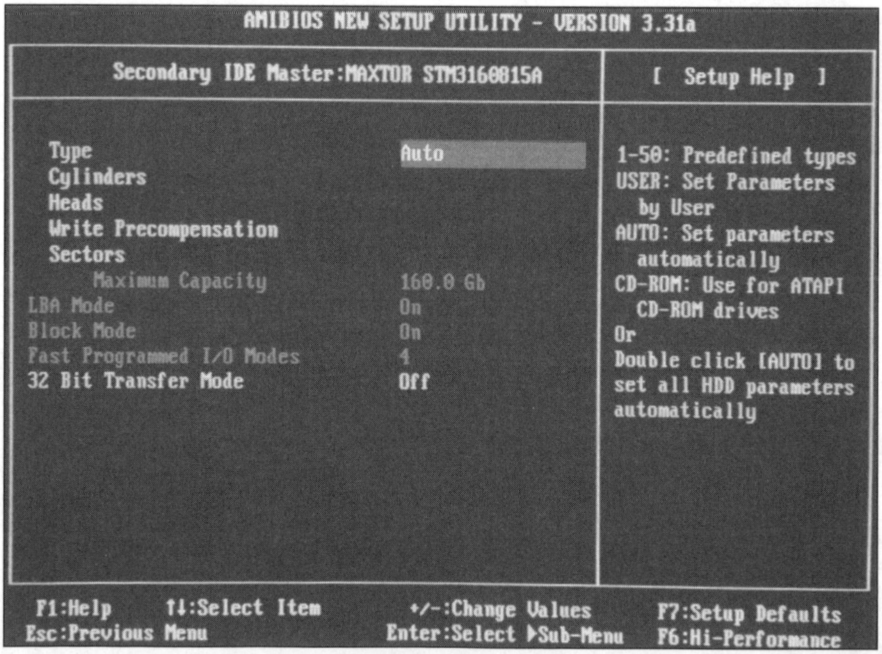

```
                AMIBIOS NEW SETUP UTILITY - VERSION 3.31a

    Secondary IDE Master:MAXTOR STM3160815A          [ Setup Help ]

    Type                          Auto           1-50: Predefined types
    Cylinders                                    USER: Set Parameters
    Heads                                           by User
    Write Precompensation                        AUTO: Set parameters
    Sectors                                         automatically
       Maximum Capacity           160.0 Gb       CD-ROM: Use for ATAPI
    LBA Mode                      On                CD-ROM drives
    Block Mode                    On             Or
    Fast Programmed I/O Modes     4              Double click [AUTO] to
    32 Bit Transfer Mode          Off            set all HDD parameters
                                                 automatically




    F1:Help      ↑↓:Select Item      +/-:Change Values    F7:Setup Defaults
    Esc:Previous Menu                Enter:Select ▶Sub-Menu  F6:Hi-Performance
```

Auto-detection is the best way to install a new PATA drive because other settings such as LBA translation, block mode (multisector transfers), and UDMA transfer rates also are configured properly. LBA is a scheme for specifying the location of data blocks on hard drives. LBA replaces earlier schemes such as cylinder-head-sector (CHS). LBA translation takes care of the conversion between older schemes such as CHS and the newer LBA scheme. This enables various hard drives to be compatible with varying BIOS programs.

NOTE   If LBA translation is turned off in the system BIOS, only 8.4GB of the hard disk's capacity is recognized by the system BIOS. If disk writes take place while a drive prepared with LBA translation is being accessed without LBA translation, data could be corrupted or overwritten.

Some BIOS programs perform the automatic detection of the drive type every time you start the system by default. Although this enables you to skip configuring the hard drive setting, it also takes longer to start the system and prevents the use of nonstandard configurations for compatibility reasons.

Depending on the system, removable-media ATAPI (ARMD) drives such as Zip and LS-120 should be configured as Not Present or Auto in the system BIOS setup or as ARMD drives depending upon the BIOS options listed. These drives do not have geometry values to enter in the system. The CD-ROM setting should be used for ATAPI CD-ROM and similar optical drives, such as CD-R, CD-RW, and DVD. Using the correct BIOS configuration for ATAPI drives enables them to be used to boot the system on drives and systems that support booting from ATAPI devices.

Configuring SATA BIOS

Before you can install an SATA hard disk to an SATA host adapter on the motherboard, you must make sure the host adapter is enabled in the system BIOS (see Figure 6-15).

After the SATA host adapter is enabled, save changes to the BIOS and shut down the system. After connecting the SATA drive to one of the onboard SATA host adapters, restart the system and reenter the BIOS setup program. Verify that the system has detected the SATA drive (see Figure 6-16). Save changes to the BIOS, restart, and prepare the hard disk for use.

Figure 6-15 Enabling an onboard SATA host adapter.

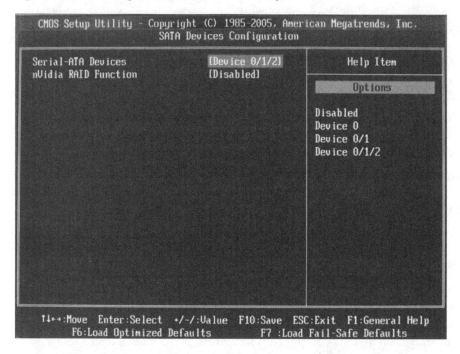

Figure 6-16 Auto-detecting an SATA hard disk.

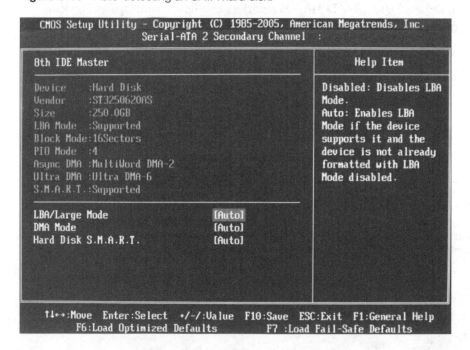

Creating an ATA or SATA RAID Array

RAID (redundant array of inexpensive drives) is a method for creating a faster or safer single logical hard disk drive from two or more physical drives. RAID arrays have been common for years on servers using SCSI-interface drives. However, a number of recent systems feature ATA RAID or SATA RAID host adapters on the motherboard. ATA and SATA RAID host adapter cards can also be retrofitted to systems lacking onboard RAID support. These types of RAID arrays are also referred to as hardware RAID arrays. RAID arrays can also be created through operating system settings, and are sometimes called software RAID arrays. However, software RAID arrays are not as fast as hardware RAID arrays.

ATA and SATA RAID types include the following:

- **RAID Level 0 (RAID 0)**—Two drives are treated as a single drive, with both drives used to simultaneously store different portions of the same file. This method of data storage is called striping. Striping boosts performance, but if either drive fails, all data is lost. Don't use striping for data drives.

- **RAID Level 1 (RAID 1)**—Two drives are treated as mirrors of each other; changes to the contents of one drive are immediately reflected on the other drive. This method of data storage is called mirroring. Mirroring provides a built-in backup method and provides faster read performance than a single drive. Suitable for use with program and data drives.

- **RAID Level 0+1 (RAID 10)**—Four drives combine striping plus mirroring for extra speed plus better reliability. Suitable for use with program and data drives.

- **RAID Level 5 (RAID 5)**—Three or more drives are treated as a logical array, and parity information (used to recover data in the event of a drive failure) is spread across all drives in the array. Suitable for use with program and data drives.

Table 6-3 provides a quick comparison of these types of RAID arrays.

Table 6-3 Comparisons of RAID Levels

RAID Level	Minimum Number of Drives Required	Data Protection Features	Total Capacity of Array	Major Benefit over Single Drive	Notes
0	2	None	2× capacity of both drives (if same size) OR 2× capacity of smaller drive	Improved read/write performance	Also called "striping"

RAID Level	Minimum Number of Drives Required	Data Protection Features	Total Capacity of Array	Major Benefit over Single Drive	Notes
1	2	Changes to contents of one drive immediately performed on other drive	Capacity of one drive (if same size); OR capacity of smaller drive	Automatic backup; faster read performance	Also called "mirroring"
10	4	Changes on one two-drive array are immediately performed on other two-drive array	Capacity of smallest drive × number of drives/2	Improved read/write performance and automatic backup	Also called "striped and mirrored"
5	3	Parity information is saved across all drives	$(x\text{-}1) \times$ capacity of smallest drive (x equals the number of drives in the array)	Full data redundancy in all drives; hot swap of damaged drive supported in most implementations	—

Motherboards that support only two drives in a RAID array support only RAID 0 and RAID 1. Motherboards that support more than two drives can also support RAID Level 0+1, and some support RAID 5 as well. RAID-enabled host adapter support varying levels of RAID.

NOTE   ATA or SATA RAID host adapters can sometimes be configured to work as normal ATA or SATA host adapters. Check the system BIOS setup or add-on card host adapter setup for details.

An ATA or SATA RAID array requires

- **Two or more identical drives**—If some drives are larger than others, the additional capacity will be ignored. Refer to Table 6-3.

- **A RAID-compatible motherboard or add-on host adapter card**—Both feature a special BIOS, which identifies and configures the drives in the array.

Because RAID arrays use off-the-shelf drives, the only difference in the physical installation of drives in a RAID array is where they are connected. They must be connected to a motherboard or add-on card that has RAID support.

NOTE Sometimes ATA RAID connectors are made from a contrasting color of plastic than other drive connectors. However, the best way to determine if your system or motherboard supports ATA or SATA RAID arrays is to read the manual for the system or motherboard.

After the drive(s) used to create the array is connected to the RAID array's host adapter, restart the computer. Start the system BIOS setup program and enable the RAID host adapter if necessary. Save changes and exit the BIOS setup program.

After enabling the RAID array host adapter, follow the vendor instructions to create the array. Generally, this requires you to activate the RAID array setup program when you start the computer and follow the prompts to select the type of array desired. (Figure 6-17 shows a typical RAID setup program.) After the RAID array is configured, the drives arc handled as a single physical drive by the system.

Figure 6-17 Preparing to create an ATA RAID array.

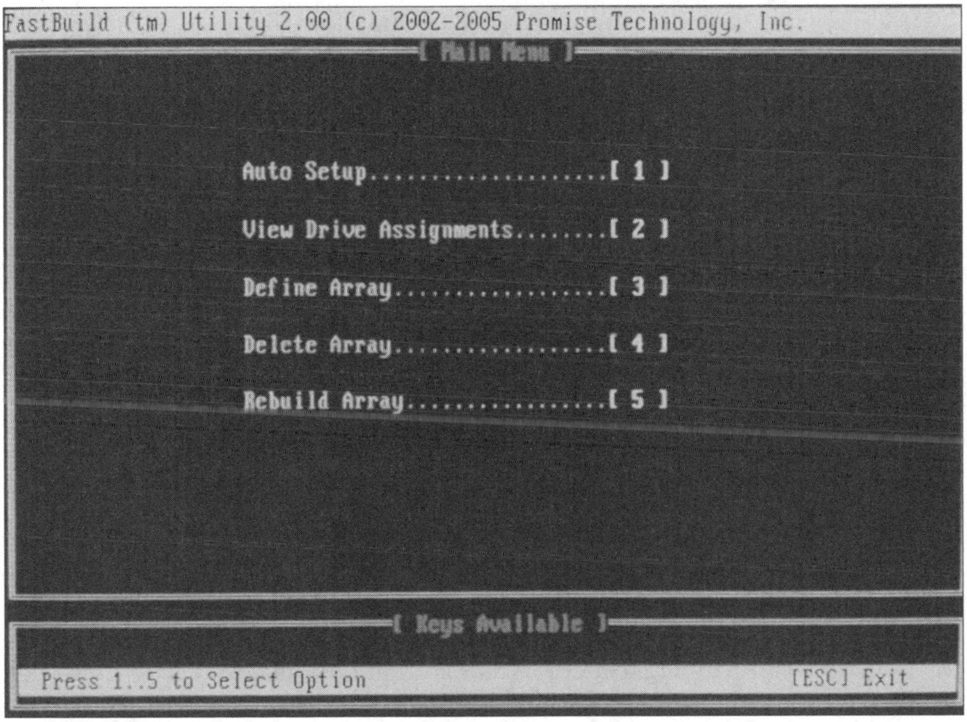

CAUTION   If one or more of the drives to be used in the array already contains data, back up the drives before starting the configuration process! Most RAID array host adapters delete the data on all drives in the array when creating an array, sometimes with little warning.

NOTE   If you want to create a striped volume (equivalent to RAID 0) in Windows XP or Windows Vista but your system does not include PATA RAID or SATA RAID host adapters, you can use Computer Management Console's Disk Management node (diskmgmt.msc).

To create a striped volume, use the New Volume Wizard from the right-click menu, and select **Striped** as the volume type. After selecting one or more additional drives and adding them to the volume, you are prompted to assign the volume a new drive letter, mount the volume to an empty NTFS folder on another drive, or do nothing. After the array is formatted, you can use it. Note that Windows cannot create a mirrored volume.

Optimizing ATA/IDE Performance

If your hard drive is stuck in first gear, so is your system. Fortunately, most systems that support LBA mode also offer several different ways to optimize the performance of IDE drives and devices. These include

- Selecting the correct PIO or DMA transfer mode in the BIOS
- Selecting the correct block mode in the BIOS
- Installing busmastering Windows drivers
- Enabling DMA mode in Windows
- Adjusting disk cache software settings

The following sections describe each of these performance optimization methods.

Selecting the PIO and DMA Transfer Modes

PATA (ATA/IDE) storage devices are capable of operating at a variety of transfer speeds. Virtually all recent hard disk and other drives support one of Ultra DMA (UDMA) modes (also known as Ultra ATA modes).

The correct speed is determined when the drive is detected by the computer during CMOS setup. However, if you use a 40-wire PATA cable, the fastest Ultra DMA speed available is Ultra DMA 33. For this reason, you should use 80-wire cables for hard disks and other PATA storage devices.

To achieve a given transfer rate, the hard disk, the host adapter (card or built-in), and the data cable must be capable of that rate. In addition, the host adapter must be configured to run at that rate.

Table 6-4 lists the most common transfer rates. Check the drive documentation or consult the drive vendor for the correct rating for a given drive.

Table 6-4   UDMA (Ultra ATA) Peak Transfer Rates

Mode	Peak Transfer Rate	PATA Cable Requirement
UDMA 2 (UDMA-33)	33.33MBps	40- or 80-wire cable
UDMA 4 (UDMA-66)	66.66MBps	80-wire cable
UDMA 5 (UDMA-100)	100MBps	80-wire cable
UDMA 6 (UDMA-133)	133MBps	80-wire cable

These modes are backward compatible, enabling you to select the fastest available mode if your system lacks the correct mode for your drive. ATA/IDE drives are backward compatible; you can select a slower UDMA mode than the drive supports if your system doesn't support the correct UDMA mode. Performance is slower, but the drive still works.

TIP Some older UDMA drives are shipped with their firmware configuration set to a lower transfer rate than the maximum supported by the drive. This helps avoid data loss that could happen if the drive is connected to a system that doesn't support the drive's maximum transfer rate. Fortunately, these drives usually include a software utility that can ratchet up the speed to the maximum allowed. If you can't find the driver disk or CD, check out the vendor's website for the utility and download it.

If a particular drive and host adapter combination is not capable of running at any UDMA speed, the system reverts to the slower PIO drive access method. PIO transfer rates are shown in Table 6-5.

Table 6-5   PIO Peak Transfer Rates

Mode	Peak Transfer Rate	Interface Type Required
PIO 0	3.33MBps	16-bit
PIO 1	5.22MBps	16-bit
PIO 2	8.33MBps	16-bit

Mode	Peak Transfer Rate	Interface Type Required
PIO 3	11.11MBps	32-bit
PIO 4	16.67MBps	32-bit

As you can see from Table 6-5, even the fastest PIO mode is only half the speed of the slowest UDMA mode.

Selecting the IDE Block Mode

IDE block mode refers to multi-sector data transfers. Originally, a PATA hard drive was allowed to read only a single 512-byte sector before the drive sent an IRQ to the CPU. Early in their history, some PATA hard drives began to use a different method called block mode, which enabled the drive to read multiple sectors, or blocks, of data before an IRQ was sent. All recent drives support block mode, and the correct value is configured when the drive is detected. If block mode is disabled, a drive that supports block mode transfers data more slowly.

NOTE Some very old ATA/IDE drives do not support block mode and run more slowly when it is enabled.

Installing IDE Busmastering Drivers

A third way to improve IDE hard disk performance is to install busmastering drivers for the IDE host interface. A busmaster bypasses the CPU for data transfers between memory and the hard disk interface. This option is both operating system–specific and motherboard/host adapter–specific.

If you have installed a new motherboard, busmastering drivers are provided on a driver CD or floppy disk. They are preinstalled on complete systems. You might find more up-to-date versions at the vendor's website or by running Windows Update. Because busmastering bypasses the CPU, be sure you are installing the correct drivers. Carefully read the motherboard or system vendor's instructions.

Enabling DMA Transfers for PATA Devices in Windows

All versions of Windows from Windows NT 4.0 (Service Pack 3 and greater) and Windows 95 through Windows Vista enable the user to allow DMA transfers between PATA devices and the system. DMA transfers bypass the CPU for faster performance and are particularly useful for optimizing the performance of both hard drives and optical drives, such as high-speed CD-ROM drives and DVD drives.

NOTE The correct busmastering drivers for your system and Windows version must be installed before you can enable DMA transfers.

Follow this procedure to enable DMA transfers for a particular IDE host adapter in Windows 2000/XP/Vista:

Step 1. Open the System Properties sheet. Right-click **My Computer** and select **Properties**, or open the **Control Panel** and select **System**.

Step 2. Click **Hardware, Device Manager**. (In Windows Vista, just click **Device Manager** under Tasks.)

Step 3. To determine which drives are connected to which host adapter, open the category containing the drives (Disk Drives for hard or removable-media drives or DVD/CD-ROM Drives for optical drives) and double-click the drive to open its Properties sheet. The location value visible on the General tab shows to which host adapter and device number the drive is connected. For example, location 0 (1) indicates the drive is connected to the primary host adapter (0) as the secondary device (1).

Step 4. Click the plus sign next to the IDE ATA/ATAPI Controllers category.

Step 5. Double-click the host adapter for which you want to adjust properties (primary or secondary IDE channel) to open its Properties sheet.

Step 6. Click **Advanced Settings**.

Step 7. To enable DMA for a particular drive, select **DMA** if available for the Transfer mode. To disable DMA, select **PIO Only** (see Figure 6-18). (In Windows Vista you would just select the checkbox labeled **Enable DMA**.)

Step 8. Click **OK**.

Step 9. Restart the computer as prompted.

If DMA is not available, you might need to install the correct busmastering driver for your system.

CAUTION Before enabling DMA or UDMA mode, check the documentation for the drive to see if it supports this mode. Enabling DMA or UDMA on a drive that does not support it can have disastrous effects.

If the drive can't go faster than UDMA 2 although it's rated for higher speeds (see Figure 6-18), you might want to change the cable. You must use the 80-wire cable to run at UDMA 4 (66MBps) or faster transfer rates. It's also okay to use the 80-wire cable for slower transfer rates.

Figure 6-18   The secondary IDE channel on this system is configured to run one drive in PIO mode and one drive in UDMA mode.

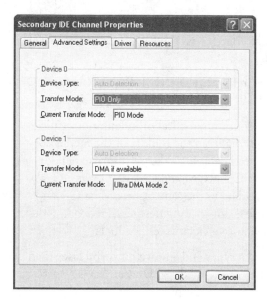

Adjusting Disk Caching Settings in Windows

Disk caches use a portion of memory to hold information flowing to and from disk drives. The system accesses the cache memory before accessing the main memory. If the information on disk is already in the cache memory, it is accessed far more quickly than if it were read from disk.

To adjust disk-cache settings for Windows 2000/XP (not Vista), follow this procedure:

Step 1.   Open the System Properties sheet and click **Advanced**.

Step 2.   Click the **Settings** button in the Performance section.

Step 3.   Click **Advanced**.

Step 4.   Click **System Cache** to use more memory on a computer that provides server features to other computers or to improve overall disk-caching performance. To avoid reducing system performance, you should enable this feature only on systems with 512MB of RAM or more.

Step 5.   Click **OK** and restart the system as prompted.

Many of today's hard drives have anywhere between 4MB and 32MB of on-board cache. The more cache memory on the hard drive, the less likely you need to adjust disk caching settings in Windows.

CD and DVD Optical Drives

Optical drives fall into two major categories:

- Those based on CD technology, including CD-ROM, CD-R (recordable CD), and CD-RW (rewritable CD)

- Those based on DVD technology, including DVD-ROM, DVD-RAM, DVD-R/RW, DVD+R/RW, and DVD±R/RW

Both CD and DVD drives store data in a continuous spiral of indentations called *pits* and *lands* on the nonlabel side of the media from the middle of the media outward to the edge. All drives use a laser to read data; DVD stores more data because it uses a laser on a shorter wavelength than CD-ROM and CD-RW drives do, allowing for smaller pits and lands and more data in the same space. Most CD and DVD drives are tray-loading, but a few use a slot-loading design. Slot-loading designs are more common in home and automotive electronics products.

CD-R and CD-RW drives use special media types and a more powerful laser than that used on CD-ROM drives to write data to the media. CD-R media is a write-once media—the media can be written to during multiple sessions, but older data cannot be deleted. CD-RW media can be rewritten up to 1,000 times. 80-minute CD-R media has a capacity of 700MB, and the older 74-minute CD-R media has a capacity of 650MB. CD-RW media capacity is up to 700MB, but is often less, depending upon how the media is formatted.

Similarly, DVD-R and DVD+R media is recordable, but not erasable, whereas DVD-RW and DVD+RW media uses a phase-change medium similar to CD-RW and can be rewritten up to 1,000 times. Typical DVD capacity is 4.7GB. DVD-RAM can be rewritten up to 100,000 times, but DVD-RAM drives and media are less compatible with other types of DVD drives and media than the other rewritable DVD types, making DVD-RAM the least popular DVD format.

Drive speeds are measured by an X-rating:

- When working with CD media, 1X equals 150KBps, the data transfer rate used for reading music CDs. Multiply the X-rating by 150 to determine the drive's data rate for reading, writing, or rewriting CD media.

- When working with DVD media, 1X equals 1.385MBps; this is the data transfer rate used for playing DVD-Video (DVD movies) content. Multiply the X-rating by 1.385 to determine the drive's data rate for reading, writing, or rewriting DVD media.

Now that we have discussed the various types of optical drives you will encounter, let's delve into the hands-on: how the drives connect to a system, and how they can be installed.

CD and DVD Drive Interfaces

Most internal CD and DVD drives use the same ATA/IDE interface used by PATA hard disks. When this interface is used by drives other than hard disks, it is often referred to as the ATAPI interface. Some recent rewritable DVD drives use the SATA interface. External CD and DVD drives typically use the USB 2.0 interface. Some internal and external CD drives used the SCSI or Parallel (LPT) interfaces, but these drives are obsolete.

Physical Installation of Optical Drives

The installation of these drives follows the standard procedure used for each interface type:

- Internal optical drives must be installed into 5.25" drive bays.

- ATAPI/IDE optical drives must be configured as master, slave, or cable select (depending upon the cable type and other drives on the same cable).

- SCSI optical drives must be set to a unique device ID.

- SATA optical drives do not require special configuration.

- USB and IEEE-1394a optical drives must be connected to ports with adequate hub power, or they must provide their own power.

If you want to play music CDs through your sound card's speakers, especially with older versions of Windows, you might need to connect a CD audio patch cable (it might be supplied with the drive or sold separately) to the CD audio jack on the sound card or motherboard audio support. Older drives support a four-wire analog cable, whereas newer drives support both the four-wire analog and newer two-wire digital cable. The digital cable provides for faster speed when ripping music CDs (*ripping* is the process of converting music CD tracks into compressed digital music files such as MP3 and WMA). Figure 6-19 shows a typical internal PATA (ATAPI) optical drive before and after connecting power, data, and music cables.

NOTE Although internal optical drives support four-wire analog audio and two-wire digital audio cables, you do not need to install these cables to permit CD audio playback unless you use versions of Windows or music playback applications that do not support ripping or playback from the ATA/IDE or SATA interface.

Figure 6-19 A typical ATAPI (PATA) internal optical drive before (top) and after (bottom) data, power, and CD music cables have been attached.

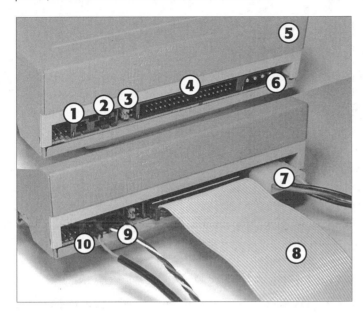

1. CD-digital audio port
2. CD-analog audio port
3. Drive jumper set to slave
4. ATA/IDE port
5. Connector legend
6. Molex power connector
7. Molex power cable
8. 40-wire ATA/IDE cable
9. CD-analog audio cable
10. CD-digital audio cable

IDE/ATAPI Optical Drive Installation Issues

On systems using PATA hard disks and ATAPI optical or removable-media drives, PATA hard disks should be connected to the primary IDE interface and other types of drives should be connected to the secondary IDE interface.

Be sure to select the specific type of drive (CD-ROM, Zip, or other; use CD-ROM for CD or DVD drives) as the drive type, when offered, in the BIOS drive setup menu. If you want to boot from an optical drive, be sure that the optical drive is specified as the first device in the boot order.

Chapter Review Questions

The following questions test your recall of the concepts described in this chapter. The answers are listed at the end of the questions in the "Answers and Explanations" section.

1. Which of the following loses its contents when you shut down the computer?

    A. Hard disk drive

    B. USB flash drive

    C. RAM

    D. ROM

2. Which memory module is much bulkier and more expensive than DRAM?

    A. SDRAM

    B. SRAM

    C. DRAM

    D. DDR

3. What type of RAM must be installed in pairs?

    A. DDR

    B. SDRAM

    C. DDR2

    D. Rambus

4. Which type of memory was the first to run in sync with the memory bus?

    A. DDR2

    B. SDRAM

    C. SRAM

    D. Rambus

5. To correctly install a DIMM or Rambus module, what should you do? (Choose all that apply.)

   A. Line up the module connectors with the socket.

   B. Verify that the locking tabs on the socket are swiveled to the outside (open) position.

   C. After verifying that the module is lined up correctly with the socket, push the module straight down into the socket until the swivel locks on each end of the socket and snap into place at the top corners of the module.

   D. None of these options is correct.

6. Which of the following is installed in all computers and is used for storing the operating system?

   A. USB drive

   B. CD drive

   C. Hard drive

   D. Firewire drive

7. What is the sector size on the platter on a hard drive?

   A. 1024 bytes

   B. 750 bytes

   C. 512 bytes

   D. 128 bytes

8. What are the two listed interfaces that are used to connect CD-ROMs and DVD-ROMs to the computer?

   A. ATA

   B. IrDA

   C. IDE

   D. EIDE

9. You have just installed a CD-ROM drive to your computer. You want to listen to music so you insert a music CD into the drive. Windows Media Player starts up, and you can see a song title and the elapsed time of the song within the player. Everything looks correct; however, for some reason you cannot hear the music. What could be the problem?

   A.   The power cable is not connected to the CD-ROM drive.

   B.   You need to connect the CD audio cable to the sound card.

   C.   You need to go the manufacturer's website for an updated CD-ROM driver.

   D.   The CD is faulty.

10. Which of the following types of RAM is PC2-8500?

   A.   SDRAM

   B.   DDR

   C.   DDR2

   D.   Rambus

11. How many pins does SDRAM have?

   A.   168

   B.   184

   C.   240

   D.   232

12. What should you *not* do when installing RAM?

   A.   Use a fair amount of force when pushing down

   B.   Touch the connectors on the bottom of the memory module

   C.   Close the locking mechanisms

   D.   Use a flashlight to check the RAM

13. Which of the following hard drive types can transmit data at a maximum of 100MBps?

   A.   ATA-5

   B.   ATA-6

   C.   ATA-7

   D.   ATA-8

14. Which of the following RAID levels uses two, and only two, disks?

   A. RAID 0

   B. RAID 1

   C. RAID 5

   D. RAID 0+1

15. What is the standard storage size of a DVD?

   A. 4.7GB

   B. 8.4GB

   C. 9.4GB

   D. 15GB

Case Study 1

Examine the RAM in your home or lab computer. List the defining characteristics of the RAM including type, storage size, speed, and maximum allowed RAM of your motherboard. Then, access memory manufacturer websites, such as www.kingston.com, to find out what types of RAM are available for your computer in the case that you want to upgrade. Keep in mind that you need to supply either the model number of the computer or the model number of the motherboard to the memory manufacturer.

Case Study 2

Examine the disks (hard drives) and discs (optical drives) in your home or lab computer. List the defining characteristics of all the drives. For example, if you have an IDE hard disk, write down the manufacturer, model, and capacity. Access the hard disk manufacturer website and locate your particular model. From the website, define the type of disk. For example, if it is an IDE hard disk, define whether it is ATA-6, ATA-7, or another version and its data transfer rate. If it is an SATA disk, define the version number and data transfer rate.

Answers and Explanations

1. C. Random access memory (RAM) loses its contents when the computer shuts down. Hard disk drives, USB flash drives, and read-only memory (ROM) are designed to retain their contents even if they are not receiving power.

2. B. SRAM, or Static RAM, is bulkier and more expensive than DRAM because it does not require electricity as often as DRAM.

3. **D.** Rambus memory that uses 32-bit RIMMs must use pairs, and unused sockets must be occupied by a continuity module.

4. **B.** SDRAM was the first memory type that was in sync with the motherboard's memory bus.

5. **A, B, C.** To correctly insert the memory modules, you should follow all the steps listed. You might also have to use a fair amount of pressure to securely lock these modules in place.

6. **C.** Hard disk drives are the most important storage device used by a personal computer. Hard disk drives store the operating system (Windows, Linux, or others) and load it into the computer's memory (RAM) at startup. Hard disk drives also store applications, system configuration files used by applications and the operating system, and data files created by the user.

7. **C.** Hard disk drives use one or more double-sided platters formed from rigid materials such as aluminum or glass. These platters are coated with a durable magnetic surface that is divided into sectors. Each sector contains 512 bytes of storage along with information about where the sector is located on the disk medium.

8. **A, C.** Most internal CD and DVD drives use the same ATA/IDE interface used by PATA hard disks. When this interface is used by drives other than hard disks, it is often referred to as the ATAPI interface.

9. **B.** If you want to play music CDs through your sound card's speakers, you might need to connect a CD audio patch cable. One end connects to the CD-ROM drive and the other end connects to the CD audio port on the sound card or motherboard. Older drives support a four-wire analog cable, whereas newer drives support both the four-wire analog and newer two-wire digital cable. If the power cable wasn't connected, the drive wouldn't have opened when you inserted the disc. CD-ROM drives normally don't need drivers installed; they are installed automatically by Windows. However you might need a soundcard driver. If the CD was faulty, Windows Media Player would not have played the song, and you wouldn't have seen the song title or the elapsed time of the song.

10. **C.** PC2-8500 (DDR2-667) is a type of DDR2 RAM.

11. **A.** SDRAM has 168 pins. DDR has 184 pins. DDR2 has 240 pins. Rambus has 232 or 184 pins.

12. **B.** When installing RAM, don't touch the bottom connectors or the chips on the side of the module if at all possible. Handle the RAM from the edges (but not the connector edge).

13. **B.** ATA-6 can transmit data at a maximum of 100MBps. ATA-5 has a max rate of 66MBps. ATA-7 has a maximum of 133MBps, and ATA-8 (SATA-II) has a maximum of 300MBps.

14. **B.** RAID 1 (mirroring) uses two disks, and two disks only. RAID 0 can use two or more disks. RAID 5 uses three or more disks. And RAID 0+1 is a combination of striping and mirroring, that needs four disks minimum.

15. **A.** A DVD's standard storage size is 4.7GB. Other sizes larger than 4.7GB require double density or double siding techniques.

Case Study 1 Solution

For example, let's say we have an Intel DP35DP motherboard and we want to install the maximum amount of RAM possible. First, we should define what type of RAM we need to install (from the motherboard's documentation). Then we should access a memory manufacturer's website to find compatible memory.

While examining the Intel DP35DP motherboard's documentation, we find that it uses DDR2 RAM and can support between 256MB and 4GB of RAM. However, in order to install the maximum of 4GB, a kit of two sticks of RAM have to be installed. The maximum RAM speed allowed by the motherboard is 800MHz. So, the next step is to access a memory manufacturer's website such as www.kingston.com. Then, we search by manufacturer (Intel), scroll down to the DP35DP model motherboard, and search. This displays a list of compatible RAM. In order to meet our goal of 4GB at 800MHz, we notice that there is only one compatible kit: KVR800D2N6K2/4G.

Another thing to keep in mind is the fact that this particular motherboard supports dual channel RAM. That means that the RAM must be installed properly within banks. These are usually color-coded. For example, on this motherboard, both RAM sticks would need to be installed into the blue slots. Both blue slots collectively form a bank.

Case Study 2 Solution

A typical computer might have an SATA hard drive and an SATA CD/DVD-ROM drive. You can find out information about the drives by accessing the Device Manager in Windows, or by using a third-party analysis program such as Belarc Advisor (www.belarc.com/free_download.html).

Or, you could open the computer, remove the drive, and read the label!

For example, a typical computer might have the following:

- SATA hard drive:

Western Digital WD5000AAKS Caviar Blue 500GB. This is an SATA v2.0 drive that can transfer 300MB of data per second. It has 8MB of cache memory. Web link:

http://www.wdc.com/en/products/products.asp?driveid=301

- SATA DVD/CD-ROM drive:

Samsung SH-223B 22x DVD-CD-ROM drive. This is a DVD writer as well. At 22x write speed, the drive can transfer up to 30MBps.

www.samsung.com/us/business/semiconductor/products/odd/oddSHS223B.html

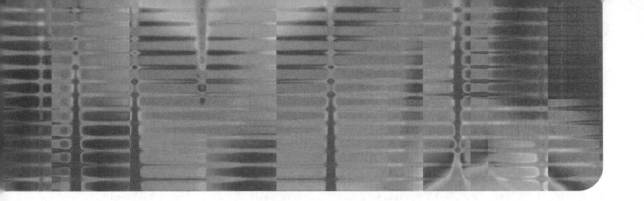

This chapter covers the following subjects:

- **Understanding BIOS, CMOS, and Firmware**—This section explains the motherboard's firmware, known as the BIOS. It also describes the relationship between the CMOS and the BIOS, and the various types of ROM you encounter.

- **Configuring the System BIOS**—This section demonstrates how to access the BIOS and modify settings—for example, RAM, processor, and video settings.

- **Power-On Self-Test and Error Reporting**—This section describes the POST and audible and visible errors that the POST reports.

- **BIOS Updates**—In this section, you learn how to upgrade the BIOS through a process known as flashing.

Computer Operation

The basic input/output system (BIOS) is an essential component of the motherboard. This boot firmware, also known as System BIOS, is the first code run by a computer when it is booted. It prepares the machine by testing it during boot-up and paves the way for the operating system to start. It tests and initializes components such as the processor, RAM, video card, magnetic disks, and optical disks. If any errors occur, the BIOS reports them as part of the testing stage, known as the power-on self test (POST). The BIOS resides on a ROM chip and stores a setup program that you can access when the computer first boots up. From this program, a user can change settings in the BIOS and upgrade the BIOS as well.

Within this chapter, you learn how the BIOS, CMOS, and batteries on the motherboard interact and how to configure and upgrade the BIOS. All of these concepts are important to learn as they are "pre-operating system" topics. If anything goes wrong in this stage, the computer won't even make it to the login screen of an operating system or any portion of the OS, for that matter.

Understanding BIOS, CMOS, and Firmware

You know what the CPU does—it does the "thinking" for the computer. But, how does the CPU "know" what kinds of drives are connected to the computer? What tells the CPU when the memory is ready to be read or written to? What turns on the USB ports or turns them off? The answer to all these questions is the BIOS. Next to the CPU, the BIOS chip is the most important chip found on the motherboard. Figure 7-1 illustrates the location of the BIOS chip on some typical systems.

The BIOS is a complex piece of firmware ("software on a chip") that provides support for the following devices and features of your system:

- Selection and configuration of storage devices connected to the motherboard's host adapters, such as hard drives, floppy drives, and CD-ROM drives

Figure 7-1   BIOS chips and CMOS batteries on typical motherboards.

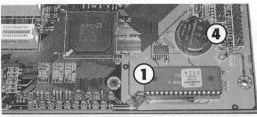

1. DIP-Type socketed BIOS chip
2. PLCC-type socketed BIOS chip
3. Surface-mounted BIOS chip
4. CR2032 CMOS batteries

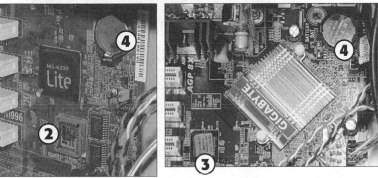

- Configuration of main and cache memory

- Configuration of built-in ports, such as PATA and SATA hard disk, floppy disk, serial, parallel, PS/2 mouse, USB, and IEEE-1394 ports

- Configuration of integrated (built into the motherboard chipset) audio, network, and graphics features when present

- Selection and configuration of special motherboard features, such as memory error correction, antivirus protection, and fast memory access

- Support for different CPU types, speeds, and special features

- Support for advanced operating systems, including networks and plug-and-play versions of Windows

- Power management

- Hardware monitoring (processor temperature, voltage levels, and fan performance)

Without the BIOS, your computer would be a collection of metal and plastic parts that couldn't interact with one another or do much of anything but gather dust.

The BIOS also performs two other important tasks:

- It runs the power-on self test (POST) when the system is started.

- It establishes a list of locations that can be used by an operating system to boot the computer (hard disk, CD or DVD drive, USB drive, floppy drive, network) and turns over control of the system by using the Bootstrap loader after completing its startup tasks.

Originally, the BIOS was stored on read-only memory (ROM) chips. This type of memory is different from random-access memory (RAM) in a few ways. Most importantly, ROM retains its contents even when the computer is shut off, whereas most types of RAM do not. Also, ROM can be read from, but not written to, whereas RAM can be read from and written to. As time progressed, ROM chips were not functional enough for the typical PC. It later progressed to a programmable ROM (PROM) chip, which enabled the user to modify settings in the BIOS. Finally, today's system BIOS resides on an EEPROM chip on the motherboard. EEPROM stands for electrically erasable programmable ROM and means that we cannot only modify settings, but also fully update the BIOS by erasing it and rewriting it in a process known as flashing.

The BIOS is the first thing that runs when you boot the PC. The BIOS's job is to identify, test, and initialize components of the system. It then points the way to the operating system so that the OS can load up and take over. Collectively, this process is known as *bootstrapping*. But the BIOS doesn't do its job alone. It works with two other important components:

- CMOS memory

- Motherboard battery (also called the CMOS battery; refer to Figure 7-1)

Throughout this chapter, you learn more about how these components work together to control system startup and onboard hardware.

Standard settings are configured by the motherboard or system vendor, but can be overridden by the user to enable the system to work with different types of hardware or to provide higher performance. CMOS memory, also referred to as non-volatile memory, is used to store BIOS settings. Do not confuse CMOS memory with system memory (RAM); CMOS memory is built into the motherboard and cannot be removed by the user.

The contents of CMOS memory are retained as long as a constant flow of DC current from a battery on the motherboard is provided. Some typical CMOS batteries are shown in Figure 7-2.

Figure 7-2   The CR2032 lithium watch battery (center) is the most common battery used to maintain CMOS settings in recent systems, but other batteries such as the Dallas Semiconductor DS12887A clock/battery chip (left) and the AA-size 3.6 volt (V) Eternacell (right) have also been used in older systems.

When the battery starts to fail, the clock starts to lose time. Complete battery failure causes the loss of all CMOS configuration information (such as drive types, settings for onboard ports, CPU and memory speeds, and much more). When this takes place, the system cannot be used until you install a new battery and re-enter all CMOS configuration information by using the CMOS configuration program.

Because the battery that maintains settings can fail at any time, and viruses and power surges can also affect the CMOS configuration, you should record important information before it is lost.

TIP   At one time, many system BIOS programs supported printing BIOS screens to a printer connected to the parallel port. Those days are gone (in fact, so are parallel printers, as well as printer ports!). However, you can still document BIOS screens the easy way: Use a digital camera set for macro (close-up) mode.

Configuring the System BIOS

The system BIOS has default settings provided by the system or motherboard maker, but as a system is built up with storage devices, memory modules, adapter cards, and other components, it is usually necessary to alter the standard settings.

To perform this task, the system assembler must use the BIOS setup program to make changes and save them to the CMOS. Originally, the BIOS setup program was run from a bootable floppy disk, but for many years most system BIOS chips have included the setup program.

Accessing the BIOS Setup Program

On most systems built since the late 1980s, the BIOS setup program is stored in the BIOS chip itself. Just press the key or key combination displayed onscreen (or described in the manual) to get started.

Although these keystrokes vary from system to system, the most popular keys on current systems include the escape (Esc) key, the Delete (Del) key, the F1 key, the F2 key, the F10 key, and various combinations of Ctrl+Alt+another specified key.

Most recent systems display the key(s) necessary to start the BIOS setup program at startup, as in Figure 7-3. However, if you don't know which key to press to start your computer's BIOS setup program, check the system or motherboard manual for the correct key(s).

Figure 7-3 The splash screens used by many recent systems display the keystrokes needed to start the BIOS setup program.

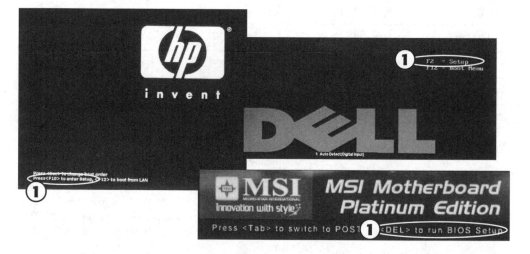

NOTE Because the settings you make in the BIOS setup program are stored in the non-volatile CMOS, the settings are often called CMOS settings or BIOS settings.

Depending on the BIOS program your motherboard uses, the key to access it is different. Table 7-1 shows the most common keys used by BIOS and motherboard manufacturers. You might notice that some computers display a splash screen when the computer first boots up. This might show the logo of the computer manufacturer or the logo of the motherboard manufacturer. In many cases during this short time period, you can press the Esc key to remove the splash screen. This then displays some details about the steps the BIOS takes while booting. Toward the bottom of the screen, it should also display the proper key to use in order to access the BIOS.

Table 7-1   Common Keystrokes Used to Start the BIOS Setup Program

BIOS	Keystrokes	Notes
Phoenix BIOS	Ctrl+Alt+Esc	—
—	Ctrl+Alt+F1	—
—	Ctrl+Alt+S	—
—	Ctrl+Alt+Enter	—
—	Ctrl+Alt+F11	—
—	Ctrl+Alt+Ins	—
Award BIOS	Ctrl+Alt+Esc	—
—	Esc	—
—	Del	—
AMI BIOS	Del	—
IBM BIOS	Ctrl+Alt+Ins* F1	*Early notebook models; press when cursor is in upper-right corner of screen.
Compaq & HP BIOS	F10	Depending on the model, the keystroke might load the Compaq or HP setup program from hard disk partition or start the setup program from the BIOS chip; press when cursor is in upper-right corner of screen.
Dell	F2	Keystroke actually loads Dell BIOS from hard disk partition.

In the following sections, we review the typical setup process, looking at each screen of a typical desktop system with an Athlon 64 x2 processor.

CAUTION BIOS programs vary widely, but the screens used in the following sections are representative of the options available on typical recent systems; your system might have similar options, but place the settings on different screens than those shown here. Laptop and corporate desktop systems generally offer fewer options than those shown here.

Be sure to consult the manual that came with your computer or motherboard before toying with the settings you find here. Monkeying with the settings can improve performance, but it can also wreak havoc on an otherwise healthy PC if you don't know what you're doing. Be warned!

BIOS Settings Overview

Table 7-2 provides a detailed discussion of the most important CMOS/BIOS settings. Use this table as a quick reference to the settings you need to make or verify in any system. Examples of these and other settings are provided in the following sections.

Table 7-2 Major CMOS/BIOS Settings

Topic	Option	Setting	Notes
Advanced	CHIP (Chipset Configuration)	Set AGP card speed and memory speed to match device speed	Nonstandard AGP or memory settings could cause instability.
Boot Sequence	Boot Sequence	Adjust as desired	To boot from bootable Windows or diagnostic CDs or DVDs, place CD or DVD (optical) drive before hard drive; to boot from USB device, place USB device before hard drive.
Memory Configuration	Memory Configuration	By SPD*	Provides stable operation using the settings stored in memory by the vendor.
		Manual settings (Frequency, CAS Latency [CL], Fast R-2-R turnaround, and so on)	Use for overclocking (running memory at faster than normal speeds) or to enable memory of different speeds to be used safely by selecting slower settings.
Processor	CPU Clock and Frequency	Set to correct settings for your processor	Faster or higher settings overclock the system but could cause instability; some systems default to low values if system doesn't start properly.
	CPU/Memory Cache	Enabled	Disable only if you are running memory testing software.

Topic	Option	Setting	Notes
Hardware Monitor	Hardware Monitor	Enable display for all fans plugged into the motherboard	Some systems, such as the example in this chapter, primarily report settings with very few options.
Integrated Peripherals	Onboard Audio, Modem, or Network	Varies	Enable if you don't use add-on cards for these functions; disable each setting before installing a replacement card.
	PS/2 Mouse	Varies with mouse type	Disable if you use USB mouse; some systems use a motherboard jumper.
	USB Legacy	Enable if USB keyboard is used	Enables USB keyboard to work outside of Windows.
	Serial Ports	Disable unused ports; use default settings for port you use	Avoid setting two serial ports to use the same IRQ.
	Parallel Port	Disable unused port; use EPP/ECP mode with default IRQ/DMA if parallel port or device is connected	Compatible with almost any recent parallel printer or device; be sure to use an IEEE-1284-compatible printer cable.
	USB Function	Enable	If motherboard supports USB 2.0 (Hi-Speed USB) ports, be sure to enable USB 2.0 function and load USB 2.0 drivers in Windows.
Misc	Keyboard	Numlock, auto-repeat rate/delay	Leave at defaults (NumLock On) unless keyboard has problems.
	PCI IRQs	Use Auto unless Windows Device Manager indicates conflict or Windows can't configure the device	Sound cards should be installed in a PCI slot that doesn't share IRQs with another slot.
	PCI/PnP IRQ, DMA, I/O Port Address Configuration (Exclusion)	Leave at defaults unless you have non-PnP ISA cards installed	No changes required on systems without ISA cards (motherboard-integrated serial, parallel, and PS/2 mouse ports are ISA but support PnP).
	Plug-and-Play OS	Enable for all except some Linux distributions, Windows NT, MS-DOS	When enabled, Windows configures devices.

Topic	Option	Setting	Notes
	Primary VGA BIOS	Varies	Select the primary graphics card type (PCIe or AGP) unless you have PCIe or AGP and PCI graphics (video) cards installed that won't work unless PCI is set as primary.
	Shadowing	Varies	Enable shadowing for video BIOS; leave other shadowing disabled.
	Quiet Boot	Varies	Disable to display system configuration information at startup.
	Boot-Time Diagnostic Screen	Varies	Enable to display system configuration information at startup.
Power Management	Power Management (Menu)	Enable unless you have problems with devices	Enable CPU fan settings to receive warnings of CPU fan failure.
	AC Pwr Loss Restart	Enable restart	Prevents system from staying down if power failure takes place.
	Wake on LAN (WOL)	Enable if you use WOL-compatible network card or modem	WOL-compatible cards use a small cable between the card and motherboard.
Security	User/Power-On Password	Blocks system from starting if password not known	Enable for security but be sure to record password in a secure place.
	Setup Password	Blocks access to setup if password not known	Both passwords can be cleared on both systems if CMOS RAM is cleared.
	Write-Protect Boot Sector	Varies	Enable for normal use, but disable when installing drives or using a multiboot system; helps prevent accidental formatting, but might not stop third-party disk prep software from working.
	Boot Virus Detection (Antivirus Boot Sector)	Enable	Stops true infections but allows multiboot configuration.

Topic	Option	Setting	Notes
Storage	Floppy Drive	Usually 3.5" 1.44MB	Set to actual drive type/capacity; some systems default to other sizes.
	PATA (IDE), SATA Drives	Varies	Auto-detects drive type and settings at startup time; select CD/DVD for CD or DVD drive; select None if drive not present or to disable an installed drive.
	LBA Mode	Enable	Disable would prevent MS-DOS or Windows from using more than 504MiB (528.5MB) of an PATA/IDE drive's capacity. Some older systems put this setting in various locations away from the standard setup screen.

* SPD (serial presence detect) is a standardized way of accessing information from memory modules. It was incorporated into many computers starting with 168-pin SDRAM. It is a hardware feature within the memory that allows the BIOS to examine and record how much RAM is present in the computer.

Automatic Configuration of BIOS/CMOS Settings

Let's be frank—after reading Table 7-2, you might be wondering, "Isn't there an easier way to configure the BIOS?" Well, actually there is, in a way.

Many BIOS versions enable you to automatically configure your system with a choice of these options from the main menu:

- BIOS defaults (also referred to as Original/Fail-Safe on some systems)
- Setup defaults (also referred to as Optimal on some systems)
- Turbo

These options primarily deal with performance configuration settings in the BIOS, such as memory timings, memory cache, and the like. The settings used by each BIOS setup option are customized by the motherboard or system manufacturer.

Use BIOS defaults to troubleshoot the system because these settings are conservative in memory timings and other options. Normally, the Setup defaults provide better performance. Turbo, if present, speeds the memory refresh rate used by the system. As you view the setup screens in this chapter, you'll note these options are listed.

CAUTION If you use automatic setup after you make manual changes, all your manual changes are overridden. Use one of these settings first (try Turbo or Setup Defaults) and then make any other changes you want.

With many recent systems, you can select Optimal or Setup defaults, save your changes, and exit, and the system works acceptably. However, you might want more control over your system. In that case, look at the following screens and make the necessary changes.

Selecting Options

On typical systems, you set numerical settings, such as date and time, by scrolling through allowable values with keys such as + and – or page up/page down. However, you select settings with a limited range of options, such as enable/disable or choices from a menu, by pressing the Enter key on the keyboard and choosing the option desired from the available choices.

Main Menu

When you start the BIOS configuration program for your system, you might see a menu similar to the CMOS Setup Utility menu shown in Figure 7-4. From this menu, you can go to any menu, select default settings, save changes, or exit the CMOS setup menu.

Figure 7-4   A typical CMOS Setup utility main menu.

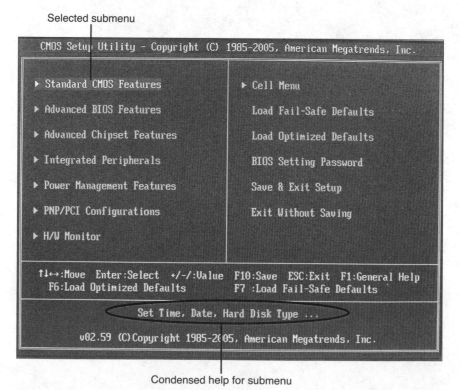

Selected submenu

Condensed help for submenu

TIP   If you need to quickly find a particular BIOS setting and you don't have the manual for the system or the motherboard, visit the system or motherboard vendor's website and download the manual. In most cases, especially with a motherboard-specific manual, the BIOS screens are illustrated. Most vendors provide the manuals in Adobe Reader (PDF) format.

Standard Features/Settings Menu

The Standard Features/Settings menu is typically used to configure the system's date and time as well as drives connected to PATA (ATA/IDE), SATA, and floppy drive interfaces on the motherboard. Figure 7-5 shows an example.

Figure 7-5   A typical CMOS Standard Features/Settings menu.

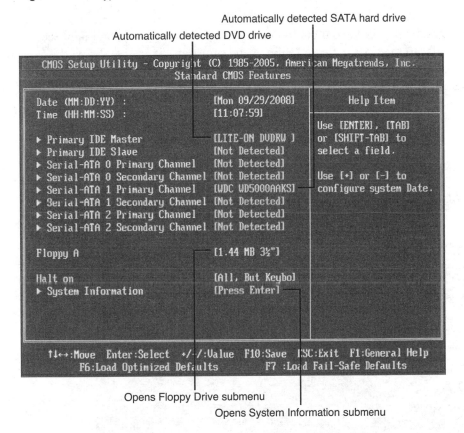

Automatically detected SATA hard drive

Automatically detected DVD drive

Opens Floppy Drive submenu

Opens System Information submenu

NOTE   Some BIOS setup programs open this menu and provide access to other menus with a top-level menu bar. Keep in mind that "Standard Features" and "Standard Settings" are just examples of the primary BIOS menu. Different BIOS programs might use a slightly different name, but usually it is shown first (to the far left of the menu bar).

PATA and SATA BIOS Configuration

Most recent systems automatically detect the drive connected to each PATA and SATA host adapter, as shown earlier in Figure 7-5. However, some systems might use manual entry of the correct settings instead. These are usually listed on the drive's faceplate or in the instruction manual.

CAUTION   Although some users recommend that you configure the settings for hard drives to user-defined, which lists the exact settings for each hard drive, this can cause a major problem in case your BIOS settings are lost due to a virus, battery failure, or other causes. If you are not an experienced user, let your computer do the work by using the Auto feature.

Floppy Drive BIOS Configuration

On systems that have an onboard floppy drive, the floppy drive must be selected manually if a different type of floppy drive is installed, or if the floppy drive is not present (see Figure 7-6).

TIP   If your system supports an internal floppy drive, but you don't use the drive, you might be able to disable the floppy controller. In such cases, you no longer need to select Disabled from the menu shown in Figure 7-6.

System Information

Some systems display system information such as processor type, clock speed, cache memory size, installed memory (RAM), and BIOS information on the standard menu or a submenu, as shown in Figure 7-7. Use this information to help determine if a system needs a processor, memory, or BIOS update.

Figure 7-6 Viewing available floppy disk drive types.

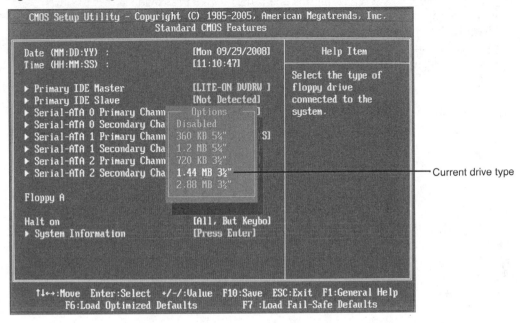

Figure 7-7 Viewing system information.

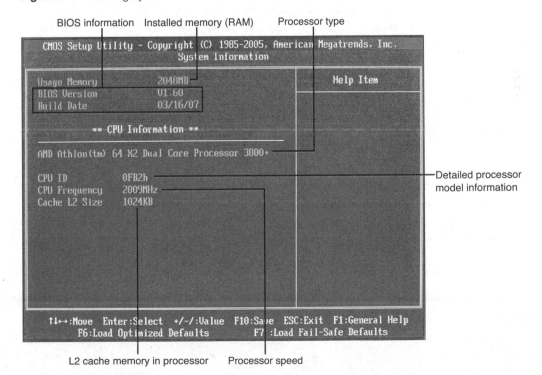

Advanced BIOS Settings/Features Menu

The Advanced BIOS Settings/Features menu typically includes settings that control how the system boots, as shown in Figure 7-8. Enabling Quick Boot skips memory and drive tests to enable faster startup. Enabling Boot Sector Protection provides some protection against boot sector computer viruses. Enabling Boot Up Num-Lock LED turns on the keyboard's Num Lock option.

The Boot Sequence submenu shown in Figure 7-9 is used to adjust the order that drives are checked for bootable media. For everyday use, follow this order:

- **First drive**—Hard disk

- **Second**—Floppy (if present) or CD/DVD drive

- **Third**—CD/DVD drive or USB device

Figure 7-8   A typical Advanced BIOS Features menu.

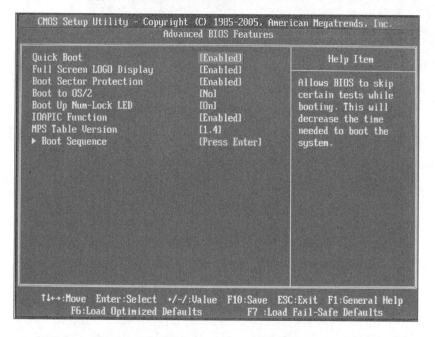

NOTE   Even when the first boot drive is set up as CD/DVD, some discs prompt the user to press a key in order to boot from the CD/DVD drive when a bootable disk is found. Otherwise, the system checks the next available device for boot files.

The order shown in Figure 7-9 is recommended for situations in which you need to boot from a CD/DVD or floppy disk drive (installing a new operating system or booting diagnostic software).

> **NOTE** If you have more than one drive in any category, you can select the boot drive from the submenus below the boot device listing.

Figure 7-9 A typical Boot Sequence submenu configured to permit booting from a CD/DVD or floppy disk.

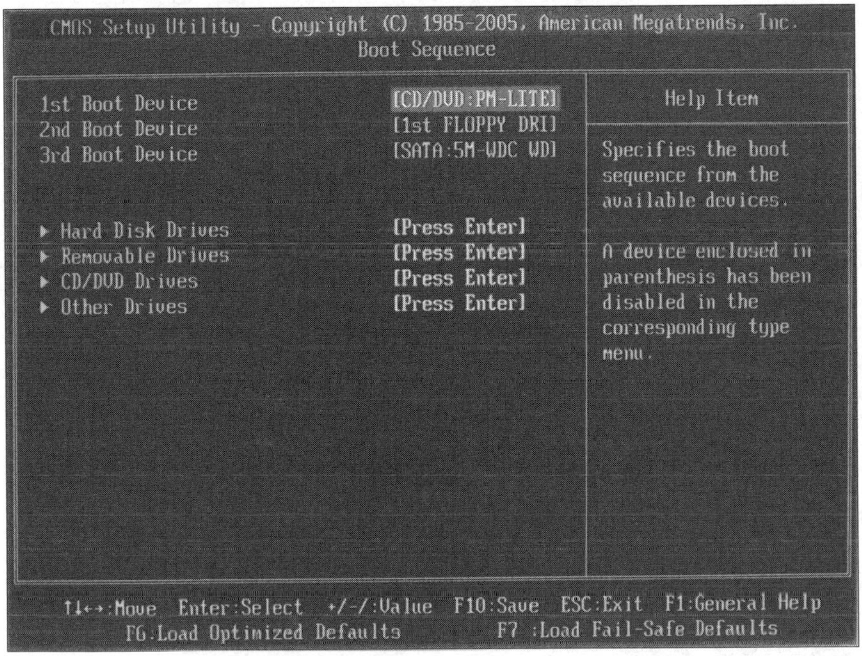

```
CMOS Setup Utility - Copyright (C) 1985-2005, American Megatrends, Inc.
                           Boot Sequence

  1st Boot Device              [CD/DVD:PM-LITE]        Help Item
  2nd Boot Device              [1st FLOPPY DRI]
  3rd Boot Device              [SATA:5M-WDC WD]    Specifies the boot
                                                   sequence from the
                                                   available devices.
  ▶ Hard Disk Drives           [Press Enter]
  ▶ Removable Drives           [Press Enter]       A device enclosed in
  ▶ CD/DVD Drives              [Press Enter]       parenthesis has been
  ▶ Other Drives               [Press Enter]       disabled in the
                                                   corresponding type
                                                   menu.




  ↑↓←→:Move  Enter:Select  +/-/:Value  F10:Save  ESC:Exit  F1:General Help
         F6:Load Optimized Defaults        F7 :Load Fail-Safe Defaults
```

Integrated Peripherals Menu

The typical system today is loaded with onboard ports and features, and the Integrated Peripherals menu shown in Figure 7-10 and its submenus are used to enable, disable, and configure them.

Note that most systems have separate settings for USB controller and USB 2.0 controller. If you connect a USB 2.0 device to a USB port on your system and you see a "This device can perform faster" error message in Windows, make sure the USB 2.0 controller or USB 2.0 mode is enabled. If USB 2.0 features are disabled in the BIOS, all of your system's USB ports run in USB 1.1 mode only.

You can configure other devices within the BIOS as well. Onboard devices that connect to ports such as IEEE-1394 and Ethernet, I/O devices such as a mouse that connect to PS/2 ports, and PATA/SATA hard drives can all be manipulated to a certain extent within the BIOS.

Figure 7-10 A typical Integrated Peripherals menu.

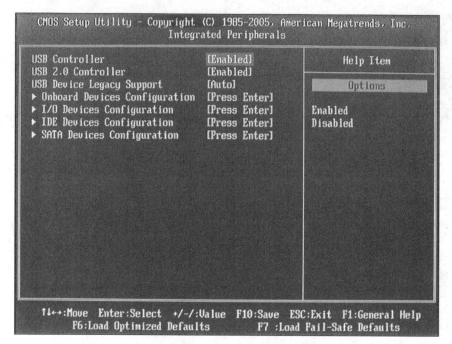

```
    CMOS Setup Utility - Copyright (C) 1985-2005, American Megatrends, Inc.
                           Integrated Peripherals

    USB Controller                [Enabled]              Help Item
    USB 2.0 Controller            [Enabled]
    USB Device Legacy Support     [Auto]                    Options
  ▶ Onboard Devices Configuration [Press Enter]
  ▶ I/O Devices Configuration     [Press Enter]        Enabled
  ▶ IDE Devices Configuration     [Press Enter]        Disabled
  ▶ SATA Devices Configuration    [Press Enter]




    ↑↓←→:Move  Enter:Select  +/-/:Value  F10:Save  ESC:Exit  F1:General Help
          F6:Load Optimized Defaults         F7 :Load Fail-Safe Defaults
```

Onboard Devices Submenu

The Onboard Devices submenu on this system, shown in Figure 7-11, is used to enable or disable newer types of ports, such as IEEE-1394 (FireWire), audio, and Ethernet LAN ports (this system has two). The onboard LAN option ROM is disabled on this system, but should be enabled if you want to boot from an operating system that is stored on a network drive.

I/O Devices Submenu

Most systems separate legacy ports such as floppy, serial (COM), and parallel port (LPT) into their own submenus, as in the I/O Devices submenu in Figure 7-12. Some systems might also have a setting for the PS/2 mouse port on this or another CMOS/BIOS menu.

Figure 7.11   A typical Onboard Devices submenu.

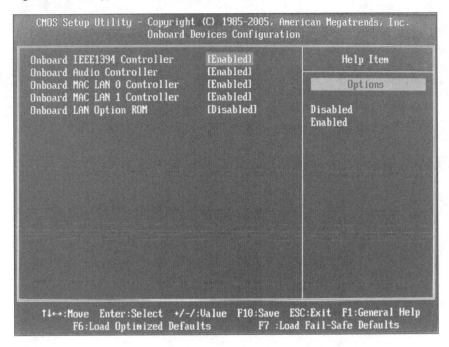

Figure 7-12   A typical I/O Devices submenu.

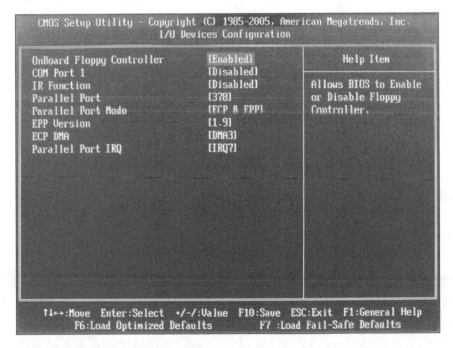

The COM (serial) port is disabled on this system because there are no devices connected to it (most devices that formerly used COM ports, such as modems, pointing devices, and printers, now use USB ports; similarly, most mice that formerly used PS/2 ports now use USB ports). The parallel (LPT) port is enabled because it is used by a printer.

NOTE You should disable ports that are not used to make it easier for the system to assign other ports, such as the ones in the Onboard Devices menu, their own hardware resources.

PATA/IDE and SATA Configuration Menus

The PATA/IDE and SATA configuration menus usually don't need adjustment, except when you need to create a redundant array of inexpensive drives (RAID) array from two or more drives.

Use the SATA configuration menu shown in Figure 7-13 to enable, disable, or specify how many SATA host adapters to make available; to enable or disable SATA RAID; and to configure SATA host adapters to run in compatible (emulating PATA) or native (AHCI) mode. AHCI permits hot-swapping of eSATA drives, and the system shown in Figure 7-13 does not list this option.

Figure 7-13 Typical SATA configuration menu.

```
CMOS Setup Utility - Copyright (C) 1985-2005, American Megatrends, Inc.
                     SATA Devices Configuration

 Serial-ATA Devices          [Device 0/1/2]          Help Item
 nVidia RAID Function         [Disabled]
                                                         Options

                                                    Disabled
                                                    Device 0
                                                    Device 0/1
                                                    Device 0/1/2




 ↑↓←→:Move  Enter:Select  +/-/:Value  F10:Save  ESC:Exit  F1:General Help
           F6:Load Optimized Defaults        F7 :Load Fail-Safe Defaults
```

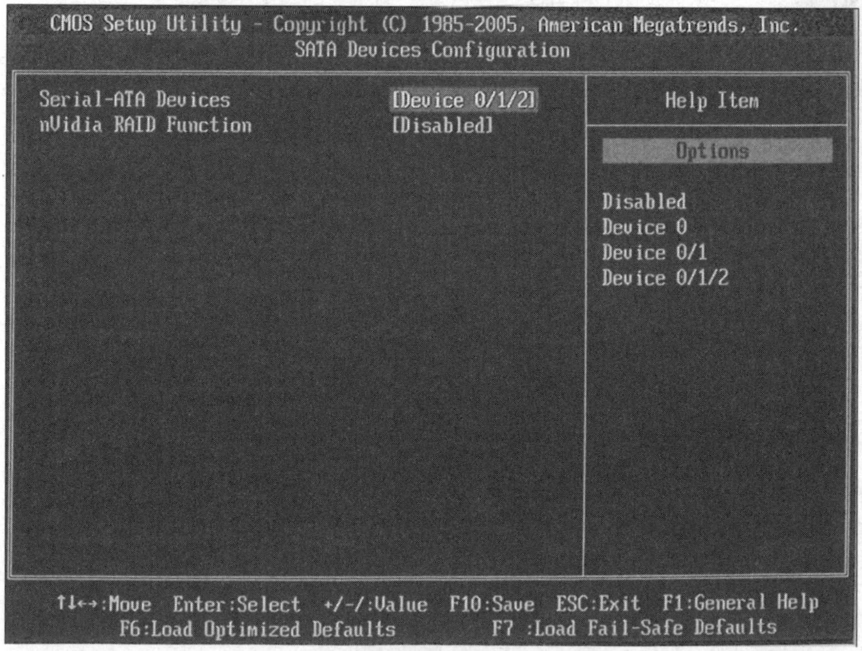

Use the PATA configuration menu shown in Figure 7-14 to enable or disable PATA/IDE host adapters and to enable or disable busmastering. Busmastering should be enabled, as disabling it causes drive access to be slow. When busmastering (the default on most systems) is enabled, the operating system must load chipset-specific drivers to permit this option to work. Many systems (but not the one shown in Figure 7-14) have two or more PATA host adapters and support RAID functions with PATA drives.

Figure 7-14 Typical PATA configuration menu.

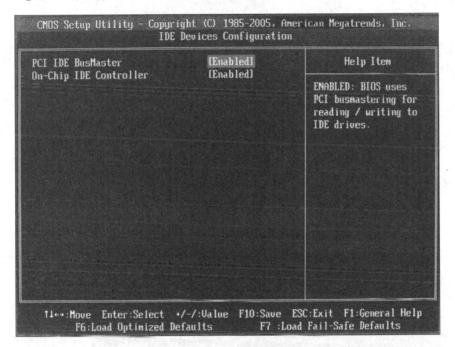

TIP To ensure that the IDE/PATA busmastering feature works properly, install the most up-to-date drivers available for the motherboard. Check the motherboard or system vendor's website for the latest drivers for the version of Windows or other operating system in use.

Power Management Menu

Although Windows includes power management features, the BIOS controls how any given system responds to standby or power-out conditions. Figure 7-15 illustrates a typical power management menu.

Figure 7-15 Typical power management configuration menu.

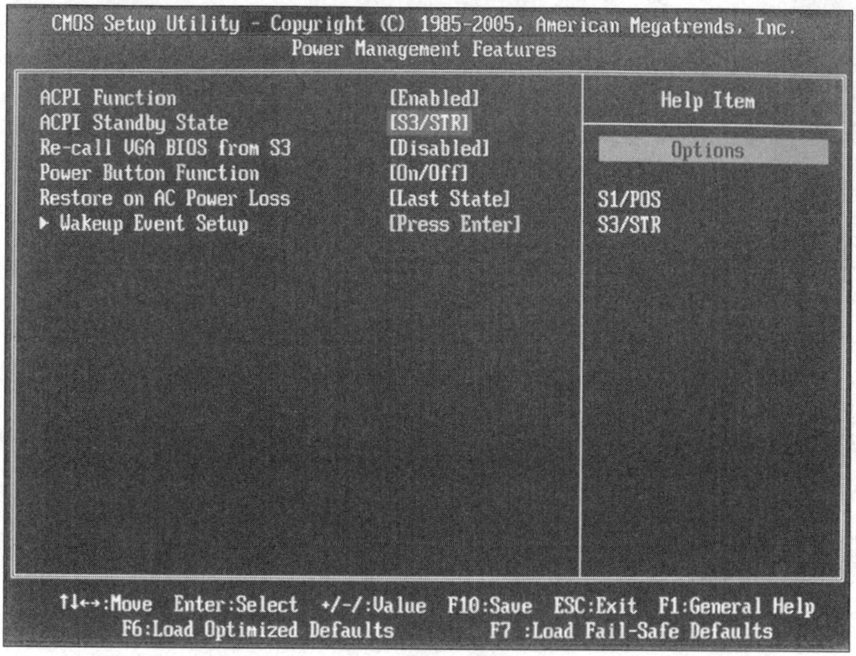

```
     CMOS Setup Utility - Copyright (C) 1985-2005, American Megatrends, Inc.
                          Power Management Features
 ┌───────────────────────────────────────────────┬──────────────────────────┐
 │  ACPI Function              [Enabled]          │        Help Item         │
 │  ACPI Standby State         [S3/STR]           │                          │
 │  Re-call VGA BIOS from S3   [Disabled]         │         Options          │
 │  Power Button Function      [On/Off]           │                          │
 │  Restore on AC Power Loss   [Last State]       │  S1/POS                  │
 │ ▶ Wakeup Event Setup        [Press Enter]      │  S3/STR                  │
 │                                                │                          │
 │                                                │                          │
 │                                                │                          │
 │                                                │                          │
 │                                                │                          │
 │                                                │                          │
 │                                                │                          │
 │                                                │                          │
 │                                                │                          │
 ├────────────────────────────────────────────────────────────────────────┤
 │  ↑↓←→:Move  Enter:Select  +/-/:Value  F10:Save  ESC:Exit  F1:General Help │
 │        F6:Load Optimized Defaults         F7 :Load Fail-Safe Defaults     │
 └──────────────────────────────────────────────────────────────────────────┘
```

ACPI is the power management function used in modern systems, replacing the older APM standard; it should be enabled. Most systems offer two ACPI standby states: S1/POS (power on standby) and S3/STR (suspend to RAM). Use S3/STR whenever possible, as it uses much less power when the system is idle than S1/POS.

You can also configure your system power button, specify how to restart your system if AC power is lost, and specify how to wake up a system from standby, sleep, or hibernation modes, as shown in Figure 7-16.

PnP/PCI Configuration Settings

The PnP/PCI Configuration dialog shown in Figure 7-17 is used to specify which graphics adapter is primary (PCI Express versus PCI or AGP versus PCI), the IRQ settings to use for PCI slots, the settings for the PCI latency timer, and which IRQ and DMA hardware resources to set aside for use by non-PnP devices.

Generally, the default settings do not need to be changed. However, if you need to make a PCI graphics adapter card—rather than a PCI Express or AGP card—the primary graphics adapter, be sure to select **PCI->PCIe** or **PCI->AGP** as appropriate.

Figure 7-16   Configuring Wakeup Events.

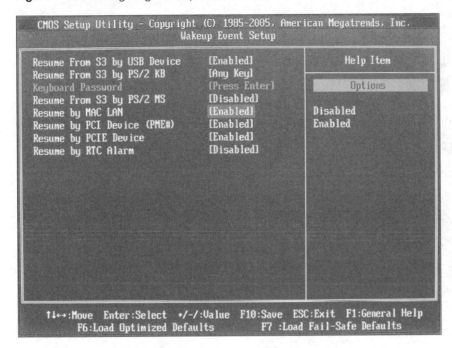

Figure 7-17   Configuring PnP/PCI settings.

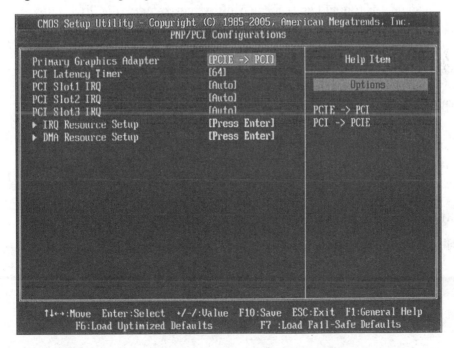

NOTE Most systems have options, as this one does, to reserve IRQ and DMA hardware resources for use by non-PnP adapters, but unless you are managing a system that has non-PnP cards installed (primarily ISA cards, which are now obsolete), there is no need to set aside those resources. If you do set them aside, you must determine the IRQs and DMAs used by these cards and reserve those settings; otherwise, non-PnP cards would not work.

Hardware Monitor

As hot as a small room containing a PC can get, it's a whole lot hotter inside the PC itself. Excessive heat is the enemy of system stability and shortens the life of your hardware. Adding fans can help, but if they fail, you have problems.

The Hardware Monitor screen (sometimes referred to as PC Health) is a common feature in most recent systems. It helps you make sure that your computer's temperature and voltage conditions are at safe levels for your computer (see Figure 7-18), and it sometimes also includes the Chassis Intrusion feature.

Figure 7-18   A typical Hardware Monitor screen.

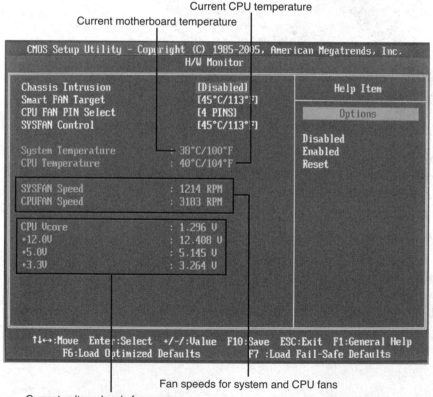

Current CPU temperature

Current motherboard temperature

Fan speeds for system and CPU fans

Current voltage levels for processor,
12V, 5V, and 3.3V connectors

Although it is useful to view temperature and voltage settings in the BIOS setup program, temperature values are usually higher after the computer has been working for awhile (after you've booted to Windows and no longer have access to this screen). Generally, the major value of this screen is that its information can be detected by Windows-based motherboard or system monitoring programs, such as the one shown in Figure 7-19. These programs enable you to be warned immediately if there are any heat- or fan-related problems with your system.

Figure 7-19   A typical Windows-based hardware monitoring program that displays information from the Hardware Monitor feature in the system BIOS.

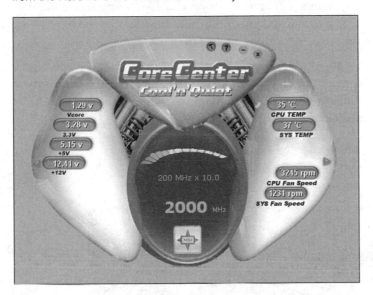

NOTE   Overheating can be caused by improper airflow through the system, a very hot room, or by a power supply that has too low a wattage rating for the devices attached to the power supply (internally or externally).

Processor and Memory Configuration

Some older processors, such as the Athlon XP, do not automatically configure the system BIOS settings for processor clock multiplier and frequency, but newer processors typically do. However, the processor configuration dialog shown in Figure 7-20 is found in performance-oriented systems and displays current settings and enables the user to adjust these and other settings to overclock the system (running its components at faster than normal settings).

Figure 7-20 A typical processor configuration screen. Options shown with * are used for over-clocking.

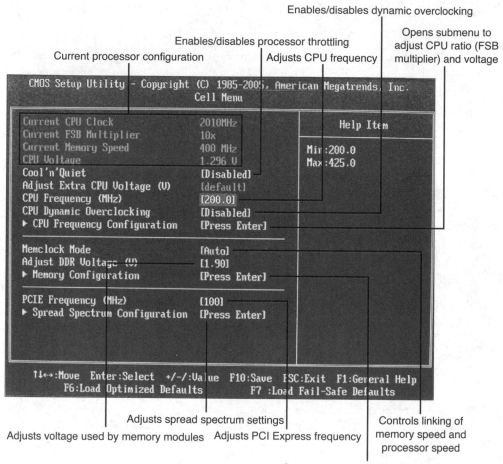

Enables/disables dynamic overclocking

Opens submenu to adjust CPU ratio (FSB multiplier) and voltage

Enables/disables processor throttling

Current processor configuration

Adjusts CPU frequency

Adjusts spread spectrum settings

Adjusts voltage used by memory modules   Adjusts PCI Express frequency

Controls linking of memory speed and processor speed

Opens memory configuration dialog

TIP Some BIOS programs "hide" the processor dialog; you must press a keystroke combination (Control+F1 is a popular choice) to reveal it. BIOS programs in laptops and corporate systems typically don't include a processor configuration dialog.

Generally, you should not adjust processor or memory timings unless you are trying to overclock a system, or if the system does not properly configure your processor or memory.

CAUTION If you make changes to processor or memory settings, and your system no longer boots or is unstable after booting, restart your system, restart the BIOS setup program, and load default or failsafe settings.

Figure 7-21 shows two views of a typical memory configuration screen. The default Auto MCT Timing Mode (see Figure 7-21A) offers limited memory adjustments, while changing the mode to Manual (see Figure 7-21B) enables many more settings and is useful primarily for overclocking and maximum-performance situations.

Figure 7-21 A typical memory configuration dialog in auto mode (A) and manual mode (B).

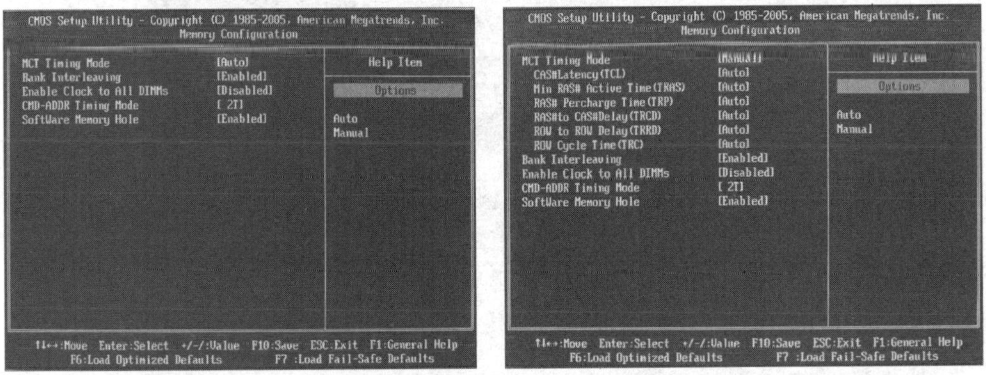

NOTE Before making any changes to memory timing, you should find out what memory modules are installed in the system and check the technical specifications at the memory vendor's website.

TIP If you want to learn more about overclocking, some useful websites include Overclockers (www.overclockers.com), Extreme Overclocking (www.extremeover-clocking.com), Maximum PC (www.maximumpc.com; www.maximumpc.com/forums/), and Tom's Hardware Guide (www.tomshardware.com).

Security Features

Security features of various types are scattered around the typical system BIOS dialogs. These include

- **BIOS password**—BIOS Settings Password or Security dialogs
- **Power-on password**—Configured through the Security dialog

- **Chassis Intrusion**—Various locations

- **Boot sector protection**—Advanced BIOS Features dialog

The BIOS password, also known as the supervisor password, protects the BIOS it-self from unauthorized access. This should be configured on every computer. In addition, it should be changed every six months or earlier.

The power-on password, also known as the user password, is a second password that can be configured in the BIOS. The user must enter this password before the BIOS allows the operating system to boot. Many organizations opt not to use this because they already have a strong username/password authentication scheme in place which resides within the operating system.

Chassis intrusion notification is when the BIOS alerts you to the fact that the computer case has been opened. In secure environments, this is an important part of overall computer security.

Boot sector protection is when the BIOS monitors the boot sector of the hard drive for viruses. If one is found, the BIOS does not allow the operating system to boot unless one of two outcomes is achieved: either the virus is removed from the hard drive (usually by some kind of bootable removable media), or if boot sector protection is disabled in the BIOS.

Some BIOS systems have other security features, such as the ability to disable USB device ports and other ports. By incorporating these various features into the security plan for your computer, you can stave off a lot of the issues that plague computer systems.

Exiting the BIOS and Saving/Discarding Changes

When you exit the BIOS setup program, you can elect to save configuration changes or discard changes. Choose the option to save changes if you made changes you want to keep (see Figure 7-22A). Choose the option to discard changes if you were "just looking" and did not intend to make any changes (see Figure 7-22B). When you exit the BIOS setup program with either option, the system restarts.

Figure 7-22   Typical exit dialogs: saving changes (A) and discarding changes (B).

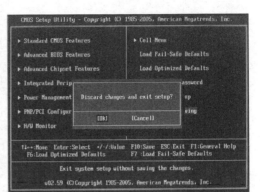

Power-On Self-Test and Error Reporting

Every time you turn on your PC, the BIOS performs one of its most important jobs: the POST (power-on self-test). The POST portion of the BIOS enables the BIOS to find and report errors in the computer's hardware.

The POST checks the following parts of the computer:

■   The CPU and the POST ROM portion of the BIOS

■   The system timer

■   Video display (graphics) card

■   Memory

■   The keyboard

■   The disk drives

You hope the POST always checks out OK. But what happens if the POST encounters a problem? The system stops the boot process if it encounters a serious or fatal error (see the following "Beep Codes" section). During the POST process, the BIOS uses any one of several methods to report problems:

■   Beep codes

■   POST error messages (displayed on the monitor)

■   POST (hex) error codes

The next sections describe each method in detail.

Beep Codes

Beep codes are used by most BIOS versions to indicate either a fatal error or a serious error. A fatal error is an error that is so serious that the computer cannot continue the boot process. A fatal error includes a problem with the CPU, the POST ROM, the system timer, or memory. The serious error that beep codes report is a problem with your video display card or circuit. Although systems can boot without video, seldom would you want to because you can't see what the system is doing.

Beep codes vary by the BIOS maker. Some companies, such as IBM, Acer, and Compaq, create their own BIOS chips and firmware. However, most other major brands of computers and virtually all "clones" use a BIOS made by one of the "Big Three" BIOS vendors: American Megatrends (AMI), Phoenix Technologies, and Award Software (now owned by Phoenix Technologies).

As you might expect, the beep codes and philosophies used by these three companies vary a great deal. AMI, for example, uses beep codes for more than ten fatal errors. It also uses eight beeps to indicate a defective or missing video card. Phoenix uses beep codes for both defects and normal procedures (but has no beep code for a video problem), and the Award BIOS has only a single beep code (one long, two short), indicating a problem with video.

Because beep codes do not report all possible problems during the startup process, you can't rely exclusively on beep codes to help you detect and solve system problems.

The most common beep codes you're likely to encounter are listed in Table 7-3.

Table 7-3   Common System Errors and Their Beep Codes

Beep Codes by BIOS Version				
Problem	**Phoenix BIOS**	**Award BIOS**	**AMI BIOS**	**IBM BIOS**
Memory	Beep sequences: 1-3-4-1 1,3,4,3 1,4,1,1	Beeping (other than 2 long, 1 short)	1 or 3 or 11 beeps 1 long, 3 short beeps	(None)
Video	(none)	2 long, 1 short beep	8 beeps 1 long, 8 short beeps	1 long, 3 short beeps, or 1 beep
Processor or motherboard	Beep sequence: 1-2-2-3	(none)	5 beeps or 9 beeps	1 long, 1 short beep

NOTE For additional beep codes, see the following resources:

- **AMI BIOS**—www.ami.com/support/bios.cfm
- **Phoenix BIOS**—www.phoenix.com/
- **IBM, Dell, Acer, other brands**—www.bioscentral.com

NOTE Don't mix up your boops and beeps! Many systems play a single short boop (usually a bit different in tone than a beep) when the system boots successfully. This is normal.

POST Error Messages

Most BIOS versions do an excellent job of displaying POST error messages indicating what the problem is with the system. These messages can indicate problems with memory, keyboards, hard disk drives, and other components. Some systems document these messages in their manuals, or you can go to the BIOS vendors' website for more information.

NOTE Keep in mind that the system almost always stops after the first error, so if a system has more than one serious or fatal error, the first problem stops the boot process before the video card has been initialized to display error messages.

POST Hex Error Codes

There are beep codes and text messages to tell you that there's a problem with your computer, but there's also a third way your PC can let you know it needs help: by transmitting hexadecimal codes to an I/O port address (usually 80h) that indicate the progress of testing and booting. The hexadecimal codes output by the BIOS change rapidly during a normal startup process as different milestones in the boot process are reached. These codes provide vital clues about what has gone wrong when your system won't boot and you don't have a beep code or onscreen message to help you. It would be handy if systems included some way to view these codes, but most do not (a few systems include a four-LED header cable that displays boot progress, but this is only a partial solution for a system that won't start properly).

To monitor these codes, you need a POST card such as the one shown in Figure 7-23, available from a variety of vendors, including JDR Microdevices (www.jdr.com) and Ultra-X (www.ultra-x.com). These cards are available in versions that plug into either the now-obsolete ISA slot or into PCI or PCI Express x1 expansion slots. The simplest ones have a two-digit LED area that displays the hex codes, whereas

more complicated (and expensive) models also have additional built-in tests. Some vendors also offer POST display devices that plug into parallel ports; these are useful for monitoring system startup without opening the case on both desktop and portable systems that include parallel ports.

Figure 7-23   This POST card plugs into a PCI slot.

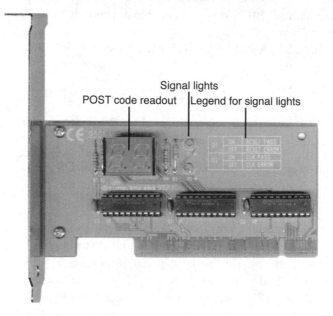

Signal lights

POST code readout   Legend for signal lights

The same hex code has different meanings to different BIOS versions. For example, POST code 31h means "display (video) memory read/write test" on an AMI BIOS, but it means "test base and extended memory" on the Award BIOS, and it is not used on Phoenix BIOS. As with other types of error messages, check your manual or the BIOS manufacturer's website for the meaning of any given code.

> **TIP**   The worst time to learn how to interpret a POST card is when your system's sick. On the other hand, the best way to learn to use a POST card is to plug it into a healthy system and watch the codes change during a normal system startup. Typically, the codes change quickly until the final code (often "FF") is reached and the system starts. On a defective system, the codes pause or stop when a defective item on the system is tested. The cards don't need to be left in systems routinely.

BIOS Updates

You can regard the BIOS chip as the "glue" that binds the hardware to the operating system. If the BIOS doesn't recognize the operating system or the hardware it communicates with, you're sure to have problems.

Because the BIOS chip bridges hardware to the operating system, you need to update the BIOS whenever your current BIOS version is unable to properly support

- New hardware, such as large SATA and PATA/IDE hard drives and different types of removable-storage drives
- Faster CPUs
- New operating systems and features
- New BIOS options

Although you can use software drivers as workarounds for hard drive BIOS limitations, a true BIOS update is the best solution for hard disk control, and the only solution if your BIOS can't handle new processors or operating systems.

If you keep your computer for more than a year or so, or if you decide to install a new processor, you might need to upgrade the BIOS. Back in the 1980s into the early 1990s, a BIOS update required a physical chip swap and, sometimes, reprogramming the chip with a device called an *EEPROM burner*. If the replacement or reprogrammed BIOS chip was installed incorrectly into the socket, it could be destroyed.

Fortunately, since the mid 1990s, you can now perform a BIOS update with software. The Flash BIOS chips in use on practically every recent system contain a special type of memory that can be changed through a software download from the system or motherboard maker.

Although Flash BIOS updates are easier to perform than the older replace-the-chip style, you still need to be careful. An incomplete or incorrect BIOS update prevents your system from being accessed. No BIOS, no boot! Regardless of the method, for maximum safety, the following initial steps are recommended:

Step 1.   Back up important data.

Step 2.   Record the current BIOS configuration, especially hard disk settings as discussed earlier in this chapter.

CAUTION   You might need to re-enter BIOS configuration information after a BIOS update, especially if you must install a different chip.

Flash BIOS Update

So you've decided you need a Flash BIOS update. Where do you get it? Don't ask the BIOS manufacturers (Phoenix, AMI, and Award/Phoenix). They don't sell BIOS updates because their basic products are modified by motherboard and system vendors.

Here are the general steps for performing a Flash BIOS update:

Step 1.   For major brands of computers, go to the vendor's website and look for "downloads" or "tech support" links. The BIOS updates are listed by system model and by version; avoid beta (pre-release) versions.

TIP   If your system is a generic system (that is, it came with a "mainboard" or "motherboard" manual and other component manuals rather than a full system manual), you need to contact the motherboard maker. Some systems indicate the maker during bootup. Others display only a mysterious series of numbers. You can decode these numbers to get the motherboard's maker. See the following websites for details:

- Wim's BIOS page (www.wimsbios.com)

- eSupport (www.biosagentplus.com)

- American Megatrend's BIOS Support page (www.ami.com/support/bios.cfm)

You can also buy replacement flash BIOS code from eSupport if you are unable to get updated BIOS code from your system or motherboard vendor.

Step 2.   Download the correct BIOS update for your system or motherboard. For generic motherboards, Wim's BIOS page also has links to the motherboard vendors' websites.

Step 3.   You might also need to download a separate loader program, or the download might contain both the loader and the BIOS image. If the website has instructions posted, print or save them to a floppy disk for reference.

Step 4.   Next, install the BIOS update loader and BIOS image to a floppy disk. Follow the vendor's instructions.

NOTE   Some BIOS updates can be done within Windows XP and Vista. If this is the case, just double-click the BIOS executable to begin the upgrade; a system restart is necessary.

Step 5.   After installation is complete, restart your system with the floppy disk containing the upgrade; make sure the floppy disk is the first item in the BIOS boot sequence. Press a key if necessary to start the upgrade process.

Some upgrades run automatically; others require that you choose the image from a menu, and still others require the actual filename of the BIOS. The BIOS update might also prompt you to save your current BIOS image to a floppy disk. Choose this option if possible so you have a copy of your current BIOS in case there's a problem.

Step 6.   After the update process starts, it takes about three minutes to rewrite the contents of the BIOS chip with the updated information.

CAUTION   While performing a Flash upgrade, make sure that you don't turn off the power to your PC and that you keep children or pets away from the computer to prevent an accidental shutdown (read: your four-year-old decides to unplug the computer). Wait for a message indicating the BIOS update has been completed before you even think about touching the computer. If the power goes out during the Flash update, the BIOS chip could be rendered useless.

Step 7.   Remove the floppy disk and restart the system to use your new BIOS features. Reconfigure the BIOS settings if necessary.

TIP   Some motherboards have a jumper on the motherboard that can be set to write-protect the Flash BIOS. Take a quick look at your documentation before you start the process and disable this jumper first. Then, reenable the write-protect jumper when you're finished with the upgrade.

Recovering from a Failed BIOS Update

If the primary system BIOS is damaged, keep in mind that some motherboard vendors offer dual BIOS chips on some products. You can switch to the secondary BIOS if the primary BIOS stops working.

If you use the wrong Flash BIOS file to update your BIOS, or if the update process doesn't finish, your system can't start. You might need to contact the system or motherboard maker for service or purchase a replacement BIOS chip.

Some BIOSs contain a "mini-BIOS" that can be reinstalled from a reserved part of the chip. Systems with this feature have a jumper on the motherboard called the Flash recovery jumper.

To use this feature, download the correct Flash BIOS, make the floppy disk, and take it to the computer with the defective BIOS. Set the jumper to Recovery, insert the floppy disk, and rerun the setup process. Listen for beeps and watch for the drive light to run during this process, because the video won't work. Turn off the computer, reset the jumper to Normal, and restart the computer.

If the update can't be installed, your motherboard might have a jumper that write-protects the Flash BIOS. Check the manual to see if your system has this feature. To update a BIOS on a system with a write-protected jumper, you must follow these steps:

Step 1.   Disable the write-protection.

Step 2.   Perform the update.

Step 3.   Reenable the write-protection to keep unauthorized people from changing the BIOS.

BIOS Chip Replacement

On motherboards whose BIOS programs can't be upgraded with software, you might be able to purchase a replacement BIOS from vendors such as eSupport or BIOSMAN (www.biosman.com). Before you order a BIOS chip replacement, consider the following:

- BIOS chip upgrades cost about $30–40 each.

- Although the BIOS will be updated, the rest of the system might still be out of date. If your system is more than two years old and is not fast enough for your needs, you might be better off buying a replacement motherboard or system.

- A replacement BIOS enables you to improve system operation without reinstalling Windows.

If you still need to update the BIOS chip itself, first verify that the vendor has the correct BIOS chip replacement. The replacement needs to

- Plug into your current motherboard; as you saw in Figure 7-1, some BIOS chips are square, and others are rectangular.

- Support your motherboard/chipset.

- Provide the features you need (such as support for larger hard disks, particular processor speeds, and so on).

It might be a different brand of BIOS than your current BIOS. If so, make sure that you have recorded your hard drive information. You need to re-enter this and other manually configured options into the new BIOS chip's setup program.

How does the BIOS vendor know what your system uses? The vendor identifies the BIOS chip you need by the motherboard ID information displayed at bootup. eSupport offers a free download utility to display this information for you. To replace the chip, follow these steps:

Step 1. Locate the BIOS chip on your motherboard after you open the case to perform the upgrade. It sometimes has a sticker listing the BIOS maker and model number. If not, go to Step 2.

Step 2. Socketed BIOS chips might be in a DIP-type package (rectangular with legs on two sides) or in a PLCC (Plastic Leaded Chip Carrier; square with connectors on four sides). Refer to Figure 7-1. The vendor typically supplies a chip extraction tool to perform the removal.

Step 3. Use the chip extraction tool to remove the BIOS chip. Don't try to remove the chip all at once; gently loosen each connected side until the chip can be lifted free.

Step 4. Remove the existing BIOS chip carefully and put it on antistatic material in case you need to reuse it in that system.

Step 5. Align the new BIOS chip with the socket. Note that a DIP-type BIOS can be installed backward (which destroys the chip when power is turned on), so be sure to align the dimpled end of the chip with the cutout end of the socket. PLCC BIOS chips have one corner cut out.

Step 6. Adjust the legs on a new DIP-type BIOS chip so it fits into the sockets, and press it down until the legs on both sides are inserted fully. Press the PLCC BIOS chip into the socket.

Step 7. Double-check the alignment and leg positions on the BIOS chip before you start the system; if the chip is aligned with the wrong end of the socket, you'll destroy it when the power comes on.

Step 8. Turn on the system, and use the new BIOS's keystroke(s) to start the setup program to re-enter any information. You might get a "CMOS" error at startup, which is normal with a new BIOS chip. After you re-enter the BIOS data from your printout and save the changes, the system runs without error messages.

NOTE A "CMOS Checksum" error is normal after you replace the BIOS chip. However, after you run the BIOS setup program and save the settings, this error should go away. If you continue to see this error, test the motherboard battery. If the battery checks out okay, contact the motherboard or system vendor for help.

Chapter Review Questions

The following questions test your recall of the concepts described in this chapter. The answers are listed at the end of the questions in the "Answers and Explanations" section.

1. What is the CMOS memory used for?

    A. Keeping the time

    B. To store BIOS settings

    C. To boot the computer

    D. None of these options is correct

2. What happens when the CMOS battery fails?

    A. All the CMOS configuration information is lost.

    B. The computer won't boot.

    C. The computer is destroyed.

    D. The motherboard is dead.

3. To make changes to the default settings in the BIOS, what must you do at startup?

    A. Press the F2 key

    B. Press Enter

    C. Press the F8 key

    D. Hold down the shift key

4. What BIOS settings allow you to automatically configure your system? (Choose all that apply.)

    A. BIOS defaults

    B. Setup defaults

    C. Turbo

    D. Function

5. Which of the following does not work when configuring or viewing BIOS settings?

   A. Esc key

   B. Enter key

   C. The + key

   D. The mouse

6. Of the following system information, which can be viewed in the BIOS? (Choose all that apply.)

   A. Installed memory (RAM)

   B. BIOS information

   C. Processor type

   D. Processor speed

   E. L2 cache memory

   F. Feature settings

7. What features can be found in the advanced BIOS settings? (Choose two.)

   A. Enable quick boot

   B. Change the clock

   C. View information

   D. Enable boot sector protection

8. In today's most recent systems, what common feature is used to help prevent excessive heat from damaging you computer?

   A. Task Manager

   B. System Monitor

   C. Hardware Monitor

   D. Drive Lock

9. Which of the following security features are included in most of the currently used BIOS programs?

A. BIOS password

B. Power-on password

C. Chassis Intrusion

D. Boot sector protection

E. All these options are correct

10. What option would you use if you are in the BIOS of your computer and you want to exit without making any changes? (Choose all that apply.)

A. Save Configuration

B. Discard Changes

C. Hit the Esc key

D. Press F8 to return to desktop

11. When you start your computer, it performs an important test. What is this test known as?

A. CPU processing

B. POST

C. A CMOS test

D. Hard drive test

12. What are BIOS beep codes used for? (Choose two.)

A. A fatal error

B. A system message

C. A serious error

D. A warning message

13. If you are installing a new drive in your computer and it is not recognized, what can you do to fix the problem?

A. Update the BIOS

B. Call the company of the new drive

C. Search for problems on the Internet

D. Refer to the information that came with the drive

14. What is the process called when upgrading the BIOS?

    A. Putting a new BIOS chip on the motherboard

    B. Removing the CMOS battery

    C. Flashing the BIOS

    D. Windows Update

15. Which of the following ROM types can be flashed?

    A. ROM

    B. PROM

    C. EPROM

    D. EEPROM

Case Study 1

You have just started up your computer. It gives off a series of loud beeps and does not boot. What would you need to do to determine what the beeps mean and how to fix the problem?

Case Study 2

Examine the motherboard of your home or lab computer. Attempt to locate the BIOS component. Then, access the motherboard manufacturer's website, download the technical manual for the motherboard, and check your findings. Most motherboard technical documents have a diagram of the motherboard pointing out each of the components. When you are finished, locate the latest flash download for your particular motherboard.

Answers and Explanations

1. B. CMOS memory, also referred to as non-volatile memory, is used to store BIOS settings and should not be confused with system memory (RAM). CMOS stands for complimentary metal-oxide semiconductor.

2. A. If the CMOS battery fails, it loses all information, such as time/date, CPU information, and drive types.

3. **A.** Most motherboards use either a function key, the Delete key, or a combination of keys to enter the BIOS setup program. Which key you use depends on the manufacture of the motherboard. F2 is a common key when entering the BIOS, as are F1, F10, and Delete. The F8 key is not used by BIOS programs; it is used by the Windows Advanced Options Boot menu when accessing options such as Safe Mode.

4. **A, B, C.** Many BIOS versions enable you to automatically configure your system with a choice of these options from the main menu.

5. **D.** Usually, you do not have access to the mouse when you are configuring the BIOS setup. You must use the keyboard.

6. **A, B, C, D, E.** The type and speed of the processor, amount of RAM, amount of cache memory, and the details of the BIOS program can all be viewed from within BIOS setup. Feature settings refers to the ability to configure various features of the operating system.

7. **A, D.** When accessing the BIOS advanced settings, some of the features available are quick boot, which skips memory and drive test to enable faster startups, and also enables protection against boot sector viruses.

8. **C.** The Hardware Monitor screen (sometimes referred to as PC Health) is a common feature in most recent systems. It helps you make sure that your computer's temperature and voltage conditions are at safe levels for your computer, and it sometimes also includes the Chassis Intrusion feature.

9. **E.** Security features of various types are scattered around the typical system BIOS dialogs. All of the features listed can be used to secure your computer systems from hackers or unauthorized personnel.

10. **B, C.** When you are in the BIOS and are not planning on making any changes, be sure to click Discard Changes after pressing Esc to prevent accidental changes.

11. **B.** Each and every time you start your computer, it goes through a test known as POST or power-on self test. If the BIOS finds any errors with the system, it notifies you by error messages known as beep codes.

12. **A, C.** Beep codes are used by most BIOS versions to indicate either a fatal error or a serious error. A fatal error is an error that is so serious that the computer cannot continue the boot process. A fatal error includes a problem with the CPU, the POST ROM, the system timer, or memory. Serious error beep codes report a problem with your video display card or circuit. Although systems can boot without video, you do not want to boot without video because you can't see what the system is doing.

13. **A.** Sometimes the BIOS does not support newer technologies. When making changes to the systems, such as adding a faster CPU or a larger SATA or PATA drive, you might need to update the BIOS.

14. **C.** When it is time for a BIOS update, go to the manufacturer's website to see if a new update has been released. Flashing the BIOS is the act of erasing all of the BIOS's current contents and writing a new BIOS to the BIOS chip. You can do this by booting off of a special floppy disk, from CD-ROM, and from within Windows. This process is now much easier than it used to be, but to be safe, you should still back up your BIOS settings before performing this task.

15. **D.** EEPROM (electrically erasable programmable read-only memory) can be erased completely so that new settings can be "flashed" to the memory chip. ROM cannot be flashed. PROM can be programmed but not erased. EPROM can be erased but uses an ultraviolet light to do so. This type of chip is uncommon in PCs.

Case Study 1 Solution

First, you need to determine who the manufacturer of the motherboard or the particular BIOS is. Then you should go to the website and download the manual for the motherboard or a copy of the beep codes for the BIOS. Reboot the computer and count the beeps and compare with the chart. It could be as easy as re-seating the RAM memory modules, or it could be a video problem.

Case Study 2 Solution

For example, information about all Intel motherboards can be found at the following link:

www.intel.com/products/motherboard/index.htm

Let's say we are using the same motherboard we used in the previous chapter case studies— the Intel DP35DP. We could go to the Intel site and search for the motherboard in a variety of ways on the website. In some cases, it might be easier to just search for the motherboard within your favorite search engine. The support page for this particular motherboard is

www.intel.com/p/en_US/support/highlights/dsktpboards/dp35dp

From here, the BIOS can be located and installed. Many motherboards allow you to update directly within Windows. However, older motherboards need to be updated with some sort of bootable removable media, such as floppy disk or CD-ROM.

Also note that all the links to technical specifications and troubleshooting are listed here. If you have issues with your motherboard or BIOS, this is an excellent resource.

This chapter covers the following subjects:

- **Types of Operating Systems**—In this section, we briefly discuss the three main types of computer operating systems you encounter: Windows, Linux, and Mac.

- **Differences in Windows Versions**—This section teaches you how to differentiate between Windows 7/Vista and XP. The graphical user interfaces (GUI) are different as well as the hardware requirements necessary to run each operating system.

- **Windows Interfaces**—This section talks about the tools you use to interface with Windows such as Windows Explorer, Computer/My Computer, Control Panel, Command Prompt, Network/My Network Places, as well as the Start menu, taskbar, and System Tray.

- **Disk Partition, File and Folder Management**—In this section, you learn about the different types of partitions (primary, extended, and so on), and how to work with, and back up, files and folders effectively.

- **System Management Tools**—Keeping the system well managed is important. This section covers tools such as Device Manager, Task Manager, Registry Editor (Regedit), and System Restore, which help to administer a sparkling Windows operating system.

Operating Systems

Until now, we have focused on hardware and sprinkled in little bits of software here and there. That's about to change. This chapter goes into depth concerning the fundamentals of Windows 7/Vista and Windows XP. When you are done with this chapter, you might even want to read it again because there is so much information packed in it.

There is a slight amount of Windows 2000 in this chapter as well; however most of the concepts and techniques used in Windows 2000 work the same way in Windows XP. Unless Windows 2000 is specifically mentioned, you can safely assume that any time XP is described, the concept is the same for Windows 2000.

You might ask why there is so much Windows XP content within this chapter. Well, even though XP is nearly a decade old, there are still a slew of companies using it. Consequently, it is very important to know. Windows Vista and Windows 7 are currently the newest operating systems by Microsoft, but they have not reached the saturation of Windows XP, even combined. Although other operating systems exist such as Macintosh and Linux, Windows is by far the most prevalent client-computer operating, and is therefore the focus of this chapter.

Note that you sometimes see references to Windows 7/Vista's "Computer" and Windows XP's equivalent "My Computer" within the same sentence. Sometimes this is written as Computer/My Computer or My Computer/Computer. The same holds true for other Windows interfaces that have undergone name changes with the advent of Windows Vista.

There is a lot of content to cover in this chapter. So, without further ado, let's demonstrate how to use and manage Windows!

Types of Operating Systems

There are many types of operating systems for computers, but the three most commonly used with standard client computers are Windows, Mac OS, and Linux. A client operating system is one that you might use at home or at the

workplace. It is generally a part of a larger network controlled by servers and other devices.

This section describes Mac OS and Linux briefly and then describes Windows, the most common client operating system, which is covered in more depth as we progress through the chapter.

Mac OS

Mac OS is the proprietary operating system used by Apple for their Macintosh computers. This operating system (and the Mac computer in general) has been a favorite of multimedia designers, graphic artists, and musicians since the 1990s. It is estimated that no more than 10% of the U.S. population uses the Mac OS.

Mac OS has used version numbers since its inception. Originally, it was simply named "System," but as of version 7.6 was titled Mac OS officially. During these early versions, the operating system could be run only on Macintosh computers that had Motorola processors. However, in 2002, Apple introduced Mac OS X (OS 10), which could be run on Macintosh computers with PowerPC or Intel processors. As of version 10.6 (known as Snow Leopard), the OS only runs on Macintosh computers with Intel platforms. Apple also updates the operating system with what are known as point releases. For example, in June of 2010, Apple released the 10.6.4 point release, updating the Snow Leopard OS and making it more secure.

Although Macintosh computers have Intel processors, they are not PCs. Likewise, the Mac OS is not compatible with PC hardware, and PC-based operating systems, such as Windows and Linux, do not normally run on Macintosh computers.

Mac OS now has specialized versions developed for devices such as the iPhone and iPod. These are streamlined OSes with a smaller footprint that use less resources.

The Mac OS (and Apple in general) is credited with making the graphical user interface (GUI) that people manipulate with a mouse and keyboard—the mainstream way of working with the computer. Mac OS X takes this to a new level by using anti-aliasing, ColorSync, and drop shadow technologies to create a more exciting and fluid interface. Mac OS uses control panels (windows with icons) to configure, troubleshoot, and maintain the computer. This is similar to the Microsoft Windows Control Panel, though different functions have varying names and locations. Some applications are ported for the Mac OS (for example, Microsoft Office for Mac) however, Mac OS uses its own web browser named Safari as opposed to Internet Explorer. Other web browsers such as Firefox can be run on Mac OS X as well.

Linux

Linux is an ever-expanding group of operating systems that are similar to Unix in their design. However, they are meant to run on PCs, gaming consoles, DVRs, mobile phones, and many other devices. Originally, Linux was designed as an alternative operating system to Windows. Currently, it is estimated that no more than 1 to 2% of the U.S. population uses Linux on PCs. However, Linux has a much larger market share when it comes to servers and other computer devices, and in those markets, the percentage is growing rapidly.

Linux was originally written by Linus Torvalds (thus the name) and can be freely downloaded by anyone. Several companies emerged, developing this free code (or a variant of the free code) into their own versions of Linux, which are referred to as distributions. Some examples of these distributions include Ubuntu, SuSE, Red Hat, and Knoppix. Although Linux is free to download, it is licensed under a General Public License, simply known as a GPL. This states that derived works can only be distributed under the same license terms as the software itself.

Linux users have the option of using one of a few GUIs that are similar to the Mac OS GUI. The two most popular GUI environments are GNOME and KDE. GNOME stands for GNU Network Object Model Environment. A graphical user interface that runs on top of the Linux operating system, it consists solely of free and open source software. Its emphasis is on simplicity and accessibility while endeavoring to use a low amount of resources. KDE previously stood for K Desktop Environment, but has since been renamed to KDE Software Compilation. The applications within the environment are meant to run on various Linux platforms but can also be compiled to run in Windows and Mac OS X. KDE is a more powerful environment that includes a web browser called Konqueror. There are many programs for Linux that are available that are just about the equivalent to Microsoft applications. For example, OpenOffice is free software that can be used to create word processing documents, spreadsheets, and so on. Newer versions of Microsoft Office are offering a limited amount of compatibility with OpenOffice documents.

The command-line functionality in most Linux distributions is in-depth and well documented, allowing a user to configure, and troubleshoot, just about anything from within the "shell" or command-line. To learn more about any commands the operating system usually has built-in manual (MAN) pages that are also accessible online.

Windows

By far, Windows is the most commonly used operating system on client computers. It is estimated that up to 90% of client computers use one of the various Windows versions. Windows is a series of operating systems released by Microsoft. Originally,

Windows was simply a GUI that was loaded on top of MS-DOS (or other DOS version). This was the case from versions 1–3, but with the advent of Windows 95, Windows became an all-in-one operating system/GUI. There are also versions of Windows used by servers (such as Windows Server 2003 and 2008) and by mobile and compact devices (such as Windows CE), but this chapter focuses on the client operating systems. The Windows operating systems that have the largest amount of usage as of 2010, in order, are Windows XP, Windows 7, and Windows Vista, according to NetMarketShare.com.

Windows incorporates many applications for the end-user including a web browser (Internet Explorer), a word processor (WordPad), a command-line interface (Command Prompt), a file-managing application (Windows Explorer), and much more. Some end-users also make extensive use of Microsoft Office (Word, Excel, Outlook, PowerPoint, and Access) and many other third-party applications. Because Windows has the highest saturation in the market, third-party application developers focus the most on compiling programs that run effectively on Windows.

Throughout the rest of this chapter, we discuss Windows in more depth.

Differences in Windows Versions

It is important to know the differences between Windows 7, Vista, and XP, and the minimum hardware requirements necessary to install each of the operating systems. We start with Windows 7/Vista and XP's graphical user interface (GUI), which is what Windows employs to interact with the user. Normally, a keyboard and pointing device such as a mouse are used to input information to the operating system's GUI, and whatever is input is shown on the screen. Basically everything you see on the display, including windows, icons, menus, and other visual indicators, is part of the GUI. Following the GUI section, we discuss system requirements for the different versions of Windows.

GUI

The Windows Vista GUI, shown in Figure 8-1, is similar to Windows 7 but different in several ways from Windows XP:

- **Windows Aero**—The Windows Vista visual experience features translucent windows, window animations, three-dimensional viewing of windows, and a modified taskbar. You can make modifications to the look of Aero by right-clicking the desktop and selecting **Personalize** and then clicking **Windows Color and Appearance**. From here, you can modify things such as the transparency of windows. To disable Windows Aero, click the **Theme** link from within the Personalize window. Then, from the Theme drop-down menu, select **Windows Classic**.

- **Welcome Center**—This window opens automatically when you first start Windows Vista. After installing the operating system, it a good starting point for running initial tasks, such as connecting to the Internet, transferring files from another computer, adding users, and learning more about Windows Vista. The Welcome Center continues to show up every time you start Windows unless you deselect the checkbox to the bottom left of the window. To open Welcome Center later, go to **Control Panel**, **System and Maintenance**.

- **Windows Sidebar and gadgets**—The Windows Sidebar in Windows Vista is a new window pane on the side of the desktop. It is primarily used to house gadgets. Gadgets are mini applications that provide a variety of services, such as connecting to the Web to access weather updates and traffic or Internet radio streams. They can also interact with other applications to streamline the Windows experience. You can download additional gadgets from Microsoft. You can modify the Sidebar by right-clicking on it and selecting **Properties**. From here, you can select whether the Sidebar starts when Windows does, place it above other Windows, change its orientation, and remove gadgets. To add gadgets, click the **+** directly over the topmost gadget. Windows 7 does away with the Sidebar by default, but gadgets are used in the same fashion and can be stored directly on the desktop.

- **Modified Start menu**—The Start menu in Windows Vista has a few changes compared to Windows XP. For example, there is a useful search field directly above the Start button. However, the Run prompt has been removed by default, but can be added by accessing the taskbar and Start Menu Properties window. The Start menu and desktop can also be configured to run in Classic mode. In Classic mode, the Start menu displays the name of the operating system along the left side in the same way that earlier versions of Windows display the name. This is usually done to optimize Windows performance.

Figure 8-1 Windows Vista's Standard desktop and Start menu (A) and Classic Desktop and Start menu (B).

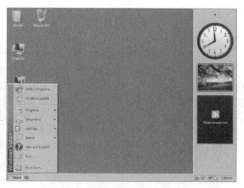

A   B

The Windows XP GUI has several differences compared to its predecessor Windows 2000:

- **Personalized start menu**—Windows XP offers a personalized start menu for each user.

- **Two-column start menu**—As shown in Figure 8-2A; the left column displays the most recently or frequently used programs and access to default applications for Internet and email, while the right column provides access to the user's documents folders and Control Panel. To see all programs, hover your mouse over **All Programs**.

- **Taskbar**—The task bar adjusts in size according to the number of programs that are running and the number of quick launch icons in use.

- **Classic mode**—Start menu and desktop can also be configured to run in a Classic mode similar to the one used by Windows 2000 (Figure 8-2B). In Classic mode, the Start menu displays the name of the operating system along the left side in the same way that earlier versions of Windows display the name.

Figure 8-2   Windows XP's standard desktop and Start menu (A) and classic desktop and Start menu (B).

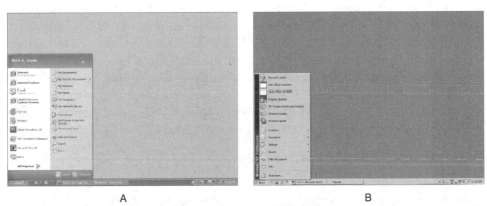

A   B

> **NOTE**   To change only the Start menu to the Classic mode, right-click the **Start** button, select **Properties**, and choose **Classic Start** menu. To change the Start menu and the desktop to the Classic mode as in Figure 8-2B, open the **Display** properties sheet, select **Themes**, and select **Windows Classic**. You can open the **Display** properties sheet from the Control Panel or by right-clicking an empty area of the desktop and selecting **Properties**.

System Requirements

System requirements for different versions of Windows vary widely. Table 8-1 compares the hardware requirements for Windows 7, Vista, XP, and 2000.

Table 8-1   Minimum Hardware Requirements for Windows 7, Vista, XP, and 2000

Component	Windows 7	Vista	XP	2000 Professional
Processor	1GHz	800MHz	233MHz	133MHz
RAM	1GB (32-bit)			
	2GB (64-bit)	512MB	64MB	64MB
Free disk space	16GB (32-bit)			
	20GB (64-bit)	15GB (20GB partition)	1.5GB (2GB partition)	650MB (2GB partition)
Other	DVD-ROM drive	DVD-ROM or CD-ROM drive	CD-ROM or DVD-ROM	CD-ROM/Floppy drive

NOTE   The specs in Table 8-1 are the *minimum* requirements. For example, Microsoft recommends a 1GHz processor for all versions of Vista, and 1GB of RAM plus a 40GB HDD for Vista Home Premium/Business/Ultimate, with similar recommendations for Win7.

You might hear the terms x86 and x64. x86 refers to older CPU names that ended in an "86." For example, the 80386 (shortened to just 386), 486, or 586 CPU and so on. Generally, when people use the term x86, they are referring to 32-bit CPUs that allow for 4GB of address space. x64 (or x86-64) refers to newer 64-bit CPUs that are a superset of the x86 architecture. This technology can run 64-bit software as well as 32-bit software and can address a maximum of 1 TB.

Windows Vista and Windows XP come in 64- and 32-bit versions, so that users from both generations of computers can run the software efficiently. Windows 2000 Professional was designed for 32-bit CPUs only.

Windows Interfaces

Windows features a variety of user interfaces, from Windows Explorer to the Start menu. The following sections discuss the major features of each.

Windows Explorer

Windows Explorer is the file-management utility used by Windows (see Figure 8-3). Windows can use Explorer to view both local drive/network and Internet content. In Windows XP, it integrates tightly with My Computer and Internet Explorer. However, in Windows 7/Vista and Windows XP systems using Internet Explorer 7 or higher, Windows Explorer launches a new process when connecting to Internet sites.

Figure 8-3 The Windows Explorer in Windows XP; the selected object's name appears in the Address bar.

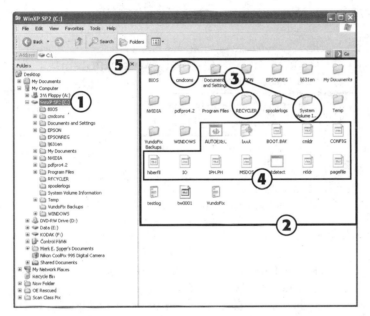

1. Selected object (C: drive)
2. Contents of C: drive (default large icons view)
3. Hidden and system folders
4. Hidden and system files
5. Click to switch to Common Tasks View

By default, Windows Explorer doesn't display hidden and system files unless the View options are changed.

You can start Windows Explorer in any of the following ways in Windows:

- From the Start menu, click **Start**, **All Programs**, **Accessories**, **Windows Explorer**.

- Open the Run prompt, type **Explorer**, and press **Enter**.

- Open My Computer to start Explorer automatically.

After you have opened Windows Explorer, you can view and organize the information in a variety of ways. In Windows XP, the Common Tasks view shows up by

default, although this can be customized to the user's needs. Windows Vista includes the stacks view, which groups files together.

Common Tasks View

When you start My Computer in Windows XP, the Common Tasks view shown in Figure 8-4 is displayed by default. The Common Tasks view displays the properties of the selected object and displays a preview when available. However, the most significant feature is the changeable task pane in the upper-left side of the display. In Windows Vista, this has been replaced by Favorite Links.

Figure 8-4 The Common Tasks view of a folder in Windows XP. The Details pane at the lower left displays a preview of the selected file as well as its properties. The File and Folder Tasks task pane at the upper left changes its name and contents to provide task options suitable for the folder or selected object.

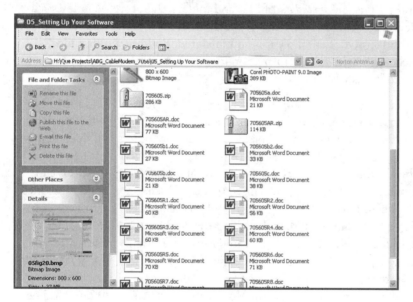

The contents and name of the task pane change according to the characteristics of the selected or displayed object. For example, display My Computer, and the task pane is titled System Tasks, with a choice of options such as View System Information, Add or Remove Programs, or Change a Setting. The contents of Other Places also changes to display related objects.

TIP   To switch between Common Tasks and Classic view, click the **Folders** icon on the toolbar.

Windows Vista Additions to Windows Explorer

The version of Windows Explorer in Windows Vista incorporates the Stacks view, which groups files according to what is specified by the user. You can click the stacks to filter the files shown in Windows Explorer. You also have the ability to save searches as virtual folders or Search Folders. Another new addition to Windows Explorer in Vista is the Details pane, which displays information relating to the currently selected file or folder.

Windows 7 Additions to Windows Explorer

The Windows 7 version of Windows Explorer incorporates *libraries*, which are user-defined collections of folders that act as logical representations of the user's content. This feature enables faster indexing and searching of important and commonly used documents, even if they are spread throughout the entire computer. This is done by analyzing file properties and *metadata* of files and folders; therefore, Windows 7 libraries are commonly known as *metafolders*. Metadata is information that describes a file's definition and structure and how it is administered. Building on that idea, metafolders such as libraries have information that describes the definition and structure of the contents within.

The Libraries portion of Windows Explorer is the default view in Windows 7. Normally, you see the Documents, Music, Pictures, and Videos libraries when opening Windows Explorer. Double-clicking a library shows all the folders and documents that are part of it, regardless of the location of the folder in which they are stored. For example, by clicking the **2 locations** link (the amount of actual locations can vary from computer to computer), you can see that the Documents library includes two locations by default: My Documents and Public Documents. You can add locations if you wish by clicking the link and clicking the **Add** button. This enables users to organize their documents and media by category, even if the files are scattered throughout the computer and beyond to locations on the network. You also can add new libraries within the main Libraries window by right-clicking **Libraries** (or right-clicking the work area) and selecting **New**, **Libraries**. After a library has been created, you can add folders to it by right-clicking it and selecting **Properties**. From there, you also can specify the default folder location to save files in a library and optimize the library.

The concept of libraries has been in use for some time, especially in media players, but Windows 7 is the first Microsoft operating system to incorporate it for use with any files. Some third-party applications might not integrate properly with Windows libraries due to programming inadequacies. If this is the case, a user will have to store the files created in that application by navigating to the actual folder where they are to be stored, bypassing the library. Always check for updates to third-party applications that might make them library-compatible.

My Computer

My Computer (known as Computer in Windows 7/Vista) is integrated tightly with Windows Explorer. My Computer is still available on all versions of Windows but many users prefer to use Windows Explorer due to its two-pane style and additional functionality. My Computer provides access to the following features and utilities:

- Open My Computer to view the local drives on your system, available network drives, the Control Panel folder, and imaging devices (see Figure 8-5). In Windows XP, use the System Tasks left pane menu to open the System properties sheet (View system information), Add or remove programs (runs Add or Remove Programs applet from Control Panel), or Change a setting (opens Control Panel). In Windows 7/Vista, these options are listed just below the menu bar.

- Right-click the My Computer icon or the My Computer option in the Start Menu to choose options such as Properties (which opens the System properties sheet), Manage (which opens the Computer Management Console), Windows Explorer, Search/Find, drive mapping, and creating shortcuts.

Figure 8-5   My Computer Window and Available System Tasks.

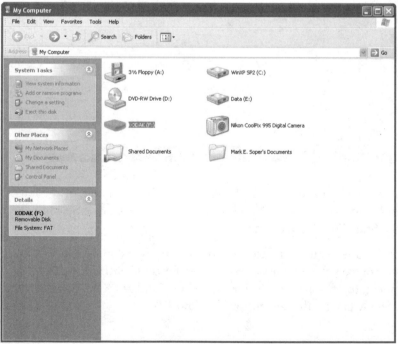

Control Panel

The Control Panel is the major starting point for adjusting the hardware and user interface settings in Windows. The Control Panel's default view is known as Category view. When you click on an icon, it displays various available tasks. Figures 8-6 and 8-7 show the Windows Vista and Windows XP versions of the Control Panel configured for Category view.

Figure 8-6   The Windows Vista Control Panel in its default Category view.

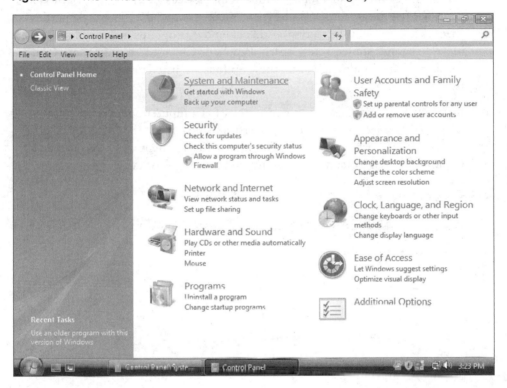

You can open the Control Panel from the Start button, My Computer, or the left window pane of Windows Explorer. (Note: If you're using the Classic Start menu, you have to click **Start**, **Settings**, **Control Panel**.)

Open any Control Panel icon or link to see current settings and make adjustments for the devices it controls. If the Classic view is used for the Control Panel folder, double-click an icon to open it. If Web view is used in Windows XP, a single click opens an icon. Single click is the default for Windows 7/Vista.

Figure 8-7   The Windows XP Control Panel in its default Category view, and the submenus triggered by each icon.

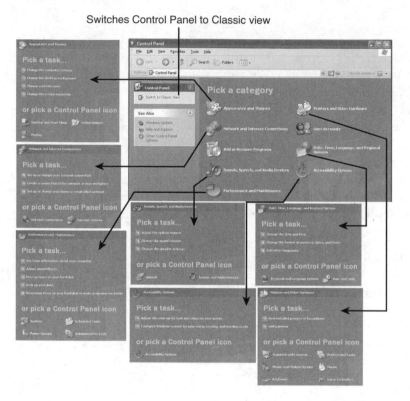

Command Prompt

Although most computer users won't use the command prompt very often, technicians use it frequently, as it enables you to

- Recover data from systems that can't boot normally.

- Reinstall lost or corrupted system files.

- Print file listings (believe it or not, you can't do this in Windows Explorer or My Computer!).

- Copy, move, or delete data.

- Display or configure certain operating system settings.

You can access the Command Prompt by navigating to **Start**, **All Programs**, **Accessories**, **Command Prompt**. In Windows 7/Vista and newer operating systems, some command-line functionality is reserved for administrators. To run the Command Prompt as an administrator, right-click it in the **Start** menu and select **Run as**

Administrator. Alternatively, the Command Prompt can be opened by accessing the Run prompt and typing **cmd.exe**.

Network

Windows 7/Vista uses the Network and Sharing Center to view connections to other computers and their shares. This is the successor to My Network Places. You can access the Network window from the Start Menu, or from within the left window pane of the Computer window. To manage network connections while in the Network window, click the **Network and Sharing Center** button. After that window is displayed, click **Manage Network Connections** (in Win7, the link is **Change Adapter Settings**). From here, you can make whatever changes you want to the network connections. Notice that by default, a network adapter is known as Local Area Connection, but you can change that name at any time. You can access many of the settings by right-clicking the network connection and selecting **Properties**.

The properties sheet for a network connection displays the protocols (for example, TCP/IP), services (such as File and Printer Sharing), and network clients installed (such as Client for Microsoft Networks), as shown in Figure 8-8.

Figure 8-8   Windows Vista Local Area Connection Properties window.

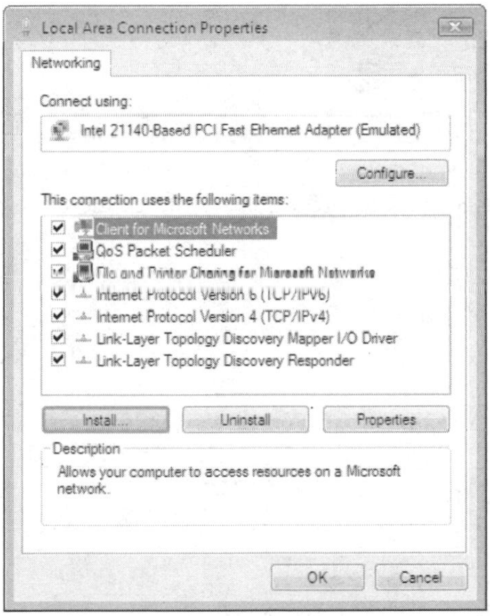

If you cannot connect to other computers on the network, keep in mind that your computer must meet the following criteria:

- Use the same protocol

- Use the same network client

- Have a unique name and unique IP address on the network

My Network Places

Windows XP uses My Network Places to manage dial-up and local area network connections. When you open My Network Places, you see a list of network locations, including those located on the local computer and on remote computers (see Figure 8-9).

Figure 8-9   Windows XP's My Network Places shows all types of shared resources, including LAN and Internet. Clicking **View Network Connections** displays connection details. Select a connection for more details.

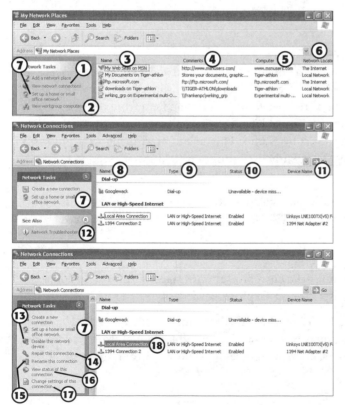

1. Click to view network connections (LAN and dial-up)
2. Displays computers in workgroup
3. Lists available network places (shared resources and connections)
4. UNC path to resource or other comments
5. Computer name and comments
6. Type of connection
7. Starts network setup wizard
8. Lists network connections by name and type
9. Lists network connection types
10. Status
11. Device providing connection (NIC, modem, and so on)
12. Starts network troubleshooter
13. Disables selected device
14. Repairs selected connection
15. Renames selected connection
16. View connection status (duration, speed, throughput)
17. Changes settings for selected connection
18. Selected connection

To view connection types (dial-up, wired network, wireless network), click **View Network Connections** in the Network Tasks pane. To configure a connection, right-click the connection and click **Properties**. To repair a connection, select it and click **Repair This Connection** from the Network Tasks pane.

Taskbar/Systray

Any open applications show up on the taskbar. However, some users don't make use of another component of the taskbar: the Quick Launch. The Quick Launch is located directly to the right of the Start button. You can enable it by right-clicking on the taskbar and selecting **Properties**, and then clicking the **Show Quick Launch** checkbox. This is disabled in Windows XP by default, but is enabled in Windows 7/Vista. It's a nice tool because the shortcuts within the Quick Launch are the same size as shortcuts on the desktop; however, you always have easy access to them.

Even before you click on the Start menu, most Windows installations already have several programs running in the System Tray (also known as the systray or SysTray), which is located in the lower-right corner of the screen, next to the clock. Microsoft also refers to this as the Notification area.

Start Menu

Even though the Start menu has a default configuration and most programs add one or more shortcuts to it when they are installed, you can add items to the Start menu, remove items from it, create or remove folders, move an item from one folder to another, and switch between large icons (default) and small icons. You can also right-click on the menu and select Sort by Name. The default Start menu in Windows XP automatically adds the most frequently used programs to a special section of the Start menu.

The Start menu is comprised of shortcuts to programs and other objects on your system. To add items to the default Windows Start menu, follow these steps:

Step 1.   Right-click the **Start** button.

Step 2.   To add a shortcut for the current user only, select **Explore**. To add a shortcut for all users, select **Explore All Users**.

Step 3.   The Start menu folder opens in the left window (see Figure 8-10); shortcuts on the Start menu are shown in the right window. To see additional Start menu folders, click the plus sign (+) next to Programs in the left window.

Figure 8-10   Preparing to add items to the default Windows XP Start menu.

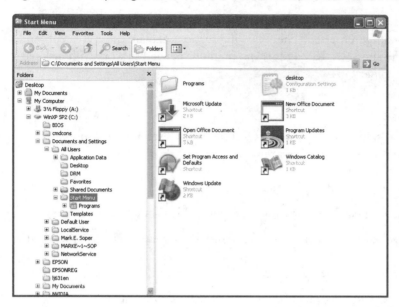

Step 4.   To create a new folder for the shortcut, click the folder in the left window where you want to create the shortcut to open it in the right window. Right-click an empty area in the right window and select **New, Folder**. Name the folder as desired.

Step 5.   To select a folder for the shortcut, click the folder in the left window. The folder's contents appear in the right window.

Step 6.   Click **File, New, Shortcut** to start the Shortcut Wizard. (This functions only if you have chosen Explore in Windows 7/Vista. Explore All Users does not allow a new shortcut.)

Step 7.   You can enter the path to the program (such as **C:\Windows\System32\cmd.exe**) or click the **Browse** button to locate the program for which you are making a shortcut. Click **Next**.

Step 8.   The shortcut name created by Windows is displayed. To keep the name created by Windows, click **Finish**. You can also change the name as desired and click **Finish**.

Step 9.   Click **OK**. The new shortcut (and new folder, if any) appear on your Start button menu.

Managing Disk Partitions, Files, and Folders

Understanding how to manage hard disks, files on all types of disks, and folders is an essential part of computer usage. The following sections explain these concepts and the command-line and GUI-based tools and methods needed to work with disk partitions, files, and folders.

Disk Partitions

An internal hard disk (PATA, SATA, or SCSI) cannot be used until it is prepared for use. There are two steps involved in preparing a hard disk:

Step 1.   Creating partitions and logical drives

Step 2.   Formatting partitions and logical drives (which assigns drive letters)

A disk partition is a logical structure on a hard disk drive that specifies the following:

- Whether the drive can be bootable

- How many drive letters (one, two, or more) the hard disk contains

- Whether any of the hard disk's capacity is reserved for a future operating system or other use

Although the name "disk partition" suggests the drive is divided into two or more logical sections, every PATA, SATA, and SCSI hard disk must go through a partitioning process, even if you want to use the entire hard disk as a single drive letter. All versions of Windows support two major types of disk partitions:

- **Primary**—A primary partition can contain only a single drive letter and can be made active (bootable). Only one primary partition can be active. Although a single physical drive can hold up to four primary partitions, you need only one primary partition on a drive that contains a single operating system. If you install a new operating system in a dual-boot configuration with your current operating system, a new version of Windows can be installed in a different folder in the same drive, or can be installed in an additional primary partition. If you want to use a non-Windows operating system along with your current operating system, it might require its own primary partition, or even special third-party software such as Norton's PartitionMagic.

- **Extended**—An extended partition differs from a primary partition in two important ways:
  - An extended partition doesn't become a drive letter itself but can contain one or more logical drives, each of which is assigned a drive letter.
  - Neither an extended partition nor any drive it contains can be bootable.

Only one extended partition can be stored on each physical drive.

You can also leave some unpartitioned space on the hard disk for use later, either for another operating system or another drive letter.

Partitioning creates drive letters; formatting creates file systems on the drive letters created during partitioning. Figure 8-11 helps you visualize how these different partitioning schemes could be used on a typical hard disk.

Figure 8-11   Typical disk partitioning schemes used for the first hard disk (first four examples) or an additional drive (last two examples).

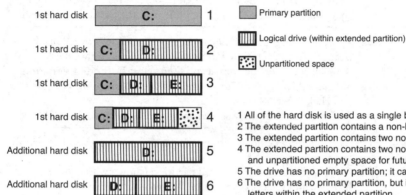

1 All of the hard disk is used as a single bootable drive letter.
2 The extended partition contains a non-bootable drive letter.
3 The extended partition contains two non-bootable drive letters.
4 The extended partition contains two non-bootable drive letters and unpartitioned empty space for future use.
5 The drive has no primary partition; it cannot be used to boot the system.
6 The drive has no primary partition, but it has two logical drive letters within the extended partition.

After a disk is partitioned, the drive letters must be formatted using a supported file system.

Using Disk Management

The Disk Management snap-in of the Computer Management console is the GUI-based application for analyzing and configuring hard drives. You can do a lot from here, as shown in Table 8-2. Try some of the configurations listed on a test computer. All you need is a drive with unpartitioned space. (For more information on how to use the Computer Management console, see the section titled "Computer Management and the MMC" later in this chapter.)

Table 8-2   Configurations in Disk Management

Configuration	Steps
Initialize a new disk	A secondary hard disk installed in a computer might not be seen by Windows Explorer immediately. To make it accessible, locate the disk (for example Disk 1), right-click **Disk 1** or **Disk 2**, and so on, and select **Initialize Disk**.

Table 8-2 Configurations in Disk Management

Configuration	Steps
Create a primary partition	1. Right-click on a disk's unallocated space (shown with a black header), and select **New Partition**, as shown in Figure 8-12. 2. Click **Next** for the wizard and then select **Primary Partition**. 3. Select the amount of unallocated space you want for the partition and click **Next**. 4. Select a drive letter. 5. Choose whether you want to format at this point. 6. Review the summary screen and if it is correct, click **Finish**. Note: For computers with limited resources, it is recommended that you hold off on formatting until after the partition is created.
Create an extended partition	1. Right-click on a disk's unallocated space (shown with a black header), and select **New Partition**, as shown in Figure 8-12. 2. Click **Next** for the wizard and then select **Extended Partition**. 3. Select the amount of unallocated space you want for the partition and click **Next**. 4. Review the summary screen and if it is correct, click Finish.
Create a logical drive	This can only be done within an extended partition that has already been created. 1. Right-click on the extended partition (shown with a green header), and select **New Logical Drive** as shown in Figure 8-13. 2. Click **Next** for the wizard. You will notice that your only option is Logical drive. Click **Next**. 3. Select the amount of unallocated space you want for the partition and click **Next**. 4. Select a drive letter. 5. Choose whether you want to format at this point. 6. Review the summary screen and, if it is correct, click **Finish**.
Format a partition/logical drive	1. Right-click the primary partition or logical drive and select **Format**. 2. In the Format x: window, select the file system and whether to do a quick format. If it is a new drive, you can select quick format. However, if the drive was used previously, you might want to leave this option unchecked. ALL DATA WILL BE ERASED during the format procedure.
Make a partition active	Right-click the primary partition and select **Mark Partition as Active**. You can have up to four primary partitions on a hard disk, but only one of them can be active.

Configuration	Steps
Convert a basic disk to dynamic	To change the size of a partition in Windows XP, to create simple and spanned volumes, or to implement RAID, the hard disk(s) need to be converted to dynamic. It's highly recommended that you back up your data before attempting this configuration. 1. Right-click the hard disk where it says Disk 0 or Disk 1 and select **Convert to Dynamic Disk**. 2. In the ensuing window, you can select multiple disks to switch over to dynamic. This can also be done in Windows 7/Vista; however, in 7/Vista, you now have the option to extend a partition, as shown next.
Extend a partition (7/Vista only)	Windows 7/Vista enables you to extend the size of a partition (volume) or shrink it within the Disk Management utility. It's highly recommended that you back up your data before attempting this configuration. 1. Right-click the volume to be extended. 2. Select **Extend Volume**. (Remember that a volume is any section of the hard drive with a drive letter.) 3. Click **Next** for the wizard and select how much space you'd like to add to the partition. 4. Select any other disks (with unpartitioned space) to combine with the first disk to create a spanned partition and click **Next**. 5. Click **Finish** at the summary screen. A reboot is not required, and this process should finish fairly quickly. You can also do this process in the Command Prompt using the Diskpart command. Note: Extended partitions are not fault tolerant. Make sure you have a backup plan in place. Note: Extended partitions are also known as extended volumes, and when covering multiple disks they are also known as spanned volumes.

In Figure 8-12, we also can see the disks at the top of the window and their status. For example, the C: partition is healthy. It also shows us the percent of the disk used, and other information such as whether the disk is currently formatting, if it's dynamic, or if it has failed. In some cases, you might see "foreign" status. This means that a dynamic disk has been moved from another computer (with another Windows operating system) to the local computer, and it cannot be accessed properly. To fix this, and be able to access the disk, add the disk to your computer's system configuration. To add a disk to your computer's system configuration, import the foreign disk (right-click the disk and then click Import Foreign Disks). Any existing volumes on the foreign disk become visible and accessible when you import the disk. For more information on the plethora of disk statuses, see the Microsoft TechNet article, "Disk Status Descriptions," at http://technet.microsoft.com/en-us/library/cc738101(WS.10).aspx

Figure 8-12   Creating a partition from unallocated disk space.

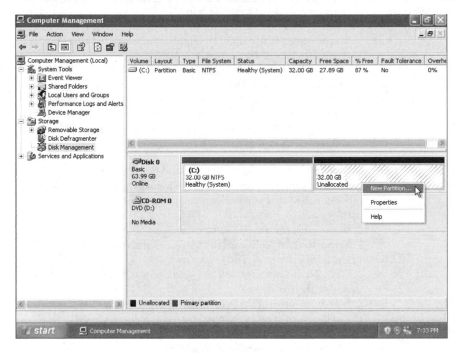

Figure 8-13   Creating a logical drive from within an extended partition.

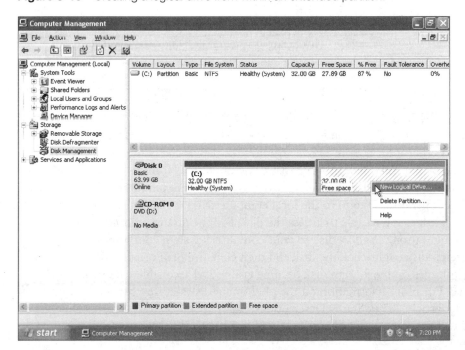

Mount Points and Mounting a Drive

You can also "mount" drives in Disk Management. A mounted drive is a drive that is mapped to an empty folder within a volume that has been formatted as NTFS. Instead of using drive letters, mounted drives use drive paths. This is a good solution for when you need more than 26 drives in your computer because you are not limited to the letters in the alphabet. Mounted drives can also provide more space for temporary files and can enable you to move folders to different drives if space runs low on the current drive. To mount a drive, follow these steps:

Step 1. Right-click the partition or volume you want to mount and select **Change Drive Letters and Paths**.

Step 2. In the displayed window, click **Add**.

Step 3. Then browse to the empty folder you want to mount the volume to, and click **OK** for both windows.

As shown in Figure 8-14, the DVD-ROM drive has been mounted within a folder on the hard drive called Test. The figure is showing the Properties window for the folder Test. It shows that it is a mounted volume, shows the location of the folder (which is the mount point), and the target of the mount point, which is the DVD drive containing a Windows Vista DVD. To remove the mount point, just go back to Disk Management, right-click the mounted volume and select **Change Drive Letters and Paths**, and then select **Remove**. Remember that the folder you want to use as a mount point must be empty, and it must be within an NTFS volume.

Figure 8-14   Empty NTFS folder acting as a mount point.

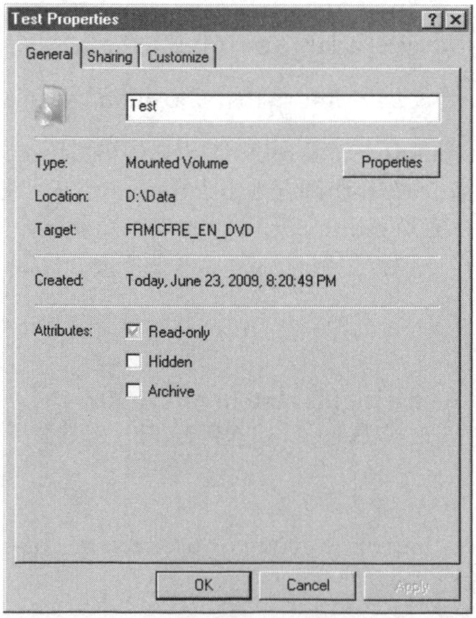

Windows File Systems

What exactly is a file system, anyway? A file system describes how data and drives are organized. In Windows, the file system you choose for a hard disk affects the following:

- The rules for how large a logical drive (drive letter) can be, and whether the hard disk can be used as one big drive letter, several smaller drive letters, or must be multiple drive letters.

- How efficiently a system stores data; the less wasted space, the better.

- How secure a system is against tampering.

- Whether a drive can be accessed by more than one operating system.

The term *file system* is a general term for how an operating system stores various types of files. Windows supports two different file systems for hard disks, FAT32 and NTFS, and supports FAT for floppy disks.

FAT32

FAT32 was introduced in 1995 and is supported by Windows 7/Vista, XP, and 2000, although NTFS is preferred. FAT32 has the following characteristics:

- The 32-bit file allocation table, which allows for 268,435,456 entries (232) per drive. Remember, an entry can be a folder or an allocation unit used by a file.

- The root directory can be located anywhere on the drive and can have an *unlimited* number of entries. Hooray!

- FAT32 uses an 8KB allocation unit size for drives as large as 16GB.

- The maximum logical partition size allowed is 2TB (more than 2 trillion bytes).

You can use FAT32 to format hard disks, flash memory, and removable media drives. However, FAT32 is recommended for hard disks *only* if the hard disk must also be accessed by dual-booting with an older version of Windows; for example, Windows 95, 98, or Me, which do not support NTFS.

NTFS

The New Technology File System (NTFS) is the native file system of Windows 7/Vista, XP, and 2000. As implemented in Windows 7/Vista and XP, NTFS has many differences from FAT32, including

- **Access control**—Different levels of access control by group or user can be configured for both folders and individual files.

- **Built-in compression**—Individual files, folders, or an entire drive can be compressed without the use of third-party software.

- **A practical limit for partition sizes of 2TB**—The same as with FAT32, although partitions theoretically can reach a maximum size of 16 exabytes (16 billion billion bytes).

- **Individual recycle bins**—Unlike FAT32, NTFS includes a separate recycle bin for each user.

- **Support for the Encrypting File System (EFS)**—EFS enables data to be stored in an encrypted form. No password, no access to files!

- **Support for mounting a drive**—Drive mounting enables you to address a removable-media drive's contents, for example, as if its contents are stored on your hard disk. The hard disk's drive letter is used to access data on both the hard disk and the removable media drive.

- **Disk quota support**—The administrator of a system can enforce rules about how much disk space each user is allowed to use for storage.

- **Hot-swapping**—Removable-media drives that have been formatted with NTFS (such as Jaz, Orb, and others) can be connected or removed while the operating system is running.

- **Indexing**—The Indexing service helps users locate information more quickly when the Search tool is used.

NOTE Windows 7/Vista, XP, and 2000 can't create a FAT32 partition larger than 32GB. However, if the partition already exists, they can use it.

Working with Folders/Directories

Windows provides two ways to work with folders (also called directories): visually, through Windows Explorer or My Computer, and at the command line (MKDIR/MD, CHDIR/CD, RMDIR/RD).

To navigate between folders in Windows Explorer, follow these procedures:

- To view the subfolders (subdirectories) in a folder (directory), click the plus (+) sign next to the folder name in the left pane of Windows Explorer.

- To view the contents of a folder (including files and other folders), click the folder in the left pane of Windows Explorer. The contents of the folder appear in the right pane.

- To navigate to the previous view, click the left-hand arrow above the address bar.

- To move to the next view, click the right-hand arrow.

- To navigate to the next higher folder in the folder hierarchy, click the up-arrow/folder button.

Figure 8-15 illustrates these concepts.

Figure 8-15   Working with folders (directories) in Windows Explorer.

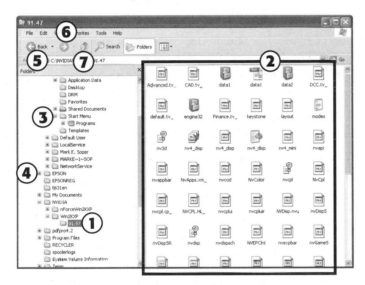

1. Selected folder
2. Contents of selected folder
3. Click to close subfolder view
4. Click to open subfolder view
5. Return to previous view
6. Advance to next view
7. Go up one level in the folder hierarchy

File Management

File management skills such as file creation, file naming, file attributes, compression, encryption, file permissions, and file types are necessary for the average computer user. The following sections discuss these skills.

Creating Files

Data files that can be accessed by registered applications can be created within the Windows Explorer/My Computer/Computer interface. To create a new file, follow these steps:

Step 1.   Open the folder where you want to create the file.

Step 2.   Right-click empty space in the right window pane and select **New** to display a list of registered file types (see Figure 8-16).

Figure 8-16   Creating a new text document on drive E:.

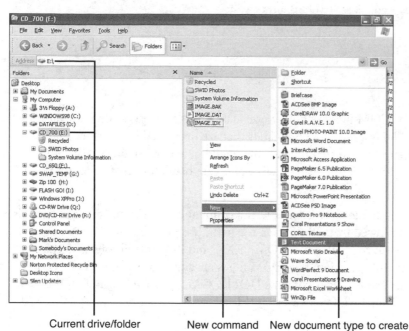

Current drive/folder   New command   New document type to create

Step 3.   Move the mouse pointer to the file type desired and click it. The new (empty) file is created in the open folder.

Step 4.   Enter a new name if desired.

Step 5.   To edit the file, double-click it.

File Types

Broadly speaking, there are two types of files used by Windows and other operating systems:

- Text

- Binary

Text files can be read with an ordinary text editor such as Notepad or Edit. However, most word processing and other types of document files, although they contain text, also contain formatting characters that a text editor cannot properly interpret.

Binary files look like gibberish when viewed in a text editor. Only the operating system (in the case of application binary files) or a compatible application (in the case of binary data files) can interpret their contents.

The following types of files can be started (executed) from a command prompt or from Windows Explorer/My Computer:

- .COM
- .EXE
- .BAT

Both .EXE and .COM files are binary executable files, whereas a .BAT file (also called a batch file) is a series of commands that are processed in sequence. Simple batch files contain the same commands that could be entered manually at a command prompt. However, it is also possible to create batch files that have conditional logic and display progress messages.

When an executable filename is entered at a command prompt, the current folder is searched first, followed by the folders in the path. If executable files in the current folder or a folder in the path have .COM, .EXE, and .BAT extensions with the same name preceding the extension, the .COM file is always launched first. For example, assume that the current folder contains DOIT.COM, DOIT.EXE, and DOIT.BAT. DOIT.COM is launched if you enter **DOIT**.

File Names and Extensions

Windows XP supports long file and folder names (LFN). LFNs can have as many as 255 characters and can contain spaces and most other alphanumeric characters, but cannot contain any of the following characters (which are used by the operating system):

```
\ / : * ? " < > ¦
```

A file can contain more than one period, but only the characters after the last period are considered the extension. In the following example, .doc is the extension:

```
mydocument.ltr.doc
```

By default, Windows hides file extensions such as .BAT, .DOC, and .EXE for registered file types. However, you can change this default in Windows Explorer/My Computer.

CAUTION Don't remove or alter the file extension if you rename a file. If you do, Windows won't be able to determine which program it should use to open the file.

Indexing

Windows 7/Vista and Windows XP offer indexing services in an attempt to help you find files faster. However, indexing too much content can lead to poorer operating system performance.

To adjust the indexing settings in Windows Vista, go to **Start, Control Panel, System and Maintenance**, and click **Indexing Options** (in Windows 7, open **Control Panel**, and in the Search field, type **Indexing Options**). From here, you can modify whether folders are indexed by clicking the **Modify** button and selecting or deselecting the folders you wish. It is not recommended to select an entire volume (such as C:), because it causes poor performance. Use indexing for specific folders where you store important data that you search for on a regular basis. If you don't want indexing at all, you can either deselect all folders that are checked or disable the indexing in general. To disable indexing altogether, follow these steps:

Step 1. Click **Start**, then right-click **Computer** and select **Manage**. This brings up the Computer Management window.

Step 2. From here, expand **Services and Applications** in the left window pane and click **Services**.

Step 3. In the right window pane, scroll down to Windows Search, right-click it, and select **Stop**. You can restart the service at any time by right-clicking and selecting Start. Check the startup type by right-clicking the service and selecting Properties. If the startup type is set to Automatic, you should change it to manual or disabled; otherwise, the service starts back up again when you restart the computer.

You can also turn off indexing for individual drives, as follows:

Step 1. Open Windows Explorer.

Step 2. Right-click the volume you want to stop indexing on (for example, C:) and select **Properties**.

Step 3. At the bottom of the window, deselect **Index This Drive for Faster Searching**.

To turn off indexing in Windows XP, follow these steps:

Step 1. Click **Start**, right-click **My Computer**, and select **Manage**. This brings up the Computer Management window.

Step 2. From here, expand **Services and Applications** in the left window pane and click **Services**.

Step 3.   In the right window pane, scroll to Indexing Service, right-click it, and select **Stop**. You can restart the service at any time by right-clicking and selecting **Start**. Check the startup type by right-clicking the service and selecting **Properties**. If the startup type is set to Automatic, you should change it to manual or disabled; otherwise, the service starts back up again when you restart the computer.

You can also turn off indexing on any volume by right-clicking the volume, selecting **Properties**, and deselecting **Allow Indexing Service to Index This Disk for Fast File Searching**.

File Permissions

Windows 7/Vista/XP/2000 systems that use the NTFS file system sometimes feature an additional tab on the file/folder properties sheet called the Security tab. It is used to control file permissions.

> **NOTE**   If Windows XP is configured to use simple file sharing, the Security tab is not visible. Simple file sharing is recommended for home and small-business networks, but reduces system security. Simple file sharing is enabled by default if the system is not connected to a domain, but is disabled automatically when the system is connected to a domain (the domain controller is used to control network security).
>
> To disable simple file sharing on a system not connected to a domain, go to either **Windows Explorer**, **My Computer/Computer**, or **Control Panel**. Click **Tools** on the menu bar, select **Folder Options**, click the **View** tab, scroll to the bottom, and clear the check mark next to **Use Simple File Sharing (Recommended)**.

The Security tab permits you to control access to the selected file or folder by granting or denying permissions shown to selected users or groups:

- **Full Control**—Enables any and all changes to a file, including deletion.
- **Modify**—File can be modified.
- **Read & Execute**—File can be read and executed.
- **Read**—File can be read.
- **Write**—File can be overwritten.
- **List Folder Contents**—When viewing the permissions of a folder, this additional permission is listed. It allows the user to *view* what is inside the folder.

The Security tab has two sections. The top section shows the users and groups that have access to the selected file or folder. You can add or remove groups or users.

The bottom section lets you specify the permissions available for the selected user or group.

DEFRAG

Over time, a hard disk becomes fragmented as temporary and data files are created and deleted. When a file can no longer be stored in a contiguous group of allocation units, Windows stores the files in as many groups of allocation units as necessary and reassembles the file when it is next accessed. The extra time needed to save and read the file reduces system performance. Windows includes a disk defragmentation tool to help regain lost read/write performance.

Defragment can be run in the following ways:

- From the Accessories menu's System Tools submenu (Disk Defragmenter)

- From a drive's properties sheet's Tools tab (Defragment Now)

- From the command line (a feature introduced in Windows XP): **defrag** (type **defrag /?** for options)

The Windows XP/2000 defragmenter features an Analyze button that determines whether defragmentation is necessary (see Figure 8-17). There is no Analyze button in Windows 7/Vista; however, it analyzes the disk automatically before defragmenting.

Figure 8-17   Disk Defragmenter's analysis indicates this drive needs to be defragmented.

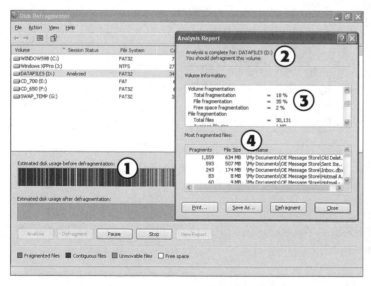

1. Visual display of drive fragmentation
2. Indicates whether defragmentation is necessary
3. Fragmentation of tested drive
4. The most fragmented files on the tested drive

> **TIP**   The narrower the colored stripes visible in the Estimated Disk Usage Before Defragmentation display, the more fragmented the drive is.

CHKDSK.EXE

Windows includes the chkdsk.exe program to check disk drives for errors. It can be run from the Windows GUI, as shown in Figure 8-18, or from the command line.

> **TIP**   It's no coincidence that Check Now is listed before Defragmentation and Backup in the Windows disk Tools menu. You should check the drive for errors *first* before you perform a defrag or backup operation.

As Figure 8-18 shows, you can also select whether to automatically fix file system errors and attempt the recovery of bad sectors with Chkdsk. If you select the option to automatically fix file system errors, Chkdsk is scheduled to run at the next restart. This is necessary because Chkdsk requires exclusive access to the drive. Chkdsk performs a three-phase test of the drive after the system is rebooted but before the Windows desktop appears.

Figure 8-18   Windows C: Properties Sheet and Check Disk Window after the Check Now button has been clicked.

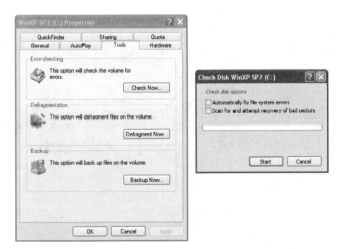

You can also run Chkdsk from the command prompt. For options, type **Chkdsk /?** from the command prompt.

In Windows 7/Vista, you need to run this command in elevated mode. Here are the two options:

- Click **Start**, **All Programs**, **Accessories**, **Command Prompt**. Right-click **Command Prompt** and select **Run as Administrator**. Click **Continue** at the permission window.

- Click **Start** and type **cmd**. Then press **Ctrl+Shift+Enter** to execute **cmd.exe** in elevated mode. Click **Continue** at the permission window.

NOTE By default, Chkdsk runs automatically at boot time if a drive is dirty (has errors); to adjust this behavior, run Chkdsk with appropriate options from the command prompt. Use **chkdsk /?** to see the options you can use.

Format

In Windows, the Format command is used primarily to re-create the specified file system on a floppy disk, removable-media disk, or a hard disk. In the process, the contents of the disk are overwritten.

Format works in different ways, depending on whether it is used on a hard or floppy disk. When Format is used on a hard drive, it creates a master boot record, two file allocation tables, and a root directory (also referred to as the *root folder*). The rest of the drive is checked for disk surface errors—any defective areas are marked as bad to prevent their use by the operating system. Format appears to "destroy" the previous contents of a hard disk, but if you use Format on a hard disk by mistake, third-party data recovery programs can be used to retrieve data from the drive. This is possible because most of the disk surface is not changed by Format.

If a floppy disk, USB flash memory drive, or removable-media disk is prepared with Format and the unconditional **/U** option is used from the command line, or the Windows Explorer Full Format option is used, sector markings (a sector equals 512 bytes) are created across the surface of the floppy disk before other disk structures are created, destroying any previous data on the disk. If the Quick Format or Safe Format option is used, the contents of the disk are marked for deletion but can be retrieved with third-party data recovery software.

NOTE The hard disk format process performed by the Format command (which creates the file system) is sometimes referred to as a high-level format to distinguish it from the low-level format used by hard drive manufacturers to set up magnetic structures on the hard drive. When floppy disks are formatted with the Full or Unconditional options, Format performs both a low-level and high-level format on the floppy disk surface.

You can use Windows Explorer to format both hard drives and floppy disks. Right-click the drive you want to format, select **Format**, and the Format options for Windows are displayed, as shown in Figure 8-19. (Windows 2000's options are almost identical, except for the lack of the MS-DOS startup disk option.)

Figure 8-19   The Windows XP Explorer Format menu for a floppy disk (left) and hard disk (right).

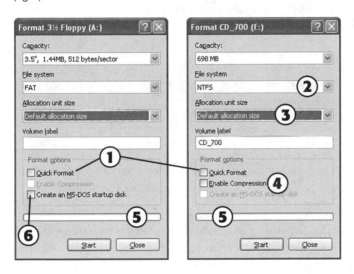

1. Reduces format time, but doesn't check for disk errors
2. Select FAT (FAT16), FAT32, or NTFS
3. Different allocation unit sizes are available with NTFS file system only
4. Compression available with NTFS file system only
5. Status bar indicates progress of format
6. Option available in Windows XP only; creates a bare-bones MS-DOS boot disk without optical drive or memory management software

Windows 2000 doesn't offer the Make an MS-DOS Startup Disk option, but is otherwise similar.

System Management Tools

The following sections discuss the major system management tools included in Windows, such as Device Manager, Task Manager, MSCONFIG.EXE, REGEDIT.EXE, Event Viewer, System Restore, and Remote Desktop.

Device Manager

Windows Device Manager is used to display installed device categories, specific installed devices, and to troubleshoot problems with devices.

To use Device Manager in Windows 7/Vista, follow these steps:

Step 1.   Click **Start**, right-click on **Computer**, and select **Properties**. This displays the System window.

Step 2.   From there, click the **Device Manager** link on the left side under Tasks.

To use the Device Manager in Windows XP/2000:

Step 1.   Open the **System Properties** window in the Control Panel, or right-click **My Computer** and select **Properties**.

Step 2.   Click the **Hardware** tab and select **Device Manager**.

NOTE   There are two other options for opening Device Manager. The first is by using the Search box within the Start menu. Just type **device manager** and then click the link for Device Manager that appears in the results box. The second is from the Computer Management console window. It opens the same way in 7/Vista and XP. To open this, right-click on **Computer** (**My Computer** in XP), and select **Manage**. This displays the Computer Management window; from there, click **Device Manager** in the left window pane. Get in the habit of using Computer Management. It has lots of common settings in one location. Another way to open Computer Management is by going to the Run prompt and typing **compmgmt.msc**.

To view the devices in a specific category, click the plus (+) sign next to the category name, as in Figure 8-20.

Figure 8-20   Device Manager with selected categories expanded.

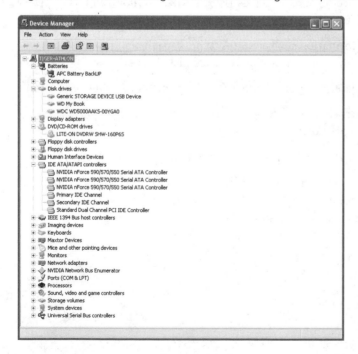

NOTE   Different systems have different categories listed in Device Manager, as Device Manager only lists categories for installed hardware. For example, the system shown in Figure 8-20 has a battery backup, so it has a Batteries category. Note also that the IDE ATA/ATAPI Controllers category also lists SATA controllers.

To see more information about a specific device, double-click the device to open its properties sheet. Device properties sheets have a General tab and some combination of other tabs:

- **General**—Displays device type, manufacturer, location, status, troubleshoot button, and usage. All devices.

- **Properties**—Device-specific settings. Applies to multimedia devices.

- **Driver**—Driver details and version information. All devices.

- **Details**—Technical details about the device (added in Windows XP SP2). All devices.

- **Policies**—Optimizes external drives for quick removal or performance. USB, FireWire, and eSATA drives.

- **Resources**—Hardware resources such as IRQ, DMA, Memory, and I/O port address. Applies to I/O devices.

- **Volumes**—Drive information such as status, type, capacity, and so on. Click Populate to retrieve information. Applies to hard disk drives.

- **Power**—Power available per port. Applies to USB root hubs and generic hubs.

- **Power Management**—Specifies device-specific power management settings. Applies to USB, network, keyboard, and mouse devices.

Figure 8-21 illustrates the Power, Driver, and General tabs.

Virtually all recent systems support Plug and Play (PnP) hardware with automatic resource allocation by a combination of the PnP BIOS and Windows. However, if you need to determine the hardware resources in use in a particular system, click **View** and select **Resources** by type (see Figure 8-22).

Figure 8-21 Selected Device Manager tabs: the Power tab for a USB hub (A); the Driver tab for an IEEE-1394 port (B); the General tab for an network controller (C).

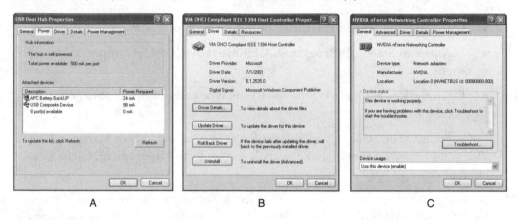

A   B   C

Figure 8-22 IRQ and DMA usage on a typical Windows XP system. ACPI power management enables IRQs above 15, and sharing of PCI IRQs 17, 20, 22, and 23 by multiple devices.

Computer Management and the MMC

We mentioned this component of Windows 7/Vista/XP a few times already, but it's worth mentioning again. Instead of hunting around for different utilities in different places in Windows, it's simpler to use the Computer Management console window

because it has most of the tools you need in one organized, two-pane window system. Here are the ways to open Computer Management:

- Click **Start**, and then right-click **Computer/My Computer** and select **Manage**.

- Navigate to **Start, All Programs, Administrative Tools, Computer Management**.

- Open the Run prompt (**Windows+R**) and type **compmgmt.msc** (a personal favorite).

In Computer Management, you find the Event Viewer, the Device Manager, Local Users and Groups, Services, and disk tools such as Disk Management. Consider using it often.

Now, to make it better, Windows 7/Vista and XP offer you the Microsoft Management Console (MMC). This is the "master" console so to speak, and you can snap in as many other console windows as you want. Add to that the fact that it saves all the consoles you snapped in and remembers the last place you were working, and this becomes a valuable and time-saving tool.

To open it, open the **Run** prompt and type **MMC**. This opens a new blank MMC. Then, to add console windows, go to **File** and then **Add/Remove Snap-in** (or press **Ctrl+M**). From there, click the **Add** button to select the consoles you want, such as Computer Management, Performance Logs and Alerts, or ActiveX Controls. You can also change the "mode" that the user works in when accessing the MMC—for example, Author mode, which has access to everything, and User mode, which has various levels of limitation. When you are finished, save the MMC, and consider adding it as a shortcut within the desktop or in the Quick Launch area, and maybe add a keyboard shortcut to open it. The next time you open it, it remembers all the console windows you added, and starts you at the location you were in when you closed the program. By default, Windows 7/Vista come with version 3.0 of the MMC, and Windows XP comes with Version 2.0. However, you can download version 3.0 for Windows XP from www.microsoft.com. Just search for "Microsoft Management Console 3.0 for Windows XP."

Task Manager

The Task Manager utility provides a useful real-time look into the inner workings of Windows and the programs that are running. There are several ways to display the Task Manager including

- Right-click the taskbar and select **Task Manager**.

- Press **Ctrl+Shift+Esc**.

- Open the **Run** prompt and type **taskmgr**.

- Press **Ctrl+Alt+Del** and select **Task Manager** from the Windows Security dialog box. (Note: This only works in Windows XP if you have turned off the Welcome Screen option.)

The Task Manager tabs include Applications (shows running applications); Processes (program components in memory); Performance (CPU, memory, pagefile, and caching stats). Windows XP adds a Networking tab (lists network utilization by adapter in use) and a Users tab (lists current users). Windows Vista adds a Services tab (displays the services on the computer and their status).

Use the Applications tab to determine if a program has stopped responding; you can shut down these programs by using the End Task button. Use the Processes tab to see which processes are consuming the most memory. Use this dialog along with the System Configuration Utility (MSConfig) to help determine if you are loading unnecessary startup applications; MSConfig can disable them to free up memory. If you are unable to shut down a program with the Applications tab, you can also shut down its processes with the Processes tab, but this is not recommended unless the program cannot be shut down in any other way.

Use the Performance tab to determine whether you need to install more RAM memory or need to increase your paging file size. Use the Networking tab to monitor the performance of your network.

The top-level menu can be used to adjust the properties of the currently selected tab and to shut down the system. Figure 8-23 illustrates these tabs. Figure 8-24 shows the newer Services tab in Windows Vista's Task Manager.

Event Viewer

If your customer is using Windows 7/Vista/XP/2000, these versions of Windows generate several log files during routine use that can be useful for determining what went wrong. Many of these can be viewed through the Event Viewer. To view the contents of the Event Viewer in Windows 7/Vista/XP/2000, right-click Computer/My Computer, click Manage and click Event Viewer. The Event Viewer captures various types of information, the three most important logs to know are: Application, Security, and System. In Windows 7/Vista, they are inside Event Viewer\Windows Logs; however, in Windows XP, these are listed directly inside of the Event Viewer.

Figure 8-23   The Windows XP version of the Windows Task Manager's Applications (A), Processes (B), Performance (C), and Networking (D) tabs.

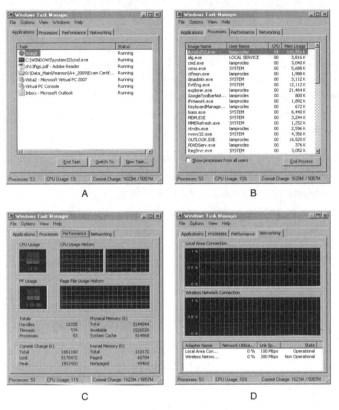

A   B

C   D

Figure 8-24   The Windows Vista version of the Windows Task Manager's Services tab.

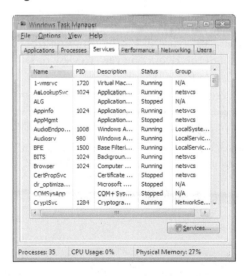

To view details about an entry in the Event Viewer, click on a log in the left window pane and entries appear in the right window pane. To open the event and view more information, double-click the event, or right-click it and select **Event Properties/ Properties**. Figure 8-25 shows the Application event viewer on a Windows XP system being used to view the details of an application error.

Figure 8-25   Viewing the details about an application error using the Application Event Viewer. The left window displays other major components of Windows XP's Computer Management Console.

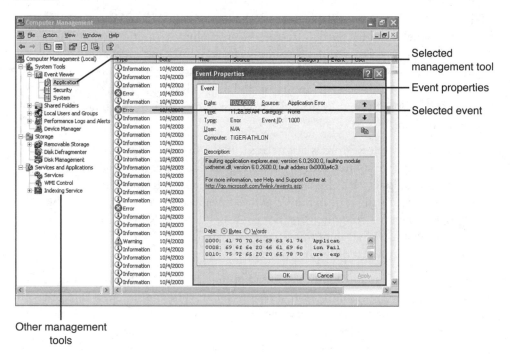

System Restore

Ever wish you had a time machine so you could go back before you installed a bad driver or troublesome piece of software? Windows 7/Vista and XP feature a time machine called *System Restore*.

System Restore enables you to fix problems caused by a defective hardware or software installation by resetting your computer's configuration to the way it was at a specified earlier time. The driver or software files installed stay on the system, and so does the data you created, but Registry changes made by the hardware or software are reversed so your system works the way it did before the installation. Restore points can be created by the user with System Restore and are also created automatically by the system before new hardware or software is installed.

To create a restore point in Windows 7/Vista, follow these steps:

Step 1.   Right-click **Computer** and select **Properties**. This opens the System Properties window.

Step 2.   Click the **System Protection** link.

Step 3.   Click the **Create** button. This opens the System Protection window.

Step 4.   Enter a name for the restore point and click **Create**.

If System Restore is not available, it might be turned off. Within Windows 7/Vista, you can enable or disable System Restore on any volume from the System Properties window/System Protection tab. Simply check or uncheck any volume that you want to enable or disable. Within Windows XP, the state of System Restore affects all drives; you can only turn the utility on and off. This is done from the System Properties window/System Restore tab. You can also change the amount of disk space it uses here.

Be aware that System Restore is not necessarily the first step you should try when troubleshooting a computer. Simply restarting the computer has been known to "fix" all kinds of issues. It's also a good idea to try the Last Known Good Configuration. You can access this within the Windows Advanced Boot Options menu by pressing **F8** when the computer first boots. Also, if System Restore doesn't seem to work in normal mode, attempt to use it in Safe Mode. Safe Mode is another option in the Windows Advanced Boot Options menu.

Be wary of using System Restore if you're fighting a computer virus or malware infection. If you (or the system) create a restore point while the system is infected, you could re-infect the system if you revert the system to that restore point. To prevent re-infection, most anti-virus vendors recommend that you disable System Restore (which eliminates stored restore points) before removing computer viruses.

Chapter Review Questions

The following questions test your recall of the concepts described in this chapter. The answers are listed at the end of the questions in the "Answers and Explanations" section.

1. Which of the following technologies is the graphical user interface used by default in Windows Vista?

   A. Windows PowerGUI

   B. Windows Aero

   C. Windows GUI version II

   D. Windows Powershell

2. Which of the following is a file management utility that is used on Windows-based operating systems?

   A. Windows Explorer

   B. File Manager

   C. Server Manager

   D. Internet Explorer

3. You are working on your Windows XP desktop computer. You need to modify your network settings. Which of the following will you use to modify this?

   A. My Computer

   B. Network Spot

   C. My Network Places

   D. My Network Manager

4. You have just been given a new hard drive with a new Windows operating system to install in a client's computer. What processes must you go through while you install the operating system on the drive? (Choose two.)

   A. Create a new partition

   B. Initialize the drive

   C. Format the drive

   D. Install the drive utility

5. You are providing some phone support for your clients. They are telling you that the video seems to be showing poorly. You need to see if there is a problem with the video card. Where would you instruct them to go to view this information?

   A. Display Properties

   B. The screensaver tab

   C. Device Manager

   D. MSCONFIG

6. What is the minimum processor requirement for Windows Vista?

   A. 133MHz

   B. 233MHz

   C. 800MHz

   D. 1GHz

7. What is the minimum RAM requirement for Windows Vista?

   A. 64MB

   B. 256MB

   C. 512MB

   D. 1024MB

8. A user wants to modify his network connection from the Windows Vista Network window. Which of the following options enable the user to do this?

   A. Task Manager

   B. Command Prompt

   C. My Network Places

   D. Network and Sharing Center

9. Which of the following operating systems uses the KDE GUI?

   A. Windows

   B. Mac OS

   C. Linux

   D. DOS

10. Which of the following operating systems can work with Intel hardware? (Select the three best answers.)

   A. Windows

   B. Mac OS version 7.6

   C. Mac OS X

   D. Ubuntu

11. According to analysts, which of the following are the three most-used versions of Windows? (Select the three best answers.)

   A. Windows 2000

   B. Windows XP

   C. Windows Vista

   D. Windows 7

12. What is the maximum number of primary partitions that a single hard drive can contain?

   A. 2

   B. 3

   C. 4

   D. 5

13. A second hard disk has been added to a computer running Windows Vista. What must be done first in order to use the drive?

   A. Initialize the drive

   B. Partition the drive

   C. Format the drive

   D. Install an operating system to the drive

14. Which of the following operating systems can extend a partition? (Select the two best answers.)

   A. Windows 2000

   B. Windows XP

   C. Windows Vista

   D. Windows 7

15. Which of the following are benefits of NTFS over FAT32? (Select the three best answers.)

   A. NTFS has a maximum partition size of 2TB

   B. NTFS has file-level security

   C. NTFS supports EFS

   D. NTFS supports disk quotas

16. What is the minimum RAM requirement for Windows 7 64-bit?

   A. 512MB

   B. 1GB

   C. 2GB

   D. 4GB

Case Study 1

Identify which operating system your home or lab computer is using. Next, identify the processor speed, amount of RAM, and hard drive space of the computer. Analyze whether the operating system can be updated to the next version. For example, if you are using Windows Vista, identify whether it can be updated to Windows 7. Use the following website for more information and aid in your analysis:

http://windows.microsoft.com/en-US/windows/downloads/upgrade-advisor

Case Study 2

Hard drives are constantly being written to. Information is on the move; programs are installed and removed, files are written and deleted. Over time, this causes fragmentation of files, resulting in a less-efficient hard drive.

Analyze your hard drive and see if it should be defragmented. Use the Disk Defragmenter tool in Windows to analyze the drive. Windows lets you know if the drive should be defragmented or not. Because disk defragmentation can be a resource-intensive process, consider running the task at a time when you won't need the computer for anything else.

Answers and Explanations

1. **B.** Windows Aero is Microsoft's new visual experience. It features translucent windows, window animations, three-dimensional viewing of windows, and a modified taskbar. You can make modifications to the look of Aero by right-clicking the desktop and selecting Personalize. Then select Windows Color and Appearance. There you can modify features such as the transparency of windows. Note: Aero is not available in Windows Vista Home Basic.

2. **A.** If you are using a Windows-based operating system, you have used this at one time or the other. You can view all files on the system as well as view network drives.

3. **C.** Windows XP uses My Network Places to manage dial-up and local area network connections. When you open My Network Places, you see a list of network connections and shared folders on the network, including those located on the local computer and on remote computers.

4. **A, C.** While you install the Windows operating system to the new drive, you must go through the partitioning and formatting steps. Almost all drives are not prepared to accept an operating system right out of the box. However, initialization happens automatically during the OS install. The primary hard drive (the one with the OS) does not need to be initialized. But, other hard drives that are added afterward need to be initialized within Disk Management.

5. **C.** For you to view the installed devices, you need to instruct the user to go to Device Manager and see if there are any errors on the display adapters.

6. **C.** The minimum processor requirement for Windows Vista is 800MHz. However, Microsoft recommends 1GHz or higher. 133MHz is the minimum processor requirement for Windows 2000 Professional, and 233MHz is the minimum for Windows XP.

7. **C.** The minimum RAM requirement for Windows Vista is 512MB. However, Microsoft recommends 1GB of RAM or higher. 64MB is the minimum RAM requirement for Windows XP/2000.

8. **D.** To manage network connections while in the Network window, click the Network and Sharing Center button. After that window opens, click the link for Manage Network Connections.

9. **C.** Linux uses the KDE GUI. Windows and Mac OS have their own GUI, and DOS is text-based with no GUI at all.

10. A, C, D. Windows and Linux distributions such as Ubuntu are meant to run on PCs. Personal computers can use hardware from many manufacturers with Intel being one of the most common. Mac OS X is written for Macintosh computers that use Intel hardware as well. Mac OS version 7.6 was the first version to be dubbed "Mac OS"; it was written for Motorola-based processors.

11. B, C, D. Windows XP, Vista, and 7 are all heavily used in the U.S. However, Windows 2000 only has a very small amount of people still using it.

12. C. A single hard drive can contain up to four primary partitions.

13. A. To do anything with the drive, it must first be initialized. Then, it can be partitioned and formatted in that order. An OS is not necessary if the first hard disk already has one.

14. C, D. Windows Vista and Windows 7 can extend partitions, but Windows 2000 and XP cannot.

15. B, C, D. NTFS supports file-level security, EFS, and disk quotas. However, although NTFS has a practical limit of 2 TB for partitions, it can theoretically be extended as far as 16 exabytes.

16. C. Windows 7 64-bit versions require a minimum of 2GB of RAM. 32-bit versions require only 1GB of RAM.

Case Study 1 Solution

For example, a Windows Vista computer could be analyzed in the following way:

1. Identify the operating system: Click **Start**, and then right-click **Computer** and select **Properties**. This displays the System window, and the Windows edition is shown at the top.

2. Identify CPU, RAM, and HD: The CPU and RAM can also be determined in the System window. However, hard drive space has to be located in either Disk Management or in Windows Explorer.

3. By accessing the following link:

   http://windows.microsoft.com/en-US/windows/downloads/upgrade-advisor

You can find out automatically whether your operating system can be upgraded to Windows 7. Factors that determine this include the CPU speed, type of CPU (32-bit or 64-bit), amount of RAM, and available hard disk space.

Case Study 2 Solution

To analyze a drive for defragmentation in Windows Vista, do the following:

1. Click **Start, All Programs, Accessories, System Tools, Disk Defragmenter**.

2. This automatically analyzes the disk. If it needs to be defragmented, Windows alerts you and you can either defragment it immediately or schedule a time to do so.

In Windows XP:

1. Click **Start**, right-click **Computer**, and then right-click **Manage**. This displays the Computer Management window.

2. Click **Disk Defragmenter**.

3. Highlight the volume (such as C) you want to analyze and click the **Analyze** button. This tells you whether you need to defragment the volume.

This chapter covers the following subjects:

- **Security Fundamentals**—This section covers the mindset you should have when securing a computer. File systems, authentication, and how to protect against malware are all dealt with in this section.

- **Data and Physical Security**—This section describes encryption types, the Local Security Policy, backups, password management, and much more.

- **Access Control Purposes and Principles**—Windows uses an Access Control Model to set what users have rights to what resources. User Access Control (UAC), NTFS permissions, and auditing are also described.

- **Installing, Configuring, and Troubleshooting Security Features**—This section demonstrates how to secure the BIOS, configure a firewall, and set up a secure wireless connection.

- **Wireless Security**—Wireless security should be foremost on an organization's mind. This section discusses encryption such as WEP and WPA. It also covers how to set up and troubleshoot wireless clients.

Basic Security

With widespread reports of security breaches, identity theft, and lost hardware, understanding how to secure computers and networks is an important skill. Computers can be protected by installing antivirus and anti-malware software, installing a firewall, and updating each of these items to the latest definitions and software release. You also can secure a computer by way of access control policies, and by implementing physical security. Mastering these objectives helps you handle the increasing challenges of computer security in the real world.

Security Fundamentals

Security is more than a set of techniques; it is a mindset. The information your clients or company stores on computers can be highly damaging to those organizations or to society at large if it falls into the wrong hands. When you understand that fact, you understand why the gamut of security techniques discussed in the following sections is necessary to protect that information.

Secure and Insecure File Systems

The decisions made about the file system used to set up a computer have a big effect on how secure that computer is against intruders. Windows 2000, XP, and Vista are designed to use the New Technology File System (NTFS) as the default file system. NTFS was designed from the start as a much more secure file system than the FAT file systems used on MS-DOS, Windows 3.x, and Windows 9x/Me.

NTFS supports the creation of user and group accounts with different levels of access to folders and files (to use this feature in Windows XP Professional, disable Simple File Sharing) and the use of the Encrypting File System (EFS) for user-specific encryption of individual files and folders (EFS support varies by Windows version). FAT file systems, such as FAT12 (floppy disks), FAT16 (small hard disks), and FAT32 (large hard disks), do not support user and group accounts, nor do they include file/folder encryption. Consequently, you should use NTFS whenever possible. Note that Windows Vista cannot be installed on

a drive that uses a FAT file system. However, Windows 2000 and Windows XP can be installed on drives that use FAT.

NOTE Windows includes the command-line Convert.exe utility for converting the file system from FAT to NTFS, and drives can be converted from FAT to NTFS during an upgrade installation of Windows. Once converted, drives cannot be changed back to FAT.

Authentication Technologies

Authentication is a general term for any method used to verify a person's identity and protect systems against unauthorized access. It is a preventative measure that can be broken down into four categories:

- Something the user knows—for example, a password or PIN

- Something the user has—for example, a smart card or other security token

- Something the user is—for example, the biometric reading of a fingerprint or retina scan

- Something the user does—for example, a signature

The devices that are used to authenticate a user, such as smart cards, biometrics, key fobs, and other products, are often referred to as *authentication technologies*.

Username/Password/PIN

Username/password or personal identification number (PIN) authentication technologies can take many forms. Some examples include

- **An authentication server on a network maintains a list of authorized users and passwords**—Only users with a recognized username and password (credentials) are allowed to access the network's resources.

- **A keypad lock on an entrance into a secure area can store a list of authorized PINs**—Only users with a recognized PIN can enter the secure area.

You can use these technologies in conjunction with other methods for additional security, such as a smart card or biometric reading.

Smart Cards

A smart card is a credit card–sized card that contains stored information and might also contain a simple microprocessor or a radio-frequency identification (RFID)

chip. You can use smart cards to store identification information for use in security applications, stored values for use in prepaid telephone or debit card services, hotel guest room access, and many other functions. Smart cards are available in contact, contactless, or proximity form factors. Key fobs containing RFID chips work in a similar fashion to proximity-based smart cards.

A smart card–based security system includes smart cards, card readers that are designed to work with smart cards, and a back-end system that contains a database that stores a list of approved smart cards for each secured location. You can also use smart card–based security systems to secure individual personal computers.

To further enhance security, smart card security systems can also require the user to input a PIN number or security password as well as provide the smart card at secured checkpoints, such as the entrance to a computer room.

Biometrics

Biometrics refers to the use of biological information, such as human body characteristics, to authenticate a potential user of a secure area. The most common type of biometric security system for PCs is fingerprint-based, but other methods include voice measurements and eye retina and iris scans.

A biometric security system uses a reader or scanner to analyze the characteristic being used for access control and digitizes it into a series of match points, a database that stores the match points of approved users, and software that determines if the information coming from the reader or scanner matches a user in the database. To prevent identity theft, biometric information is usually encrypted.

Biometrics are increasingly being used to prevent unauthorized access to desktop and laptop PCs. Many laptop and portable PCs now include fingerprint readers and biometric software, and USB-based fingerprint readers can be added to desktop and laptop PCs. Some fingerprint readers require the users to swipe the finger across the reader, while others use a pad that the user pushes, similar to the way a fingerprint is placed on an ink pad.

Protection Against Viruses and Malware

Protection against viruses and malware is a necessary protection for every type of computing device, from portable PC to server. Computer protection suites that include antivirus, anti-malware, anti-adware, and anti-phishing protection are available from many vendors, but some users prefer a "best of breed" approach that uses the best available products in each category.

These programs can use some or all of the following techniques to protect users and systems:

- Real-time protection to block infection

- Periodic scans for known and suspected threats

- Automatic updating on a frequent (usually daily) basis

- Renewable subscriptions to obtain updated threat signatures

- Links to virus and threat encyclopedias

- Inoculation of system files

- Permissions-based access to the Internet

- Scanning of downloaded files and sent/received emails

The most important thing you can remember when attempting to protect against viruses and malware is to keep your anti-malware application up to date. The second most important item is to watch out for unknown data, whether it comes via email, or USB flash drive, or from elsewhere.

Software Firewalls

A software firewall is a program that examines data packets on a network to determine whether to forward them to their destination or block them. You can use firewalls to protect only against inbound threats (one-way firewall) or against both unauthorized inbound and outbound traffic (two way firewall). The standard firewall in Windows XP and Windows Vista is a one-way firewall. However, many third-party firewall programs, such as Zone Alarm, are two-way firewalls.

NOTE Windows Vista's firewall can also be used in two-way mode by modifying its configuration through the Windows Firewall with Advanced Security Microsoft Management Console (MMC) snap-in. For details, see http://technet.microsoft.com/en-us/library/cc507848.aspx.

You can configure a software firewall to permit traffic between specified IP addresses and to block traffic to and from the Internet except when permitted on a per-program basis.

Corporate networks sometimes use a proxy server with a firewall as the sole direct connection between the Internet and the corporate network and use the firewall in the proxy server to protect the corporate network against threats.

Hardware Recycling and Deconstruction

Even after a computer has reached the end of its useful life, the hard disk it contains represents a potential security risk. To prevent confidential company or client information from being accessed from a computer that is being disposed of for resale, recycling, or deconstruction for parts, you can use one of the following methods:

- Remove the hard disk(s) and destroy their platters with a hammer or other device, then recycle the scrap. Use this method when preserving the hard disk as a working device is not necessary.

- Overwrite the hard disk(s) with a program that meets or exceeds recognized data-destruction standards such as the U.S. Department of Defense 5220.22-M (7 passes) or Peter Guttman's 35-pass maximum security method. These programs destroy existing data and partition information in such a way as to prevent data recovery or drive forensics analysis. Use this method when maintaining the hard disk as a working device is important (such as for donation or resale). You can use a variety of commercial and freeware programs for this task, which is variously known as disk scrubbing or disk wiping.

You also should handle external hard disks in one of these ways when disposing of them. To prevent information from being recovered, you can physically destroy or bulk-erase floppy disks that contain sensitive information. To protect information on CD or DVD media, shredding is recommended.

Data and Physical Security

Even if the computer network is secure, a PC and its information is not completely secure if you overlook data and physical security issues. The following sections help you understand how to ensure that you properly deal with these potential security risks.

Data Access Local Security Policy

The Local Security Policy window provides access to a variety of policies that you can use to protect data residing on the system. In Windows Vista/XP/2000, you can access this by navigating to the **Start** menu and then choosing **Control Panel**. Verify that you are in Classic view, double-click **Administrative Tools**, and then double-click **Local Security Policy**. Alternatively, you can press **Windows+R** to open the **Run** prompt, and type **secpol.msc**.

These policies include

- **Enable auditing**—Open the **Local Policies** section of the Security Settings dialog, and click **Audit Policy**. Now, enable auditing for a policy. For example, to audit user access to files, folders, and printers, double-click the **Audit Object Access** policy and checkmark the **Success and Failure** options. Then click **OK** to save your changes. (In some operating systems, these are checkmarked already.) To specify a file, folder, or printer to audit, use the object's Auditing tab (located in the Advanced dialog of the object's Security tab). For details, see Microsoft Knowledge Base article 310399 at http://support.microsoft.com/. This function is available on Windows XP only if Simple File Sharing is disabled. Success and Failure information is stored in the Event Viewer's Security logfile.

- **Shutdown: Clear Virtual Memory Pagefile**—The pagefile might store passwords and user information. By enabling this option, you can prevent this information from being used to compromise the system.

- **Take ownership of files or other objects**—This setting is located in **Security Settings**, **Local Policies**, **User Rights Assignments**. By default, this is set to the Administrators group, but to reduce the chance of ownership changes by unauthorized persons, modify this to just one account; for example, the primary account on the computer.

- **Turn on Ctrl+Alt+Del**—The actual name of this policy is "Interactive logon: Do not require Ctrl+Alt+Del." By disabling this policy, the actual Ctrl+Alt+Del screen appears before logging in, a valuable security feature that can deter would-be hackers from getting into the system and accessing its data.

TIP   For other security settings, see the Windows XP security checklists at LabMice.net (http://labmice.techtarget.com/articles/winxpsecuritychecklist.htm) and the Computer Protection Program at the Berkeley Lab (www.lbl.gov/cyber/systems/wxp-security-checklist.html).

Encryption Technologies

Microsoft includes two types of built-in encryption with some of their versions of Windows. The Encrypting File System (dependent on an NTFS-formatted volume) is used to encrypt individual files and folders. BitLocker is used to encrypt an entire disk.

Encrypting File System

Windows 2000, Windows XP Professional, Windows Vista Business/Enterprise/Ultimate, and Windows 7 Ultimate editions include support for EFS. You can use EFS to protect sensitive data files and temporary files and can applied it to individual files or folders (when applied to folders, all files in an encrypted folder are also encrypted).

EFS files can be opened only by the user who encrypted them, by an administrator, or by EFS keyholders (users who have been provided with the EFS certificate key for another user's account). Thus, they are protected against access by hackers.

Files encrypted with EFS are listed with green filenames when viewed in Windows Explorer or My Computer. Only files stored on a drive that used the NTFS file system can be encrypted.

To encrypt a file, follow this process:

Step 1.   Right-click the file in Windows Explorer or My Computer and select **Properties**.

Step 2.   Click the **Advanced** button on the General tab.

Step 3.   Click the empty **Encrypt Contents to Secure Data** checkbox.

Step 4.   Click **OK**.

Step 5.   Click **Apply**. When prompted, select the option to encrypt the file and parent folder or only the file as desired and click **OK**.

Step 6.   Click **OK** to close the properties sheet.

To decrypt the file, follow the same procedure, but clear the Encrypt Contents to Secure Data checkbox in Step 3.

NOTE   To enable the recovery of EFS encrypted files in the event that Windows cannot start, you should export the user's EFS certificate key. For details, see the Microsoft TechNet article Data Recovery and Encrypting File System (EFS) at http://technet.microsoft.com/en-us/library/cc512680.aspx.

BitLocker Encryption

To encrypt an entire disk, you need some kind of full disk encryption software. There are several currently available on the market; one developed by Microsoft for Windows Vista is called *BitLocker*—available only on Windows Vista Ultimate and Windows Vista Enterprise editions. This software can encrypt the entire disk,

which, after complete, is transparent to the user. However, there are some requirements for this, including

- A Trusted Platform Module (TPM): a chip residing on the motherboard that actually stores the encrypted keys.

  or

- An external USB key to store the encrypted keys. Using BitLocker without a TPM requires changes to Group Policy settings.

  and

- A hard drive with two volumes, preferably created during the installation of Windows. One volume is for the operating system (most likely C:) that will be encrypted; the other is the active volume that remains unencrypted so that the computer can boot. If a second volume needs to be created, the BitLocker Drive Preparation Tool can be of assistance and can be downloaded from Windows Update.

BitLocker software is based on the Advanced Encryption Standard (AES) and uses a 128-bit encryption key.

Backups

Securing backups prevents them from being misused by unauthorized users. Some backup applications include an option to password-protect the backup files so they can be restored only if the user provides the correct password. If you use a backup program that does not support password protection (such as Windows 2000 and XP's integrated NTBackup.exe), you must physically secure the backup media or drive to prevent it from access by unauthorized users.

Data Migration

The process of migrating data from one system to another, such as during the replacement of an old system by a new system, provides another potential security risk if you do not perform the data migration in a secure manner.

If possible, perform the data migration with a direct network or USB connection between the old and new computers. If this is not possible, make sure you use a migration program that can password protect the migration file. The Files and Settings Transfer Wizard in Windows XP automatically provides a password after collecting information from the old computer. This password must be used on the new computer before the migration file can be accessed.

If you use other migration programs, check their documentation to determine whether and how password protection is provided.

Data and Data Remnant Removal

After data is migrated to the new computer, you should clear the old computer of data or data remnants. If the computer will no longer be used, you can use a full-disk scrubbing program to wipe out the entire contents of the hard disk, including the operating system. For details, see the section "Hardware Recycling and Deconstruction," earlier in this chapter.

However, if the computer will still be in use with its current operating system, you can use software that overwrites only data files and "empty" disk space (no-longer-allocated disk space that might still contain recoverable files). Programs such as Norton Wipe Info (included as part of Norton System Works and Norton Utilities), McAfee Shredder (included in various McAfee programs), and others offer options to wipe files and folders, "empty" disk space, or an entire disk drive.

Password Management

PC users should use passwords to secure their user accounts. Through the local security policy and group policy in Windows, you can set up password policies that require users to do the following:

- Change passwords periodically (Local Policies, Security Options)
- Be informed in advance that passwords are about to expire (Account Policies, Password Policy)
- Enforce a minimum password length (Account Policies, Password Policy)
- Require complex passwords (Account Policies, Password Policy)
- Prevent old passwords from being reused continually (Account Policies, Password Policy)
- Wait a certain number of minutes after a specified number of unsuccessful logins has taken place before they can log in again (Account Policies, Account Lockout Policy)

To make these settings in Local Security Settings, open the Security Settings node and navigate to the appropriate subnodes (shown in parentheses in the preceding list). In Group Policy (gpedit.msc), navigate to one of the following as appropriate:

- Computer Configuration, Windows Settings, Security Settings, Account Policies, Password Policy

- Computer Configuration, Windows Settings, Security Settings, Account Policies, Account Lockout Policy

- Computer Configuration, Windows Settings, Security Settings, Local Policies, Security Options

Locking a Workstation

You should lock your computer whenever you are not at the keyboard. The ability to lock the computer depends upon each user being assigned a password. You can use the following methods to lock a computer:

- To automatically lock the computer after the screen saver is enabled, do the following:
  - In Windows XP/2000, select the **On Resume, Password Protect** check box. This option is located on the Display properties sheet's Screen Saver tab.
  - In Windows Vista, select the **On Resume, Display Logon Screen** check box. This option is located in the Screen Saver Settings window, which can be accessed from Control Panel, Personalization.

- To lock the computer immediately, press **Windows key+L** on your keyboard, or press **Ctrl+Alt+Del** and select **Lock Computer**.

To log back on to the computer, provide your username and password or password (if your user name is already displayed) when prompted.

Incident Reporting

In addition to enabling auditing of local security policy settings and checking the audit logs periodically, organizations should also set up and follow procedures for reporting security-related incidents. These incidents could include the following:

- Repeated attempts to log into password-protected accounts

- Unlocked doors to areas that should be secure, such as computer or server rooms, backup media storage, or network wiring closets

- Unknown clients detected on wireless networks

- Viruses and malware detected on clients or servers

- Unauthorized access in the form of denial-of-service (DoS) and other malicious attacks, remote access Trojans (RATs), and the detection of unrecognized network sniffers

Organizations have varying procedures when it comes to incident reporting. One common process for incident reporting and response includes the identification and containment of problems, then evidence gathering and further investigation. Afterwards, the process usually includes procedures for the eradication of threats, and recovery from them. Finally, documentation and monitoring procedures are common to attempt to avoid the same issues in the future.

Social Engineering

Social engineering is a term popularized by the career of successful computer and network hacker Kevin Mitnick, who used a variety of methods to convince computer users to provide access to restricted systems. Some of these methods include

- **Pretexting**—Pretending to be from the company's help desk, telephone, or Internet provider, or an authorized service company and asking the user to provide login credentials to enable routine maintenance to be performed or to solve an urgent computer problem.

- **Phishing**—Setting up bogus websites or sending fraudulent emails that trick users into providing personal, bank, or credit card information. A variation, phone phishing, uses an interactive voice response (IVR) system that the user has been tricked into calling to trick the user into revealing information.

- **Trojan horse**—Malware programs disguised as popular videos or website links that trap keystrokes or transmit sensitive information.

- **Baiting**—Leaving physical media (such as a CD, DVD, or USB drive) that appears to be confidential information lying around. The media autoruns when inserted and can deliver various types of malware, including backdoor access to a company's computer network.

Although antivirus and antiphishing programs and features in the latest web browsers can stop computer-based social engineering exploits, pretexting can only be stopped by users who refuse to be gulled into letting down their guard. Teach users to do the following:

- Ask for ID when approached in person by somebody claiming to be from "the help desk," "the phone company," or "the service company."

- Ask for a name and supervisor name when contacted by phone by someone claiming to be from "the help desk," "the phone company," or "the service company."

- Provide contact information for the help desk, phone company, or authorized service companies and ask users to call the authorized contact person to verify that the service call or phone request for information is legitimate.

- Log into systems themselves and then provide the tech the computer, rather than giving the tech login information.

- Change passwords immediately after service calls.

- Report any potential social engineering calls or in-person contacts, even if no information was exchanged. Social engineering experts can gather innocuous-sounding information from several users and use it to create a convincing story to gain access to restricted systems.

Access Control Purposes and Principles

Controlling access to files, folders, printers, and physical locations is essential for system and network security. The following sections discuss the purposes and principles of access control.

Operating System Access Control

Operating system access control in Windows 2000, XP, and Vista requires the use of the NTFS file system. To use access control in Windows XP Professional, the default Simple File Sharing setting must also be disabled.

User, Administration, and Guest Accounts

There are three standard account levels in Windows:

- **Limited (known as Standard user accounts in Windows Vista and Restricted users in Windows 2000)**—Limited accounts have permission to perform routine tasks. However, these accounts are blocked from performing tasks that involve system-wide changes, such as installing hardware or software. (Windows Vista permits Standard user accounts to perform some UAC-restricted tasks, such as adding hardware, if they can provide an administrator password.)

- **Administrator**—Users with an administrator account can perform any and all tasks.

- **Guest**—The guest account level is the most limited. A guest account cannot install software or hardware or run already-existing applications and cannot access files in shared document folders or the Guest profile. The Guest account is disabled by default. If it is enabled for a user to gain access to the computer, that

access should be temporary, and the account should be disabled again when the user no longer requires access.

When a user is created using the Users applet in Windows, the user must be assigned a limited (Standard) or Administrator account. Guest accounts are used for visitors.

User Account Control (UAC)

User Account Control (UAC) is a security component of Windows Vista that keeps every user (besides the actual Administrator account) in standard user mode instead of as an administrator with full administrative rights—even if the person is a member of the administrators group. It is meant to prevent unauthorized access, as well as avoid user error in the form of accidental changes. With UAC enabled, users perform common tasks as non-administrators, and when necessary, as administrators, without having to switch users, log off, or use Run As.

Basically, UAC was created with two goals in mind:

- To eliminate unnecessary requests for excessive administrative-level access to Windows resources

- To reduce the risk of malicious software using the administrator's access control to infect operating system files

When a standard end-user requires administrator privileges to perform certain tasks such as installing an application, a small pop-up UAC window appears, notifying the user that an administrator credential is necessary. If the user has administrative rights and clicks Continue, the task is carried out, but if the user does not have sufficient rights, the attempt fails. Note that these pop-up UAC windows do not appear if the person is logged on with the actual Administrator account.

You can turn UAC on and off by going to **Start**, **Control Panel**, **User Accounts and Family Safety**. Then select **User Accounts**, and **Turn User Account Control On or Off**. From there, you can turn UAC on and off by checking or unchecking the box. If a change is made to UAC, the system needs to be restarted. Note that if you are using the Classic view in the Control Panel, User Accounts and Family Safety is bypassed.

Groups

You can assign users in Windows 2000, XP, and Vista/Win7 to different groups, each with different permissions. The Local Policy (local PCs) and Group Policy (networked PCs connected to a domain controller) settings can restrict PC features by group or by PC. Aside from the Administrator, User, and Guest groups (whose

corresponding accounts were explained previously), there is one additional group you should know: the Power Users group. Power users have more permissions than standard users, but fewer permissions than administrators. Power users can install drivers, run non-certified programs, and in general modify computer-wide settings. Because of this, members of the Power Users group might be able to expose the computer to security risks, such as running a Trojan horse program or executing a virus. Be especially careful which users are added to the Power Users and Administrators groups. Because the Power Users group can be a security risk, Microsoft has decreased the amount of "power" these users have in Windows Vista and Win7. For example, power users can no longer customize file associations the way they did in Windows XP.

Permissions Actions, Types, and Levels

You assign permissions for folders, files, and printers via the Security tab of the object's properties sheet. Folder and file permissions vary by user type or group, and can include the following:

- **Full Control**—Complete access to contents of file or folder. When Full Control is selected, all of the following are selected automatically.

- **Modify**—Change file or folder contents.

- **Read & Execute**—Access file or folder contents and run programs.

- **List Folder Contents**—Display folder contents.

- **Read**—Access a file or folder.

- **Write**—Add a new file or folder.

Each permission has two settings: Allow or Deny. Generally, if you want a user to have access to a folder, you add them to the list and select **Allow** for the appropriate permission. If you don't want to allow them access, normally you simply don't add them. But in some cases, an explicit **Deny** is necessary. This could be because the user is part of a larger group that already has access to a parent folder, but you don't want the specific user to have access to this particular subfolder. This leads us to permission inheritance.

Permission Inheritance and Propagation

If you create a folder, the default action it takes is to inherit permissions from the parent folder. So any permissions that you set in the parent are inherited by the subfolder. To view an example of this, locate any folder within an NTFS volume (besides the root folder), right-click it and select **Properties**, access the **Security** tab, and click the **Advanced** button. Toward the bottom of the window, you see an

enabled checkbox named Inherit from Parent the Permission Entries That Apply to Child Objects. This means that any permissions added or removed in the parent folder are also added or removed in the current folder. In addition, those permissions that are being inherited cannot be modified in the current folder. To make modifications to the permissions, you would need to deselect the **Inherit from Parent the Permission Entries That Apply to Child Objects** checkbox. When you do so, you have the option to copy the permissions from the parent to the current folder or remove them entirely. So by default, the parent is automatically propagating permissions to the subfolder and the subfolder is inheriting its permissions from the parent.

You can also propagate permission changes to subfolders that are not inheriting from the current folder. To do so, select the **Replace Permission Entries on All Child Objects** with entries shown here that apply to Child Objects checkbox. This might all seem a bit confusing; just remember that folders automatically inherit from the parent unless you turn inheriting off—and you can propagate permission entries to subfolders at any time by selecting the **Replace** option.

Moving and Copying Folders and Files

Moving and copying folders have different results when it comes to permissions. Basically, it breaks down like this:

- If you *copy* a folder on the same or to a different volume, the folder inherits the permissions of the parent folder it was copied to (target directory).

- If you *move* a folder to a different location on the same volume, the folder retains its original permissions.

Components

Use the Security tab on a printer's properties sheet to restrict access to the printer. To restrict access to other components, such as CD or DVD drives, use Local Policy or Group Policy settings.

Restricted Spaces

To prevent users from accessing restricted spaces, such as computer or server rooms or LAN wiring closets, use physical access restriction devices, such as smart cards or key fobs.

Auditing and Event Logging

Windows 2000, XP, and Vista all support auditing and event logging, both of which enable you to find out what issues affecting security might be taking place on a particular computer.

Event logs are enabled by default, while auditing of files, folders, and printers must be enabled by the system administrator. When auditing is enabled, success and failure entries for audited devices are stored in the Security log.

To view event logs in these versions of Windows, follow these steps:

Step 1.   Right-click **My Computer** (2000, XP) or **Computer** (Vista) and select **Manage**. The Computer Management console opens.

Step 2.   Expand the Event Viewer node. It contains four subnodes: Application, Internet Explorer, Security, and System.

Step 3.   Select the desired node to see events (see Figure 9-1).

Figure 9-1   Viewing the Application Event log.

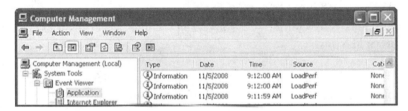

Step 4.   To view details of a particular event, double-click the event (see Figure 9-2).

Figure 9-2   Viewing the details of an application hang in the Application Event log.

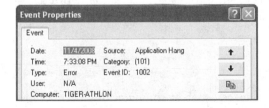

To enable auditing, see the section "Data Access Local Security Policy," earlier in this chapter.

Periodically, you should clear event logs. Before clearing these logs, you might want to archive their contents. For details, see Microsoft Knowledge Base article 308427 at http://support.microsoft.com.

Installing, Configuring, and Troubleshooting Security Features

The following sections help you understand how to set up and configure major security features.

BIOS Security Features

Several common BIOS features can be used to help prevent unauthorized access to the computer. These include

- **Boot sector virus protection**—Enable this feature to prevent boot sector viruses and malware from infecting the system hard disk.

- **Boot sequence**—Place the system hard disk first in the boot order to prevent unauthorized users from booting from a floppy disk, CD, or DVD.

- **BIOS setup password**—Enable this feature to prevent unauthorized users from altering BIOS setup information.

NOTE In the event that the setup password is mislaid, you can reset the CMOS chip used to store BIOS settings with a jumper on the motherboard, or by removing the battery for several minutes.

- **BIOS HDD Password**—On a semi-related note, many laptops come equipped with drive lock technology; this may simply be referred to as an HDD password. If enabled, it prompts the user to enter a password for the hard drive when the computer is first booted. If the user of the computer doesn't know the password for the hard drive, the drive locks and the OS does not boot. An eight-digit or similar hard drive ID usually associates the laptop with the hard drive that is installed. On most systems, this password is clear by default, but if the password is set and forgotten, it can usually be reset within the BIOS. Some laptops come with documentation clearly stating the BIOS and drive lock passwords.

If you are unable to boot from CD, DVD, or floppy disk to perform PC maintenance or troubleshooting, change the boot sequence to place removable media earlier in the boot order than the system hard disk.

If the BIOS setup program is protected by a password and the password is lost, you can clear the password on most desktop systems by using the BIOS clear jumper on the motherboard or by removing the battery for several seconds.

CAUTION   Some laptops use the password to permanently restrict access to only the password holder. In such cases, the password cannot be bypassed. See the documentation for your laptop or portable system before applying a BIOS password to determine whether this is the case.

Software Firewalls

You can configure software firewalls, such as the firewalls incorporated in Windows XP SP2 and SP3, and Windows Vista, to permit specified applications to pass through the firewall, to open specific ports needed by applications, or to block all traffic. Whenever possible, it's easier to permit traffic by application rather than by UDP or TCP port numbers.

To enable the Windows Firewall while permitting exceptions, click **On** (recommended) and leave the Don't Allow Exceptions checkbox cleared (see Figure 9-3). To block all incoming traffic (recommended when the computer is used in a public location, such as a hotel or restaurant), click the **Don't Allow Exceptions** checkbox.

Figure 9-3   The Windows Firewall's General tab (Windows XP).

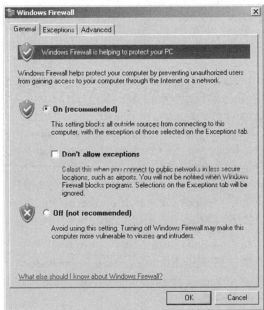

Turn off the Windows Firewall only if directed by an installer program, or if you prefer to use a third-party firewall.

Click the **Exceptions** tab shown in Figure 9-4 to view programs that are permitted to access your computer (checked programs). Click **Add Program** to add a program, or **Add Port** to add a TCP or UDP port number to the list of Exceptions.

Figure 9-4   The Windows Firewall's Exceptions tab (Windows XP).

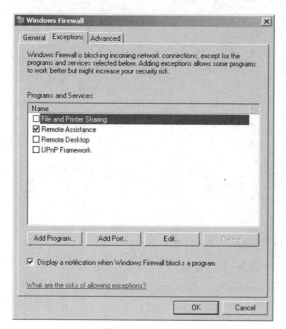

To revoke an exception temporarily, clear the checkbox. To remove the program or port from the list of Exceptions, select the program or port and click **Delete**. Use **Edit** to change the program, port number, or scope (list of IP addresses) for the selected item.

Use the Advanced tab (see Figure 9-5) to specify which connections are protected by Windows Firewall, to set up a security log, to set up ICMP for messaging between networked computers, and to reset Windows Firewall's defaults.

Troubleshooting Software Firewalls

If users are unable to connect to shared folders on your system, or if you are unable to use programs that require inbound connections, you might have one of the following situations:

- **Your firewall is configured to block all connections (No exceptions setting)**—Turn the Windows Firewall on but clear the **No Exceptions** checkbox.

Figure 9-5   The Windows Firewall's Advanced tab (Windows XP).

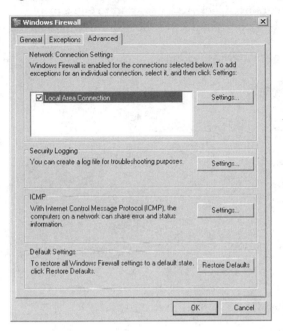

- **A Windows Firewall is blocking x program dialog has appeared**—Click **Unblock** to permit the program access to your system.

- **Your firewall does not have an exception set up for the program**—With the Windows Firewall, open the Exceptions tab and make sure the program that is being blocked is listed and is checked. Click an empty checkbox to reenable an exception. Use Add Program to add the program. To enable Windows Firewall to permit access to your computer's shared files and printers, File and Printer Sharing must be on the Exceptions list and the exception must be enabled.

- **You might have two firewalls (Windows Firewall and a third-party firewall, or two third-party firewalls) running and one or both of them are blocking connections**—Turn off one of the firewall programs and configure the other one properly.

- **You did not open the correct TCP or UDP ports for a program**—Generally, it's easier to set up exceptions by adding a program. However, in some cases, you might need to use Add Port to set up the exceptions needed. Be sure to specify each of the port numbers and the correct port type for each port number.

Ports are usually the culprit when it comes to firewall troubleshooting. If a person cannot ping your computer, yet you can access the network and the Internet, and people need to access your system remotely, consider checking the ports of your firewall.

File Systems (Converting from FAT32 to NTFS)

Windows 2000 and Windows XP can be installed on either FAT32 or NTFS file systems. However, the FAT32 file system lacks the security and user/group permissions features of NTFS. To convert a FAT32 drive to NTFS so you can use NTFS's security and user/group permissions features, use the command-line Convert.exe program:

Step 1.   Click **Start**, **Run**.

Step 2.   Enter **cmd.exe** and click **OK** to open a Windows command prompt session.

Step 3.   To convert drive C:, enter **convert c: /fs:ntfs**.

Malicious Software Protection

Windows XP and Windows Vista include Windows Defender, which provides real-time and scan-based protection against malware types such as Trojan horses and worms. However, for complete protection, you also need to install an antivirus program.

To determine whether antivirus, anti-malware, and firewall programs are running properly and are up to date, open the Security Center in Control Panel (see Figure 9-6). It reports the status of both Microsoft and third-party security programs.

TIP   When you install third-party security programs that support Security Center, you are asked if you want Security Center or the third-party security program to report potentially dangerous conditions. To avoid duplicate warnings, select the option to use Security Center to provide warnings.

Types of Malware and Infection Methods

Malware types and infection methods you should understand include

- **Trojan horse**—Programs that purport to be useful utilities or file converters, but actually install various types of harmful programs on your computer, including spyware, remote access, and rootkits

Figure 9-6   The Windows XP Security Center.

- **Rootkits**—A concealment method used by many types of malware to prevent detection by normal antivirus and anti-malware programs

- **Spyware**—Software that spies on system activities and transmits details of Web searches or other activities to remote computers

- **Remote access**—Programs that enable unauthorized control of your system; can be used to set up networks of compromised computers known as botnets

- **Adware**—Software that displays pop-up ads and banners related to your Web searches and activities

- **Grayware**—General term for dialers, joke programs, adware, and spyware programs

Training Users in Malware Protection

Users should be educated in how to do the following:

- Keep antivirus, antispyware, and anti-malware programs updated

- Scan systems for viruses, spyware, and malware

- Understand major malware types and techniques

- Scan removable-media drives (CDs, DVDs, USB drives, and floppy disks) for viruses and malware

- Configure scanning programs for scheduled operation

- Respond to notifications when viruses, spyware, or malware have been detected

- Quarantine suspect files

- Report suspect files to the help desk and to the software vendor

- Removal of malware

- Disable antivirus when needed (such as during software installations) and to know when to reenable antivirus

- Use antiphishing features in web browsers and email clients

Training users can be difficult. Many employees in a company say that they don't have time for training, and might be hard to get through to. However, a small amount of time spent training can create a more productive atmosphere in general. Consider getting a person with training experience to help you. You could also consider webinars or computer-based training modules that users can complete on their own time.

Wireless Security

If an organization runs a wireless network, wireless security should be foremost on their mind. The best way to secure a wireless network is to use encryption such as WEP, WPA, or better yet, WPA2. Strong passphrases between the wireless clients and the wireless access point (wireless AP) are also important to consider. Sometimes, wireless clients are not able to connect to the wireless network properly; this section also covers how to troubleshoot those wireless clients.

WEP and WPA Encryption

An encrypted wireless network relies on the exchange of a passphrase between the client and the wireless access point (AP) or router before the client can connect to the network. There are three standards for encryption: WEP, WPA, and WPA2.

Wireless equivalent privacy (WEP) was the original encryption standard for wireless Ethernet (Wi-Fi) networks. It is the only encryption standard supported by most IEEE 802.11b-compliant hardware. Unfortunately, WEP encryption is not strong enough to resist attacks from a determined hacker. There are several reasons this is true, including key length (64-bit WEP uses a ten-character hex key, and 128-bit WEP uses a 26-character hex key) and the use of unencrypted transmissions for

some parts of the handshaking process. Because WEP encryption is not secure, you should not use it to "secure" a wireless network.

As a replacement to WEP, Wi-Fi Protected Access (WPA) was developed a few years ago. It is available in two strengths: WPA (which uses TKIP encryption) and the newer, stronger WPA2 (which uses AES encryption). WPA and WPA2's encryption is much stronger than WEP, supports a key length from 8 up to 63 alphanumeric characters (enabling the use of punctuation marks and other characters not permitted with WEP) or 64 hex characters, and supports the use of a RADIUS authentication server in corporate environments.

NOTE In some environments, WPA and WPA2 are both referred to as WPA, so the encryption method selected during wireless security configuration determines whether WPA or WPA2 has been chosen.

Because all clients and wireless APs or wireless routers on a wireless network must use the same encryption standard, use the strongest standard supported by all hardware.

Ideally, all wireless networks should be secured with WPA2 (WPA has been cracked, although cracking WPA is much harder than cracking WEP). However, the use of WPA2 encryption might require upgraded drivers for older network adapters and upgraded firmware for older wireless APs or wireless routers. Wi-Fi Certified adapters and wireless APs or wireless routers must support WPA2 as of March 13, 2006.

TIP There are various ways to create a strong passphrase for use with a WPA or WPA2 network. Some vendors of wireless APs and wireless routers include a feature sold under various brand names that is compliant with the Wi-Fi Protected Setup standard (also known as Easy Config). If this cannot be used on some hardware, you can obtain a dynamically generated strong passphrase at Gibson Research Corporation's Perfect Passwords website: www.grc.com/passwords.htm.

Copy and paste the passphrase provided into Notepad or another plain-text editor and then copy or paste it into the configuration dialog for a wireless AP, wireless router, and wireless client as needed.

Configuring Wireless Clients

After configuring a wireless AP or wireless router to provide WEP, WPA, or (preferably) WPA2 encryption, you must configure wireless clients with the same encryption information. You can set up clients manually or automatically. Note that

each wireless client connecting to a wireless AP or wireless router must use the same encryption standard and passphrase and specify the SSID used by the wireless AP or wireless router.

Windows XP SP2 and newer versions include a Wireless Network Setup Wizard. You can use this wizard to set up a brand-new wireless network or to add a client to an existing wireless network. To run the wizard, follow this procedure:

Step 1.   Click **Start**, **All Programs**, **Accessories**, **Communications**, **Wireless Networking** Wizard. At the introductory screen, click **Next** to continue.

Step 2.   In the Create a Name for Your Wireless Network dialog (see Figure 9-7), enter the service set identifier (SSID) you want to use for your network. You can create an SSID up to 32 characters.

Step 3.   Select whether you want to automatically assign a network key (default) or manually assign a network key. Use the manual option if you are adding your system to an existing network. If you use the manual option, you are prompted to enter your wireless network's existing WEP or WPA key later (see Step 6).

Step 4.   By default, the wizard uses WEP encryption; to use WPA encryption, click the **Use WPA Encryption** check box. Click **Next** to continue. Note that you see an error dialog onscreen if your network hardware is already connected to your system and it does not support WPA. Click **OK** to continue.

Step 5.   If you select the default "automatic" option shown in Figure 9-7, you can select from two options to save your settings: a USB flash (keychain) drive or manual network setup. The USB flash memory drive option can be used by any devices that support Microsoft Connect Now. Such devices automatically read the XML-format network setup files from the USB flash memory drive when the drive is connected to the device.

Step 6.   If you select the option to enter a network key yourself, you see the dialog shown in Figure 9-8. Enter the network key and then reenter it. Click **Next** to continue.

Figure 9-7   Creating an SSID and selecting network encryption with the Windows XP SP2 Wireless Network Setup Wizard.

Select this option to enter an existing network key

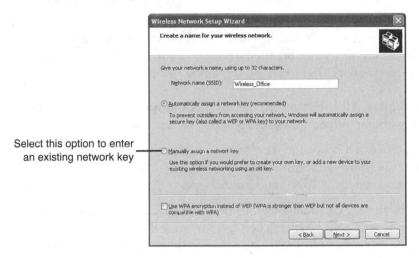

Figure 9-8   Entering a WEP key manually with the Windows XP Wireless Network Setup Wizard.

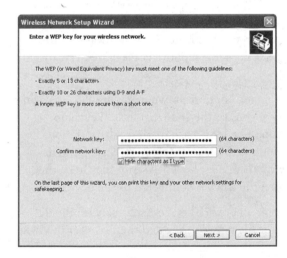

Step 7.   On the following screen, select the option to store the network settings to a USB flash drive or to configure the network manually.

Step 8.   If you selected the option to store the network settings on a USB flash drive, insert the drive when prompted. Click **Next**. A dialog displays the setup files as they are transferred to the flash drive.

Step 9.   Follow the instructions shown in Figure 9-9 to transfer the settings from the USB flash drive to your wireless access point (or router) and other network client PCs and devices. Click **Next** to continue.

Figure 9-9   How to transfer settings to other computers and devices.

Step 10.   At the end of the process, the wizard displays a "completed successfully" dialog. If you transferred settings to other devices using the USB flash memory drive (Step 9), the devices are listed by name.

Step 11.   Click the **Print Network Settings** button to open the settings in Notepad (see Figure 9-10).

Step 12.   Click **File, Save As** and name the file to create a backup of your settings, or click **File, Print** to make a printout that you can use to manually enter the settings on your wireless access point, router, or other network clients.

Troubleshooting Wireless Clients

If you are unable to connect to a wireless network, check the following settings:

■   **You might have selected the wrong SSID from the list of available wireless networks**—If you did not change the default SSID for your wireless AP or wireless router to a custom name, you might be trying to connect to the wrong wireless network. If you are entering the SSID for a non-broadcast network, double-check your spelling, punctuation, and capitalization.

Figure 9-10   Using Notepad to view, save, or print your settings.

- **If the network is encrypted, you might have selected the wrong encryption type or entered the wrong passphrase**—Be sure to select the same encryption type and enter the same passphrase as those used on the wireless AP or wireless router.

- **If you are connecting directly to another wireless device using an ad-hoc connection, you might have specified the wrong channel**—Both devices in an ad-hoc connection must use the same channel.

- **If you have not connected to the network before and you are not using a dual-channel (2.4GHz and 5GHz) wireless adapter, you might not have the correct adapter for the network**—This is much more likely if you have an 802.11a (5GHz) wireless adapter, as there are relatively few wireless networks using this standard.

- **If you have not connected to an 802.11g network before and you are using an 802.11b wireless adapter, the network might be configured to permit only 802.11g clients**—To permit both 802.11b and 802.11g clients to connect to an 802.11g network, configure the network security to use WEP and make sure the network is set as mixed rather than G-only. See the router or wireless AP documentation for details.

Unused Wireless Connections

As you make connections to wireless networks, Windows XP and Windows Vista can store the connections for reuse. Periodically, you should review this list of connections and delete connections you no longer need. By removing unused connections, you prevent your system from connecting to wireless networks that might not be secure.

To view the list of stored connections in Windows XP, follow these steps:

Step 1.   Open **My Network Places**.

Step 2.   Click **View Network Connections** in the Network Tasks pane.

Step 3.   Right-click your wireless network connection and select **Properties**.

Step 4.   Click the **Wireless Networks** tab. Your connections are listed.

Step 5.   To delete an unused connection, select it and click **Remove** (see Figure 9-11).

Figure 9-11   Windows XP's Wireless Networks dialog lists the connections you have made to various networks.

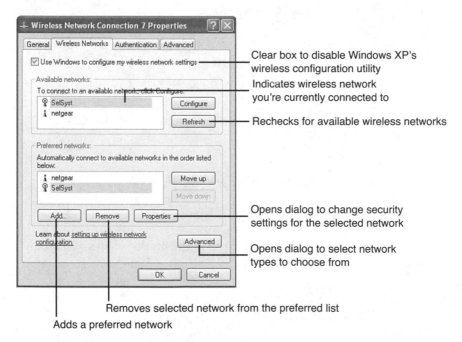

Step 6.   Repeat Step 5 until you have deleted all of the unused connections you no longer need.

Step 7.   Click **OK** to close the dialog.

To view the list of stored connections in Windows Vista, follow these steps:

Step 1.   Open **Control Panel**.

Step 2.   Click **Network and Internet**.

Step 3.   Open **Network and Sharing Center**.

Step 4.   Click **Manage Wireless Networks** in the Tasks pane. Your connections are listed.

Step 5.   To delete an unused connection, select it and click **Remove** (see Figure 9-12).

Figure 9-12 Windows Vista's Wireless Networks dialog lists the connections you have made to various networks.

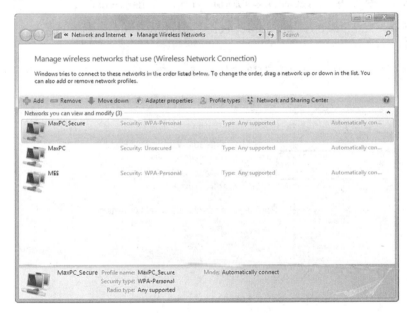

Step 6.   Repeat Step 5 until you have deleted all of the unused connections you no longer need.

Step 7.   Click the red **X** to close the dialog.

Chapter Review Questions

The following questions test your recall of the concepts described in this chapter. The answers are listed at the end of the questions in the "Answers and Explanations" section.

1. Which type of authentication technology uses a credit card–sized device that stores information about the user?

   A. Smart card '

   B. Credit card

   C. Keyless entry

   D. Biometrics

2. What technology uses human body characteristics as a way of allowing users into a secured area?

   A. Smart card

   B. Biometrics '

   C. PIN number

   D. Keyless entry

3. What are special products that can protect you from viruses and malware?

   A. Antivirus software

   B. Malware protection

   C. Phishing protection

   D. All of these options are correct '

4. Which of the following can help protect your computer from inbound and outbound attacks?

   A. Gateway

   B. Router

   C. Software firewall ,

   D. Hub

5. What are the three standards for encryption of wireless networks?

   A. WEP ·

   B. WPA ·

   C. WAP

   D. WPA2 ·

6. Windows 2000, Windows XP, and Windows Vista come with which type of encryption technology?

   A. NAT

   B. EFS ·

   C. User account

   D. WEP

7. You are using a computer with Windows Vista Enterprise installed. You need to encrypt the entire disk for security purposes. What technology allows you to do this?

   A. IPsec

   B. EFS

   C. BitLocker ·

   D. L2TP

8. When attackers ask questions to obtain information, what is this type of attack called?

   A. Social engineering ·

   B. System hacking

   C. Spam

   D. Spyware

9. You are working on a Windows Vista computer. You keep getting messages from the operating system asking you for permissions. What is the name of this new feature?

   A. User State Migration

   B. User Account Control ·

   C. User State Control

   D. User Account Information

10. Your company has a desktop that has a BIOS password assigned. The user who was in charge of the computer has left the company. What would you need to do to resolve this issue?

   A. Use a password reset CD.

   B. Reset the BIOS to the defaults.

   C. You cannot do this.

   D. Remove the jumper from the motherboard.

11. A thumb print would be an example of which of the following?

   A. Smart card

   B. Biometrics

   C. Antivirus

   D. WPA

12. You need to recycle a hard disk. Which of the following steps should you take?

   A. Destroy the hard disk

   B. Format the hard disk

   C. Overwrite the hard disk

   D. Remove the hard disk

13. Where can auditing be enabled on a Windows computer?

   A. Control Panel

   B. Command Prompt

   C. Local Security Policy

   D. Windows Explorer

14. Which of the following types of encryption does BitLocker use by default?

   A. WPA

   B. WEP

   C. TPM

   D. AES

15. Which of the following methods should be employed when it comes to password management? (Select the three best answers.)

   A. Enforce a minimum password length '

   B. Require complex passwords

   C. Prevent old passwords from being reused •

   D. Change passwords every year •

Case Study 1

Examine the wireless network adapter in your home or lab computer. Define which wireless encryption technique it is using. This is most likely WEP, WPA, or WPA2. You might also see TKIP or AES protocols in use. The best configuration of these options would be WPA2 with AES. If your network adapter is not set to this, examine why this is and list the steps you can take to increase the level of encryption in use. Keep in mind that the wireless network adapter and the wireless access point that it connects to must "handshake," meaning they must agree on, and be compatible with, the same encryption protocols.

Case Study 2

You are called to a customer's computer. The customer complains of pop-up messages, and they are being redirected to websites that they do not want to go to. You must fix this problem as soon as possible. What would you need to do to get the computer back up and running?

Answers and Explanations

1. **A.** A smart card contains user information and when used with a pin number to secure workstations gives you better security.

2. **B.** Biometrics is a technology that can use fingerprints, voice, and retina scans as an authentication method.

3. **D.** All of the listed products can help in the prevention of viruses, malware, and phishing scams. These need to be turned on and kept up to date to be effective.

4. **C.** A software firewall is a program that examines data packets on a network to determine whether to forward them to their destination or block them. You can use firewalls to protect against inbound threats only (one-way firewall) or against both unauthorized inbound and outbound traffic.

5. **A, B, D.** The three standards are WEP, WPA, and WPA2. All are used to encrypt data on wireless networks.

6. **B.** Windows Vista, XP, and 2000 have a built-in encryption protocol called the Encrypting File System. After it's applied, it can only be accessed by the user who created it and administrator or the EFS key holders.

7. **C.** Windows Vista Ultimate and Enterprise include the option to use BitLocker Drive Encryption, which can encrypt an entire hard disk drive without a user's knowledge.

8. **A.** Social engineering is a simple and very easy way to get information from someone inside a company. By simply calling on the phone and pretending to be someone else, a person can get information that should not be given out. Training users is the best way to prevent this kind of attack.

9. **B.** User Account Control (UAC) is a security component of Windows Vista that keeps every user (beside the actual Administrator account) in standard user mode instead of as an administrator with full administrative rights, even if he is a member of the administrators group.

10. **D.** If the BIOS setup program is protected by a password and the password is lost, you can clear the password on most desktop systems by using the BIOS clear jumper on the motherboard or by removing the battery for several seconds.

11. **B.** A thumb print (and thumb print scanner) is an example of biometrics.

12. **C.** If you are recycling a hard disk, be sure to use special overwriting software that destroys any old data on the disk (this is known as sanitizing). Destroying the entire disk renders it useless and therefore un-recyclable. Formatting the hard disk does not necessarily remove all information on the disk. Simply removing the disk is not enough; it needs to be sanitized in some way.

13. **C.** The Local Security policy is where functions such as auditing can be enabled.

14. **D.** BitLocker uses the Advanced Encryption Standard (AES) by default. WPA and WEP are wireless encryption standards. TPM stands for Trusted Platform Module, a chip that resides on the motherboard that stores encrypted keys.

15. **A, B, and C.** Passwords should be complex and have a minimum length. Also, the use of old passwords should be discouraged, at least for some set time limit. Changing passwords often is important. Many organizations enforce the changing of passwords every month or sooner.

Case Study 1 Solution

Examination of the wireless adapter can occur in one of two places: in Windows or in third-party software. In Windows, you can access the wireless adapter in the **Network Connections** window. You can access third-party software from **Start, All Programs**. However, they can both usually be accessed from the System Tray. Locate the wireless icon, right-click it, and select Properties in most cases. This enables you to re-configure the wireless encryption method. Some wireless network adapters cannot go beyond WPA without an additional software solution. Consider upgrading the entire wireless network adapter if this is the case. Finally, the encryption level used on the wireless client must match that of the wireless access point. If the wireless AP needs to be updated, you can do that by connecting to it with a browser over the network. Some wireless APs need an updated ROM file in order to utilize the latest encryption standards.

Case Study 2 Solution

First, you would determine what operating system the client is using. If the person is using Windows Vista or XP SP2, you can run Windows Defender to clean the obvious malware (Windows Defender is not included in Windows XP by default but can be downloaded from Microsoft's website). You can also use a third-party software program to remove the spyware from the computer. After the problem is resolved, be sure to install an anti-malware product to the computer. This helps to prevent the problem from happening again.

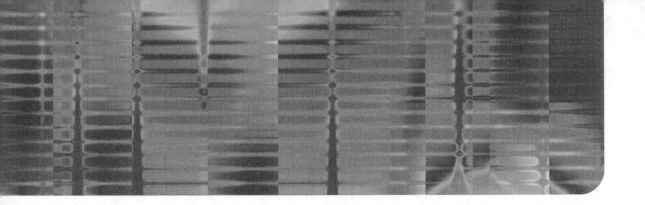

This chapter covers the following subjects:

- **PC Tools**—This section describes the basic tools that should be part of every PC technician's toolkit.

- **Preventing Electrostatic Discharge**—This section describes damages that can result from electrostatic discharge (ESD) and ways to prevent it.

- **Using a Troubleshooting Process**—This section describes a typical six-step troubleshooting process, which you can use when you are called upon to troubleshoot basic problems with a computer or other device. It can help to guide you as you figure out problems.

- **Determining Whether a Problem Is Caused by Hardware or Software**—This section discusses a computer's subsystems, and components, in an effort to help you differentiate between hardware and software-related issues. It also covers important topics such as backing up data, recording configurations, and more.

- **Troubleshooting Windows**—To troubleshoot Windows effectively, you need to know how to recover from errors and be able to identify and analyze the problem efficiently. This section covers common problems you might encounter in Windows, how to troubleshoot boot-up errors, how to fix application issues, and how to decipher error codes and messages.

- **Where to Go for More Information**—Information related to technical issues can be found in many places, including the manufacturer's website, PC books, online computer magazines, and search engines. Be sure to read through this section to find out where to go for those technical solutions!

Troubleshooting

Everyone has seen or heard of a computer hardware error or Windows error. On the hardware side, issues are less common, but devices can fail, or they could be defective when they are first purchased, or perhaps they are not compatible with the rest of the computer. On the software side, operating systems such as Windows can have hundreds of different errors and failures. And it's not just Windows; every operating system fails at some point—it's just a matter of time. Windows can have lots of different kinds of errors, from boot errors, to non-critical application errors, to complete failures of Windows known as stop errors. A good troubleshooter is able to discern whether the problem is software or hardware related and analyzes and repairs all of these problems.

In an effort to aid the PC technician, Windows offers tools such as the Windows Repair Environment, Recovery Console, Advanced Boot Options menu, and Microsoft Help and Support, formerly known as the Knowledge Base (MKSB), which we refer to often in this chapter. The Help and Support website is chock full of articles about all kinds of problems you see in the field; you can access it at http://support.microsoft.com. We cover all these tools and much more throughout this chapter in an attempt to make you a well-rounded troubleshooter.

PC Tools

A technician's best tools are his or her senses and hands. However, a technician needs hardware tools to open the PC and to install and replace components. There are several personal computer (PC) tools that should be a part of every technician's toolkit, including

- **Phillips and straight-blade screwdrivers**—Used when hex drivers are not compatible; non-magnetic preferred

- **Torx drivers**—Required for some Compaq models; non-magnetic preferred

- **Hex drivers**—Used for opening and closing cases and securing and removing cards and motherboards; non-magnetic preferred

- **3-claw parts retrieval tool**—Retrieves loose parts from computer interior; prevents lost parts, which can lead to dead shorts

- **Hemostat clamps**—Replaces tweezers for inserting and removing jumper blocks and cables

- **Needle-nose pliers**—Straightens bent pins

- **Eyebrow tweezers**—Replaces normal tweezers in toolkit for removing and replacing jumpers

- **Penlight**—Illuminates dark cases

- **Magnifier**—Makes small parts and markings easier to read

- **Jeweler's screwdriver set**—Enables repairs to devices that use small screws

You can buy toolkits that contain many of these items, but don't hesitate to supplement a kit you already have with additional items from this list or other items you find useful. Figure 10-1 illustrates some important tools.

Figure 10-1   Typical tools used by computer technicians.

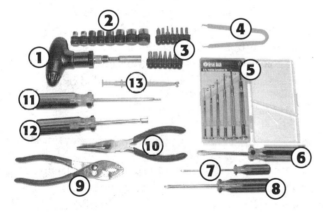

1. Screwdriver with removable tips (shown in #2 and #3)
2. Hex driver tips
3. Screw and Torx tips
4. Chip puller (also useful for removing keytops)
5. Jeweler's screwdriver set
6. Flat-blade screwdriver
7. Small Phillips-head screwdriver
8. Phillips-head screwdriver
9. Pliers
10. Needle-nose pliers
11. Torx driver
12. Hex driver
13. 3-claw parts retrieval tool

Preventing Electrostatic Discharge

Electrostatic discharge (ESD) occurs when two objects of different voltages come into contact with each other. The human body is always gathering static electricity, more than enough to damage a computer component. ESD is a silent killer. If you were to touch a component without proper protection, the static electricity could

discharge from you to the component, most likely damaging it, but with no discernable signs of damage. Worse yet, it is possible to discharge a small amount of voltage to the device and damage it to the point where it works intermittently, making it tough to troubleshoot. It only takes 30 volts or so to damage a component. On a dry winter day, you could gather as much as 20,000 volts when walking across a carpeted area! Ouch! There are several ways to equalize the electrical potentials, allowing you to protect components from ESD:

- **Use an antistatic wrist strap**—The most common kind is inexpensive and only takes a moment to put on and connect to the chassis of the computer (an unpainted portion of the frame inside the case). By using an antistatic wrist strap, you are constantly discharging to the case's metal frame instead of to the components that you handle. Of course, the chassis of the computer can only absorb so much ESD, so consider another earth-bonding point to connect to or try to implement as many other antistatic methods as possible. Most wrist straps come equipped with a resistor (often 1 megaohm) that protects the user from shock hazards when working with low-voltage components. This is considered the most important part of a PC toolkit.

  More advanced types of wrist straps are meant to connect to an actual *ground*; a ground strip or the ground plug of a special dedicated AC outlet. These are used in more sophisticated repair labs. Do not attempt to connect the alligator clip of a basic wrist strap (purchased at an office store), to the ground plug of an outlet in your home.

- **Touch the chassis of the computer**—Do this to further discharge yourself before handling any components. This is also a good habit to get into for those times when an antistatic strap is not available.

- **Use an antistatic mat**—Place the computer on top of the antistatic mat and connect the alligator clip of the mat to the computer's chassis in the same manner that you did with the wrist strap. (Some people stand on the mat and connect it to the computer.)

- **Use antistatic bags**—Adapter cards, motherboards, and so on are normally shipped in antistatic bags. Hold on to them! When installing or removing components, keep them either inside or on top of the bag until you are ready to work with them.

Remember: ESD need only happen once and that $500 video card you are trying to install is toast!

Using a Troubleshooting Process

It is necessary to approach computer problems from a logical standpoint. To best accomplish this, PC technicians implement a troubleshooting methodology (or maybe more than one). There are several different troubleshooting methodologies available; the following is an example of a common six-step troubleshooting process. This process works well for just about any troubleshooting you might do.

Step 1.   Ascertain what the problem is.

Step 2.   Write down probable causes of the problem.

Step 3.   Determine if theories are correct through testing.

Step 4.   Create and implement a plan to resolve the problem.

Step 5.   Verify that the problem has been fixed; employ preventative measures.

Step 6.   Document the entire process.

As you attempt to troubleshoot computer issues, think in terms of this six-step process. Plug the problem directly into these steps.

For example, in Step 1 you might identify an issue; maybe the computer won't turn on. For Step 2, a probable cause could be that the computer is not plugged in to the AC outlet. Instead of keeping everything inside your head, consider writing down one or more probable causes on paper. To test the theory in Step 3, you would plug the computer in. If it works, then great, but if it doesn't, you would go back to Step 2 and establish a new theory, or work through your list of possible theories you had written out earlier. When you have reached a theory that tests positive, move on to Step 4 and establish the plan of action based on that theory, and then implement your solution. (Keep in mind that many plans of action are more complicated than just plugging the computer in! Perhaps the AC outlet was loose, which would require a licensed electrician to fix it.) Next, in Step 5, you want to *test*. Always test and verify that the system is functioning correctly. If need be, implement preventative measures; for example, re-route the power cable so that it is out of the way and can't be disconnected easily. Finally, in Step 6, you want to document what has happened, and how you fixed the problem. In many companies, documentation begins right when you first get a troubleshooting call (or trouble ticket), and the documentation continues throughout the entire process. You can track documentation on paper, or in an online system; it depends on your company's procedures. Be sure to keep track of what happened, why it happened, and how you fixed the problem.

Because computer failures happen to the customer (who usually is less technically aware than you of the possible causes for the problem), you must work with the

customer to create a complete list of symptoms so that you can find the right solution quickly and accurately. To do this, you need to

- Carefully observe the customer's environment to look for potential causes of computer problems, such as interference sources, power problems, and user error.

- Ask the customer what (if anything) has changed recently about the computer or its environment. Anything from new hardware or software being installed, new telephone or network being installed, or even a new coffee maker or air-conditioning unit could be at the root of the problem. A simple way to ask this would be to say, "What has changed since the last time it (the PC) worked?"

- Determine what tasks the customer was performing on the PC. You can determine this not only by asking the customer questions, but by reviewing system log files, browser history, and so on.

- Ask the customer detailed questions about the symptoms, including unusual system behavior, such as noises or beeps, office events taking place around the same time, onscreen error messages, and so on.

TIP Windows generates several log files during routine use that can be useful for determining what went wrong. Many of these can be viewed through the Event Viewer. To view the contents of the Event Viewer, right-click **Computer/My Computer**, click **Manage**, and click **Event Viewer**. The Event Viewer captures three types of information: application errors, security audits, and system errors.

Because some types of computer problems aren't easy to replicate away from the customer site, your customer might see system problems you never do, even if you attempt to reproduce the problem.

TIP Remember, troubleshooting is the art and science of quickly and accurately determining what is wrong with a customer's system. Troubleshooting is an art because every technician brings his or her own experience and personality to the task. Troubleshooting is also a science because you can apply a definite method that brings you a great degree of success.

Determining Whether a Problem Is Caused by Hardware or Software

The oldest dilemma for any computer technician is determining whether a problem is caused by hardware or software. The widespread use of Windows operating systems makes this problem even more acute than it was when MS-DOS was the predominant standard, because all hardware in a Windows system is controlled by Windows device drivers.

A troubleshooting cycle is a method that you can use to determine exactly what part of a complex system, such as a computer, is causing the problem. The troubleshooting cycle used in this section goes into more depth than the six-step troubleshooting process described in the preceding section. The first step is to determine the most likely source of the problem. The client interview helps you determine which subsystem is the best place to start solving the problem. In the previous example, the printing subsystem was the most likely place to start.

A *subsystem* is the combination of components designed to do a particular task, and it can include hardware, software, and firmware components. Use Table 10-1 to better understand the nature of the subsystems found in any computer.

Table 10-1   Computer and Peripheral Subsystems and Their Components

Subsystem	Hardware	Software	Firmware
Printing	Printer, cable, parallel, or serial port	Printer driver in Windows application	BIOS configuration of port
Display	Graphics card, monitor, cables, port type, motherboard (integrated video)	Video drivers in Windows	Video BIOS, BIOS configuration of video type, boot priority
Audio	Sound card, microphone, speakers, speaker and microphone cables, CD analog and digital cables to sound card, motherboard integrated audio	Audio drivers in Windows	BIOS configuration of integrated audio
Mouse and pointing device	Mouse or pointing device, serial or mouse port, USB port	Mouse driver in Windows	BIOS port configuration, USB legacy configuration
Keyboard	Keyboard, PS/2 or USB port	Keyboard driver in Windows	BIOS keyboard configuration, USB legacy configuration

Subsystem	Hardware	Software	Firmware
Storage	Drives, data cables, power connectors, USB, IEEE-1394 or SCSI cards, or built-in ports	Storage drivers in Windows	BIOS drive configuration, BIOS configuration of built-in PATA, SATA, USB, IEEE-1394 ports, RAID functions
Power	Power supply, splitters, fans, cables	Power-management software (Windows)	BIOS power-management configuration
CPU	CPU, motherboard	System devices	BIOS cache and CPU configuration
RAM	RAM, motherboard	(none)	BIOS RAM timing configuration settings
Network	NIC, motherboard, USB port (for USB devices), cable	Network configuration files and drivers	BIOS PnP and power management, BIOS configuration of integrated network port or USB port
Modem	Modem, motherboard or serial port or USB port, cable	Modem drivers, application	BIOS PnP, power management, BIOS port configuration

You can see from Table 10-1 that virtually every subsystem in the computer has hardware, software, and firmware components. A thorough troubleshooting process takes into account both the subsystem and all of its components.

There are a few other techniques to consider when troubleshooting, including which components to check first, common points of failure, the fact that a device is known to be working doesn't necessarily mean it's new, and to keep track of your solutions.

What Components to Check First

As the previous subsystem list indicated, there's no shortage of places to start in virtually any subsystem. What's the best way to decide whether a hardware, software, or firmware problem is the most likely cause? Typically, hardware problems come and go, whereas software and firmware problems are consistent. Why? A hardware problem is often the result of a damaged or loose wire or connection; when the connection is closed, the component works, but when the connection opens, the component fails. On the other hand, a software or firmware problem causes a failure under the same circumstances every time.

Another rule of thumb that's useful is to consider the least-expensive, easiest-to-replace item first. In most cases, the power or data cable connected to a subsystem is the first place to look for problems. Whether the cable is internal or external, it is almost always the least-expensive part of the subsystem, can easily come loose, and can easily be damaged. If a cable is loose, has bent pins, or has a dry, brittle, or cracked exterior, replace it.

When new software or new hardware has been introduced to the system and a problem results immediately afterward, that change is often the most likely cause of the problem.

Hardware conflicts such as IRQ, I/O port address, DMA channel, and memory address, or conflicts between the software drivers in the operating system are typical causes of failure when new hardware is introduced. New software can also cause problems with hardware, because of incompatibilities between software and hardware or because new software has replaced drivers required by the hardware.

Points of Failure on the Outside of the Computer

The front of the computer might provide valuable clues if you're having problems with a system. In case of problems, check the following common points of failure for help:

- **Can't read CD or DVD media**—The drive door on the CD-ROM or other optical drive might not be completely closed or the media might be inserted upside down; press the eject button to open the drive, remove any obstacles, reseat the media, and close the drive.

> **TIP**   You can also eject optical media with Windows Explorer/My Computer. Right-click the drive and select **Eject**. If the drive doesn't eject the media, there could be a problem with the drive's data cable, cable connection, or power connection.

- **Can't shut down the computer with the case power switch**—The case power switch is connected to the motherboard on ATX, BTX, and other modern desktop systems, not directly to the power supply as with older designs. The wire might be loose or connected to the wrong pins on the motherboard. Keep in mind that most systems require you to hold in the power button for about four seconds before the system shuts down. If the computer crashes, you might need to shut down the computer by unplugging it or by turning off the surge suppressor used by the computer. Some ATX and BTX power supplies have their own on-off switches.

- **Can't see the drive access or power lights**—As with the case power switch, these lights are also connected to the motherboard. These wires might also be loose or connected to the wrong pins on the motherboard.

- **Can't use USB, IEEE-1394, or other ports on the front of the system**—Some systems have these ports on the front of the computer as well as the rear. Front-mounted ports are connected with header cables to the motherboard. If the cables inside the case are loose, the ports won't work. If the ports are disabled in the system BIOS, the ports won't work.

As you can see from this section, in many situations, you need to open the case to resolve a problem, even though the symptoms might first manifest themselves outside the computer.

"Known-Working" Doesn't Mean "New"—Best Sources for Replacement Parts

To perform parts exchanges for troubleshooting, you need replacement parts. If you don't have spare parts, it's very tempting to go to the computer store and buy some new components. Instead, take a spare system that's similar to the "sick" computer, make sure that it works, and then use it for parts. Why? Just because it's new doesn't mean it works.

For example, you might replace an alternator on a car with a brand-new, lifetime-warranty alternator that ends up failing in less than a week. Whether it's a cable, a video card, a monitor, or some other component, try using a known-working item as a temporary replacement rather than brand new.

> **TIP**   Rather than give away, sell, or discard working video cards, hard disks, and other components you have replaced with faster, bigger, better upgrades, keep at least one of each item to use as a replacement for testing purposes or as a backup in case the upgrade fails.

If you don't have spare parts, use a spare system if possible rather than knocking another working system (and user) out of action by "borrowing" parts from an operational system. Use the same brand and model of system for known-working spares if possible, because the components inside are more likely to be identical to the "sick" system you are diagnosing.

Swapping from an identical or nearly identical system is especially important if the system you are diagnosing uses proprietary components or is a laptop computer.

Keeping Track of Your Solutions

Make a practice of keeping detailed notes about the problems you solve. If your company has a help-desk system with tracking capabilities, use it. Even if the best you can do is write up your findings, you can use desktop search tools to find the answers to the same problems that might arise later.

Be sure to note symptoms, underlying problems, workarounds, and final resolutions. To help capture the information, you need

- Use the Windows Screen Capture feature (press the **PrtScn** button and copy the clipboard contents into Paint or another image editor) to grab screens.

- Use the Save As Web Archive feature in Internet Explorer to grab web pages complete with text and links as one file.

Your documentation might be a mix of printed documents, saved documents, written documents, saved web pages, saved emails, and so on. Or, you might use a trouble ticket system to keep track of all conversations, emails, and steps taken to resolve problems. This all depends on your organization's policies and procedures. Be sure to acquaint yourself with the procedures early on.

Troubleshooting Windows

A damaged Windows installation prevents the computer from getting any work done. It is important for a technician to know how to recover an operating system by using the Advanced Boot Options menu and recovery environments, such as Windows Vista's WinRE and Windows XP's Recovery Console. A technician should also know how to restore a system using Windows Vista's Complete PC Backup, and Windows XP's Automated System Restore, as well as the System Restore utility. Understanding the tools provided in Windows for troubleshooting the operating system helps you solve real-world problems.

Recovering an Operating System

If Windows does not start properly, you have a variety of options you can use to get it working again:

- If the problem is caused by the most recent change to Windows, you can use the Last Known Good Configuration startup option to get things working again.

- If you are not sure of the problem, you can use Safe Mode or other advanced boot options to help diagnose the problem.

- If Windows does not boot, you can use the Windows Recovery Environment (WinRE) for Windows Vista/Win7, or the Recovery Console for Windows XP/2000 to fix the problem.

- If Windows does not boot and needs to be restored, there are various tools that can be implemented including Complete PC Backup (Vista), ASR System Restore (XP), and the Emergency Repair Disk (2000).

The following sections discuss these tools in detail.

Last Known Good Configuration, Safe Mode, and Other Advanced Boot Options

If you are unable to start Windows Vista/XP/2000 but don't see an error message, the problem could be caused by a driver or startup program, video driver problems, or problems with the system kernel. Windows offers various advanced boot options to help you correct startup problems. To access these startup options, press the **F8** key immediately after the computer starts up; this brings up the Windows Advanced Boot Options menu (which you might also see referred to as advanced startup options), as shown in Figure 10-2.

Figure 10-2   Windows Vista Advanced Boot Options menu.

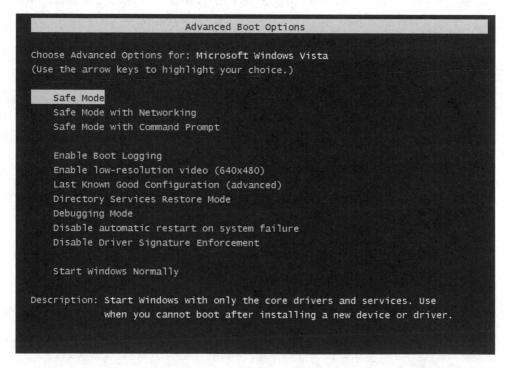

Windows Vista/XP/2000 offers the following startup options as part of the Advanced Boot Options menu (also known as the ABOM):

- **Safe Mode**—Starts system with a minimal set of drivers; can be used to start System Restore or to load Windows GUI for diagnostics.

- **Safe Mode with Networking**—Starts system with a minimal set of drivers and enables network support.

- **Safe Mode with Command Prompt**—Starts system with a minimal set of drivers but loads command prompt instead of Windows GUI.

- **Enable Boot Logging**—Creates a ntbtlog.txt file.

- **Enable low-resolution video (640×480)**—Uses a standard VGA driver in place of a GPU-specific display driver, but uses all other drivers as normal. (This is called *Enable VGA Mode* in Windows XP/2000.)

- **Last Known Good Configuration**—Starts the system with the last configuration known to work; useful for solving problems caused by newly installed hardware or software.

- **Directory Services Restore Mode**—Used to restore a domain controller's active directory (Windows Server). Even though it is listed, it is not used in Windows Vista/XP/2000.

- **Debugging Mode**—An advanced diagnostics tool that enables the use of a debug program to examine the system kernel for troubleshooting.

- **Disable automatic restart on system failure (Vista only)**—Prevents Windows from automatically restarting if an error causes Windows to fail. Choose this option only if Windows is stuck in a loop where Windows fails, attempts to restart, and fails again.

- **Disable driver signature enforcement (Vista only)**—Allows drivers containing improper signatures to be installed.

- **Start Windows Normally**—Used to boot to regular Windows. This option is listed in case a user inadvertently presses F8, but does not want to use any of the Advanced Boot options.

If Windows Vista fails to start properly and then restarts automatically, it normally displays the Windows Error Recovery screen and gives you the following options: Safe Mode, Safe Mode with Networking, Safe Mode with Command Prompt, Last Known Good Configuration, and Start Windows Normally. This means that Windows has acknowledged some sort of error or improper shut down and offers a truncated version of the Advanced Options Boot menu.

Table 10-2 lists typical problems and helps you select the correct startup option to use to solve the problem.

Table 10-2   Using the Windows Vista/XP/2000 Advanced Boot Options Menu

Problem	Windows Version	Startup Option to Select	Notes
Windows won't start after you install new hardware or software.	Vista, XP, 2000	Last Known Good Configuration	Resets Windows to its last-known working configuration; you need to reinstall hardware or software installed after that time.
Windows won't start after you upgrade a device driver.	Vista, XP, 2000	Safe Mode	After starting the computer in Safe Mode, open the Device Manager, select the device, and use the Rollback feature to restore the previously used device driver. Restart your system. Uses VGA resolution but retains the color settings normally used.
Windows won't start after you install a different video card or monitor.	Vista, XP, 2000	Enable low-resolution video (640×480)/Enable VGA Mode	Most video cards should be installed when your system is running in VGA Mode. If a video error occurs, use this option, and then the Display Properties window to select a working video mode before you restart.
Windows can't start normally, but you need access to the Internet to research the problem or download updates.	Vista, XP, 2000	Safe Mode with Networking	You can use Windows Update and the Internet, but some devices won't work in this mode. This mode also uses 640×480 resolution, but retains the color settings normally used.
Windows doesn't finish starting normally, and you want to know what device driver or process is preventing it from working.	Vista, XP, 2000	Enable Boot Logging	This option starts the computer with all its normal drivers and settings and also creates a file called **ntbtlog.txt** in the default Windows folder (usually C:\Windows for Vista/XP or C:\WINNT for 2000). Restart the computer in Safe Mode and open this file with Notepad or Wordpad to determine the last driver file that loaded. You can update the driver or remove the hardware device using that driver to restore your system to working condition.

Table 10-2 Using the Windows Vista/XP/2000 Advanced Boot Options Menu

Problem	Windows Version	Startup Option to Select	Notes
Windows is loading programs you don't need during its startup process.	Vista/XP	Boot computer in Normal Mode (or Safe Mode if the computer won't start in Normal Mode); click **Start, Run**; then type **MSConfig**.	Use MSConfig to disable one or more startup programs, and then restart your computer. You can also use MSConfig to restore damaged files, or to start System Restore to reset your computer to an earlier condition.

There is only a small window of time available to press F8; it's right between the BIOS and when the normal operating system boots. Press F8 repeatedly right after the BIOS POST begins. It is important to note that the Last Known Good Configuration option is only helpful before a successful logon occurs. After a user logs on, that becomes the last known good logon. It is recommended that you attempt to repair a computer with the Advanced Boot Options *before* using Windows Vista's System Recovery Options, or Windows XP/2000's Recovery Console.

Windows Recovery Environment (WinRE)

Windows Recovery Environment (WinRE) is a set of tools included in Windows 7, Windows Vista, Windows Server 2008, and other upcoming Windows operating systems. It takes the place of the Recovery Console used in Windows XP/2000. Also known as System Recovery Options, WinRE's purpose is to recover Windows from errors that prevent it from booting. There are two possible ways to access WinRE:

- **Option 1**—Booting to the Windows Vista DVD

- **Option 2**—Booting to a special partition on the hard drive that has WinRE installed

The first option is more common with an individual computer that has Windows Vista installed; for example, if you performed a clean installation with the standard Windows Vista DVD and made no modifications to it. To start WinRE, make sure that the DVD drive is first in the boot order of the BIOS, boot to the Windows Vista DVD (as if you were starting the installation), choose your language settings and click **Next**, and then select **Repair Your Computer**, which you find at the lower-left corner of the screen.

CAUTION Important! Do not select **Install Now**. That would begin the process of reinstalling Windows Vista on your hard drive.

The second option is used by OEMs (original equipment manufacturers) so that users can access WinRE without having to search for, and boot off of, a Windows Vista DVD. These OEMs (computer builders and system integrators) preinstall WinRE into a special partition on the hard drive, separate from the operating system, so that the user can boot into it at any time. Compare this to the older Recovery Console that was installed into the same partition as the operating system. To access WinRE that has been preinstalled, press **F8** to bring up the Advanced Boot Options menu, highlight **Repair Your Computer**, and press **Enter**. If you don't see Repair Your Computer in the Advanced Boot Options menu, then it wasn't installed to the hard drive, and you have to use option 1, booting from the Vista DVD. Note that you can still use option 1 even if WinRE was installed to the hard drive; for example, in a scenario where the hard drive installation of WinRE has failed.

NOTE The process to install WinRE to the hard drive is a rather complicated one. However, if you are interested, here is a link that gives the basics of installing WinRE: http://blogs.msdn.com/winre/archive/2007/01/12/how-to-install-winre-on-the-hard-disk.aspx.

Regardless of which option you selected, at this point a window named "System Recovery Options" should appear, prompting you to select an operating system to repair. Most users only have one listed. Highlight the appropriate operating system in need of repair and click **Next**. The options at your disposal display as shown in Figure 10-3. Table 10-3 describes these options in more depth.

Figure 10-3 Windows Vista System Recovery Options window.

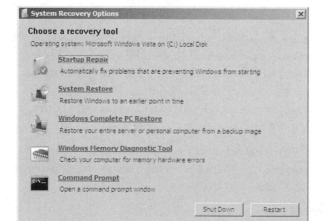

Table 10-3   Description of the Windows Vista System Recovery Options

System Recovery Option	Description
Startup Repair	When clicked, this automatically fixes certain problems, such as missing or damaged system files that might prevent Windows from starting correctly. When you run Startup Repair, it scans your computer for the problem and then tries to fix it so your computer can start correctly.
System Restore	Restores the computer's system files to an earlier point in time. It's a way to undo system changes to your computer without affecting your personal files, such as email, documents, or photos. Note: If you use System Restore when the computer is in Safe Mode, you cannot undo the restore operation. However, you can run System Restore again and choose a different restore point if one exists.
Windows Complete PC Restore	This restores the contents of a hard disk from a backup. Windows Complete PC Backup and Restore is only included with Vista Business and Vista Ultimate.
Windows Memory Diagnostic Tool	Scans the computer's memory for errors.
Command Prompt (Replaces the Recovery Console in XP/2000)	Advanced users can use the Command Prompt to perform recovery-related operations and also run other command-line tools for diagnosing and troubleshooting problems. Puts the user into a directory called X:\Sources. Works much like the previous Recovery Console in Windows XP/2000, with the addition of a few new commands.

Recovery Console

The Windows Recovery Console is a special command-line interface that is designed for copying files and performing disk repairs. It is used by Windows XP and 2000. In Windows 2000, you can use the Recovery Console as an alternative to the Emergency Repair process, such as if you need to restore only one system file. Windows XP lacks the Emergency Repair provision, so understanding how to use the Recovery Console is even more important.

Use Recovery Console when the system cannot start from the hard disk because of missing or corrupted boot files, or when other types of missing system files prevent the computer from starting in Safe Mode.

To start Windows XP's Recovery Console, you have two options:

- **Option 1**—Boot your system with the Windows XP CD and run the Recovery Console as a repair option.

- **Option 2**—While the system is working properly, install the Recovery Console from the Windows XP CD-ROM. It appears automatically as a startup option when you restart your computer.

To start Recovery Console from the Windows XP CD, follow these steps:

Step 1.   Boot the system from the Windows XP CD.

Step 2.   When prompted, press **R** to start the Recovery Console. (In Windows 2000, you press **R** for Repair and then **C** for the Recovery Console.)

To log in to Recovery Console:

Step 1.   Select the installation to log into. (Do this by pressing the number that corresponds to the operating system.)

Step 2.   Provide the administrator password for the system.

To copy Recovery Console from the Windows XP/2000 CD:

Step 1.   While Windows is running, insert the Windows CD into the CD or DVD drive.

Step 2.   Click **Start, Run**.

Step 3.   In the Run prompt, type *x:\i386\winnt32.exe /cmdcons* where *x* is the drive letter for the CD or DVD drive.

Step 4.   To confirm the installation, click **Yes** in the Windows Setup dialog box describing Recovery Console.

Step 5.   Restart the computer. The next time that you start your computer, Microsoft Windows Recovery Console appears on the startup menu. Select it to start Recovery Console.

NOTE   For Windows XP Professional x64 Edition, the path to use in Step 3 is *x:\amd64\winnt32.exe /cmdcons*.

NOTE   If the C: partition or the boot sector of the hard drive is damaged, you will most likely not be able to boot to the Recovery Console on the hard drive. In this case, you have to use Option 1 and boot off the CD-ROM.

The Recovery Console contains some of the same commands that are available in the normal command-line interface, along with additional commands that are necessary only for repairing the installation.

> **CAUTION**   The Recovery Console permits access to only the following locations:
>
> - The root folder (root directory)
> - The %SystemRoot% (Windows) folder and its subfolders
> - The Cmdcons folder
> - Removable media drives, such as CD and DVD drives
>
> In other words, you *cannot* use the Recovery Console to access files not stored in these folders, such as users' data files.

Using System Restore with Advanced Boot Options

If you cannot boot into Windows XP, try starting your computer using the Safe Mode option and then click the **System Restore** link. Click **Restore My Computer to an Earlier Time**, select a previous restore point, and click **Next**. This returns your system to a previous state.

You can also start a System Restore with Safe Mode with the Command Prompt option. If you are prompted to select an operating system, use the arrow keys to select the appropriate operating system for your computer, and then press **Enter**. Log on as an administrator or with an account that has administrator credentials. At the command prompt, type `%systemroot%\system32\restore\rstrui.exe`, and then press **Enter**. Follow the instructions that appear on the screen to restore your computer to a functional state.

Using Windows Vista's Complete PC Backup

Complete PC Backup is the successor to Windows XP's Automated System Recovery. It backs up an entire image of your system to the removable media of your choice; for example, DVD. To create a backup of your PC with Vista's Complete PC Backup, follow these steps:

Step 1.   Start the Complete PC Backup by going to **Start, All Programs, Accessories, System Tools, Backup Status and Configuration**.

Step 2.   Click the **Complete PC Backup** button.

Step 3.   Select **Create a Backup Now** and follow the directions. Have media ready that can hold an image of your operating system; for example, DVD-R. Be ready; this is a sizeable image.

To restore a system from the backup, follow these steps:

Step 1.   Insert the installation disc and then restart the computer. (Make sure that the DVD drive is listed first in the BIOS boot order.)

Step 2.   Press any key when prompted in order to boot off of the DVD.

Step 3.   Choose your language settings and then click **Next**.

Step 4.   Click **Repair Your Computer**.

Step 5.   Select the operating system you want to repair (usually there is only one), and then click **Next**.

NOTE   If you are restoring a 64-bit system using a 32-bit Complete PC backup or a 32-bit system using a 64-bit Complete PC backup and have more than one operating system installed, do not select an operating system. If an operating system is selected by default, clear the selection by clicking a blank area of the window, and then click **Next**.

Step 6.   On the System Recovery Options menu, click **Windows Complete PC Restore** and then follow the instructions. Insert the last DVD of the backup set when prompted to do so.

Using Automated System Recovery (ASR) (Windows XP)

Windows XP Professional does not include a true disaster-recovery backup program. However, the Automated System Recovery (ASR) option in NTBackup does enable you to restore the system state (user accounts, hard disk configuration, network configuration, video settings, hardware configuration, software settings, and operating system boot files).

To create an ASR backup with NTBackup, follow these steps:

Step 1.   Switch to Advanced Mode (if NTBackup starts in Wizard mode) and click the **Automated System Recovery Wizard** button (see Figure 10-4).

Figure 10-4   Preparing to start the ASR Wizard.

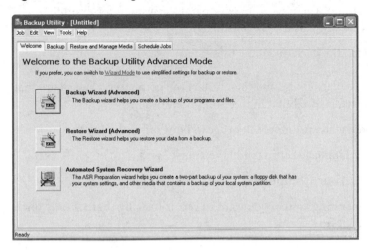

Step 2.   The Automated System Recovery Preparation Wizard's opening dialog appears. Click **Next** to continue.

Step 3.   Specify where to store the backup, and click **Next**.

Step 4.   Click **Finish** to complete the wizard. The backup starts. Provide a floppy disk when prompted to store configuration files.

The floppy disk created by the ASR Wizard contains three files that store information about storage devices (asr.sif), Plug and Play (PnP) information (asrpnp.sif), and a list of system state and critical files that were backed up (setup.log).

To restore a system with ASR, you need the following:

- The Windows XP Professional distribution CD

- The ASR backup

- The ASR floppy disk

- A supported floppy drive

If the computer does not have provision for a floppy drive connected to a floppy drive controller, there are a few USB floppy drives that are supported. The USB floppy drives that Microsoft supports for installing Windows XP (and for ASR) are listed in Microsoft Knowledge Base article 916196, available at http://support.microsoft.com.

Follow this procedure:

Step 1.   Start the system with the Windows XP Professional CD.

Step 2.   Press **F2** when prompted to start Automated System Recovery.

Step 3.   Insert the ASR floppy disk.

Step 4.   Provide backup files when prompted.

After completing the ASR restore, you need to reinstall your applications and restore your most recent backup to return your system to service.

Diagnosing and Troubleshooting Other Problems

The ability to diagnose and troubleshoot problems depends upon a combination of technical skills and the ability to interact with clients. Often, a combination of what clients tell you (or don't tell you) and your own detective skills are needed to solve a computer problem.

Identifying the Problem: User Interview

The client interview is the all-important first step in solving any computer troubleshooting situation. During this interview, you need to determine the following facts:

- The software in use at the time of the problem
- The hardware in use at the time of the problem
- The task the customer was trying to perform at the time of the problem
- The environment in the office or work area at the time of the problem
- If new software or hardware has been added to the computer or network
- If any changes have been made to the system configuration
- If other users are having the same or similar problems

The number-one question you're trying to answer is, "What changed since the last time it worked?" Sometimes the client can tell you what changed, and sometimes you must "ask" the computer what changed.

Analyzing the Problem

Depending on the clues you receive in the initial interview, you should go to the client's work area prepared to perform a variety of tests. You must look for four major issues when evaluating the customer's environment:

- Event logs and services

- Symptoms and error codes (might require you to try to reproduce the problem)

- Power issues

- Interference sources

You can select from the tests listed in Table 10-4 based on your evaluation of the most likely sources of problems. You might need to perform several tests to rule out certain problems.

Table 10-4 Troubleshooting Tests and Requirements

Test	Requires
Power	Multimeter, circuit tester
BIOS beep and error codes	List of BIOS codes, POST card
Printer self-test	Printer and paper
Windows bootlog	Start Windows with Bootlog option enabled
I/O Port tests	Connect loopback plugs and run third-party diagnostics
Video tests	Run third-party diagnostics
Hardware resources	Windows Device Manager
Device drivers	Windows Device Manager

The multimeter is a must-have for any PC technician. This device tests the voltage of any device in your computer. It can also test watts, amps, and ohms (some can even take the temperature!). When testing power connections in the computer and AC outlets, be sure to have one of these handy.

Identifying the Problem: Logs and Services

If the client interview alone doesn't point you in the right direction, check event logs and services.

Event Logs

You can view event logs by running the Computer Management Console (press **Windows+R** to open the Run prompt and type `compmgmt.msc`). Event logs are stored in branches of the Event Viewer. Look for Error messages (marked with a white X on a red circle) first, and then Warnings (yellow triangle). Frequent errors or warnings that point to the same program or device can indicate a serious problem (see Figure 10-5).

Figure 10-5   Viewing an error message in the Application event log.

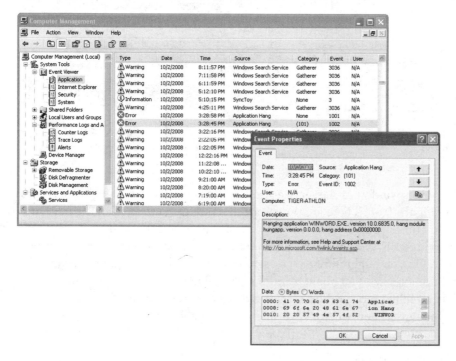

Services

Many Windows features, such as printing, wireless networking, and others, depend upon services. To see if a needed service is running, open the Services and Applications node of the Computer Management Console and click **Services**. Check the Status column for the service needed (see Figure 10-6). To start a stopped service, right-click it and select **Start**. Alternatively, you could click the **Start** button on the tool bar, or double-click the service and click the **Start** button from the Properties window.

Figure 10-6   A common service in the Computer Management window and its Properties window.

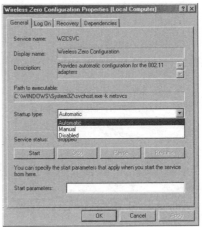

1. Start Service button
2. Right-click menu
3. Status of service

The Properties window of the service also enables you to change the startup type, as shown in Figure 10-6. There are three startup types: Automatic, Manual, and Disabled. Sometimes you might need to set a service to Automatic so that the service starts automatically every time the computer boots; many services are set this way by default. Or, you might want to set a service to Manual so that you have control over it. In other cases, you might want to set it to Disabled; for example, disabling the insecure Telnet service. This service is disabled by default in Windows Vista and XP, but you never know who or what might have enabled it.

Recording Symptoms and Error Codes

If you don't find event logs useful, services are running properly, and your tests rule out power and interference, you must proceed to tests that focus on the hardware or software that appears to be the most likely cause of the problem.

Which test or diagnostic routine is the best one to start with? Before you perform any specific tests, review the clues you gathered from the client. Here's an example: a document in Microsoft Word would print to a laser printer, but a project in Adobe InDesign would not.

Because all Windows-based programs use the same Windows printer driver, we can rule out the printer driver. Printer hardware or driver failures would prevent all software programs from printing; however, in this case, printing works from some

programs but not others when the same printer and printer drivers are in use. Before you can solve this problem, you need more information about the printer. It's time to use the printer's self-test (a technique listed earlier in Table 10-4) for more information about the printer.

A laser printer's self-test usually indicates the amount of RAM on board, the emulation (HP or PostScript), and firmware revisions. The amount of RAM on board is critical, because laser printers are page printers: The whole page must fit into the laser printer's RAM to be printed.

Thus, there are two variables to this printing problem: the size of the RAM in the printer and the size of the documents the user is trying to print. The self-test reveals the printer has only the standard amount of RAM (2MB) on board. This amount of RAM is adequate for text, but an elaborate page can overload it. A look at the InDesign document reveals that it has a large amount of graphic content, whereas the Microsoft Word document is standard-sized text only with a minimal use of bold and italic formatting.

Your theory is to add RAM to the printer, and it can print the brochure. If you don't have a suitable RAM module, how can you prove it?

Because Microsoft Word printed a text-only document flawlessly, you might be able to convince your client from that fact alone that the printer isn't "broken" but needs a RAM upgrade—or a workaround.

Devising a workaround that helps the printer work is good for client satisfaction and proves that your theory is correct. Have the client adjust the graphics resolution of the printer from its default setting to a lower amount, such as from 1,200 dpi to 600 dpi or from 600 dpi to 300 dpi, and print the brochure again. If a lack of printer memory is the cause of the problem, reducing the brochure's dots per inch for graphics objects enables the brochure to print. The client looks at the lower print quality, and if the client is not satisfied with the lower print quality caused by lower graphics resolution, at that point you can recommend the RAM upgrade. Point out the provision for RAM upgrades in the printer manual if necessary. Remember, you're not selling anything, but solving problems.

If the printer does not print at all, other tests from Table 10-4 are appropriate, such as the I/O port loopback test or hardware resources check.

Checking Configurations and Device Manager

To check system configuration, use the following methods:

- To check integrated hardware, restart the system, start the BIOS configuration program, and examine the appropriate settings.

- To check Windows version, memory size, and processor speed, open the System properties sheet in Windows. The General tab lists this information.

- To check hardware resources, driver versions, and device status, open the Device Manager and open the properties sheet for any given device.

- To check program information, open the application program and use its Help, About option to view program version and service pack or update level.

Common Problems

The following sections discuss how to deal with common computer problems, including

- STOP (blue screen) errors

- Auto restart errors

- System lockups

- I/O device problems

- Application install or start/load problems

- Stalled print spooler

- Incorrect or incompatible print driver

STOP (Blue Screen) Errors

STOP errors (also known as blue screen of death or BSOD errors) can occur either during start up or after the system is running. The BSOD nickname is used because the background is normally blue (or sometimes black) with the error message in white text. Figure 10-7 displays a typical BSOD.

NOTE   Regardless of when a STOP/BSOD error occurs, your system is halted by default. To restart the computer, you must turn off the system and turn it back on. But, before you do that, record the error message text and other information so you can research the problem if it recurs. It is possible for the system to restart on its own.

BSOD errors can be caused by any of the following:

- **Incompatible or defective hardware or software**—Start the system in Safe Mode and uninstall the last hardware or software installed. Acquire updates before you reinstall the hardware or software. Exchange or test memory.

Figure 10-7 A typical STOP (BSOD) error. You can look up the error by name or by number.

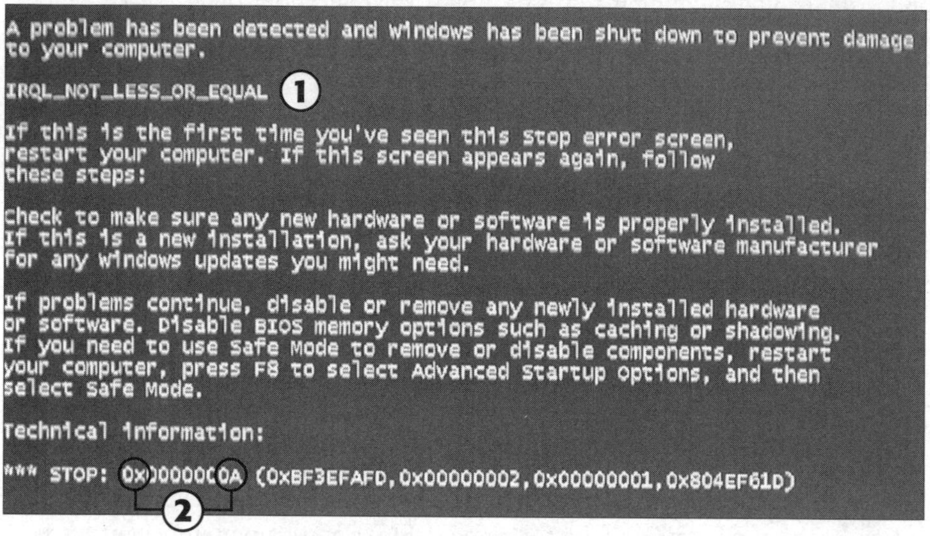

```
A problem has been detected and windows has been shut down to prevent damage
to your computer.

IRQL_NOT_LESS_OR_EQUAL  (1)

If this is the first time you've seen this stop error screen,
restart your computer. If this screen appears again, follow
these steps:

Check to make sure any new hardware or software is properly installed.
If this is a new installation, ask your hardware or software manufacturer
for any windows updates you might need.

If problems continue, disable or remove any newly installed hardware
or software. Disable BIOS memory options such as caching or shadowing.
If you need to use safe Mode to remove or disable components, restart
your computer, press F8 to select Advanced Startup Options, and then
select Safe Mode.

Technical information:

*** STOP: 0x0000000A (0xBF3EFAFD,0x00000002,0x00000001,0x804EF61D)
                 (2)
```

1. Enter this text as shown to look up the error by name
   at http://support.microsoft.com or third-party websites.
2. STOP errors are often listed as 0x followed by the last
   two digits in the error code, such as 0x0A in this example.

- **Registry problems**—Select Last Known Good Configuration as described earlier in this chapter and see if the system starts.

- **Viruses**—Scan for viruses and remove them if discovered.

- **Miscellaneous causes**—Check the Windows Event Viewer and check the System log. Research the BSOD with the Microsoft Knowledge Base.

To determine the exact cause of the error, you must

Step 1. Record the exact error message before restarting the computer.

Step 2. Research the error at Microsoft's Knowledge Base (http://support.microsoft.com) if the BSOD keeps happening.

TIP Unfortunately, you can't take a screen capture of a BSOD for printing because a BSOD completely shuts Windows down. However, if you have a digital camera handy, it makes a great tool for recording the exact error message. Just be sure to use the correct range setting to get the sharpest picture possible (normal or close-up, often symbolized with a flower icon). Turn off the flash on the camera and use ISO 400 to enable handheld shooting in dim light.

Application Troubleshooting

Application troubleshooting involves dealing with applications that cannot be installed or cannot start.

If you can't install an application, here are some reasons why—and some solutions:

- **Not enough disk space on C: drive**—Use the Custom Installation option, if available, to choose another drive, delete old files in the default `Temp` folder, or free up space by deleting .chk files created by `ScanDisk` or `Chkdsk` in the root folder.

- **Computer doesn't meet minimum requirements for RAM or CPU speed**—Check for installation program switches to turn off speed and RAM checks, or, better still, upgrade the system to meet or exceed minimums.

- **No more space available in root folder**—A FAT16 drive with 256 entries in the root folder cannot create any more folders or files in the root. Install to another folder, or convert the drive to FAT32 or NTFS to eliminate this limitation. Keep in mind that a long file name (LFN) can use up multiple entries in the root folder.

- **Application incompatible with version of Windows in use**—Although most recent commercial applications are designed to be installed on several different Windows versions, some older commercial applications and some custom applications might not support a particular Windows version. If an update to a compatible version is available, update the application and try the installation again with an updated version. If no updated version is available, you can either use a different program or install a virtualization environment such as Microsoft's Virtual PC, install an operating system supported by the application, and install the application itself. The virtualized operating system and application run in a window on the host PC.

NOTE   To learn more about virtualization and Virtual PC, visit the Virtual PC website at www.microsoft.com/windows/virtual-pc/default.aspx.

CAUTION   Even if you choose another drive rather than the default system drive (usually C:) for the application, a severe shortage of space on the system drive can still prevent a successful installation. That's because shared files are often installed on various areas of the default system drive.

Using Task Manager

Windows Vista/XP/2000 can display the Windows Task Manager (see Figure 10-8) when you press **Ctrl+Alt+Del** (select **Task Manager** from the Windows Security dialog box).

Figure 10-8   The Windows XP version of the Windows Task Manager's Applications (top left), Processes (top right), Performance (bottom left), and Networking (bottom right) tabs.

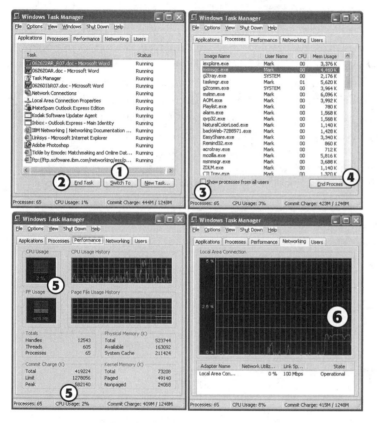

1. Click to switch tasks
2. Click to end selected task
3. Click to show processes for all users
4. Click to end selected process
5. Current CPU usage
6. Network usage history

Use the Applications tab to determine if a program has stopped responding; you can shut down these programs. Use the Processes tab to see which processes are consuming the most memory. Use this dialog along with the System Configuration Utility (MSConfig) to help determine if you are loading unnecessary startup applications; MSConfig can disable them to free up memory. If you are unable to shut down a program with the Applications tab, you can also shut down its processes with the Processes tab, but this is not recommended unless the program cannot be shut down in any other way.

Use the Performance tab to determine whether you need to install more RAM memory or need to increase your paging file size. Use the Networking tab to monitor the performance of your network.

The top-level menu can be used to adjust the properties of the currently selected tab and to shut down the system.

Troubleshooting with Device Manager

If your computer has devices that are malfunctioning in a way that Device Manager can detect, or has devices that are disabled, they are displayed as soon as you open Device Manager. For example, in Figure 10-9, the Ports (COM and LPT) category displays a malfunctioning port, COM 2, indicated by an exclamation mark (!) in a yellow circle. The parallel printer port, LPT1, has been disabled, as indicated by a red X. If the malfunctioning or disabled device is an I/O port, such as a serial, parallel, or USB port, any device attached to that port cannot work until the device is working properly.

Figure 10-9   Windows XP Device Manager displaying disabled and malfunctioning devices.

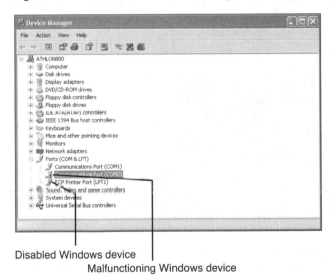

Disabled Windows device
Malfunctioning Windows device

Not every problem with a device shows up in Device Manager, but most problems with resource conflicts or drivers are displayed here.

To troubleshoot problems with a device in Device Manager, open its Properties sheet by double-clicking the device. Use the General tab shown in Figure 10-10 to display the device's status and to troubleshoot a disabled or malfunctioning device.

Figure 10-10   A problem device's General properties. If the device's General Properties sheet lacks a solution button, look up the Device Manager error code and take appropriate action manually.

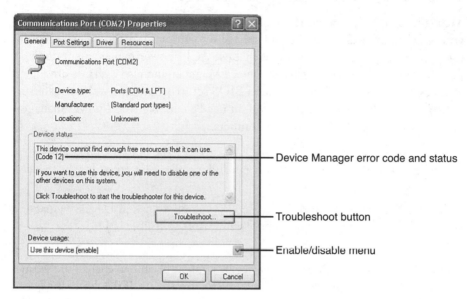

Device Manager error code and status

Troubleshoot button

Enable/disable menu

When you have a malfunctioning device such as the one in Figure 10-10, you have several options for resolving the problem:

- Look up the Device Manager code to determine the problem and its solution (see Table 10-5 for a few examples).

Table 10-5   Examples of Some Device Manager Codes and Solutions–

Device Manager Code Number	Problem	Recommended Solution
Code 1	This device is not configured correctly.	Update the driver.
Code 3	The driver for this device might be corrupted, or your system might be running low on memory or other resources.	Close some open applications. Uninstall and reinstall the driver. Install additional RAM.
Code 10	Device cannot start.	Update the driver. View MSKB article 943104 for more information.
Code 12	This device cannot find enough free resources that it can use. If you want to use this device, you need to disable one of the other devices on this system.	You can use the Troubleshooting Wizard in Device Manager to determine where the conflict is, and then disable the conflicting device. Disable the device.

- Click the **Troubleshoot** button (if any) shown on the device's General Properties tab; the button's name and usage depends upon the problem. Table 10-5 lists the codes, their meanings, and the solution button (if any).

- Manually change resources. If the nature of the problem is a resource conflict, you can click the Resources tab and change the settings and eliminate the conflict if possible. Most recent systems that use ACPI power management don't permit manual resource changes in Device Manager and also override any changes you might make in the system BIOS setup program. On these systems, if resource conflicts take place, you might need to disable ACPI power management before you can solve resource conflicts.

- Manually update drivers. If the problem is a driver issue but an Update Driver button isn't available, open the Driver tab and install a new driver for the device.

NOTE These are just a few examples of the codes you might see in Device Manager. For a complete list, see the link http://support.microsoft.com/kb/310123.

If the device has a conflict with another device, you might be able to change the settings in the device's Properties page/Resources tab (see Figure 10-11). If the device is a legacy (non-PnP) device, you might need to shut down the system and reconfigure the card manually before you can use Device Manager to reset its configuration in Windows.

Figure 10-11 The parallel port's current configuration (A) conflicts with another port. By selecting another configuration (B), the conflict is resolved.

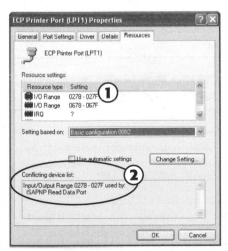 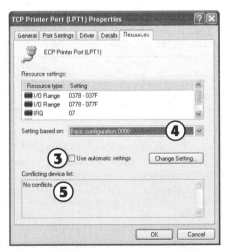

1. Conflicting resource (I/O port address)
2. Conflicting device
3. Can solve most configuration conflicts when selected
4. Selects from various preconfigured settings
5. Conflict resolved

You can also use the Device Manager to disable a device that is conflicting with another device. To disable a device, follow these steps:

Step 1.   Click the plus (+) sign next to the device category containing the device.

Step 2.   Right-click the device and select **Disable**.

or

Step 1.   Right-click the device and select **Properties**.

Step 2.   On the General tab, look for the Device Usage display at the bottom of the window. Click the menu and select **Do Not Use This Device (disable)**. Refer to Figure 10-10. If you prefer to solve the problem with the device, click the **Troubleshoot** button.

Depending on the device, you might need to physically remove it from the system to resolve a conflict. To use the Device Manager to remove a device, follow these steps:

Step 1.   Click the plus (+) sign next to the device category containing the device.

Step 2.   Right-click the device and select **Uninstall**.

Step 3.   Shut down the system and remove the physical device.

or

Step 1.   Right-click the device and select **Properties**.

Step 2.   Access the Driver tab, and click the **Uninstall** button.

Step 3.   Shut down the system and remove the physical device.

Where to Go for More Information

After you've gathered as much information as possible, you might find that you still need more help. User manuals for components often are discarded, software drivers need to be updated, and some conflicts don't have easy answers. Use the following resources for more help:

- **Manufacturers' websites**—Most system and component manufacturers provide extensive technical information via the World Wide Web. You should have the Adobe Reader program in its latest version available to be able to read the technical manuals you can download (Adobe Reader is a free download from

www.adobe.com). These sites often contain expert systems for troubleshooting, specialized newsgroups, downloadable driver updates, and other help for problems.

- **Printed manuals**—Although many vendors have switched to web-based or Adobe Reader (PDF) manuals, some vendors still provided printed manuals or quick-reference diagrams. Be sure to file these in a way that permits quick access when needed.

- **Web-based or PDF manuals on disc**—Many vendors, especially those that use CDs or DVDs to distribute device drivers or utility programs for hardware, now put their user or reference manuals on the same medium. To view a web-based manual, open the file with your web browser. To view a PDF manual, open the file with Adobe Reader, Adobe Acrobat, or other PDF viewer/editor.

- **Help for "orphan" systems and components**—It's frustrating to need information about a system whose manufacturer is no longer around. Sites such as www.download.com and www.windrivers.com provide information and drivers for orphan systems and components.

- **Online computer magazines**—If your back-issue collection of major computer magazines is missing some issues, or even if you've never subscribed to the print versions, you can find a lot of technical content from the major magazine publishers online: www.pcmag.com (*PC Magazine*), www.pcworld.com (*PC World*), and www.maximumpc.com (*Maximum PC*) are just three of my favorite resources.

- **Third-party news and information sites**—Tom's Hardware (www.tomshardware.com), AnandTech (www.anandtech.com), The Register (www.theregister.co.uk), and iXBT Labs (http://ixbtlabs.com/) are just a few of the websites you can use for product reviews, news, and insights.

- **Book series**—Scott Mueller's *Upgrading and Repairing PCs* (www.upgradingandrepairingpcs.com) can be a lifesaver. With nearly 2.5 million copies sold, it's still the single best source of information about desktop computer hardware, old and new. Other books in the series, such as *Upgrading and Repairing Laptops* and *Upgrading and Repairing Microsoft Windows, Second Edition*, are also valuable. The *Upgrading and Repairing Networks* text is recommended for improving your network skills. When it comes to Windows, try Que's *Special Edition Using* and *In Depth* series (www.quepublishing.com).

- **Search engines**—Google (www.google.com), Yahoo! (www.yahoo.com), Good-search (www.goodsearch.com), Bing (www.bing.com), and others and aggregators such as Dogpile (www.dogpile.com) are among the fastest ways to locate specific resources for further research. Currently, of these, my favorite is Google. Google is fast, finds text in many types of online content (not just HTML web pages, but also Adobe Acrobat, Microsoft Word, and others), can search newsgroups, and finds image and video files as well. Use its Advanced Search feature to narrow your search; you can even search a particular website only. Click the **Cached** button to see the site as Google last saw it if the current contents aren't what you need or the website is down. Go to **http://groups.google.com** to search or browse Usenet newsgroups.

With so many sources of information available in print and online, there's no reason to stop learning. To succeed and enjoy yourself, take every opportunity to learn more.

Chapter Review Questions

The following questions test your recall of the concepts described in this chapter. The answers are listed at the end of the questions in the "Answers and Explanations" section.

1. You have just installed an updated driver for your video card. You reboot the system and, for some reason, Windows does not start. What could you do to fix this problem?

   A. Press **F8** at boot and select the Last Known Good Configuration.

   B. Select **Ctrl+Alt+Del** at the BIOS screen.

   C. Create a boot disk on a floppy disk.

   D. Reboot the computer and hope it comes back up.

2. You are working on a computer running the Windows Vista operating system. You get a boot error. What is an option you can use to recover your system to normal?

   A. NTBACKUP

   B. System Restore

   C. ASR Disk

   D. WinRE

3. You are working on a computer running the Windows XP operating system. You receive a boot error that the NTLDR is missing or corrupt. Which of the following could you use to restore the file?

   A. Copy and paste from the CD

   B. The Recovery Console

   C. The NTBACKUP program

   D. Use the advanced boot options

4. You have just set up a new user's computer that is running the Windows XP operating system. This user wants to make sure that the computer's system state can be restored in the event of a failure. What system recovery option would you want to set up?

   A. Automated System Recovery

   B. Emergency Repair Disk

   C. There is not one

   D. Complete PC Backup

5. Which of the following gives you the ability to recover an operating system if you have a system boot failure? (Choose all that apply.)

   A. WinRE

   B. Last Known Good Configuration

   C. Recovery Console

   D. All of these options are correct

6. You are the technician for your company. You are in charge of maintaining all desktop computers. You need to keep your systems updated. Which of the following would you need to do to maintain these computers? (Choose all that apply.)

   A. Install the latest service pack

   B. Defragment your computer

   C. Install all hotfixes

   D. Install antivirus updates

7. You have a user who is having problems with her PC. You inspect the computer and find that the computer is not running an up-to-date service pack. Where would you go to get the service pack?

   A. openoffice.org

   B. msn.com

   C. update.microsoft.com

   D. Your favorite search engine

8. You are working as a desktop technician for your company. You have been asked to come up with a way to protect all users' documents in case they are deleted. Which of the following should you do?

    A. Create system restore points on all computers

    B. Schedule backups

    C. Save all data to a removable drive

    D. Send all documents to a remote location

9. You are the desktop technician for your company. You have been asked to come up with a plan to minimize the downtime of users' workstations in case of failure during working hours. What should you do to make this happen?

    A. Create a NTBACKUP schedule

    B. Perform a system state backup

    C. Create an image backup of the system

    D. Set up a system restore point

10. What is the second step of the six-step troubleshooting process mentioned in this chapter?

    A. Ascertain what the problem is

    B. Determine whether theories are correct through testing

    C. Document the entire process

    D. Write down probable causes of the problem

11. What is the third step of the six-step troubleshooting process?

    A. Ascertain what the problem is

    B. Determine whether theories are correct through testing

    C. Document the entire process

    D. Write down probable causes of the problem

12. Which of the following is not a method for preventing ESD?

    A. Touch the chassis of the computer

    B. Use an antistatic wrist strap

    C. Increase temperature

    D. Use antistatic bags

13. Which kind of tool should you use to test for power supply problems?

   A. Device Manager

   B. Multimeter

   C. CPU-Z

   D. POST card tester

14. A BSOD is also known as which of the following?

   A. Disabled device

   B. Virus

   C. Critical error

   D. Stop error

15. What does an exclamation point in the Device Manager signify?

   A. Disabled device

   B. Malfunctioning device

   C. Unknown device

   D. Missing device

Case Study 1

There are many ways to troubleshoot and repair a computer. How you troubleshoot the computer depends on the type of symptoms you discern. However, one of the common ways to troubleshoot the computer is to enlist the aid of the Windows Advanced Boot Options Menu (ABOM). Reboot your computer. Immediately after the BIOS starts, press **F8** to view the ABOM. Write down the various options you see and attempt to define them and list the possible reasons you might use each one. Use the information in this chapter as well as Microsoft's TechNet website (http://technet.microsoft.com/en-us/default.aspx) as resources.

Case Study 2

You are a technician for your company. You have been having problems with a user's computer hard drive. The user is losing her data. You need to come up with a solution to keep the user's documents from being deleted. You do not have a network server to store the user's data. What should you do to prevent this from happening?

Answers and Explanations

1. **A.** If you are unable to start Windows Vista/XP but don't see an error message, the problem could be caused by a driver or startup program, video driver problems, or problems with the system kernel. When pressing F8, Windows XP and Vista display the Advanced Boot Options menu, which includes various options, such as Safe Mode, VGA Mode, and Last Known Good Configuration, which helps you correct startup problems.

2. **D.** WinRE is a set of tools included in Windows Vista, Windows Server 2008, and other upcoming Windows operating systems. It takes the place of the Recovery Console used in Windows XP/2000. Also known as System Recovery Options, WinRE's purpose is to recover Windows from errors that prevent it from booting.

3. **B.** The Windows Recovery Console is a special command-line interface that is designed for copying files and performing disk repairs. It is used by Windows XP and 2000. In Windows 2000, you can use the Recovery Console as an alternative to the Emergency Repair process, such as if you need to restore only one system file. Windows XP lacks the Emergency Repair provision, so understanding how to use the Recovery Console is even more important.

4. **A.** The Automated System Recovery (ASR) option in NTBackup enables you to restore the system state (user accounts, hard disk configuration, network configuration, video settings, hardware configuration, software settings, operating system boot files). The Emergency Repair Disk (ERD) is used in Windows 2000, and Complete PC Backup is used in Windows Vista. Windows XP Professional does not include a true disaster-recovery backup program like Complete PC Backup.

5. **D.** All the listed options are valid for recovering an operating system if the system does not boot. WinRE is the Windows Vista Recovery Environment, which has several options to repair boot failure. The Last Known Good Configuration is one of the Advanced Boot Options that can be accessed by pressing F8 in any version of Windows. You can install the recovery console from the Windows XP CD-ROM. After it's installed, it becomes part of the boot selection in the boot.ini file.

6. **A, C, D.** To keep a computer updated, and you should install the latest service pack, which can be downloaded from the Internet or installed from CD; install any hotfixes and security updates through Windows Update; and install antivirus updates, which is usually accomplished by setting the AV updates to download and install automatically.

7. **C.** In this case, you need to go to the Windows update site and download the latest service pack and any additional patches and hotfixes that are listed on the update webpage.

8. **B.** You should always have some sort of backup schedule for your user documents to prevent permanent loss of their data. You can use the NTBACKUP tool to set up these backups.

9. **C.** If you create an image backup of the system, you can easily restore the computer to its original state in about 20 minutes or so. This has become a great tool for technicians to use if a hard drive fails or you are unable to bring the system back online.

10. **D.** The second step of the six-step troubleshooting process in this chapter is to write down probable causes of the problem. Ascertaining the problem is the first step. Determining if theories are correct is the third step. Documentation is the sixth and last step, although you might document throughout the entire process.

11. **B.** The third step of the troubleshooting process is to determine whether theories are correct through testing. Ascertaining the problem is the first step. Documentation is the sixth and last step. Writing down probable causes is the second step.

12. **C.** Increasing temperature is not a method of preventing ESD. Instead, you should increase the humidity if at all possible.

13. **B.** A multimeter can test power supplies and other electrical devices and confirms proper voltage among other things.

14. **D.** A BSOD (Blue Screen of Death) is also known as a Stop error.

15. **B.** An exclamation point signifies a malfunctioning device. Disabled devices are shown with a red X. Unknown devices are shown with a question mark. Missing devices are not shown at all.

Case Study 1 Solution

The ABOM varies between different versions of Windows. For example, Windows Vista should display the following options:

- **Safe Mode**—Starts system with a minimal set of drivers; can be used to start System Restore or to load Windows GUI for diagnostics. Also used to run virus scans.

- **Safe Mode with Networking**—Starts system with a minimal set of drivers and enables network support. Great for when drivers are not working properly and the computer can only boot in Safe Mode, but you also need access to the Internet to download drivers.

- **Safe Mode with Command Prompt**—Starts system with a minimal set of drivers but loads command prompt instead of Windows GUI. Great when your testing and diagnosis need only be done in the command-line.

- **Enable Boot Logging**—Creates a ntbtlog.txt file. This helps to further analyze and diagnose problems with drivers. You would boot to this option first. This creates the ntbtlog.txt file. Then, reboot into safe mode to analyze the file.

- **Enable low-resolution video (640×480)**—Uses a standard VGA driver in place of a GPU-specific display driver, but uses all other drivers as normal. (This is called *Enable VGA Mode* in Windows XP/2000.) This helps you troubleshoot video problems; however, everything else runs as normal.

- **Last Known Good Configuration**—Starts the system with the last configuration known to work; useful for solving problems caused by newly installed hardware or software. The Last Known Good (LKG) Configuration is the configuration that the computer had as of the last successful login.

- **Directory Services Restore Mode**—This is used to restore a domain controller's active directory (Windows Server). Even though it is listed, it is not used in Windows Vista/XP/2000.

- **Debugging Mode**—This is an advanced diagnostics tool that enables the use of a debug program to examine the system kernel for troubleshooting.

- **Disable automatic restart on system failure**—Prevents Windows from automatically restarting if an error causes Windows to fail. Choose this option only if Windows is stuck in a loop where Windows fails, attempts to restart, and fails again. This is in offered in newer versions of Windows only.

- **Disable driver signature enforcement**—Allows drivers containing improper signatures to be installed. This can be used when a known-good driver from a third-party is not being accepted by Microsoft. This is in offered in newer versions of Windows only.

- **Start Windows Normally**—This can be used to boot to regular Windows. This option is listed in case a user inadvertently presses F8, but does not want to use any of the Advanced Boot Options. It doesn't have any real troubleshooting functionality.

Case Study 2 Solution

First, you might want to run some sort of diagnostic program on the user's hard drive. If you find the drive is good, you should set up some type of backup strategy using the NTBACKUP tool. Because you don't have a network server to store the user documents, you should back up the data to a USB or some other type of removable disk. This helps keep the user's data safe from deletion and make her very happy.

This chapter covers the following subjects:

- **Network Models**—This section defines the client/server and peer-to-peer networking models and explains the differences between the two.

- **Internet Connectivity Technologies**—This section defines services such as dial-up, ISDN, DSL, cable, and satellite. It also talks about LAN connectivity to the Internet.

- **TCP/IP Applications and Technologies**—This section covers the various protocols and services that run within the scope of TCP/IP; for example, HTTP, email, and FTP.

- **Installing Network Interface Cards**—This portion shows how to install PCI network adapters.

- **Cable and Connector Types**—This section defines twisted-pair cable, coaxial, fiber optic, and the different connectors each of those cables use.

- **Network Devices**—This section covers the differences between a hub and a switch, as well as the devices that allow data to flow past the LAN and out to the Internet.

- **Configuring TCP/IP**—This section demonstrates how to configure TCP/IP, and covers IPv4 addressing concepts.

- **Using Network Command-Line Tools**—You should know how to use ping, ipconfig, and tracert. Learn it here!

Networks

A network is a group of computers, peripherals, and software that are connected to each other and can be used together. Special software and hardware are required to make networks work.

Two or more computers connected together in the same office are considered a LAN (local area network). LANs in different cities can be connected to each other by a WAN (wide area network). The Internet represents the world's largest network, connecting both standalone computers and computers on LAN and WAN networks all over the world.

At one time, it was necessary to use a network operating system (NOS) such as Novell NetWare to enable networking. However, current operating systems, including Windows, include the components needed for networking.

Windows 7, Vista, XP, and Windows 2000 include the following NOS features, enabling systems running these operating systems to be used either as network clients or as peer network servers:

- **Client software**—Enables systems to connect with other networks. Windows XP/2000 can connect to Windows and Novell NetWare networks, among others, and Windows Vista connects to Windows networks only by default. The most common example of this is the Client for Microsoft Networks component of Windows.

- **Network protocols**—Windows XP/2000 can utilize TCP/IP, IPX/SPX, and NetBEUI. Windows Vista/Win7 use TCP/IPv4 and TCP/IPv6 by default, as these are by far the most common.

- **File and print sharing**—Enables Windows systems to act as peer servers for Windows and Novell NetWare networks.

- **Services**—Enables specialized network services, such as shared printers, network backup, and more.

In essence, adding a computer to a network requires installing a network adapter (either wired or wireless), configuring the adapter in the operating system, making additional TCP/IP configurations, and testing the connection to

the network and the Internet. This chapter discusses how to do all of these things. It also gets into the basics of network cables and connectors, network devices, and the various TCP/IP applications and configurations you should know.

Network Models

As the network features found in Windows suggest, there are two major network models:

■   Client/server

■   Peer-to-peer

It's important to understand the differences between them so that you can identify which works more efficiently in various environments.

Client/Server

Most departmental and larger networks are client/server networks, such as the one illustrated in Figure 11-1. The networks controlled by Windows Server 2003, Windows 2000 Server, and Novell NetWare servers are examples of client/server networks.

The roles of each computer in a client/server network are distinctive, affecting both the hardware used in each computer and the software installed in each computer. In a client/server environment there are many advantages, including centralized administration, better sharing capabilities, scalability, and possibly increased security.

Servers

A *server* is a computer on the network that provides other computers (called *clients* or *workstations*) with access to resources, such as disk drives, folders, printers, modems, scanners, and Internet access. Because these resources can be used by different computers over the network, they are called shared resources.

Servers can also be used for different types of software and tasks. For example, application servers run tasks for clients, file servers store data and program files for clients, and mail servers store and distribute email to clients.

Servers typically have more powerful hardware features than typical PCs, such as SCSI or SATA RAID arrays or network attached storage for hard disk storage, larger amounts of RAM, hot-swap power supplies, and server-optimized network adapters. However, because servers are not operated by an individual user, they often use low-performance integrated or PCI video and might be managed remotely rather than with a keyboard or monitor connected directly to the server.

Figure 11-1 A typical client/server network.

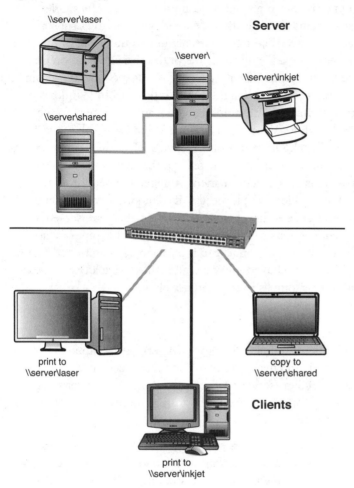

Clients

A *client* is a computer that uses the resources on a server. Typical examples of client computers include Windows Vista, XP, and 2000. Depending on the network operating system in use, clients and servers can be separate machines or a client can act as a server and a server can act as a client. Clients can refer to servers either by assigning drive letters to shared folders or by using a Universal Naming Convention (UNC) path name to refer to the server, as shown in Figure 11-1.

In the figure, \\server\shared is an example of a shared folder. It is also an example of a UNC path. The double-backslash precedes a computer name. The single backslash precedes the sharename. (This is often denoted with variables such as \\computername\sharename, or \\IPaddress\sharename.) So the name of the computer the client connects to is "server," and the name of the shared folder on that computer is called "shared." Mapping is the process of making a connection from the client computer to the remote share. You do it in Windows from Windows Explorer, or in the Command Prompt. For example, if you want to connect to the \\server\shared folder in Windows Vista, you can open Windows Explorer and then access **Tools, Map Network Drive**. From there, you select the drive letter you would like to use for the connection and type the path to the share—once again in this case, \\server\shared. This creates a permanent, mapped connection to the share that can be accessed in Windows Explorer just like any other volume on the local computer; the only difference is that the contents in the share are served up remotely. You can also map connections to shares in the Command Prompt by using the **net use** command. For example, to connect to the previously mentioned share, you would type **net use \\server\shared**, or you could add a drive letter to utilize **net use P: \\server\shared**, as long as P: is not in use already.

Peer-to-Peer

The network features built into Windows allow for peer servers: Computers can share resources with each other, and machines that share resources can also be used as client workstations. As with client/server networking, resources on peer servers can be accessed via UNC (as shown in Figure 11-1) or by mapping drive letters and printer ports on a client to server resources.

As Figure 11-2 shows, if mapped drive letters and printer ports are used in a peer-to-peer network, the same resource has a different name, depending on whether it's being accessed from the peer server (acting as a workstation) itself or over the network. In Figure 11-2, the system on the top shares its external hard disk drive with the system on the bottom, which refers to the shared hard disk drive as F:\. The system on the bottom shares its printer with the system on the top, which has mapped the shared printer to LPT2.

The peer server loads file and printer-sharing software to make printers and drives or folders available to others. Because a peer server is also used as a workstation, it is equipped in the same way as a typical workstation or standalone PC.

Figure 11-2   A simple two-station peer-to-peer network, in which each computer acts as a peer server to the other.

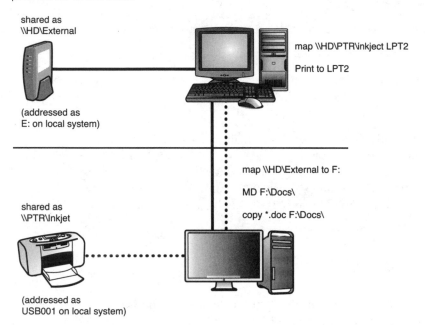

shared as
\\HD\External

map \\HD\PTR\inkject LPT2

Print to LPT2

(addressed as
E: on local system)

map \\HD\External to F:

MD F:\Docs\

shared as
\\PTR\Inkjet

copy *.doc F:\Docs\

(addressed as
USB001 on local system)

Internet Connectivity Technologies

One of the best reasons to create a network of any size is to provide access to the Internet. The many types of connectivity technologies that can be used for Internet access are discussed in the following sections.

TIP   As you review the following sections, try to determine which type of Internet connections you use at home and at your workplace.

Modems and Dial-Up Internet Connectivity

Until the late nineties, dial-up networking (DUN) had been the most common way for home and small businesses to connect to the Internet. Dial-up connections are often referred to as analog connections because the device used to make the connection is an analog modem, which connects to the Internet through an ordinary telephone line. Every time you connect to the Internet with a dial-up modem, you are making a network connection.

A modem sending data modulates digital computer data into analog data suitable for transmission over telephone lines to the receiving modem, which demodulates the

analog data back into computer form. Modems share two characteristics with serial ports:

- Both use serial communication to send and receive information.
- Both often require adjustment of transmission speed and other options.

In fact, most external modems require a serial port to connect them to the computer; some external modems use the USB port instead.

NOTE Properly used, the term *modem* (modulator-demodulator) refers only to a device that connects to the telephone line and performs digital-to-analog or analog-to-digital conversions. However, other types of Internet connections such as satellite, wireless, DSL, and cable Internet also use the term *modem*, although they work with purely digital data. When used by itself in this book, however, *modem* refers only to dial-up (telephone) modems.

Modems come in five types:

- **Add-on card**—Add-on card modems for desktop computers, such as the one shown in Figure 11-3, fit into a PCI expansion slot.
- **External**—External modems plug into a serial or USB port.
- **PC Card**—PCMCIA (PC Card) modems are sometimes built in a combo design that also incorporates a 10/100 Ethernet network adapter.
- **Motherboard-integrated**—Many recent desktop computers have integrated modems, as do many notebook computers.
- **Mini-PCI card**—Some notebook computers that appear to have built-in modems actually use modems that use the mini-PCI form factor and can be removed and replaced with another unit.

Although some high-end add-on card and PC Card modems have a hardware UART (universal asynchronous receiver transmitter) or UART-equivalent chip, most recent models use a programmable *digital signal processor (DSP)* instead. Modems with a DSP perform similarly to UART-based modems, but can easily be reprogrammed with firmware and driver updates as needed. Low-cost add-on card and PC Card modems often use *HSP (host signal processing)* instead of a UART or DSP. HSP modems are sometimes referred to as Winmodems or soft modems because Windows and the computer's processor perform the modulation, slowing down performance. HSP modems might not work with some older versions of Windows or non-Windows operating systems.

Figure 11-3 A typical PCI internal modem. Note the two RJ-11 connectors on the rear of the modem: They enable you to plug a phone into the modem so you can use the modem or your telephone.

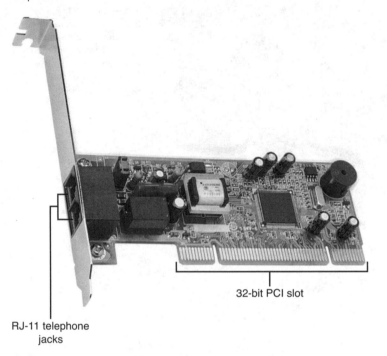

32-bit PCI slot

RJ-11 telephone
jacks

External modems, such as the one shown in Figure 11-4, must be connected to a serial or USB port. Serial port versions require an external power source (USB modems are usually powered by the USB port or hub), but the portability and front-panel status lights of either type of external modem make them better for business use in the minds of many users.

ISDN Internet Connectivity

ISDN (Integrated Services Digital Network) was originally developed to provide an all-digital method for connecting multiple telephone and telephony-type devices, such as fax machines, to a single telephone line and to provide a faster connection for teleconferencing for remote computer users. A home/small office-based connection can also provide an all-digital Internet connection at speeds up to 128Kbps. Line quality is a critical factor in determining whether any particular location can use ISDN service. If an all-digital connection cannot be established between the customer's location and the telephone company's central switch, ISDN service is not available or a new telephone line must be run (at extra cost to you!).

Figure 11-4   A typical external modem that connects to a serial port. Note the reset switch, which enables the user to reset the modem without turning off the computer.

1. Status/activity lights
2. RJ-11 connector for telephone pass-through
3. RJ-11 telephone cable
4. Power cable
5. 9-pin serial cable
6. Reset switch

NOTE   The telephone network was originally designed to support analog signaling only, which is why an analog (dial-up) modem that sends data to other computers converts digital signals to analog for transmission through the telephone network. The receiving analog modem converts analog data back to digital data.

ISDN Hardware

To make an ISDN connection, your PC (and any other devices that share the ISDN connection) needs a device called an ISDN terminal adapter (TA). A TA resembles a conventional analog modem. Internal models plug into the same PCI, ISA, and PC Card slots used by analog modems, and external models use USB or serial ports. External TAs often have two or more RJ-11 ports for telephony devices, an RJ-45 port for the connection to the ISDN line, and a serial or USB port for connection to the computer.

Setting Up an ISDN Connection

ISDN connections (where available) are provided through the local telephone company. There are two types of ISDN connections:

- Primary Rate Interface (PRI)

- Basic Rate Interface (BRI)

A PRI connection provides 1.536Mbps of bandwidth, whereas a BRI interface provides 64Kbps (single-channel) or 128Kbps (dual-channel) of bandwidth. BRI is sold to small businesses and home offices; PRI is sold to large organizations. Both types of connections enable you to use the Internet and talk or fax data through the phone line at the same time.

A direct individual ISDN connection is configured through the network features of Windows with the same types of settings used for an analog modem connection. You configure a network-based ISDN connection through the network adapter's TCP/IP properties window. For more information, see "Configuring TCP/IPv4," later in this chapter.

TIP Most telephone companies have largely phased out ISDN in favor of DSL, which is much faster and less expensive.

Broadband Internet Services (DSL, Cable, Satellite)

Broadband Internet service is a blanket term that refers to the following Internet access methods: digital subscriber line (DSL), cable, and satellite. All of these methods provide bandwidth in excess of 300Kbps, and current implementations are two-way services, enabling you to use your telephone while accessing the Internet.

NOTE Other types of broadband Internet service, including direct wireless (using microwave transceivers) and powerline, are not as common, but you might encounter them in some areas.

Digital Subscriber Line (DSL)

DSL (Digital Subscriber Line) can piggyback on the same telephone line used by your telephone and fax machine, or it can be installed as a distinctly separate line. Either way, DSL requires a high-quality telephone line that can carry a digital signal. For home use, DSL is designed strictly for Internet access. But for business use, DSL can be used for additional services and can be used in site-to-site scenarios between organizations.

There are two major types of DSL: ADSL (Asynchronous DSL) and SDSL (Synchronous DSL). Their features are compared in Table 11-1.

Table 11-1   Common DSL Services Compared

Service Type	Supports Existing Telephone Line	User Installation Option?	Typical Downstream Speeds	Typical Upstream Speeds	Typically Marketed To
ADSL	Yes	Yes	384Kbps to 6Mbps	128Kbps to 384Kbps	Home, small-business
SDSL	Not typically	No	384Kbps to 2.0Mbps	Same as downstream speed	Larger businesses and corporations

NOTE   Downstream refers to download speed; upstream refers to upload speed. SDSL gets its name (Synchronous DSL) from providing the same speed in both directions; ADSL is always faster downstream than upstream.

A device known as a DSL modem is used to connect your computer to DSL service. DSL modems connect to your PC through the RJ-45 (Ethernet) port or the USB port. The rear of a typical DSL modem that uses an Ethernet (RJ-45) connection is shown in Figure 11-5.

Figure 11-5   The rear of a typical DSL modem with a power port (top left), RJ-45 data port to the PC (top center), and an RJ-11 telephone line port (top right). The RJ-45 cable is shown at bottom left, and the RJ-11 cable is shown at bottom right.

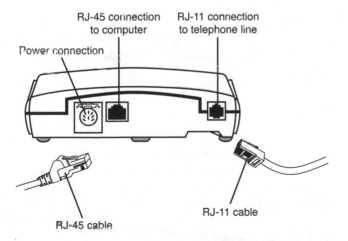

As Figure 11-5 indicates, a typical home DSL connection uses the same telephone lines as ordinary telephone equipment. However, your telephone can interfere with the DSL connection. To prevent this, in some cases a separate DSL line is run from

the outside service box to the computer with the DSL modem. Or, small devices called microfilters are installed between telephones, answering machines, fax machines, and other devices on the same circuit with the DSL modem. Microfilters can be built into special wall plates, but are more often external devices that plug into existing phone jacks, as shown in Figure 11-6.

Figure 11-6   A typical self-installed DSL setup. The DSL vendor supplies the DSL modem (center) and microfilters that attach between telephones and other devices and the wall outlet (right).

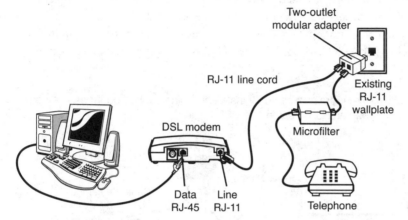

Some DSL connections are configured as an always-on connection similar to a network connection to the Internet. However, many vendors now configure the DSL connection as a PPPoE (point-to-point protocol over Ethernet) connection instead. A PPPoE connection requires the user to make a connection with a username and password.

NOTE   Windows Vista and Windows XP have native support through its Network Connection Wizard. With older versions of Windows, the vendor must provide setup software.

Cable Internet

Cable Internet service piggybacks on the same coaxial cable that brings cable TV into a home or business. A few early cable ISPs used internal cable modems, which supported one-way traffic. (The cable was used for downloads and a conventional telephone line was used for uploads and page requests.) Virtually all cable Internet service today is two-way and is built upon the fiber-optic network used for digital cable and music services provided by most cable TV vendors.

Cable Internet can reach download speeds anywhere from 1Mbps up to 10Mbps or faster. Upload speeds are typically capped at 128Kbps, but some vendors now offer faster upload speeds in some plans.

NOTE You can have cable Internet service without having cable TV.

Some cable TV providers use the same cable that carries cable TV for cable Internet service, while others run a separate cable to the location. When the same cable is used for both cable TV and cable Internet service, a splitter is used to provide connections for cable TV and Internet. The splitter prevents cable TV and cable Internet signals from interfering with each other. One coaxial cable from the splitter goes to the TV or set-top box as usual; the other one goes into a device known as a cable modem. Almost all cable modems are external devices that plug into a computer's 10/100 Ethernet (RJ-45) or USB port. Figure 11-7 shows a typical cable Internet connection.

Figure 11-7 A typical cable modem and cable TV installation. The cable modem can be connected to the computer through an RJ-45 cable or a USB cable.

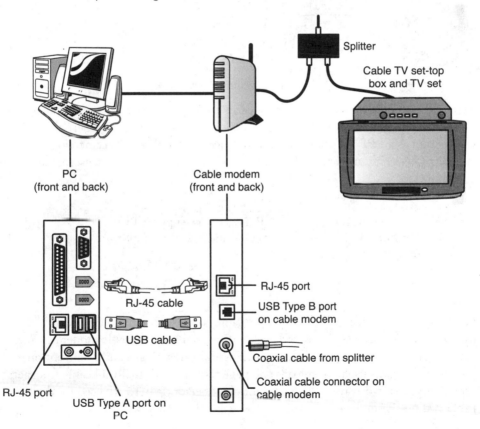

A cable Internet connection can be configured through the standard Network properties sheet in Windows or with customized setup software, depending upon the ISP.

Satellite

Satellite Internet providers, such as HughesNet (previously known as DirecWAY, and, before that, as DirecPC), Starband, and WildBlue use dish antennas similar to satellite TV antennas to receive and transmit signals between geosynchronous satellites and computers. In some cases, you might be able to use a dual-purpose satellite dish to pick up both satellite Internet and satellite TV service.

NOTE   Geosynchronous satellites orbit the Earth's equator at a distance of more than 22,000 miles (approximately 35,000 kilometers). Because of their orbit and altitude, they remain in the same location in the sky at all times. In the Northern Hemisphere, you need an unobstructed view of the southern sky to make a connection. In the Southern Hemisphere, you need an unobstructed view of the northern sky to make a connection.

Satellite Internet services use external devices often called satellite modems to connect the computer to the satellite dish. They connect to the USB or Ethernet (RJ-45) port in a fashion similar to that used by DSL or cable modems.

The Federal Communications Commission (FCC) requires professional installation for satellite Internet service because an incorrectly aligned satellite dish with uplink capabilities could cause a service outage on the satellite at which it's aimed. Setup software supplied by the satellite vendor is used to complete the process.

LANs and Internet Connectivity

A LAN is an ideal way to provide Internet access to two or more users. However, a LAN by itself cannot connect to the Internet. Two additional components must also be used with a LAN to enable it to connect to the Internet:

- **An Internet access device**—This could be a dial-up modem, but more often a broadband connection such as DSL, cable, or satellite is used.

- **A router**—This device connects client PCs on the network to the Internet through the Internet access device. To the Internet, only one client is making a connection, but the router internally tracks which PC has made the request and transmits the data for that PC back to that PC, enabling multiple PCs to access the Internet through the network.

NOTE   As an alternative to a router, some small networks use a gateway, which is a PC configured to share its Internet connection with others on the network. Windows 2000 and later versions support this feature, known as Internet Connection Sharing. Note that wireless access devices known as gateways actually resemble routers.

TCP/IP Applications and Technologies

Transport Control Protocol/Internet Protocol (TCP/IP) is a multiplatform protocol used for both Internet access and for LANs. TCP/IP is used by Novell NetWare 5.x and later, and Windows 7/Vista/XP/2000 as the standard protocol for LAN use, replacing NetBEUI (used on older Microsoft networks) and IPX/SPX (used on older versions of Novell NetWare). Using TCP/IP as a network's only protocol makes network configuration easier because users need to configure only one protocol to communicate with other network clients, servers, or with the Internet.

TIP   Most networking you perform in the real world uses TCP/IP. TCP/IP is also the most complex network to configure, especially if you need to use a static IP address. Make sure you understand how it works!

TCP/IP actually is a suite of protocols used on the Internet for routing and transporting information. The following sections discuss some of the application protocols that are part of the TCP/IP suite, as well as some of the services and technologies that relate to TCP/IP.

ISP

An ISP (Internet service provider) provides the connection between an individual PC or network and the Internet. ISPs use routers connected to high-speed, high-bandwidth connections to route Internet traffic from their clients to their destinations.

HTTP/HTTPS

Hypertext Transfer Protocol (HTTP) is the protocol used by web browsers, such as Internet Explorer and Netscape Navigator, to access websites and content. Normal (unsecured) sites use the prefix http:// when accessed in a web browser. Sites that are secured with various encryption schemes are identified with the prefix https://.

NOTE Most browsers connecting with a secured site also display a closed padlock symbol onscreen.

SSL

Secure Socket Layers (SSL) is an encryption technology used by secured (https://) websites. To access a secured website, the web browser must support the same encryption level used by the secured website (normally 128-bit encryption) and the same version(s) of SSL used by the website (normally SSL version 2.0 or 3.0).

TLS

Transport Layer Security (TLS) is the successor to SSL. SSL3 was somewhat of a prototype to TLS and was not fully standardized. TLS was ratified by the IETF in 1999. However, many people and companies might still refer to it as SSL.

HTML

Hypertext Markup Language (HTML) is the language used by web pages. An HTML page is a specially formatted text page that uses tags (commands contained in angle brackets) to change text appearance, insert links to other pages, display pictures, incorporate scripting languages, and provide other features. Web browsers, such as Microsoft Internet Explorer and Netscape Navigator, are used to view and interpret the contents of web pages, which typically have file extensions such as .HTM, .HTML, .ASP (Active Server pages generated by a database), and others.

You can see the HTML code used to create the web page in a browser by using the View Source or View Page Source menu option provided by your browser. Figure 11-8 compares what you see in a typical web page (top window) with the HTML tags used to set text features and the underlined hyperlink (bottom window). The figure uses different text size and shading to distinguish tags from text, and so do most commercial web-editing programs used to make web pages.

Tags such as <P> for paragraphs are used by themselves, and other tags are used in pairs. For example, <A HREF...> is used to indicate the start of a hyperlink (which will display another page or site in your browser window), and </A> indicates the end of a hyperlink.

NOTE The World Wide Web Consortium (www.w3c.org) sets the official standards for HTML tags and syntax, but major browser vendors, such as Microsoft and Netscape, often modify or extend official HTML standards with their own tags and syntax.

Figure 11-8   A section of an HTML document as shown in a browser.

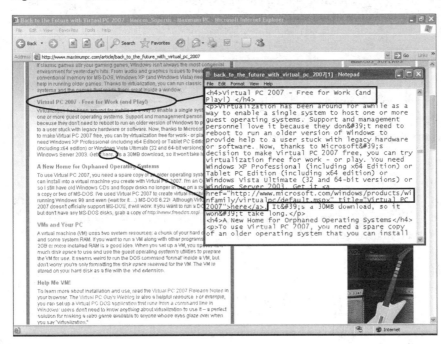

FTP

File Transfer Protocol (FTP) is a protocol used by both web browsers and specialized FTP programs to access dedicated file transfer servers for file downloads and uploads. When you access an FTP site, the site uses the prefix ftp://.

Windows contains `ftp.exe`, a command-line FTP program; type **FTP**, press **Enter**, and then type **?** at the FTP prompt to see the commands you can use.

FTP sites with downloads available to any user support anonymous FTP; if any credentials are required, it's typically the user's email address as a password (the username is preset to anonymous). Some FTP sites require the user to log in with a specified username and password.

TIP   Although you can use Windows' built-in FTP client for file uploads and downloads with both secured and unsecured FTP sites, you should consider using third-party FTP products such as FileZilla (http://filezilla-project.org/) or WS_FTP Pro (www.ipswitchft.com/products/ws_ftp_professional/). These programs enable you to create a customized setup for each FTP site you visit, and they store passwords, server types, and other necessary information. They also enable faster downloads than typical web browsers running in ftp:// mode.

Telnet

Telnet enables a user to make a text-based connection to a remote computer or networking device and use it as if he were a regular user sitting in front of it, rather than simply downloading pages and files as he would with an http:// or ftp:// connection.

Windows contains a command-line Telnet program. To open a connection to a remote computer, enter a command such as

`telnet a.computer.com`

To use other commands, open a command prompt, type `telnet`, and press the **Enter** key. To see other commands, type ?/help.

> **NOTE**   The remote computer must be configured to accept a Telnet login. Typically, TCP port 23 on the remote computer must be open before a login can take place.

> **NOTE**   Telnet is not very secure, especially when used by default. Therefore, it is recommended to use other more secure protocols such as SSH.

SSH

Secure Shell (SSH) allows data to be exchanged between computers on a secured channel. This protocol offers a more secure replacement to FTP and Telnet. The Secure Shell server housing the data you want to access has port 22 open.

DNS

The domain name system (DNS) is the name for the network of servers on the Internet that translate domain names, such as www.informit.com, and individual host names into their matching IP addresses. If you manually configure an IP address, you typically provide the IP addresses of one or more DNS servers as part of the configuration process.

> **CAUTION**   Can't access the site you're looking for? Got the wrong site? You might have made one of these common mistakes:
>
> - **Don't assume that all domain names end in .com**—Other popular domain name extensions include .net, .org, .gov, .us, .cc, and various national domains such as .uk (United Kingdom), .ca (Canada), and many others.
>
> - **Don't forget to use the entire domain name in the browser**—Some browsers add the www. prefix used on most domain names, but others do not. For best results, spell out the complete domain name.

If you want a unique domain name for either a website or email, the ISP that you use to provide your email or web hosting service often provides a registration wizard you can use to access the domain name registration services provided by various companies such as VeriSign.

A domain name has three major sections, from the end of the name to the start:

- The top-level domain (.com, .org, .net, and so on)

- The name of the site

- The server type; www indicates a web server, ftp indicates an FTP server, mail indicates a mail server, and search indicates a search server

For example, Microsoft.com is located in the .com domain, typically used for commercial companies. Microsoft is the domain name. The Microsoft.com domain has the following servers:

- www.microsoft.com hosts web content, such as product information.

- support.microsoft.com hosts the Microsoft.com support website, where users can search for Knowledge Base (KB) and other support documents.

- ftp.microsoft.com hosts the File Transfer Protocol server of Microsoft.com; this portion of the Microsoft.com domain can be accessed by either a web browser or an FTP client.

Many companies have only WWW servers, or only WWW and FTP servers.

NOTE   Some small websites use a folder under a domain hosted by an ISP:
www.anisp.com/~asmallsite

Email

All email systems provide transfer of text messages, and most have provisions for file attachments, enabling you to send documents, graphics, video clips, and other types of computer data files to receivers for work or play. Email clients are included as part of web browsers, and are also available as limited-feature freely downloadable or more-powerful commercially purchased standalone email clients. Some email clients, such as Microsoft Outlook, are part of application suites (such as Microsoft Office) and also feature productivity and time-management features.

TIP Users who travel away from corporate networks might prefer to use a web-based email account, such as Hotmail, or use Outlook Web Access to get access to email from any system with a properly configured web browser.

To configure any email client, you need

- The name of the email server for incoming mail
- The name of the email server for outgoing mail
- The username and password for the email user
- The type of email server (POP, IMAP, or HTTP)

Some email clients and servers might require additional configuration options.

To access web-based email, you need

- The website for the email service
- The username and password

The following sections describe three email protocols: SMTP, POP, and IMAP.

SMTP

The Simple Mail Transfer Protocol (SMTP) is used to send email from a client system to an email server, which also uses SMTP to relay the message to the receiving email server.

POP

The Post Office Protocol (POP) is the more popular of two leading methods for receiving email (IMAP is the other). In an email system based on POP, email is downloaded from the mail server to folders on a local system. POP is not a suitable email protocol for users who frequently switch between computers, because email might wind up on multiple computers. The POP3 version is the latest current standard. Users that utilize POP3 servers to retrieve email typically use SMTP to send messages.

TIP For users who must use POP-based email and use multiple computers, a remote access solution, such as Windows Remote Desktop or a service such as GoToMyPC, is recommended. A remote access solution enables a user to remotely access the system that connects to the POP3 mail server so he or she can download and read email messages, no matter where he or she working.

IMAP

The Internet Message Access Protocol (IMAP) is an email protocol that enables messages to remain on the email server so they can be retrieved from any location. IMAP also supports folders, so users can organize their messages as desired.

To configure an IMAP-based email account, you must select IMAP as the email server type, and specify the name of the server, your user name and password, and whether the server uses SSL.

Ports

We've mentioned several types of ports so far. When making networking connections to other computers a port is a number that identifies a network application. For two computers to communicate they must both use the same protocol. In order for an application to send or receive data, it must use a particular protocol designed for that application, and open up a port to make a connection to another computer. For example, let's say you want to visit www.google.com. You open a browser and type http://www.google.com. The protocol being used is HTTP, and it makes the connection to the web server: google.com. The HTTP protocol selects an unused port on your computer (known as an outbound port) to send and receive data to and from google.com. On the other end, google.com's web server has a specific port open at all times ready to accept sessions. In most cases, the web server's port is 80, which corresponds to the HTTP protocol. This is known as an inbound port. Table 11-2 displays some common protocols and their corresponding inbound ports.

Table 11-2   Common Protocols and Their Ports

Protocol	Port Used
FTP	21
SSH	22
Telnet	23
SMTP	25
HTTP	80
POP3	110
HTTPS	443

Installing Network Interface Cards

Although many recent computers include a 10/100 or 10/100/1000 Ethernet port or a Wireless Ethernet (WLAN) adapter, you often need to install a network interface card (NIC) into a computer you want to add to a network.

To install a Plug and Play (PnP) network card, follow this procedure:

Step 1. Turn off the computer and remove the case cover.

Step 2. Locate an available expansion slot matching the network card's design (most use PCI, but some servers and workstations might use PCI-X or PCI Express).

Step 3. Remove the slot cover and insert the card into the slot. Secure the card in the slot.

Step 4. Restart the system and provide the driver disk or CD-ROM when requested by the system.

Step 5. Insert the operating system disc if requested to install network drivers and clients.

Step 6. The IRQ, I/O port address, and memory address required by the card are assigned automatically.

Step 7. Test for connectivity (check LED lights, use a command such as ping, and so on) and then close the computer case.

Cable and Connector Types

There are four major types of network cables:

- Unshielded twisted pair (UTP)
- Shielded twisted pair (STP)
- Fiber-optic
- Coaxial

Network cards are designed to interface with one or more types of network cables, each of which is discussed in the following sections.

NOTE   Serial (RS-232) null modem and parallel (LPT) crossover cables can be used with direct parallel or direct serial connections (also known as direct cable connection), which are special types of two-station networking included in Windows that use standard network protocols but do not use network cards.

Infrared (IR) ports built into many notebook computers can also be used with direct serial connection.

UTP and STP Cabling

Unshielded twisted pair (UTP) cabling is the most common of the major cabling types. The name refers to its physical construction: four twisted pairs of wire surrounded by a flexible jacket.

UTP cable comes in various grades, of which Category 5e (Cat5e) is the most commonly found installation of the standard cabling grades as of 2010. Cat5e cabling is suitable for use with both standard 10BaseT and Fast Ethernet networking, and can also be used for Gigabit Ethernet networks if it passes compliance testing.

Shielded twisted pair (STP) cabling was originally available only in Cat4, which was used by the now largely outdated IBM token-ring networks. STP uses the same RJ-45 connector as UTP, but includes a metal shield for electrical insulation between the wire pairs and the outer jacket. It's stiffer and more durable, but also more expensive and harder to loop through tight spaces than UTP. Type 1 STP cable used by older token-ring adapters has a 9-pin connector. STP cabling is also available in Cat5, Cat5e, and Cat6 for use with Ethernet networks. It is used where electromagnetic interference (EMI) prevents the use of UTP cable.

Figure 11-9 compares the construction of STP and UTP cables.

Table 11-3 lists the various types of UTP and STP cabling in use and what they're best suited for.

Table 11-3   Categories and Uses for UTP and STP Cabling

Category	Network Type(s) Supported	Supported Speeds	Cable Type, Notes
1	Telephone, DSL, HomePNA	Up to 100Mbps (HomePNA)	UTP; one wire pair
2	LocalTalk	Up to 4Mbps	UTP; obsolete; one wire pair
3	10BASE T Ethernet	Up to 10Mbps	UTP; obsolete; replace with Cat5, Cat5e, or Cat6; four wire pairs

Category	Network Type(s) Supported	Supported Speeds	Cable Type, Notes
4	Token ring	Up to 16Mbps	Shielded twisted pair (STP); one wire pair
5	10BASE-T, 100BASE-T, 1000BASE-T	Up to 1,000Mbps	UTP, STP; four wire pairs
5e	10BASE-T, 100BASE-T, 1000BASE-T	Up to 1,000Mbps	Enhanced version of Cat5; available in UTP, STP; four wire pairs
6	10BASE-T, 100BASE-T, 1000BASE-T	Up to 1,000Mbps	Handles higher frequencies than Cat5; available in UTP, STP
7	10BASE-T, 100BASE-T, 1000BASE-T	Up to 1,000Mbps	Uses 12-connector GG45 connector (backward-compatible with RJ-45); available in UTP, STP

Figure 11-9   An STP cable (left) includes a metal shield and ground wire for protection against interference, while a UTP cable (right) does not.

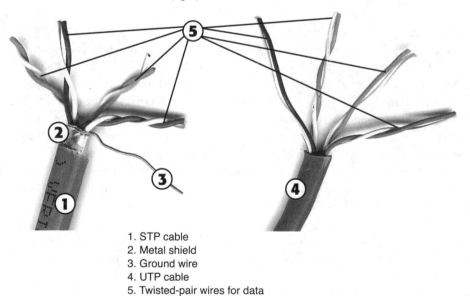

1. STP cable
2. Metal shield
3. Ground wire
4. UTP cable
5. Twisted-pair wires for data

Figure 11-10 compares Ethernet cards using UTP (or STP), thin coaxial, and thick coaxial cables and connectors to each other.

Figure 11-10   Combo UTP/BNC/AUI Ethernet network cards (left and right) compared with a UTP/STP-only Ethernet card (center) and cables.

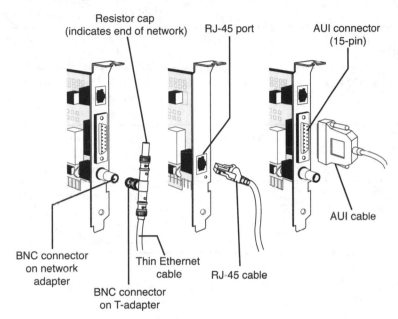

The connector used by Ethernet cards that use UTP or STP cable is commonly known as an RJ-45 connector. RJ stands for registered jack; the RJ-45 has eight contacts that accept eight wires, also known as pins. It resembles a larger version of the RJ-11 connector used for telephone cabling. UTP cabling runs between a computer on the network and a hub or switch carrying signals between the two. The hub or switch then sends signals to other computers (servers or workstations) on the network. When a computer is connected to a hub or switch, a straight-through cable is used. This means that both ends of the cable are wired the same way. If a computer needs to be connected directly to another computer, a crossover cable, which has a different pin configuration on one end, is used. Keep in mind that between the computer and the hub or switch, there might be other wiring equipment involved; for example, RJ-45 jacks, patch panels, and so on. UTP and STP cable can be purchased in prebuilt form or as bulk cable with connectors, so you can build the cable to the length you need. Figure 11-11 compares RJ-11 and RJ-45 connectors.

NOTE Although RJ-45 is the common name for the UTP Ethernet connector, this is a misnomer; the proper name is 8P8C (8 position, 8 contact). Don't confuse it with the RJ-45S connector, an eight-position connector, used for telephone rather than computer data. An RJ-45S jack has a slightly different shape than the connector used for Ethernet, and includes a cutout on one side to prevent unkeyed connectors from being inserted into the jack.

To see drawings of the RJ-45S jack and other telephone jacks, see www.siemon.com/us/standards/13-24_modular_wiring_reference.asp.

Figure 11-11   RJ-11 connector (left) compared to RJ-45 connector (right).

Hubs connect different computers with each other on the network. See "Network Devices," later in this chapter for more information.

You can purchase UTP and STP cable in prebuilt assemblies or can be built from bulk cable and connectors.

Fiber-Optic Cabling

Fiber-optic cabling transmits signals with light rather than with electrical signals, which makes it immune to electrical interference. It is used primarily as a backbone between networks. Fiber-optic cable comes in two major types:

- **Single-mode**—Has a thin core (between 8 and 10 microns) designed to carry a single light ray long distances.

■ **Multi-mode**—Has a thicker core (62.5 microns) than single-mode; carries multiple light rays for short distances.

You can purchase fiber-optic cabling prebuilt, but if you need a custom length, you should have it built and installed by experienced cable installers because of the expense and risk of damage. Some network adapters built for servers are designed to use fiber-optic cable. Otherwise, media converters are used to interconnect fiber optic to conventional cables on networks.

NOTE When Ethernet is run over fiber-optic cables, the letter *F* is used in place of *T* (twisted pair) in the name. For example, 10BASE-F is 10Mbps Ethernet running on fiber-optic cable, 100BASE-F is 100Mbps Ethernet running on fiber-optic cable, and so on.

Coaxial Cabling

Coaxial cabling is the oldest type of network cabling; its data wires are surrounded by a wire mesh for insulation. Coaxial cables, which resemble cable TV connections, are not popular for network use today because they must be run from one station directly to another rather than to or from a hub/switch.

Coaxial cabling creates a bus topology; each end of the bus must be terminated, and if any part of the bus fails, the entire network fails.

The oldest Ethernet standard, 10BASE5, uses a very thick coaxial cable (RG-8) that is attached to a NIC through a transceiver that uses a so-called "vampire tap" to connect the transceiver to the cable. This type of coaxial cable is also referred to as Thick Ethernet or Thicknet.

Thin Ethernet, also referred to as Thinnet, Cheapernet, or 10BASE2 Ethernet was used for low-cost Ethernet networks before the advent of UTP cable. The coaxial cable used with 10BASE2 is referred to as RG-58. This type of coaxial cable connects to network cards through a T-connector that bayonet-mounts to the rear of the network card using a BNC connector. The arms of the T are used to connect two cables, each running to another computer in the network.

If the workstation is at the end of a network, a terminating resistor is connected to one arm of the T to indicate the end of the network (refer to Figure 11-10). If a resistor is removed, the network fails; if a station on the network fails, the network fails.

Two other types of coaxial cable are common in cable Internet, satellite Internet, and fixed wireless Internet installations:

- **RG-59**—Used in older cable TV or satellite TV installations; 75-ohm resistance. Also used by the long-obsolete Arcnet LAN standard.

- **RG-6**—Uses same connectors as RG-59, but has a larger diameter with superior shielding; used in cable TV/Internet, satellite TV/Internet, and fixed wireless Internet/TV service; 75-ohm resistance.

Plenum and PVC

The outer jacket of UTP, STP, and coaxial cable is usually made of PVC (polyvinyl chloride), a low-cost durable vinyl compound. Unfortunately, PVC creates dense poisonous smoke when burned. If you need to run network cable through suspended ceiling or air vents, you should use more-expensive plenum cable, which produces less smoke and a lower level of toxic chemicals when burned.

Connector Types

Most coaxial cables, including RG-58, RG-59, and RG-6 use a BNC (Bayonet Neill-Concelman) connector. RG-58 uses a T-adapter to connect to a 10BASE2 Ethernet adapter. RG-11 (Thicknet) cable is connected to an Ethernet card by means of an external transceiver, which attaches to the AUI port on the rear of older Ethernet network cards. The transceiver attaches to the cable with a so-called "vampire tap."

10BASE-T, 100BASE-T, and 1000BASE-T Ethernet cards using copper wire all use the RJ-45 connector shown earlier in Figure 11-11, as do newer token-ring, some ISDN, and most cable Internet devices. DSL devices often use the RJ-11 connector shown earlier in Figure 11-11, as do dial-up modems.

To attach a cable using RJ-11 or RJ-45 connectors to a network card or other device, plug it into the connector so that the plastic locking clip snaps into place; the cable and connector fit together only one way. To remove the cable, squeeze the locking clip toward the connector and pull the connector out of the jack. Some cables use a snagless connector; squeeze the guard over the locking clip to open the clip to remove the cable.

Fiber-optic devices and cables use one of several connector types. The most common include

- **SC**—Uses square connectors

- **ST**—Uses round connectors

- **FC**—Uses a round connector

See Figure 11-12. If you need to interconnect devices that use two different connector types, use adapter cables that are designed to match the connector types and other characteristics of the cable and device.

Figure 11-12   SC, FC, and ST fiber-optic cable connectors compared.

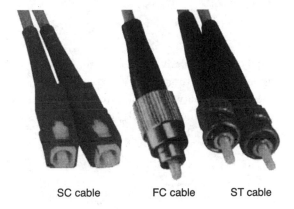

SC cable   FC cable   ST cable

Network Devices

Hubs connect different computers with each other on an Ethernet network based on UTP or STP cabling. A hub has several connectors for RJ-45 cabling, a power source, and signal lights to indicate network activity. Most hubs are stackable, meaning that if you need more ports than the hub contains, you can connect it to another hub to expand its capabilities.

A hub is the slowest connection device on a network because it splits the bandwidth of the connection among all the computers connected to it. For example, a five-port 10/100 Ethernet hub divides the 100Mbps speed of Fast Ethernet among the five ports, providing only 20Mbps of bandwidth to each port for Fast Ethernet and 10/100 adapters, and only 2Mbps per port for 10BASE-T adapters. A hub also broadcasts data to all computers connected to it.

A switch resembles a hub but creates a dedicated full-speed connection between the two computers that are communicating with each other. A five-port 10/100 switch, for example, provides the full 10Mbps bandwidth to each port connected to a 10BASE-T card and a full 100Mbps bandwidth to each port connected to a Fast Ethernet or 10/100 card. If the network adapters are configured to run in full-duplex mode and the switch supports full-duplex (most modern switches do), the Fast Ethernet bandwidth on the network is doubled to 200Mbps, and the 10BASE-T bandwidth is doubled to 20Mbps. Switches can be daisy-chained in a manner similar to stackable hubs, and there is no limit to the number of switches possible in a network.

Hubs and switches are the only connectivity equipment needed for a workgroup LAN. However, if the network needs to span longer distances than those supported by the network cabling in use or needs to connect to another network, additional connectivity equipment is needed.

■ **Repeater**—A repeater boosts signal strength to enable longer cable runs than those permitted by the "official" cabling limits of Ethernet. You can use hubs and switches as repeaters.

NOTE Windows Vista/XP features built-in bridging capabilities. You can also use a wireless router with a built-in switch to create a single network with both wired and wireless clients.

■ **Router**—A router is used to interconnect a LAN to other networks; the name suggests the device's similarity to an efficient travel agent, who helps a group reach its destination as quickly as possible. Routers can connect different types of networks and protocols to each other (Ethernet, token ring, TCP/IP, and so on) and are a vital part of the Internet. Router features and prices vary according to the network types and protocols supported.

Switches and routers make up the basic infrastructure of most LANs. Although other equipment is necessary for different types of connections and environments, these two are the most commonly found devices in a server room. Just remember that the switch generally connects one or more computers to each other. The router connects one or more networks to each other.

Configuring TCP/IP

The TCP/IP protocol, although it was originally used for Internet connectivity, is now the most important network protocol for LAN as well as larger networks. To connect with the rest of a TCP/IP-based network, each computer or other device must have a unique IP address. If the network connects with the Internet, additional settings are required.

There are two ways to configure a computer's TCP/IP settings:

■ Server-assigned IP address

■ Static IP address

Table 11-4 compares the differences in these configurations.

Table 11-4   Static Versus Server-Assigned IP Addressing

Setting	What It Does	Static IP Address	Server-Assigned IP
IP address	Identifies computer on the network	Unique value for each computer	Automatically assigned by DHCP server
DNS configuration	Identifies domain name system servers	IP addresses of one or more DNS servers, host name, and domain name must be entered	Automatically assigned by server
Gateway	Identifies IP address of device that connects computer to Internet or other network	IP address for gateway must be entered; same value for all computers on network	Automatically assigned by server
WINS configuration	Maps IP addresses to NetBIOS computer names; used with Windows NT 4.0 and earlier versions	IP addresses for one or more WINS servers must be entered if enabled	Can use DHCP to resolve WINS if necessary

All versions of Windows default to using a server-assigned IP address. As Table 11-4 makes clear, this is the preferable method for configuring a TCP/IP network. Use a manually assigned IP address if a Dynamic Host Configuration Protocol (DHCP) server (which provides IP addresses automatically) is not available on the network—or if you need to configure a firewall or router to provide different levels of access to some systems and you must specify those systems' IP addresses.

NOTE   Routers, wireless gateways, and computers that host an Internet connection shared with Windows's Internet Connection Sharing or a third-party sharing program all provide DHCP services to other computers on the network.

To configure TCP/IP in Windows, access the Internet Protocol Properties window; this window contains several dialogs used to make changes to TCP/IP. Note that these dialogs are nearly identical in Windows XP and Windows Vista. To open the General tab of the Internet Protocol Properties window, open **Network Connections**, right-click the network connection, select **Properties**, click **Internet Protocol (TCP/IP)** in the list of protocols and features, and click **Properties**.

TCP/IP Configuration with a DHCP Server

Figure 11-13 shows the General tab as it appears when a DHCP server is used.

Figure 11-13 The General tab is configured to obtain IP and DNS server information automatically when a DHCP server is used on the network.

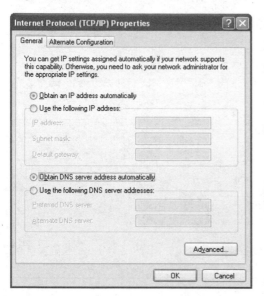

NOTE To determine the IP address, default gateway, and DNS servers used by a system using DHCP addressing, open a command prompt and enter the `ipconfig` `/all` command.

To learn more about using ipconfig, see "Using ipconfig" in this chapter.

TCP/IP Alternate Configuration

The Alternate Configuration tab shown in Figure 11-14 is used to set up a different configuration for use when a DHCP server is not available or when a different set of user-configured settings are needed, as when a laptop is being used at a secondary location. By default, automatic private IP addressing (APIPA) is used when no DHCP server is in use. APIPA assigns each system a unique IP address in the 169.254.x.x range. APIPA enables a network to perform LAN connections when the DHCP server is not available, but systems using APIPA cannot connect to the Internet.

You can also use the Alternate Configuration tab to specify the IP address, subnet mask, default gateway, DNS servers, and WINS servers. This option is useful if this system is moved to another network that uses different IP addresses for these servers.

Figure 11-14   The Alternate Configuration tab is used to set up a different IP configuration for use on another network, or when no DHCP server is available.

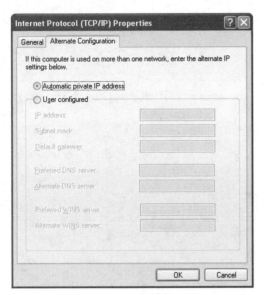

TCP/IP User-Configured IP Address, DNS Addresses, and Advanced Settings

When a DHCP server is not used, the General tab is used to set up the IP address, subnet mask, default gateway, and DNS servers used by the network client (the information shown in Figure 11-15 is fictitious).

Figure 11-15   The General tab of the TCP/IP properties sheet when manual configuration is used.

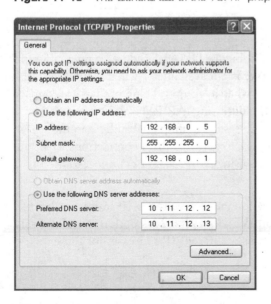

Click the **Advanced** button shown in Figure 11-15 to bring up a multitabbed dialog for adding or editing gateways (IP Settings), DNS server addresses (DNS), adjusting WINS resolution (WINS), and adjusting TCP/IP port filtering (Options). These options can be used whether DHCP addressing is enabled or not. Figure 11-16 shows these tabs.

Figure 11-16 The tabs used for Advanced TCP/IP Settings.

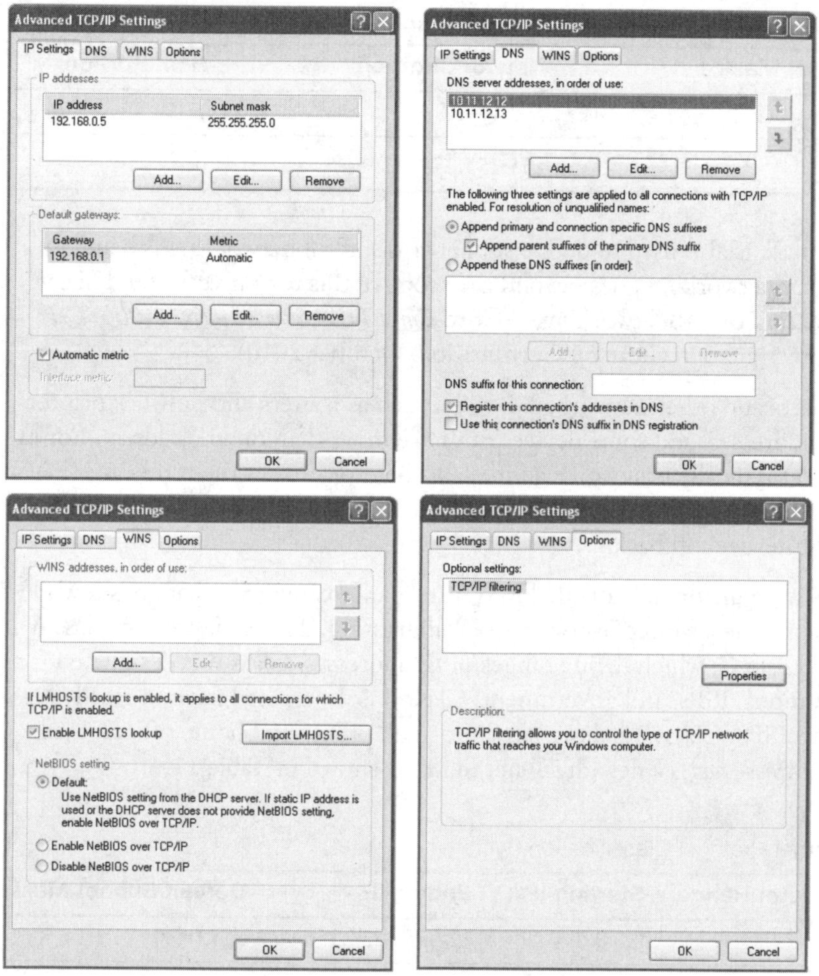

Understanding IP Addressing, Subnet Masks, and IP Classes

An IPv4 address consists of a group of four numbers that each range from 0 to 255, for example: 192.168.1.1. IP addresses are divided into two sections: the network portion, which is the number of the network the computer is on, and the host portion, which is the individual number of the computer. Using the IP address we just

mentioned as an example, the 192.168.1 portion is typically the network number, and .1 is the host number. A subnet mask is used to distinguish between the network portion of the IP address, and the host portion. For example, a typical subnet mask for the IP address we just used would be 255.255.255.0. The 255s correspond to the network portion of the IP address. The 0s correspond to the host portion, as shown in Table 11-5.

Table 11-5   An IP Address and Corresponding Subnet Mask

IP Address/Subnet Mask	Network Portion	Host Portion
192.168.1.1	192.168.1	1
255.255.255.0	255.255.255	0

The subnet mask is also used to define subnetworks, if subnetworking is being implemented. Subnetworking goes beyond the scope of this text; if you would like more information on subnetworking, refer to *CompTIA Network+ (N10-004) Cert Guide* by Mike Harwood (Pearson Certification, October 2010).

Both computers and other networked devices, such as routers and network printers, can have IP addresses, and some devices can have more than one IP address. For example, a router typically has two IP addresses—one to connect the router to a LAN, and the other that connects it to the Internet, enabling it to route traffic from the LAN to the Internet and back.

IP addresses were historically divided into three major categories that are shown in this book to provide a simple overview of IP addressing. Those classes are Class A, Class B, and Class C, which define ranges of IP addresses. Class A is designated for large corporations, ISPs, and government. Class B is designated for mid-sized corporations and ISPs. Class C is designated for small offices and home offices. Each class of IP addresses uses a default subnet mask, as shown in Table 11-6.

Table 11-6   Internet Protocol Classification System

Class	First Octet Range	Starting IP	Ending IP	Default Subnet Mask
Class A	1–127	0.0.0.0	127.255.255.255	255.0.0.0
Class B	128–191	128.0.0.0	191.255.255.255	255.255.0.0
Class C	192–223	192.0.0.0	223.255.255.255	255.255.255.0

NOTE The 127 network is reserved for testing. This is known as the loopback; for example, 127.0.0.1. The usable starting IP for Class A is actually 1.0.0.0.

In any given network, the first and last addresses are reserved and cannot be assigned to computers or other hosts. For example, in the 192.168.1.0 network, 192.168.1.1 through 192.168.1.254 can be assigned, but 192.168.1.0 is reserved for the network number, and 192.168.1.255 is reserved for something called the broadcast.

Each number in an IP address is called an octet. An octet is an 8-bit byte. This means that in the binary numbering system the number can range from 00000000–11111111. For example, 255 is actually 11111111 when converted to the binary numbering system. Another example: 192 equals 11000000.

NOTE To convert numbers from decimal to binary and vice-versa, use the Windows calculator. Press **Windows+R** to bring up the Run prompt and then type **calc**. This runs the Windows Calculator. From here, click **View** on the menu bar and select **Scientific**. Now you notice radio buttons on the upper left that enable you to change between numbering systems. Simply type any number and then select the numbering system you want to convert it to.

In a Class A network, the first octet is the network portion of the IP address, and the three remaining octets identify the host portion of the IP address. Class B networks use the first and second octets as the network portion, and the third and fourth octets as the host portion. Class C networks use the first three octets as the network portion and the last octet as the host portion of the IP address. Table 11-7 gives one example IP address and subnet mask for each class.

Table 11-7 Internet Protocol/Subnet Mask Examples for Classes A, B, and C

Class	IP Address/Subnet Mask	Network Portion	Host Portion
Class A	10.0.0.1	10	0.0.1
	255.0.0.0	255	0.0.0
Class B	172.16.0.1	172.16	0.1
	255.255.0.0	255.255	0.0
Class C	192.168.1.100	192.168.1	100
	255.255.255.0	255.255.255	0

See a pattern? The size of the network portion increases in octets, and the host portion decreases as you ascend through the classes. As time goes on, you see more patterns like this within TCP/IP.

WINS Configuration

Windows Internet Naming Service (WINS) matches the NetBIOS name of a particular computer to an IP address on the network; this process is also called *resolving* or *translating* the NetBIOS name to an IP address. WINS requires the use of a Window Server that has been set up to provide the resolving service. If WINS is enabled, the IP addresses of the WINS servers must be entered.

If the IP address is provided by a DHCP server, or if a WINS server is used, you need to enter the correct WINS settings (refer to Figure 11-16).

The network administrator informs you of the correct settings to use on this dialog.

Gateway

A *gateway* is a computer or device (such as a router) that provides a connection between a LAN and a wide area network (WAN) or the Internet. Computers that use a LAN connection to connect to the Internet need to enter the IP address or addresses of the gateways on this tab (refer to Figure 11-15) if the computer doesn't use DHCP to obtain an IP address.

DNS Configuration

The Internet uses the domain name system (DNS) to map domain names, such as www.microsoft.com, to their corresponding IP address or addresses. A computer using the Internet must use at least one DNS server to provide this translation service. Use the DNS Configuration tab to set up the computer's host name, domain name, and DNS servers (refer to Figure 11-15) if the computer doesn't use DHCP to obtain an IP address.

NOTE Most ISPs and networks have at least two DNS name servers to provide backup in case one fails. Be sure to enter the IP addresses of all DNS servers available to your network. In Windows, these are referred to as preferred and alternate DNS servers.

Using Network Command-Line Tools

Windows contains several command-line tools for troubleshooting and configuring the network. These include the following:

- **ipconfig**—Displays detailed TCP/IP configuration about your Windows NT/2000/XP system

- **ping**—Tests TCP/IP and Internet connections

- **tracert**—Traces the route between a specified website or IP address and your PC

- **net**—Displays and uses network resources

- **nslookup**—Displays detailed information about DNS

The following sections describe these tools. Keep in mind that during this section, when the term "IP address" is used, it is referring to IPv4 addresses. IPv6 addresses are being (slowly) implemented that enable all manner of devices to be networked in the future.

Using ipconfig

The **ipconfig** command-line utility is used to display the computer's current IP address, subnet mask, and default gateway (see Figure 11-17). The **ipconfig** command combined with the /all switch shows more information including the DNS server address and MAC address, which is the hexadecimal address that is burned into the ROM of the network adapter.

Figure 11-17   ipconfig /all displays complete information about your TCP/IP configuration.

```
C:\WINDOWS\system32\cmd.exe

C:\>ipconfig /all

Windows IP Configuration

        Host Name . . . . . . . . . . . . : laptop_musicxpc
        Primary Dns Suffix  . . . . . . . :
        Node Type . . . . . . . . . . . . : Unknown
        IP Routing Enabled. . . . . . . . : No
        WINS Proxy Enabled. . . . . . . . : No

Ethernet adapter Local Area Connection:

        Connection-specific DNS Suffix  . :
        Description . . . . . . . . . . . : Marvell Yukon 88E8055 PCI-E Gigabit
troller
        Physical Address. . . . . . . . . : 00-1E-68-55-BA-01
        Dhcp Enabled. . . . . . . . . . . : No
        IP Address. . . . . . . . . . . . : 10.254.254.202
        Subnet Mask . . . . . . . . . . . : 255.255.255.0
        Default Gateway . . . . . . . . . : 10.254.254.1
        DNS Servers . . . . . . . . . . . : 10.254.254.1

Ethernet adapter Wireless Network Connection:

        Media State . . . . . . . . . . . : Media disconnected
        Description . . . . . . . . . . . : Intel(R) Wireless WiFi Link 4965AGN
        Physical Address. . . . . . . . . : 00-1D-E0-70-2C-47

C:\>
```

TIP   If you're having problems seeing other computers on the network or connecting to the Internet on a network that uses server-assigned IP addresses, type `ipconfig /release` and press **Enter**, and then type `ipconfig /renew` and press **Enter** to obtain a new IP address from the DHCP server on your network.

Using ping

Windows can use the `ping` command to test TCP/IP, check for connectivity to other hosts on the network, and check the Internet connection for proper operation. The `ping` command is a more reliable way to check an Internet connection than opening your browser because a misconfigured browser could cause you to think that your TCP/IP configuration is incorrect.

To use `ping` to check connectivity with another host on the network, follow this procedure:

Step 1.   Open a command-prompt window.

Step 2.   Type `ping IPaddress` or `ping servername` to ping another host on the network, and then press **Enter**. For example, to ping a router, typical syntax would be `ping 192.168.1.1`.

To use `ping` to check your Internet connection, follow this procedure:

Step 1.   Start your Internet connection. If you use a LAN to connect to the Internet, you might have an always-on connection.

Step 2.   Open a command-prompt window.

Step 3.   Type `ping IPaddress` or `ping servername` and press **Enter**. For example, to ping a web server called www.erewhon.net, type `Ping www.erewhon.net`.

By default, `ping` sends four data packets from your computer to any IP address or server name you specify. If your TCP/IP connection is working properly, you should see a reply from each ping you sent out indicating how quickly the signals traveled back from the target and the IP address or URL of the target. The replies indicate that the host is alive. Any other message indicates a problem; for example the "Request timed out" or "Destination host unreachable" messages require further troubleshooting. Keep in mind that if it's the local computer that is configured incorrectly, you might not be able to "ping" anything! Also watch for the amount of time the ping took to reply back. A longer latency time could indicate network congestion. Conversely, the lower the time in milliseconds (ms), the faster your connection. Connection speeds vary a great deal due to various factors, such as Internet

network congestion, server speed, and the number of relays needed to transfer your request from your computer to the specified server. To check relay information, use the tracert command.

Using tracert

The tracert command is used by Windows to trace the route taken by data traveling from your computer to an IP address or website you specify. By default, tracert checks up to 30 hops between your computer and the specified website or IP address. To use tracert to check the routing, follow this procedure:

Step 1.   Start your Internet connection. If you use a LAN to connect to the Internet, you might have an always-on connection.

Step 2.   Open a command-prompt window.

Step 3.   Type **tracert *IP address*** or **tracert *servername*** and press **Enter**. For example, to trace the route to a Web server called www.erewhon.tv, type **Tracert www.erewhon.tv. Tracert** displays the IP addresses and URLs of each server used to relay the information to the specified location, as well as the time required.

To see help for the tracert command, type **tracert** without any options and press the **Enter** key.

Using the net Command

Windows includes the net command for use in displaying and using network resources from the command line. Some of the net commands you can use include

- **net help**—Displays help for a net option; for example, use Net Help View for help with the net view command.

- **net use**—Maps a network drive to a shared resource on the network; for example, net use Q: \\Tiger1\shared. In this example, Q: behaves just like any other drive letter, such as C:, D:, and so on. The only difference is that it redirects to another computer on the network.

- **net view**—Displays other hosts on the network.

- **net helpmsg *errorcode#***—Displays the meaning of any Microsoft error code.

To display a complete list of net commands, type **net /? ¦More** from the command prompt.

Using nslookup

nslookup is a command-line tool used to determine information about the DNS. When nslookup is run without options, it displays the name and IP address of the default DNS server before displaying a DNS prompt. Enter the name of a website or server to determine its IP address; enter the IP address of a website or server to determine its name. Enter a question mark (?) at the prompt to see more options; type **exit** and then press **Enter** to exit the program.

Chapter Review Questions

The following questions test your recall of the concepts described in this chapter. The answers are listed at the end of the questions in the "Answers and Explanations" section.

1. The Windows operating system uses two major types of networks. Which of the following are the two?

   A. Client/server

   B. Node server

   C. Peer-to-peer

   D. IP network model

2. One reason for implementing a network is to be able to share the Internet. Which of the following methods can connect a network to the Internet? (Choose all that apply.)

   A. Dial-up modem

   B. ISDN modem

   C. DSL modem

   D. Cable modem

3. Which of the following technologies are part of the TCP/IP suite? (Choose all that apply.)

   A. HTTP/HTTPS

   B. SSL

   C. TLS

   D. Ethernet

4. You have been asked by your company to create and install a network. You have decided that you are using Cat5e. What type of cable does Cat5e use? Choose all that apply.

   A. STP

   B. Coaxial

   C. UTP

   D. Thin net

5. Which of the following devices would you need if a client asks you to connect his computer to a network? (Choose two.)

   A. A NIC

   B. A wireless card

   C. AGP adapter card

   D. A BNC connector

6. You have been asked by your company to upgrade all hubs to switches. How would this upgrade change the existing network?

   A. The network will be slower

   B. There is no difference in speeds

   C. A switch creates a dedicated full-speed connection

   D. You do not need to have NICs

7. You have been asked by a company to analyze their network. You find several hubs and switches within the network. Which of the following additional devices might you find in this network?

   A. Routers

   B. Bridges

   C. Repeaters

   D. VLAN technology

8. You have been contacted by a client that is having problems connecting to the Internet. Where would be a good place to start the troubleshooting process?

   A. File and Print Sharing

   B. Install NWLink protocol

   C. Configure the DHCP server

   D. TCP/IP configuration

9. What is the name of the service that must be installed on a Windows computer to be able to connect to a network?

   A. Client Services for NetWare

   B. AppleTalk Protocol

   C. Client for Microsoft Networks

   D. NDS

10. A user with your company is having connectivity problems. You need to diagnose the problem as soon as possible. You call the client and walk her through finding the IP address. What should you do next?

  A. Run `ipconfig /release`

  B. Run `ipconfig /flushdns`

  C. Ping the IP address of the client's computer

  D. Walk her through how to ping the server

11. A user is unable to access the network. Which of the following could cause this to happen? (Choose all that apply.)

  A. Damage to cables

  B. A faulty network card

  C. The boot files are corrupt

  D. Connecting a high-speed NIC to a low-speed port

12. Which of the following operating systems are typically considered to be "client" operating systems? (Select the two best answers.)

  A. Windows XP

  B. Windows Server 2008

  C. Windows Vista

  D. UNC

13. Which of the following offers the highest download data transfer rate?

  A. DUN

  B. BRI ISDN

  C. Cable

  D. SDSL

14. Which of the following is a commonly used TCP/IP protocol on the Internet?

  A. ISP

  B. HTTP

  C. HTML

  D. Telnet

15. Which of the following resolves domain names to IP addresses?

   A. DNS

   B. SSH

   C. HTTP

   D. POP

Case Study 1

Examine your home or lab network. Define its main characteristics. Answer the following questions:

   Is it client/server or peer-to-peer?

   Do the computers connect in a wired fashion or wireless?

   What is the maximum speed of those connections?

   What kind of Internet connection is being used, and what is its maximum speed?

   What protocols are being utilized?

By using the `ipconfig/all` command, you can discern a good deal of information. But you also need to use your eyes, research on the Internet, and possibly run some LAN and Internet tests.

Case Study 2

You have a computer that has an issue with connecting to network resources such as a printer or share on a server. What are some of the tests you can perform to fix this problem so the user can continue working?

Answers and Explanations

1. A, C. The Windows operating system uses two types of networks. One is a client/server network, meaning that client computers need to contact a domain controller to work. A peer-to-peer network is used in smaller networks where the expense is a factor, no centralized administration is necessary, or if the organization doesn't have the resources to support a client/server network.

2. A, B, C, D. Although the older dial-up modems are going by the wayside, they are still used. The newer technologies such as an ISDN, cable, and DSL more commonly connect today's networks to the Internet.

3. **A, B, C.** The TCP/IP protocol suite includes many protocols including the Hypertext Transfer Protocol (HTTP), HTTP Secure (HTTPS), Secure Sockets Layer (SSL), and its successor Transport Layer Security (TLS). Ethernet is a network architecture commonly used, upon which TCP/IP runs.

4. **C.** UTP cable comes in various grades, of which Category 5e is the most common of the standard cabling grades. Category 5e cabling is suitable for use with both standard 10BaseT and Fast Ethernet networking and can also be used for Gigabit Ethernet networks if it passes compliance testing.

5. **A, B.** Although many recent computers include a 10/100 or 10/100/1000 Ethernet port or a wireless Ethernet adapter, you might need to install a network interface card (NIC) into a computer you want to add to a network. This card is normally installed to a PCI x1 slot or a PCI slot; however, AGP is used for video only.

6. **C.** A switch resembles a hub but creates a dedicated full-speed connection between the two computers that are communicating with each other. By doing this, it upgrades the speed of the existing network.

7. **A, B, C.** Hubs or switches are the only connectivity equipment needed for a workgroup LAN. However, if the network needs to span longer distances than those supported by the network cabling in use or needs to connect to another network, additional connectivity equipment is needed. A repeater is used to carry the signals even farther than normal. You can also use a bridge to connect two networks together. A router can be used to connect two or more networks.

8. **D.** The TCP/IPv4 protocol, although it was originally used for Internet connectivity, is now the most important network protocol for LAN as well as larger networks. To connect with the rest of a TCP/IP-based network, each computer or other device must have a unique IP address. If the network needs to connect with the Internet, additional settings might be required.

9. **C.** If your computer needs to connect to a Windows network, you must verify that the Client for Microsoft Networks is installed. Usually this is installed by default, but if not, it can be added within the Properties window of the appropriate network connection; the Windows CD is required.

10. **C.** After you have discerned the IP address of the client's computer, ping that IP address to see if it is alive. If you get replies, then the client computer has network connectivity. If your ping times out, then you need to troubleshoot the issue further.

11. **A, B.** If a user reports that he or she cannot connect to the network, check cables, connectors, and other network hardware. A disconnected cable is a common culprit. A faulty connector or network card could also be the cause. Replace any damaged cables and connectors.

12. **A, C.** Windows XP and Vista are client operating systems. Windows Server 2008 is a Microsoft server product (although it can act as a client, it is typically referred to as a server). UNC stands for universal naming convention; this type of path can be used to make connections to network resources.

13. **C.** Cable Internet connections have the highest average data transfer rate followed by SDSL, BRI ISDN, and then DUN.

14. **B.** HTTP (Hypertext Transfer Protocol) is the most commonly used Internet protocol. The only other protocol listed in the answers is Telnet, which is insecure and not commonly used. ISP stands for Internet service provider. HTML stands for Hypertext Markup Language, the most commonly used language for programming websites.

15. **A.** DNS (Domain Name System) resolves domain names such as www.google.com to their corresponding IP addresses. SSH stands for Secure Shell, a decent alternative to Telnet. HTTP is Hypertext Transfer Protocol. POP stands for Post Office Protocol, one of the most common email protocols.

Case Study 1 Solution

A typical home network is peer-to-peer. However, today even some small offices have client/server networks. Let's use a typical peer-to-peer home network as an example.

This network might have four computers in total, one of them a laptop, plus a few other devices that use the network such as a DVR, Blu-Ray player, or gaming console. Quite often, these connections are wireless, but if the router is near a TV, it might be easier (and less expensive) to simply connect DVRs and similar equipment that is nearby with a patch cable. The maximum speed of these connections usually are either 100Mbps or 1Gbps. The Internet connection is most likely cable Internet (or DSL), with a typical maximum download speed of around 5Mbps, and maximum upload speed of 1Kbps. The most common protocol to be used by far would be HTTP. However, users might also connect with FTP (for transferring files), and SMTP and POP3 (for sending and receiving email).

The `ipconfig/all` command on a typical network would probably tell you that the computers are on an IP network number such as 192.168.1.0, that their subnet mask is 255.255.255.0, and that they are connecting to a gateway/DNS server at an address such as 192.168.1.100. The command would also tell you the network name (workgroup name if it is indeed peer-to-peer), and whether IPv6 is also being used.

Case Study 2 Solution

First, you would need to make sure that file and print sharing is turned on for the system. If that is turned on, the next thing would be to check the permissions to see if you are even allowed to connect to the resource. After you have determined that one of these issues have been fixed, you can then recheck to see whether the access is working.

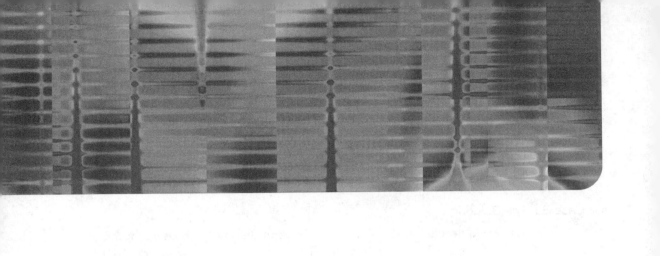

Index

Numerics

A

B

Q-R

T

 **FREE Online Edition**

Your purchase of **Computer Structure and Logic** includes access to a free online edition for 45 days through the Safari Books Online subscription service. Nearly every Pearson IT Certification book is available online through Safari Books Online, along with more than 5,000 other technical books and videos from publishers such as Addison-Wesley Professional, Cisco Press, Exam Cram, IBM Press, O'Reilly, Prentice Hall, Que, and Sams.

SAFARI BOOKS ONLINE allows you to search for a specific answer, cut and paste code, download chapters, and stay current with emerging technologies.

Activate your FREE Online Edition at
www.informit.com/safarifree

> **STEP 1:** Enter the coupon code: CSBXZAA.

> **STEP 2:** New Safari users, complete the brief registration form.
> Safari subscribers, just log in.

If you have difficulty registering on Safari or accessing the online edition, please e-mail customer-service@safaribooksonline.com